Active Learning for Fours

Debby Cryer

Thelma Harms

Adele Richardson Ray

Frank Porter Graham Child Development Center
University of North Carolina, Chapel Hill, North Carolina

Dale Seymour Publications
Parsippany, New Jersey

Senior Editor: Lois Fowkes

Design Manager: Jeff Kelly

Production/Manufacturing Director: Janet Yearian

Production/Manufacturing Coordinator: Barbara Atmore

Cover and text design: Paula Shuhert

Illustrations: Cynthia Swann Brodie

        Jane McCreary

        Joel Snyder

        Rachel Gage

Dale Seymour Publications®
An imprint of Pearson Learning
299 Jefferson Road, P.O. Box 480
Parsippany, New Jersey 07054-0480
www.pearsonlearning.com
1-800-321-3106

Dale Seymour Publications® is a registered trademark of Dale Seymour Publications, Inc.

Cheerios is a registered trademark of General Mills, Inc.
Lego is a registered trademark of Interlego AG, Switzerland.
X-acto is a registered trademark of Hunt X-acto, Inc.

ISBN 0-201-49400-0
9 10 11 12 13 14-ML-07 06 05 04 03

Dedication

In the years that we have been involved in early childhood education, we have spent countless hours observing and talking with children and their teachers. In reality, every child who has shown us delight or interest in an activity has had a part in the creation of this book. And every teacher who has searched for and implemented activity ideas that we see children enjoying has had a part in the creation of this book.

The children whom we have known in closest relationships—our sons and daughters, nephews and nieces (and now grandchildren, too!), children of friends, and those we have taught in our own classrooms—have also had a great influence on our work. They have allowed us to watch, in a most personal way, the amazing details of human development. They have given us messages about developmental appropriateness that we could never have learned in any other way.

It is to all of these children and teachers, and to all who will use Active Learning activities in the future, that we dedicate this book.

Contents

Activities for Physical Development

Creative Activities

Activities for Learning from the World Around Them

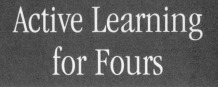

Active Learning
for Fours

Planning for Fours

Quality Care for Fours

Four-year-olds are usually thought of as the "senior class" in most early childhood programs. They talk more clearly than younger children, can follow directions quite well, and usually help teachers in many ways. They really seem to understand what is going on. They are usually very responsible, but like most "seniors," they also test limits. Sometimes teachers feel that Fours have outgrown the early childhood program, especially at the end of the year. It is often hard to remember that Fours are still very young and need lots of affection and patience, as well as an adult's protection from dangers.

Children develop many skills while they are four. They seem to leap ahead in their thinking and understanding. They are well-coordinated and take pride in being able to swing, do a somersault, or hop around on one foot. Fours can remember longer nursery rhymes and learn the words and actions to songs that have several verses. They enjoy playing in small groups and are more able to cooperate with friends than the younger children are. Most Fours can manage their personal care, such as toileting, fastening buttons, or eating all by themselves. And if there is a problem, they can usually ask for the help they need. A program for Fours should provide lots of activities so that children can practice all the skills that they are proud of doing by themselves and learn new skills, too.

Fours need quality early childhood programs. There are a variety of programs for Fours, including full-day child care, preschools in the public schools, private full-day or half-day preschools, Head Start, and others. It is impossible to separate care from education in programs for Fours. Quality programs help children develop both their minds and bodies in a safe and healthy place. Providing quality care is not an easy job. That is why caregivers have to use everything they do during the day to help children feel good about themselves while they learn social and thinking skills. It is not enough to see that children are fed, clean, and safe from harm. Meeting the child's basic health and safety needs is only custodial care. Developmental care tries to meet all the needs of the growing child, including love, guidance, and learning, as well as basic care.

Even though they are so able in many ways, Fours still have so much to learn. They need to practice getting along with others and taking care of themselves independently. Just as important, they need to continue improving many skills in thinking and talking. The key to working with Fours is to remember that they are learning all the time. They will learn more if we give them safe ways to explore and help them think and talk about what they are doing.

The Active Learning Series

The Active Learning Series is made up of activity books for infants, one-, two-, three-, four-, and five-year-olds. Each of these books contains a planning guide and four activity sections. In addition, *Active Learning for Children with Disabilities: A Manual for Use with the Active Learning Series* describes how to adapt activities in all of the books.

Active Learning for Fours has many ideas for working with children whose abilities match those usually developed between 48 and 60 months of age. The book is divided into five sections, which are listed below.

Planning for Fours

This section has ideas for setting up your room and schedule to provide good early childhood education and avoid problems. It includes ways of handling Fours that help them develop self-discipline. It shows how to plan activities so that things will run smoothly, and includes a Fours Can List of things four-year-olds are usually able to do.

Activities for Listening and Talking

This section has ideas to help you make the best use of talking with and listening to Fours individually and during large- and small-group times all through the day. It also has play ideas using books, pictures, and puppets. Activities are numbered 1 through 104.

Activities for Physical Development

This section has ideas to develop the large muscles in the legs, arms, and back. These muscles help children run, balance, and climb. It also has ideas to develop the small muscles in the hands and fingers. Activities are numbered 105 through 188.

Creative Activities

This section has activities with art and carpentry, blocks, dramatic play, and music. These activities help to develop the senses, the imagination, and pleasure in creation. Activities are numbered 189 through 361.

Activities for Learning from the World Around Them

This section has activities that focus on nature and science, the senses, size, shape, color, and numbers. These activities help children enjoy and learn about the world around them. Activities are numbered 362 through 471.

Sharing Ideas with Parents

Parents are interested in what you do with their children. It makes a parent feel good to know that you have been paying special attention to his or her child. You can share the ideas in this book with parents in many ways.

- Have a relaxed talk with each child's parents every day. Tell parents about the activities their child likes.

- Have things on hand for parents to borrow and read. Cut out articles from magazines and put them in folders. Include articles in other languages, if necessary, so that there is something for everyone. Let parents know that you have materials they can borrow.

- Call state offices and agencies for free materials on child care topics. They may have materials on meals and snacks for preschoolers, children's growth and development, getting ready for kindergarten, or ways parents can spot problems.

- Have a meeting for parents. Show a film or slides and talk about helpful ideas for raising children. Topics such as handling behavior problems, activities for Fours, or moving on to kindergarten will interest parents of Fours. Your local community college may be able to help with speakers, films, and other resources.

- Work closely with parents so that children benefit from the feeling of trust and warmth you share with their families.

- Set up a parents' bulletin board to post current information about center activities, notices about parenting education, and fun things to do with children.

- Make sure that you display pictures on the bulletin board and around the room of all races and ethnic groups so that everyone feels welcome and included.

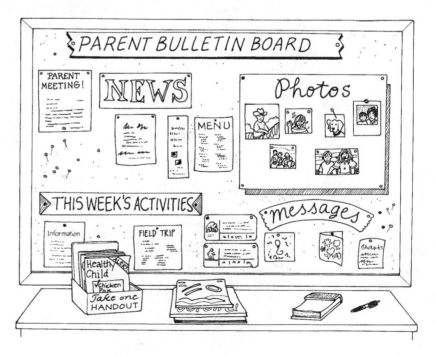

Helping Fours Feel Special

Fours need to know that you really care about them. They know this from your interest and friendly attention. They feel good when you look into their eyes as you talk to them and really pay attention as they talk to you. Fours become frustrated and angry when you are rough or unfriendly, force them to do things they do not enjoy, or ignore their feelings. The way you relate to the children in your care is very important. It helps shape the way the children see themselves.

Developmental care means showing children that you value and like them. Throughout this book, you will find ideas to help children feel special. Emotional support is built into all the activities. In order to help Fours feel good about themselves, keep the following points in mind:

- Treat children as individuals rather than as a big group. Arrange the room and most activities so that children are in small groups. Then it is easier to relate to each child.

- Talk with Fours often. It builds a happy relationship.

- Look right into a child's eyes when you talk together. It helps the child feel important and special.

- Use the child's name when you talk together. It makes what you say more personal.

- Listen to your Fours. They are trying to tell you about what interests them. Carry on conversations with them.

- Use a kind tone of voice and gentle touch. Help children when they ask. It shows you care.

- Use routines, such as meals and naps, as times to talk and relate to the children. It gives them special attention while they get personal care.

- Show delight in the things Fours can do. It helps them feel proud of what they can do by themselves.

- Even when you have to correct your Fours or stop what they are doing, remember to handle them with respect so that they always to feel loved.

Giving Fours Practice with Words

Fours need words for different things. They need words to *understand* what you and others are saying. They need words to *think* about things. They also need words to *talk* to others about their ideas. Your job is to help Fours get practice with words in all these different ways.

You are helping a child understand words and ideas when you read stories, talk about what is happening in a picture, describe what a child is doing, and answer a child's questions.

Often we see Fours thinking aloud as they play. They may tell about what the make-believe people are doing or talk in the different voices of the make-believe people. They may talk about the steps they take as they solve a problem. This kind of talk is thinking out loud. It guides children's actions and helps them develop what will become silent thinking later on. While they are little, children need to think aloud as they play. Encourage them to talk about their actions.

You will find that it helps children to remember how to do something if you talk them through an action while you show them what to do. For example, if you are showing a child how to use watercolors, you can model what to do by saying, "See, I dip the paintbrush into the clean water. Then I wipe the extra water off on the side of the cup. Now I stroke the brush across the color I want to use." By talking, you have helped the child think aloud.

Fours usually understand many more words than they use when they talk. Asking simple questions is a good way to give children practice in using more words. Try to ask your Fours open-ended questions that need more than a one-word answer. The word you use to start a question gives you a clue to the type of answer the child will be practicing:

- "What," "who," and "when" start questions that ask for information. Children will usually answer "what," "who," and "when" questions with one or two words. You can encourage them to say more by repeating their answer and waiting for them to add some other ideas. "What did you build with the blocks?" "A house." If they do not add more, you can say, "Tell me more about your house."

- "How" starts a question that asks a child to remember step by step what happened. Children usually need to use a longer sentence to answer this kind of question. "How did we make the pancakes?" asks for a step-by-step description. "How did you build this farm with the blocks?" asks the child to remember what he used and what he did.

- "Why" starts a question that asks for a reason or a cause. "Why" questions are hard for many Fours to answer. Start with simple questions, such as "Why is the boy in this story sad?" If the child can't answer, you can remind him about what happened and look back at the pictures. Then ask the question again: "Now, can you tell me why he's sad?"

Fours also like to imagine and think about things they have not experienced. When you read stories about imaginary adventures, such as *Curious George* by H. A. Rey in which George, the monkey, flies over the city holding on to a bunch of balloons, you might ask how the children think it feels to fly, as well as what they think might happen next in the story.

In the activities in this book, there are many examples of questions to use with Fours and topics to talk about with them. Try out some of these ideas and notice which ones help the children to talk most. Remember, the important thing is to make children feel free to talk. You can do that if you listen to them, discuss things with them, and show that you enjoy what they tell you.

Handling Problems

Although four-year-olds are competent in many ways, they can also test the patience of many adults. It helps if you can see the everyday difficulties you have with Fours as signs of growth. For example, Fours can become frustrated or angry when things do not go as they wanted, but you know that they are working hard on developing new skills and working toward goals they set. Sometimes it takes only a little help from you to make things turn out right. Fours can often become rough or dangerous in their active play, but they are really finding new ways to challenge their muscles. You might need to help them find safe challenges outdoors. Fours often go beyond the limits, but they are really trying to become more independent. If you give them many choices and things they can do alone, they can take pride in their independence without pushing limits. They sometimes exclude or pick on another child as they work on developing the skill to get along well with others and figure out how to make friends. When you can appreciate the steps that Fours are taking, it becomes easier to cut down on some of the difficult times.

Fours are just beginning to work out problems by talking things through. They are learning to listen to another person's point of view, think about the feelings of others, and see how their actions affect things. But they often need an adult to help make this work. Fours can use words well and can (but do not always) remember much of what you say to them. They are full of love, excited about learning, and enjoy friends more than ever. Like all young children, they are not good at waiting with nothing to do, and when they get tired or hungry, everything falls apart.

It is important to have a few clear rules with Fours and stick to them. Too many rules are confusing. Patience and kindness are the way to work with children. If the adult gets angry, the children will show anger or fear. Children who are screamed at or spanked learn to hit and scream at others. Punishment that shames or frightens a child hurts the entire adult-child relationship. Remember, Fours are copycats and are copying the way you treat them. That's how they learn. So you need to be sure that you do what you want them to copy.

The best way to handle problems with Fours is to plan ahead so that there are fewer chances for things to go wrong. Plan ahead to have enough safe play space, interesting toys, and fun activities so that children won't get frustrated and strike out. But planning ahead will not do away with all the problems. Some Fours have to be watched more closely than others. You will get to know the signs before a child hits someone else, and that's the time to stop him if you can. If you stop things early by reminding the children about the words or actions they need to use, you can prevent a lot of fights.

You will get to know which children need to have you close to them because they do more hurting. The child who hurts needs lots of love to help him grow. When problems happen, step in, and make it clear that you don't allow the troublesome behavior. Then help the child figure out what he did, how it made others feel, how he felt, and what he can do the next time so that things work out better. Also be sure to make it clear that you still love him.

Here are some suggestions for handling the common problems of four-year-olds.

Problems Around Routines

Have each four-year-old help as much as possible with routines—hanging up her own coat, helping set the table for lunch, helping serve herself, and putting toys back where they belong.

When you are changing activities, avoid having all the children change at the same moment. Whenever you can, help a few children at a time to finish up and start the new activity rather than all at the same time. This makes it easier to prevent a rush when you're changing activities.

Give children choices as often as you can. Sometimes a big problem can be helped by giving a child a choice that she can make. For example, if a child is noisy at story time, ask her if she wants to listen with the group or quietly look at books in the book corner.

Don't rush during routines such as toileting or meals. This puts pressure on the children and causes upsets.

Keep children actively involved before meals. Have them help with getting meals and snacks ready. Allow children to play until the food is ready. If needed, use songs, finger plays, and stories to prevent waiting with nothing to do before meals.

Treat things with a light touch. Too much control is as bad as not enough control. Make sure children know the important limits, but be flexible within those limits.

Don't insist too much or threaten something you can't carry out. You will only back yourself into a corner. Remember, the child really has the final say about what he will eat or whether he will play well with another child.

Remember that many Fours no longer need naps. Provide a quiet time, space, and activities for children who do not go to sleep, but continue naps for those who still need them.

Give children notice before a change in activity is coming: "You are having a good time building with blocks. You may play for a little while longer before it is clean-up time." Remind them again about two minutes before they have to finish up. Whenever possible, let Fours finish up what they are doing and then move on to the next activity in their own time.

Making It Easier to Say Good-bye

By the time children are four, they have usually become used to saying good-bye. But separating from parents can be a problem that pops up time after time in children's lives as they begin to understand things in new ways. Fours often have problems with saying good-bye, even when they have separated easily for months. It is very important to take the child's feelings seriously, just as you would do with a younger child.

For new children, help both parent and child feel at ease with you before the child's first day. Have the parent bring the child in for a few short visits at fun times before she leaves him. Then the child will feel at ease with you and the new place. Invite parents to visit or drop in any time while the child is with you.

Encourage parents to stay a while when the child is dropped off and help the child get settled into an activity. Be sure parents tell their children good-bye and never sneak off, even if it may seem to be the easiest thing at the time.

Visit children in their homes if they are having a hard time saying good-bye.

Have a new child bring something from home to keep with him or have the parent leave something that is hers, such as a book or scarf, with the child so that he can hold it whenever he wishes.

Tell a "good-bye to mommy/daddy" story to all the children, using little dolls or flannelboard pieces. Remember to tell the children that the sad feelings the dolls have are OK, and that the dolls have happy feelings as they have fun with friends and others who care for them.

Help the child become involved in play with a special friend. But let him know you will still be there if he needs you.

Have a special toy or story ready for the child who finds it hard to have her parent leave. Be ready to give lots of warm attention. Remember to give that child plenty of attention during the rest of the day.

Help the child write a note (you write down what the child wants to say) or make a special picture to give the parent at the end of the day.

Encourage parents to stay a bit at pick-up time. Then the child can show the parent where he played and what he did all day.

Don't be surprised if problems with the parent's leaving start over again after a vacation or an illness. Always handle these problems with kindness.

Hurting and Fighting

Because fours are good talkers, they are discovering that they can really hurt others with words. It's important to help children understand how the feelings of others are affected when cruel words are used. Be careful to never use hurtful words yourself, and do not make a huge fuss when children are fighting. Instead, discuss problems calmly, helping children figure out ways to avoid problems the next time.

Always watch the children closely and stop things before they get out of hand. If you see things in time, you can help the child to solve the problem without hurting others. Sometimes you can avoid problems. For example, you can remind the child to get his own blocks from the shelf instead of taking another child's.

If a child tends to fight a lot, be aware of when problems start and why. Help him to use the words he needs to solve the problem and to understand the feelings he and others have when problems happen.

Make sure there are enough interesting activities out at the same time so that children don't have to fight over the most popular ones. Use a waiting list for the most popular activities. Continue special activities several days in a row so that all of the children get one or more chances until they are no longer interested.

Make sure children have enough space to play. Crowding causes fights.

Remind children how to ask by saying easy words such as "please show me," or "may I." Play an asking game at group time so that your Fours can practice taking turns.

Make sure you set a good example. *Never* hit a child who has hit someone else; never scream or kick things around. Children will copy what you do, not what you tell them to do.

Emotional Upsets

Although Fours usually do not have the tantrums that Twos have, they can become very angry or upset. This is most likely to happen when a child is hungry, tired, too hot, trying to do something that is very hard, or when there is too much (or too little) going on.

Avoid problems by stopping an upsetting situation as soon as you can, before the child loses control.

Show the children that you still love them as you help them work through their anger safely. Most children don't like being angry or upset any more than you do. Keep yourself calm; don't let yourself get angry or aggressive.

Pick out a safe, cozy place for the child to quiet down and get control. Suggest in a calm way that the child use this place if she needs to. Make sure that you can see the child and that she is not a danger to herself or others. As soon as the child is calm, help her come out and join the group. Do not make a big fuss about it.

If anger is violent and happens often, talk to a child development specialist, a mental health consultant, or a social worker. Some problems are too hard for you to handle alone. The agency that supervises your center can suggest someone. If possible, get the person to come in and see the child in your group. There may be something in your program or schedule that is setting off the child's problems.

Be sure to talk to the parents to find out if the same type of problem happens at home. Ask how the parents handle the child and what works well. Decide on one way to handle problems at home and at school.

In a few cases, the help of a professional consultant may be needed to plan a special program for a child who often has difficulties. Work with the parents and consultant to plan and carry out the program at home and at school.

Sharing and Taking Turns

Have plenty of the most popular toys and materials so that Fours do not always have to share. Remember that sharing can be difficult, even for adults.

When a child remembers to share or take turns, praise her and tell her you like sharing and taking turns. When you share something or give someone a turn, call the children's attention to it: "Now it's Becky's turn. See, I'm sharing."

Make a game of taking turns: you take a turn, then give the children their turns.

Use a "waiting list" or sign-up sheet for each activity center and for taking turns using a popular toy. Put the sheet down low where the children can see you print their names on it. Encourage children to write their own names as they become able. Check off each child's name as he finishes his turn and send him to get the next child on the list. This works well as long as there are other interesting activities to do while the child waits his turn.

Always continue a special activity until each interested child has had a turn. If children know that they will have enough time to have a turn, they will not crowd or be tense about taking turns.

Using Naughty Words

Listen to the words Fours hear in your program. If you do not want the child to say certain words, then be sure those words are not used by the staff or children. Children say the words they hear others use.

Avoid emotional reactions to the "naughty" words a child might say. If you get annoyed, angry, or punish the child, that gives attention to the naughty word, and the word will be repeated more often. Giving children attention for something they do encourages them to do it again. It does not matter whether the attention is positive or negative. So, never punish a child for using an unacceptable word.

If you want to explain to the child that a word should not be repeated, do this gently, and give the child a better word to use the next time. Then be very patient and remain calm. The child will have to spend a long time learning that he can't use some words, even though others may say them. This is very confusing for Fours.

Sometimes one child teases another child by using naughty words or by calling names. The satisfaction of having the other child cry or become angry is enough attention to keep the teasing going. Teach the children to ignore teasing and naughty words. Tell them that it will stop if they walk away and pay no attention to the one who is teasing. Make sure to give attention for the good things the child who teases says and does. Give support to the child who is hurt.

Growing Up Too Fast

Remember that Fours are still very young children, even though they may not think so. Be realistic about what you expect or allow. Also work with the parents so that they don't expect too much.

Some Fours may still need a reminder to use the toilet. Don't make a fuss or worry if a child has an accident. Use a light touch and encourage the child to be independent in changing clothes and helping to clean up.

Set up the spaces used by children so that they can do as much as possible by themselves. But remember that you must still ensure the children's health and safety.

Tips on Handling Problems

- Make a few clear rules for safety and how to treat others. Explain why the rules are important. Always stick to these rules.

- If four-year-olds are doing something you or others don't like, help them figure out what to do instead. Help them remember the rules and think about how their actions make others feel.

- Encourage Fours to use words instead of hitting or fighting. You may need to help them remember the words to use.

- When children use words to hurt others' feelings, help them see how their actions make others feel. Then help them figure out better ways to solve problems.

- Talk with the children about the feelings people have and how actions can cause others to feel either happy or sad. Help them understand that feelings are fine, but hurting is not.

- Have plenty of the materials and toys you expect children to use as they play together, such as blocks or art materials. Then children will better be able to play together without fighting.

- Have more than one of the most popular toys, such as tricycles or other riding toys. Encourage the children to help figure out a fair way to share these toys; for example, start a waiting list.

- Take Fours outdoors every day to play in a safe area. Leave enough indoor space for active play, too.

- Keep groups of children small by using several activity centers in the room at the same time. Crowding causes fights.

- Be sure there are interesting activities in many areas of the room so that children do not fight over the one new activity.

- Allow Fours to choose what they want to do much of the day. Keep whole-group activities short.

- Make sure lunch and nap are early enough so that Fours don't get too hungry or tired. If you are stuck with a fixed meal schedule, make sure they can have a small, healthful snack when they are hungry.

- Keep Fours from having to wait with nothing to do. Have some books to look at, sing a song, or do a finger play if they must wait. Never crowd children into one small area to wait.

- Use imagination, humor, and a light touch to prevent emotional upsets. Step in early, before things get out of hand. Take children outside or to another room; a change of scene sometimes puts a new look on things.

- Keep a special eye on the child who hits or hurts others. Then you will be able to catch that child when you see he is frustrated or angry and help him before he hurts someone. Also make sure to catch the child being good and to praise the many positive things he does.

- Be calm. Comfort a hurt child, but also keep loving and caring for the one who hurts others. He needs you to help him grow.

Making Time for Activities in the Schedule

The way you use the time children spend with you is called the *schedule*. Everything that is done for care and play needs its own time in the schedule. You must plan ahead to make time for both care and play.

When you are gone and someone else is taking care of the children, he or she will need to know the schedule. If you write down the main things you do and when you do them, then others who care for your children can do things at the same time. Your Fours will expect certain things to happen every day in the same order. If things go on as they should, it makes them feel more relaxed, even if you are not with them.

The most important thing about a schedule is that it helps you think ahead. Then you can plan many activities for both morning and afternoon and get the things that you will need ready ahead of time. Any schedule should be flexible so that you can take advantage of all the interesting things that come up.

Use routines, such as naps, meals, and snacks, as times to give a child personal attention. With a little planning, some of the activities in this book can be done during routine care and will not add much work for you. Routines are good times to talk to individual children and teach self-help skills. As you use the activities, make sure to choose some that can be done during routines.

As much as you can, try to let Fours choose their own activities and decide whether to play by themselves or in small groups. Try not to have all of them do things together in a large group. Expecting lots of young children to do things together is frustrating to both the teacher and the children.

You will need to have many safe things to play with in different parts of the room so that all the children don't crowd together to play with the same thing at the same time. If you share a space with another group, try to schedule different times to use the space. For example, take your children outside and arrange for the other group to be inside at that time.

Make sure your schedule has outdoor play times and indoor play times every day. Also make sure to schedule a balance of quiet play times and active play times. Plan a short time for a story, finger plays, and nursery rhymes once or twice a day. Have music times often. Fours love to dance, play instruments, and sing songs.

Changing from one activity to another, or making transitions, can be hard for Fours. Big changes, such as the transition between lunch and nap or between indoor and outdoor time, must be carefully planned. Try to let children finish up one or two at a time and move on to the next activity instead of all moving on at once.

If you have someone help you, it is easier to let the children finish up one at a time and send them on to the next activity. For example, as each child finishes lunch, he can go to wash up and brush his teeth with another adult. Then that adult can take a small group with her to the next thing on the schedule. By that time, the rest of the children will probably be finished with lunch. You can take that small group to the bathroom and on to the next activity.

Even if you are alone, it helps to have everything ready for the next activity so that you can get the children started on the new activity quickly. It is hard for Fours to wait with nothing to do.

While you are taking care of the children, don't take the time to clean up completely. The children can help you clear away what you have to. You can come back and do the rest when children are asleep or after most of them have left for the day. When the children are there, give them your full attention. This is easier when you teach the children to do a lot of the work for themselves.

Always have a few extra ideas ready that you can use in case you need them. It is better to have too many activities planned than too few. Fours can go through activities very quickly, so have the materials prepared for some extra things to do. During bad weather it helps to have some new materials to put out and some active games to play indoors.

Self-Directed and Teacher-Directed Activities

Fours want to do things by themselves. When Fours are free to choose and do their own activities, the activities are *self directed*. Self-directed activities are possible when there are plenty of toys and materials on low shelves for children to use independently. Toys and materials should be changed regularly to add new interest and challenge to play areas. During the day, remind Fours to pick up and put away toys in the proper place as they finish using them. This keeps the toys ready for others to use. If everything is a jumble, the children soon lose interest. Also, when the room is kept in order, cleanup is easier at the end of the day.

You need to be right there with the children when they do activities that require lots of help or close supervision. These activities are *teacher directed*. Teacher-directed activities need to be done at times when you are free to work with the children. Fingerpainting or cooking are examples of activities that should be teacher directed. Once children have become competent at doing some teacher-directed activities, they might be added to the self-directed activities that children can choose freely. If you have enough self-directed toys out at all times, children will have a lot to keep them busy. Then you can bring out the teacher-directed activities at scheduled times.

Helping Children Get Ready for School

Fours are still a long way from first grade, where they will be expected to learn to read, write, and do simple addition and subtraction. The best way for you to help them get ready for school work is by doing activities such as those in this book, as well as many other play activities that enrich children's lives. In this book, you will notice that children are *not* given worksheets to do. They are *not* pushed to read, write, or learn numbers. They are not expected to sit quietly for long times. Instead, children are given many chances to follow their interests through hands-on activities that help them see the importance and usefulness of reading and writing. There are many activities that let children play with numbers so that they find out how numbers work. And children have lots of time to learn how to get along well with others and collect information about the world. Of course, children are encouraged to read, write, or listen quietly as they become interested and able, but for four-year-olds, this is not the most important part of getting ready for school.

Activity Tips

Set up the children's indoor space for play.

- Divide and organize big spaces into play areas with low shelves and other furniture. Keep in mind where the sink, doors, and windows are as you plan areas.

- Be sure adults can supervise the areas easily.

- Set up four or more activity centers with plenty of safe toys and materials for children to use in self-directed activities. Some activity centers to include are a book corner, blocks, playhouse, puzzles and put-together toys, art, science, and a quiet corner with a rug and a few soft pillows.

- Set up the areas to help Fours learn to do things for themselves. Have plenty of safe toys and materials on low shelves for Fours to use.

- Separate the quiet centers from the active centers. Help the children enjoy quiet play as well as active play so that they won't get too tired.

- Label shelves and other toy containers with clear pictures.

- Keep toys organized. Put the same kind of toys in one area and toys with small pieces in dishpans or boxes.

- Set up an indoor active play area with some safe large-muscle play things. This lets the Fours move around indoors, especially in bad weather.

- Plan indoor walking pathways so that children and adults can move safely among activity areas without disrupting play.

Plan ahead to make things go smoothly.

- Plan new activities that you will add to ongoing activity centers ahead of time and write them on a planning form.

- Choose activities to match children's skills. If an activity turns out to be too hard, try an easier one.

- Plan when and where you will do each activity.

- Include quiet and active, indoor and outdoor, small-group and individual activities.

- Add new activities to old favorites.

- Always have extra activities ready in case you need them.

- Set special materials out ahead of time and make sure you have enough materials for all the Fours who want to take part.

Activity Tips
Continued

Keep Fours interested, active, and learning.

- Allow four-year-olds to choose their activities much of the day.
- Help Fours remember how to take out, use, and put away the toys correctly.
- Keep Fours from having to wait with nothing to do.
- Have enough toys so that children don't have to wait a long time for turns.
- Give children practice talking about what they and others are doing. Help them think things through by asking some questions.
- Remember to look into the child's eyes as you talk and listen. This gives each child a turn to be special.

Slowly help Fours learn to be part of a group.

- Keep large group times very short, ten to fifteen minutes. Have two smaller groups instead of one big group if you can.
- Encourage but don't force a child to be part of a group. Give the child a choice of a quiet alternative while the rest of the group is together.
- If a group activity you planned isn't working, stop and try something else.

Make everything you do count twice.

- Use routines such as eating and getting up from naps as a time to talk with a few children. Try doing some of the activities at this time.
- Use the same materials to do more than one activity.
- Repeat the same activity several days in a row so that all the children who want to can try it.
- Make sure that there is a wide variety of activities so that every child can find something of interest.
- Once you have introduced materials for an activity, place them on a shelf in an activity center for children to use independently.
- Try the same activity with all the Fours who are at about the same level.
- Let the children learn to do as much as they can by themselves: setting the table, serving themselves, putting toys away.

Activity Tips
Continued

Avoid indoor health and safety problems.

■ Cover electrical outlets, put safety locks on cabinets with poisons or other dangerous items, be sure there are mats under indoor climbing equipment.

■ Have children pick things up and put them away as they go along.

■ Let the Fours do activities that need to be closely watched, such as cooking or carpentry, only while you are there with them. Make sure that dangerous items, such as knives or hot plates, are out of reach when you can't watch carefully.

■ Have plenty of toys and materials. Provide more than one of the most popular toys and use a fair system for sharing. A waiting list helps Fours take turns. Divide toys (Lego Bricks® or watercolor markers) into several small boxes so that there is a set for each child who needs one.

■ Make the room safe so that Fours won't hurt themselves when playing.

■ Remember that even if you set things up to be safe, accidents can still happen. Be alert and make sure you always keep the children within your sight and hearing.

■ Wash your hands and have the children wash theirs often, especially after using the toilet or blowing noses and before meals and water play.

■ See pages 30–34 for outdoor health and safety ideas.

Gathering or Group Time

Fours can be gathered together in a larger group once or twice a day to sing, take part in short talks, or listen to a story. Keep them together only as long as everybody is really interested. Usually with young Fours, that means only 10 to 15 minutes. Older Fours might stay for 15 to 25 minutes if they are really involved in what is happening. If you have someone working with you, it is best to divide a big group into two smaller groups. The smaller the group, the easier it is to have a good gathering time and for children to take part in what you do.

Sample Schedule

The main purpose of a schedule is for you to think and plan ahead so that the day will go smoothly and things will get done. You can change this schedule to fit your Fours' needs. Remember to be flexible and follow the children's needs and interests.

Children arrive:	Greet each child and parent Self-directed activities in activity centers Use toilet and wash hands individually, as needed
Mid-morning:	Wash hands, help prepare snack, set table Breakfast or snack Short group time
Late morning:	Planned play time: self-directed activities for some children, teacher-directed activities for others Clean up after play time Planned large-muscle play outdoors or indoors Gathering or group time: stories, music, talking about activities Routines before lunch (washing hands, setting tables)
Mid-day	Lunch
Early afternoon:	Clean up after lunch Get ready for nap Nap or quiet activities for non-nappers
Mid-afternoon:	Napping Fours get up Routines (toileting, dressing, putting cots away) Snack Planned play time: self-directed activities for some children, teacher-directed activities for others

Late afternoon:	Outdoor play time
	Self-directed activities in activity centers
	Routines (getting children's things ready to send home)
	Talk with parents/children at pick-up time

After most children are gone:	Clean up
	Discuss day with staff and plan for tomorrow
	Set up for next day

Making Spaces Safe and Healthy for Fours

If you do all you can to avoid health and safety problems, you will feel more relaxed and enjoy your work with the children more. Although Fours understand some safety rules, they still need safe spaces to use. Child-proofing the room and the outdoor area where children play takes a lot of thought. Think about what you can do to make it safe for your Fours at all times.

You have to be very careful with four-year-olds. In their active play they want to challenge themselves and do not always see dangers. They forget safety rules when their attention is on something else. Yet you can't always be close by, and you want to encourage Fours to do things by themselves. These questions will help you start thinking about child-proofing the spaces used by Fours.

How can I block off the windows, doors, stove, and electrical outlets so that the children can't get hurt?

Where can I lock away medicines, cleaning materials, and other harmful things?

Where can I store things I don't want Fours to use by themselves?

Where can I put things that need supervision so that it's easy to get them out often for use when I can watch?

Is everything I have left out safe for Fours to use by themselves?

How can I make everything they will climb on safe?

Can I see what all the children are doing from every place in the room or outdoor area?

Tips on Health and Safety

- Never leave Fours alone. They need to be supervised by an adult at all times.

- Be sure that *all* areas used at any time by the children are safe. If children must go through a hallway or other space outside of the room to get from one place to another, make sure those areas are just as safe as the rest of children's space.

- Check to be sure that fire exits are not blocked and that the paths to the exits are clear. Have regular fire and emergency drills so that children and staff know what to do.

- Make sure gates and doors are closed so that Fours can't wander outside of safe areas.

- Cover all electrical outlets.

- Buy toys you can easily keep clean. Wash toys in dishwashing detergent and water when necessary. Rinse well. Let toys dry in the air.

- Make sure all the materials are safe for children to put in their mouths (nontoxic paints, fabrics, and dyes).

- Do not store toys in a toy chest with a heavy lid that can fall down. Use open, low shelves that are fixed so that they can't fall over.

- Check all toys for sharp edges, splinters, and other hazards that develop as toys get old.

- Make sure that outdoor areas are free of tall grass, weeds, and harmful insects and are fenced in for safety.

- Be sure that there is plenty of cushioning material under climbing equipment and that there is enough space around the equipment to make a safe fall area.

- Cover the sandbox to keep animals out.

- Put up strong fences to keep Fours away from windows, stoves, and other dangers.

- Teach children to flush toilets as soon as they are used. Check on toilets yourself. Disinfect once daily.

- Wash your hands with soap after you help children go to the toilet or wipe their noses. Remind the children to wash their hands, too. Handwashing cuts down on germs and illness.

- Set up children's cots or mats for resting in a well-ventilated area, with 36 inches between each cot or mat.

- Be sure to read the Notes in the activities for more health and safety ideas.

Making the Most of Your Space

Fours need a lot of space in which to move around. There never seems to be enough usable space for play when you care for a group of young children. Planning how to best use space can help, even though it may not solve all the problems. Look around your room and ask yourself the following questions.

What can I store outside the room?

How can I move the furniture around to open up space for play?

Are there any large spaces that are wasted during most of the day and where children do rough play?

How can I divide my space into different areas but still supervise all the children?

What activities are better outdoors than indoors?

Where can children do large-muscle play in rainy weather?

Tips for Routine Care

- Use all the space you have. Put away anything you aren't using. Try to get routine care furnishings, such as cots, that stack well.

- Make sure routine care areas take up as little space as possible. Use routine care spaces and furnishings for play whenever possible. For example, use eating tables for art and small-muscle play when it is not time to eat. Put cots out in play spaces when it is nap time instead of having cots set up all the time.

- Remember that cots should be about 36 inches apart to cut down on the spread of germs.

- Give each child a storage space for his coat, spare clothes, and artwork.

Tips for Play

- Set up four or more safe activity centers for play, some for quiet play and some for more active play. Remember to put some soft pillows and toys in one quiet area. If possible, include an area for large-muscle play, too.

- Arrange the schedule so that children spend most of the day playing in activity centers, either indoors or outdoors.

- Have plenty of safe toys and materials on low, open shelves in the activity centers so that Fours can get them by themselves. Have a plentiful supply (two or more toys or several sets of the same materials) of the most popular things to cut down on fighting.

- Change the toys in the activity centers often.

- Have some very low tables in the activity centers for drawing, puzzles, and other table-top toys. Make sure chairs are small and strong, and that the children's feet rest on the floor when they sit down. (These can also be used for meals and snacks.)

- Set up a safe, fenced-in outdoor area. Take the children out every day. Riding toys, balls, swings, a slide, climber, and a sandbox with toys to use work well outdoors. Adding pretend play props, art, water, and a carpentry bench makes the outdoors even better.

Making Activity Centers

Activity centers are the heart of a good early childhood program. They set the stage for most of the learning that your Fours will do every day. Schedules should be arranged so that children spend most of their indoor time in activity centers. Once your space is set up with basic toys and equipment in activity centers, you can add all kinds of special activities to the centers.

An activity or interest center is a place where the toys, open, easy-to-use storage, and play space have been set up for a special kind of play. For example, you might set up a dramatic play center, a book center, a block center, an art center, or a music center. Some activity centers can be set up outdoors, too.

Make sure that each activity center has the following things.

■ Open shelves so that children can get the toys and put them back by themselves

■ Furnishings such as soft pillows to sit on in the book area, a flat rug on the floor in the block area, an easel or art table in the art area

■ Any other things that will make the materials in the center easy and safe to use, such as a large towel under the water table, plastic aprons for the children to wear, a throw rug spread under the sand table, and a place to dry paintings

Activity Centers Fours Can Enjoy Every Day

■ Art Center with paints, paper, crayons, watercolor markers, safe scissors, tape, glue, paste, and play dough

■ Block Center with different kinds of unit blocks (wooden or plastic) and toy animals, trucks and cars, and airplanes to use with blocks

■ Book Center with a soft, cozy place to look at books, puppets, and picture and story games

■ Large-Muscle Center with a small climber, crates or cubes for children to use for building obstacle courses, a low balance beam, large hollow blocks, and mats for supervised rolling and tumbling

■ Math Center with lots of small things to count; number, shape, and size games for counting, matching, sorting, and comparing; number/shape/size books and pictures; pencils or markers; and paper

■ Music Center with quiet rhythm instruments, a toy piano, a tape recorder with earphones, and tapes

- Science and Nature Center with things from nature such as stones, seeds, or flowers; living example of the animal world, such as caterpillars or goldfish; magnets; magnifying glasses; and books and pictures

- Dramatic Play Center with dishes, pots and pans, play sink, play stove, a small table and chairs, dolls and doll beds, dress-up clothes, an unbreakable mirror, play telephones and other things commonly used in the home; other props, such as a toy cash register, a typewriter, or hats to use during pretend play

- Puzzle and Small-Muscle Center with many kinds of puzzles (some harder and some easier), beads to string, pegs with pegboards, and toys with pieces that go together and pull apart such as Lego Bricks®

- Sand and Water Center with a water table, a sand table, lots of containers of different sizes and shape, strainers, shovels, and pails

Tips for Setting up Centers

- Before you make up your mind about where to put activity centers, look at your indoor and outdoor space. Decide which activity centers to have indoors and which outdoors. The set-up may change with the seasons.

- Decide which activity centers should be out permanently because they get daily use and which ones can be stored in activity boxes that are rotated into centers. For example, you may want to have a permanent block center, but you may rotate cooking activities into the science center.

- Put messy activity centers near water and centers that need to be protected from people walking around the room away from pathways and away from doors. Activities that need privacy and quiet can be put in corners.

- Remember to keep pathways clear for children and adults to walk around and between activity centers.

- Set up quiet activities like books and art away from noisy activities like music and blocks.

- It is important to keep toys and materials neat and organized so that the centers don't get cluttered. Have plenty of materials for children to use, but do not put too many materials out on shelves at the same time.

- Fours enjoy toys that have many small pieces. Keep toys with many pieces organized in clearly labeled activity boxes so that it is easy to change what is out and keep sets of materials together.

- Make sure puzzles and other put-together toys have all their pieces before they are put away. Put-together toys with missing pieces are very frustrating to Fours and should not be used.

Stretching Space with Activity Boxes

When you put everything you need for one kind of activity into a box or dishpan, you have made an activity box. This helps you keep many different things ready for children to play with without taking up much room. Activity boxes help you set up new activities quickly because you don't have to run around at the last minute to find the toys you need. You can store activity boxes in a closet or on a shelf. The activity boxes hold things to add variety to materials you have out every day in the activity centers. Label each box so that you know what's inside. A picture on the box will help the children know what's inside.

As you and the children put things back into an activity box, make sure that all the pieces are there and that they are clean. If you are careful to do that, you can count on the materials being in good shape the next time you need them. You will find many ideas for indoor and outdoor activity boxes as you read the activities in this book.

Outdoor Play

Outdoor play is relaxing and joyful for children. They can move around and be noisy and messy or talk and play quietly with friends in an out-of-the-way corner. Both active and quiet play areas should be a part of the playground.

Be sure to set up an outdoor play space and use it every day as the weather permits. Check to see that the area is safe:

- Make sure all equipment is safe and in good repair. Check for splinters, exposed nails, and broken pieces.

- Climbing equipment should not be too high for the Fours, and should be spaced far enough apart so that if children fall they will not hit other pieces of equipment.

- When you buy equipment, make sure it has been tested for safety.

- Provide sufficient cushioning material, such as sand or wood chips, under climbing equipment and swings. The amount of cushioning material needed will depend on how high the equipment is and the type of cushioning material being used.

- Install each piece of equipment away from other equipment so that a child who falls will not hit anything else.

- Be sure all equipment is firmly anchored so that it will not fall.

- Check to be sure that slides and other metal equipment are not too hot or cold for children to use safely. If possible, position slides so that they are not in full sun.

- Check for exposed cement or sharp rocks where children are playing.

- Arrange pathways and play areas so that children who are walking from one area to another or playing are not near swings or speeding riding toys.

- Have a fence around the area so that it is easier to keep the children safely inside and keep dangers out.

Be sure the outdoor play space is free of any health problems:

- Have weeds cut, be sure none of the plants are poisonous, and get rid of harmful bugs.

- Before you take the children out each day, check to see that there is no trash in the area.

- Cover the outdoor sandbox to prevent animals from using it. Even if the whole playground is covered in sand, have a separate area for sand play that can be covered and is not near active play. Encourage children to use this clean sand area.

- Be sure there is shade on sunny days and use sunscreen on children if needed. Be sure to have parent's permission when using sunscreen.

- Take sanitary precautions with any water play. Use clean water that is running or changed often, have children wash hands before water play, and use a hose or water slide rather than a pool.

It is very important that all children can easily use the playground and the equipment in it, no matter what their physical abilities are. A child who uses a walker or wheelchair needs to find challenging chances for exercise and play. This takes special planning. When you buy new equipment, make sure it can be used by children with disabilities even if you do not have such a child in your program at the time. If you do not have the right equipment for a child with physical disabilities, ask for advice from a professional who is working with the child. Often it takes very little to make the equipment right or to add some new activities.

A storage shed in the outdoor area is handy for storing wheel toys and activity boxes. A rolling cart or wagon for carrying activity boxes with balls, wheel toys, sand toys, and other materials makes bringing things outdoors easier. The children can help take things out. If you are doing a special activity, be sure to set it up ahead of time. Once the outdoor area is set up, you will only need to get the children out and back inside again.

Outdoor space can also be organized into activity centers. Some of the centers you have outdoors will be fixed, but others can be changed and moved from indoors to outdoors. Fours enjoy the following outdoor activity centers:

- Climbing center with safe climber, sturdy boxes, and boards to build an obstacle course

- Sandbox center with play dishes, shovels, and pails
- Water play center with a sprinkler in hot weather, and a water play table or buckets and tubs for washing baby dolls and doll clothes and playing with dishes and pans on warm days
- Art center where the easel or painting table can be brought out and where messy activities such as fingerpainting can be done
- Active play centers where children can use wheel toys such as tricycles and wagons, play with balls of different sizes, or dance to music.

Trips

Fours like to see new things, but any trip outside the play yard needs a lot of planning. Don't even think of taking a trip until every child feels secure about coming to the center. Ask parents and other helpers to come along on a trip so that you have enough adults to keep the children safe.

Walking trips are easier than bus or car trips. A car trip is a big job because each child must have his own seat belt or safety seat to be really safe, and that often means using a van or several cars. Anyway, most Fours like a short walk to a nearby place just as well as a longer trip. Even for a walking trip, you should have at least one adult for every four or five children. Be sure all children have partners that they hold hands with as they walk because Fours can still wander off and get into danger. Adults should be at the front and back of the group and hold the hand of any children who need more supervision. Walking trips should be short so that children don't get tired or bored. Before the trip, make sure children know the safety rules and talk about things you might see. Point these things out as you take your walk.

Get written permission from parents for any trip that takes children away from the center. Tell the parents when you will be going, where you will be going, when you will be back, and if they need to do anything special for their children that day. Remind parents again the day before the trip.

You don't even have to take Fours away from the center to have some interesting trips. Try a trip to another part of your building, such as the office or kitchen. A trip in your own play yard can be fun if you take a small group out at a time when the other children are indoors. Do something different on a play yard trip, such as catching insects or collecting leaves.

Fours are still very young children and do not need to be taken on big trips. Frequent walks in the neighborhood where children and adults share their discoveries work well with Fours. Later in the year, when they are almost five, plan several short trips in your community. A picnic or longer trip at the end of the year is a special treat and is best when children's families can be involved.

Whether the trip is close or far, there should be follow-up activities to extend the learning from the trip. You can help the children remember what they experienced and do fun activities that let the children show what they know from the trip. There are ideas for activities to use after trips in the activities section of this book.

Three Steps in Planning Activities for Fours

1. Plan and set up activity centers indoors and outdoors with basic toys and materials that most Fours will enjoy. Arrange the schedule so that children spend most of their day playing in these centers. Select activities from the various sections of this book to do in each of the activity centers to keep the centers interesting and challenging.

2. Find out what each child is interested in and the skills each is working on. The "Fours Can" list can help you learn about each of your Fours. Plan activities from this book that are right for each child and show the child how to do them. You can work with a child individually on these activities during the planned activity times in your schedule while other children are busy with activities they have chosen for themselves. These activities can be placed into the activity centers and done by any interested children.

3. Find out what interests lots of your Fours. Then plan special units about these topics. Add activities that go with these topics to the basic activity centers.

Planning Activities Around Topics

Many teachers find that it helps planning when they pick a topic and look for activities to do on that topic. In the first years of school, teachers often plan units on subjects such as community helpers and the family. You can do this, too. However, units go best when you remember to respond to your four-year-olds' own interests.

The most successful activities are those that build on the interests of the children in your group. Just about any topic is fine, as long as the children enjoy thinking and talking about it. It does not matter if they did the same topic when they were younger or that they will do it again when they are older. The topic is right for Fours as long as the children show curiosity, challenge, and excitement as they move beyond what they already know.

Units can last only a few days or go on for several weeks. For example, you may notice that the children are fascinated with the new baby they see when a mom comes in to pick up her older child, so you do a unit on all kinds of babies.

As part of the unit, you could put picture books about many kinds of babies, including animal pups and cubs, into the book corner and put pictures of babies up where the children can see them. Parents might bring in their children's baby pictures, and you might bring in one of your baby pictures, too. You could talk about babies with the children to see what they can tell you and then give them more information. You might add lots of baby things, such as real plastic baby bottles and baby clothes, to the Dramatic Play Center and baby animal puzzles and picture-matching games to the Puzzle and Small-Muscle Center. You might ask a parent to come in with a baby and talk about all the things the baby needs and can do.

Once you pick a topic, you can find related activities in the sections of this book, including stories, songs, and finger plays. Pages 36 and 37 list some topics that can be used to build a unit. You can add your own ideas, too.

Myself	
	■ what I like, what I used to like
	■ my toys
	■ my clothes
	■ what I look like

Who lives at my house	
	■ parents
	■ grandparents
	■ brothers and sisters
	■ other adults and children
	■ pets

Mothers and babies	■ animal babies
	■ human babies
	■ when I was a baby
	■ baby brothers and sisters and friends
The weather	■ cold/warm, rainy/sunny
	■ clouds
	■ clothes we wear in different weather
	■ where we play in different weather
	■ seasons
Animals	■ birds, amphibians, reptiles, mammals
	■ pets
	■ zoo animals
	■ farm animals
	■ animal families
Nature	■ water, rivers, ponds, ocean
	■ mountains, valleys, and hills
	■ rocks, pebbles
	■ plants and flowers
	■ sun, moon, and stars
Going places	■ on the ground: walking, running; cars, trucks, buses, bicycles, trains; riding different animals
	■ in the air: airplanes, helicopters, hot air balloons
	■ in the water: swimming, boats, submarines
Health and safety	■ healthful eating
	■ brushing teeth, washing hands, bathing
	■ fire safety
	■ traffic safety
Our neighborhood	■ people in our community
	■ where we live, types of homes
	■ stores: grocery, pet, book, department, shopping center
	■ restaurants
	■ library
	■ fire station

Helping to save the earth	■ saving energy: water, electricity
	■ recycling waste
	■ keeping our environment clean

Moving on to kindergarten	■ where will we be going
	■ riding a school bus
	■ eating in a school cafeteria
	■ kindergarten activities
	■ new friends
	■ visiting kindergartens in small groups

Sample Unit

As an example of how you might choose related activities on a topic for a month, let's think through how a unit on "Going Places" might work. This example is for a long unit with many topics. Some of your units may be much shorter and last only a few days or a week.

MONTHLY UNIT TOPIC

GOING PLACES

Week 1 — People and animals can move from place to place by using their bodies.

Talk about how people can move all by themselves: walking, running, hopping, skipping, rolling.

Where do children and their families go when they walk?

How fast or slow can children move in many different ways?

How do animals move?

How do people use animals to go places?

Materials and Activities

Children look at magazine pictures and books that show people walking, running, jumping, and so on.

Children figure out as many ways as they can to move from one spot to another.

Children create a book about how people move to put into book area.

Use a stopwatch to time children as they move.

Have toy people and horses, elephants, camels, and so on in the block area.

Put dress-ups, hobby horse toys, and props in the Dramatic Play Center that encourage pretending to ride animals.

Do music and movement activities that are about moving in different ways.

Week

2

Talk about all the different ways to move using wheels: trucks, cars, buses, bicycles, baby strollers, motorcycles, subways, trains.

How do children's families go places using vehicles with wheels?

What do cars need to go?

How do people use trucks to move small and big things ?

What vehicles move on tracks?

Talk about safety while riding in cars: seat belts, car safety seats.

Materials and Activities

Add trucks and many other wheel toys to the block area.

Add a train set to the block area.

Put books on wheeled vehicles in the book area.

Children create a book about wheeled vehicles.

Take children on a field trip to a gas station.

Put together toys that have wheels.

Put a stroller, car safety seat for dolls, and toy steering wheel in the Dramatic Play Center.

Set up a pretend car or bus using chairs in rows with pretend seat belts.

Use riding toys in the outdoor area with a pretend gas station, some road signs.

Take children on a field trip to ride on a bus.

People can travel in water.

Talk about how people travel across water.

Talk about water safety: knowing how to swim, wearing life vests.

Discuss swimming or boating experiences children have had with their families.

Talk about different types of boats: sailboats, motor boats, paddle boats, huge ships.

Talk about animals that swim: fish and others that live in the water, such as whales or seals, and also animals that are able to swim, such as dogs.

Materials and Activities

Provide pictures of and books about different boats, submarines, rafts, and people swimming.

Put boat and swimming props (small paddles, life vests, flippers, face masks) in the Dramatic Play Center.

Display photographs or child-drawn pictures of children and their families swimming or boating.

Do a float/sink activity. Provide toy boats and people for the water table. Make boats in the carpentry area for the water table.

Put toy boats in the block area.

Put a small, safe rowboat in the outdoor area.

Teach songs about rowing boats.

Go on a field trip to take a boat ride.

Week

4

Talk about airplanes, rocket ships, hot air balloons, helicopters.

How do people travel in the air?

Talk about jobs people do at airports.

What happens on airplane trips?

Talk about animals and insects that fly: birds, bats, butterflies, bees, mosquitoes, and others.

Materials and Activities

Provide pictures of and books about different ways to fly.

Children can make rocket ships or airplanes out of wood and other scraps.

Put airplanes and toy airports in the block area.

Go on a field trip to an airport.

Children can pretend to be airplanes taking off, flying, landing.

Children can fold paper airplanes and play with them outside.

Children can spot many kinds of birds taking off, flying, and landing.

Teach songs about flying.

Weekly and Daily Planning

Unit activities are fun and can add special excitement to a classroom. But it is important to remember that a wide range of activities are really needed in a good early childhood program. When you plan for the week, remember that you will need to provide many self-directed and teacher-directed activities for the children every day in addition to the unit activities. The unit can help you bring many different ideas and facts to the children's attention. The repetition in a unit also helps four-year-olds learn some basic ideas and words. But you will need to plan other activities for children to do both indoors and outdoors while unit activities are being done. Also, be sure to keep a unit going as long as children show interest.

When you get down to practical planning for children, you need to think of what you will do day by day. Making a daily plan can help you think of activities that you can add to the children's play in the activity centers or to group activities. The daily plan can help you think of new toys or materials to bring out on a given day, and ways to change activity centers by using some different activity boxes. In your daily plan, try to include activities from all four sections of this book.

There is a sample form for a weekly plan on pages 47 and 48. You could put your completed plan up on the wall as a reminder. Also, use the plan as a guide when you get your materials ready for the next day.

Planning for Individual Children

Every four-year-old is an individual with his or her own pattern of abilities. No two children of the same age will be able to do exactly the same things. By using the "Fours Can" lists on pages 53 and 54, you can find some of the things each one of the children can do. Using the "Fours Can" lists, take a few minutes to watch each one of your Fours and write down what he or she can do.

The "Fours Can" lists are not meant to be used to screen for problems. They cannot tell you how fast or slow a child is developing. These lists can only help you notice more of what a child can do. Without the help of a list, you usually see only the big advances a child makes. A list can help you become a better observer so that you see more of the little advances a child is working on every day.

When you know some of the things children in your group can do, then you will know which activities in this book will best suit them. For each of the activities in this book, a "Fours Can" is listed that tells what skill the activity will let the child practice. If you think a child can do that skill or is trying to learn to do it, then try the activity.

In some groups there will be a wider range of abilities because children with disabilities have been included. The activities in the various books of the *Active Learning Series* have been used successfully in classrooms that include children with disabilities. It is especially important to look at the Fours Can lists before using an activity with a child who has a disability. You may need to use activities from the book on Threes for some children or simplify the activities in this book for Fours. Depending on the disability, you may need to change the activity slightly or provide special equipment so that the child can be successful. Lots of helpful ideas can be found in *Active Learning for Children with Disabilities* by Bailey, Cryer, Harms, Osborne, and Kniest, published by Addison-Wesley Publishing Company.

When you plan, try to think of several children who would enjoy the activity you choose. Jot down their names on the written planning form so that you will remember to encourage them to try the activity. Sometimes there will be one or two children that you plan to include in a special teacher-directed activity. During a slow time of day, try that special activity with the children. You might try it when some children are napping and others are up, or when some children have left for the day. The important thing is to plan some activities that are right for each child in your group every day.

Most of the activity ideas in this book can be introduced to children, and then the toys and materials needed for the activity can be placed in an activity center. The children will be able to choose the activity to do over and over again until they are no longer interested. You will find that children will show their friends how to use the materials, too.

Writing an Activity Plan

It is easy to do a written activity plan using the activities in this book. Each activity has a number and a name. Just put the number and name of the activity you want to use in the right place on the planning form. You will probably be able to use the same activity for a small group of children who are able to do the same things. Jot down the names of the children near the activity to remind you.

On pages 47 and 48, there is a weekly planning form. Post your weekly plan where you can see it. Having the children's names on the written plan helps you make sure that you are keeping each child in mind. If anyone else has to take over for you, things will go more smoothly with a written plan.

Your written plan should list the *new* activities you want to try. You will also want to repeat old familiar activities that went well before because Fours enjoy repeating activities. The reason for planning is to be ready with a lot of activities and materials. It is better to plan too much than too little. Always have some extra things ready in case you need them. This way the children will be active, happy, and learning new things all day, during routines and at play times. When you have written your activity plan, look it over and ask yourself the following questions:

Have I used routines such as meals and snacks to help children learn whenever possible?

Have I planned for both morning and afternoon playtimes?

Have I planned outdoor play activities daily, weather permitting?

Are self-directed activities and toys available all through the day?

Remember in carrying out your written plan to prepare for activities by getting the materials together, going over the instructions, and thinking of questions to ask the children and things to talk about for different activities.

On the next four pages you will find a sample Activity Plan form. The first one is filled in to show you how to use it. Copy the blank form if you wish and change it to fit your needs. If you are already using a written plan form and you are happy with it, by all means stay with it. Remember, this is only a sample to help you come up with the written planning form for Fours that suits you best.

Activity Plan

Write the names of the activities you plan for the different activity areas in your classroom. If there are specific children who will benefit especially from an activity you plan, write their names next to the activity and encourage them to take part.

Activity Areas	Monday	Tuesday	Wednesday	Thursday	Friday
Large Group Time 87, 100	Guess the Word	Work Our Dads and Moms Do Emma, Fred, Jimmy, Jinsy	Work Our Dads and Moms Do Susie, Dave, Nicky, Amanda	Work Our Dads and Moms Do Vanessa, Mark, Brooke, Paul	Guess the Word

Activity Centers	Monday	Tuesday	Wednesday	Thursday	Friday
Books 26, 34, 36, 41	Using Picture Word Recipes to Cook	Using Picture Word Recipes to Cook	Typing Emma, Jimmy	Letter Stamps Jinsy, Nicky	Making Family Posters
Art 218, 220, 240	Fingerpaint Prints	Picture Stories Susie, Dave	Picture Stories Vanessa Paul Mark	Sand Casting	Sand Casting
Blocks 263, 264, 265, 274	Build Around Me Brooke, Paul	Build Around Me	Making Signs for the Block Area Jinsy, Nicky	Block Stories	How We Move As We Build Paul
Music 322, 337, 340, 341, 344	Choose and Play Tapes Emma	Seeing Words for Songs	Play Your Kazoo	Guess the Instrument	Matching Sounds
Dramatic Play 307, 311	Grocery Store	Restaurant Play	Restaurant Play	Restaurant Play	Restaurant Play, Grocery Store

Activity Centers	Monday	Tuesday	Wednesday	Thursday	Friday
Large Muscles 121, 122, 125	Outdoor Basketball Susie Dave Brooke	Plastic Hoop Places Amanda Vanessa	Tents Paul	Tents Paul	Outdoor Basketball Susie Dave Brooke
Small Muscles 164, 165, 166, 167, 184	Opening and Closing Containers Paul	Clothespin Work Paul	Rolling Small Cards Paul, Brooke	Beads and Strings Activity Box	Telephone Wire Jewelry Emma, Jimmy
Science/Nature 388, 389, 392, 394	Taking Care of Classroom Pets Jinsy, Fred	Differences in Trees	Sink or Float Game	Experimenting with Flashlights Paul	Taking Care of Classroom Pets Vanessa, Mark
Math 418, 421, 461, 469	Money Matching and Sorting Games	Money Matching and Sorting Games	Ring Board Sorting Game Amanda	Matching Written Numbers Jinsy	What Number Are You Feeling? Emma, Jimmy
Other P.M. Group		Nicky's mom visits to talk about her job			Emma's dad visits to talk about his job
Other	A.M. snack— children eat what they cooked	A.M. snack— children eat what they cooked			P.M. Snack— Emma's birthday (special snack)

Activity Plan

Write the names of the activities you plan for the different activity areas in your classroom. If there are specific children who will benefit especially from an activity you plan, write their names next to the activity and encourage them to take part.

Activity Areas	Monday	Tuesday	Wednesday	Thursday	Friday
Large Group Time					

Activity Centers	Monday	Tuesday	Wednesday	Thursday	Friday
Books					
Art					
Blocks					
Music					
Dramatic Play					

Activity Centers	Monday	Tuesday	Wednesday	Thursday	Friday
Large Muscles					
Small Muscles					
Science/Nature					
Math					
Other					
Other					

Finding the Right Activities

The activities for Fours have been broken into two age groups. Each age group is shown with a picture.

stands for what a child 48 to 54 months can do.

stands for what a child 54 to 60 months can do.

Every activity has one of these two pictures to make it easy to pick out the right activities for the children in your care. You can use these activities for a four-year-old who is developing normally, more slowly, or faster than usual. Just choose an activity based on what each child *can do.* Each activity in this book tells what the four-year-old should be able to do in order to take part in the activity. Remember, what the child can do is more important in choosing the right activity than the child's age.

The first activities in each section are easier than those that come later. For example, in the first sorting activities in the Math section, children are asked to sort by color; later they sort by size or shape.

On pages 53 and 54, you will find a list of many things Fours can do in each of the two age groups. Take time to look at these pages. It may surprise you to see what you can or can't expect from Fours.

When You Start to Use the Activities

- Look at the "Fours Can" lists. Watch and think about each child. What can each one do?

- Pick out the best "Fours Can" picture for each of your children. This will help you plan for each one of them.

- Which children seem to be on a similar level in large- and small-muscle skills, in listening and talking, and in play interests? Plan some activities for those small groups.

- Look at all four activity sections and ask yourself the following questions:

  Which activities do I have the materials for?

  Which activities do I think each child will be able to enjoy?

Which activities do I have time to do?

Which activities would I like to start with?

Can I relate any of these activities to a unit topic?

- Encourage children to try the activities. Show children how to do the activity if needed. Whenever possible add the activity to a center for any interested children to use.

- Go back over the plan at the end of the week, and ask yourself these questions about how things went.

Which activities went best?

Which activities did not go well and why?

Do I need to make any changes in the interest centers?

Do I need to make any changes in the daily schedule?

Do I need to make any new activity boxes?

Writing Your Own Activities

Some of the activities you will find in this book may be familiar to you. That's because parents and caregivers have always used many of the activities to encourage children to grow and learn. There will also be some activities you've never used before. That's why activity books such as this one keep you on your toes with lots of new ideas. And there may be some activities that you have enjoyed doing with Fours that are not in this book. As you remember them, write them down in the blank activity boxes at the end of each section. This will make it easier to remember and use the activities again as you write your activity plans.

When you work with four-year-olds, you will find that you have to think up some of your own activities to meet children's needs, suit their interests, and make the best use of the toys you have on hand. Here's how to write your own activities.

- First, think about what one child can do. Use the "Fours Can" lists to help focus on a skill the child would like to practice.

- Next, think about what you need to do to help the child practice the skill: Ask yourself the following questions:

Will the activity be teacher- or child-directed?

What toys, equipment, or other materials will I need?

Where will the activity work well?

How long will the activity take?

How many children can take part in the activity?

Will I have to get things ready ahead of time?

Exactly what must I do to make the activity happen?

What kinds of things can I say to help with the child's learning?

■ Write your activity in a blank space on the planning form. Try it out to see how it works. Make changes if you need to.

Activity Checklists

At the beginning of each activity section in this book, you will find a checklist. The checklist is to help you see how well the setting you create for children meets their needs for learning in that area. It's a good idea to use these checklists to see what the strengths and weaknesses of your setting are for each type of activity in the book. Then you can see where improvements are needed. The checklists can be your guide for making changes.

You can do all the checklists at one time if you wish, or pick one or two to work on at first and then do the others when you are ready. As you carefully read each statement on the checklists, look around your preschool setting and think about the things you do with the children.

Carefully follow these directions as you do the checklists.

1. On each checklist you will find that the statements are followed by check boxes under two age ranges. Note the ages of the children in your setting and rate the statements for those ages.

2. If you find much evidence that a statement is *true* for an age group, put a check in the box.

3. If you find clear evidence that a statement is *not true*, put an X in the box.

   Make notes next to a statement if you are not sure about whether it should get a check or an X.

If people who do not work in your classroom want to use the checklists, they will need to spend enough time observing in your room to really find out what they need to know. It takes about two hours in a morning to get most of the information needed to complete all the checklists. If the other observers do not see or hear everything needed to complete the checklists, then they will have to set aside time to ask you some questions about your preschool setting. However, they should be sure to observe first.

Observers may see things differently from the way you do. If there is a chance to talk about the differences, both of you will probably end up with some good new ideas.

"Fours Can" Lists

The following pages give you more information on what Fours can do. It is important to remember that these lists are only general guidelines and cannot be used to find out whether a child is or is not developing typically. These lists are not a screening test. If you are worried about a child in your care, you should advise the parents to find a professional who can do some special tests. The parents could talk to their family doctor for suggestions. Or they could find out about special services by asking the child care professionals who come to your center, such as the child care specialist, social worker, or early childhood special educator.

The "Fours Can" lists are meant to help you become more aware of some of the things most four-year-olds can do. The lists are actually made up of many of the "Fours Can" indicators from the activities. Without a list to follow, it is hard to be aware of the new little steps each child takes. But these new little steps are what we need to encourage in order to help children grow. We want to help each child practice these small advances as she plays with toys, listens to stories, answers our questions, and takes part in all the play activities. Then the big advances will come more easily in their own time.

Fours Can List

48 MONTHS

From 48 to 54 months, some things Fours can do are

- stand on one foot for ten seconds
- name three shapes
- use many words (more than 1500)
- remember some things seen in a picture or in a group of objects
- ask lots of questions
- test adult limits frequently
- enjoy playing with other children more than playing alone
- walk on a balance beam
- ask for help when needed
- tell what their artwork is
- repeat rhymes, songs, or dances
- get dressed without much help
- jump backward
- try to imitate someone who draws a square
- draw a person with three parts
- know some prepositions, such as *in front of, under, behind,* or *on top of*
- walk downstairs, alternating feet
- recognize some colors
- catch a bounced ball
- play alone for 20–30 minutes
- know the name of a penny, nickel, dime
- fasten buttons quite well
- eat well with fork, cut easy foods with knife
- usually stay dry through the night
- jump over things

54 MONTHS
- recognize own name in print

Fours Can List

54 MONTHS

From 54 to 60 months, some things Fours can do are

- hop on one foot at least five times
- cut out a big circle
- tell you what some words mean
- brush teeth quite well
- draw a person with six parts
- ask permission to use things that belong to others
- do well in small groups of three or four
- lace shoes
- show correct number of objects, up to five
- taunt others by calling names
- play cooperatively in small groups often
- say "I'm sorry" to others
- do a somersault
- behave well in public most of time
- tell the opposite of some words
- tell a familiar story
- tell the color of many things
- give understandable home address
- draw some simple things we can recognize
- take part in a large group for a short time
- cut and paste simple shapes
- say when a sound is loud or soft
- say whether two words rhyme
- usually manage all toileting skills alone
- use four or five words in a sentence
- count to ten
- recognize a few printed words
- tell on others who do naughty things
- jump over knee-high obstacles with both feet together
- print own name but not clearly

60 MONTHS
- print a few capital letters

Active Learning
for Fours

Activities for
Listening and Talking

Index

of Activities for Listening and Talking

Here's Why

Words are important to four-year-olds as a way of telling you what they think and how they feel. Words also help children solve problems and remember. Four-year-olds are able to do more with words every day. Their sentences are getting longer, and they are putting more words and ideas together. They ask many questions, and answer some questions, too. But Fours still have lots to learn before they can talk clearly. In fact, children are usually about six years old before they can be easily understood. You can help Fours continue to practice talking by asking questions, listening with interest, and adding to what they say.

In the Books/Pictures/Pre-Reading/Pre-Writing section you will find ideas for using pictures to help your Fours practice some new thinking skills, such as naming, matching, guessing, and comparing. You will also find activities in which Fours get the warm, personal experiences with books that make learning to read more fun later on. Children will begin to understand that what they say can be written down and read back to them in many activities.

The Conversation and Group Talk activities give you ideas for helping Fours use talking to get along with others, share feelings and ideas, work on self-help skills, follow directions, and show what they know and remember. Some of the activities in this section are just for fun as you and the Fours play with words together. Listening and talking should be a big part of everything you do with children. The activities in this book can get you started helping Fours improve their skills with words.

Throughout the day, conversations will happen as part of the children's activities. It is also important to bring a small group of Fours together to talk about something of interest so that they can learn how to take turns as they listen and talk. On page 127 there are tips about making group discussions go smoothly with Fours.

Materials and Notes

Books/Pictures/Pre-Reading/Pre-Writing

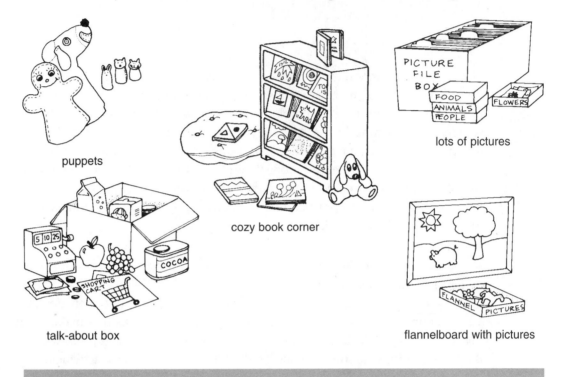

puppets

cozy book corner

lots of pictures

talk-about box

flannelboard with pictures

- Remember that listening and talking about many new experiences is the best way for Fours to get ready to read and write when they are ready.

- Give interested children lots of chances to try writing or reading when they choose. But spend most of your time encouraging Fours to do fun, interesting activities that enable them to learn many words and talk a lot.

- Do most book activities with small groups of children. Read often to a few Fours in the Book Center. Have large-group story times that do not last very long. Be sure children are uncrowded and comfortable when they listen to stories.

- Use lots of books and pictures in all areas of the room to show information about topics you are discussing with the children.

- Many of the activity ideas for younger and older Fours can be used with either age-group. This is because they are open ended and can be challenging to children of a wide range of abilities.

- Give children many chances to tell stories about pictures, activities, and so on. Write down exactly what they say as they watch you write. Read their words back to them.

Activity Checklist

Books/Pictures/Pre-Reading/Pre-Writing

Book and picture activities for Fours use sturdy picture books, simple picture games, and pictures in the room that add information to what you talk about with Fours. Fours enjoy being read to and looking at books on their own. They are likely to notice the letters and words printed in books, but most are not ready to read yet. They enjoy easy picture games. They like to retell or pretend to read familiar stories and to make up their own. Fours begin to understand that what they say can be written down and read when adults write their stories and then read them back. Some older Fours may want to write some letters and words.

Check for each age group

	48–54 months	54–60 months
1. Many pictures are placed where children can see and touch them. New pictures and books are added often.	❐	❐
2. Most pictures show things that are interesting to the children and that the children talk about with adults.	❐	❐
3. A cozy book area, with a variety of sturdy, well-kept books is available to the children most of the day.	❐	❐
4. Pictures and books show people of different races, ages, cultures, and abilities in positive nonsexist ways.	❐	❐
5. Adults and children often talk about pictures.	❐	❐
6. Adult reads with children every day, mostly in small groups, but also during larger group times.	❐	❐
7. Children use simple picture games, puppets, and flannelboards with teacher help when needed.	❐	❐
8. Children see many printed words, such as names on cubbies or picture/word labels on toy shelves.	❐	❐
9. Children often have what they say written down for them by an adult. The child sits where he can see the letters printed correctly, not sideways or upside down. The adult reads back what the child has said.	❐	❐
10. Interested children are encouraged to read and write some letters in their names, and other simple words. Children who are not interested are not pushed to take part in these activities.	❐	❐

1

Fours can

- look at books on their own

Using the Book Center

Set up a Book Center for your Fours to use. (See Book Center Ideas on page 84.) Talk with the children about how to use books carefully and how to clean up the center when finished.

Add books that come from the library, books the children have made, and photo albums of the children in your group. Have a special little place where children can safely put books they bring from home. Talk with the children about taking special care of these books the others wish to share.

🏠 indoors   🕐 5–20 minutes   **#** 1–4 Fours

2

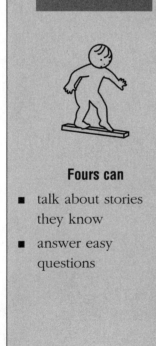

Fours can

- talk about stories they know
- answer easy questions

Read and Ask

Read a short story to a group of Fours. (See Story Times Ideas, page 84.) As you finish reading a page, see if the children can answer some questions about what is happening. Hold the book up so that children can see the pictures. Then use questions that ask what, who, where, when, why, and how things are happening in the story.

Why did Sal have no blueberries in her bucket?
Why was Little Bear's Mom frightened?
What do you think Sal and her mom will do with their blueberries?

Encourage children to listen while the others talk. Give all children a chance to answer.

🏠 in or out   🕐 5–15 minutes   **#** 1–10 Fours

3

The Class Book

Have your Fours help you make a <u>book</u> with a page for each child. On each child's page, write his or her name. Then talk with each Four so that you can write down what he or she tells you about favorite things to do, places to go, and other ideas for the page. Add <u>photos of each child</u> or pictures children draw. Read the book to small groups of children. As they get to know it well, let them tell you about their friends.

Whose page is this? It says she likes to play with blocks. That's right, it's Patricia.
This is Marika's page.
Do you remember what Marika likes to do?

Put the book in the Book Center so that the children can look at it by themselves.

Fours can

- retell familiar stories
- learn that what they say can be written and read

🏠 indoors   🕐 5–15 minutes   # 2–6 Fours

4

Poster Making

Have your Fours help you make picture posters to go with the ideas you talk about. For example, if you are talking about spring flowers, make posters that show different kinds. Cut out lots of the <u>pictures</u> you need from <u>magazines</u> and <u>catalogs</u>. Then your Fours can look at them and help you glue the ones they like onto a large sheet of sturdy <u>paper</u>.

Talk with the children about the pictures as you work. Write down some of the things they say on the poster, too. Read their words back to them. Have the children help hang up the posters when they are done. Look at the posters and talk about them often. Take them down after a week or two, but save them to look at again.

Fours can

- talk about pictures
- learn that what they say can be written and read

🏠 indoors   🕐 15–25 minutes   # 1–8 Fours

5

Fours can

- talk about things they know
- guess easy riddles

Picture Card Riddle Game

Use a set of picture cards that have many different pictures. Show your Fours two pictures of things they know about. Encourage the children to talk a little about the two pictures. Then give clues about one of the pictures and see if anyone can guess which picture you are talking about.

This creature has eyes, a nose, and a mouth.
Hmmm, Some of you think it's the fish, and some think it's the rabbit.
Here's another clue. It has fur.
Right! It's the rabbit, Joseph!

Give your Fours chances to take turns giving the clues and guessing. Show three or four pictures to make the game more challenging.

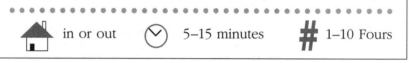

🏠 in or out   🕐 5–15 minutes   # 1–10 Fours

6

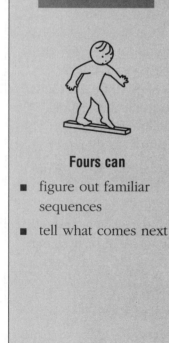

Fours can

- figure out familiar sequences
- tell what comes next

Sequence Card Story

Buy or make a set of easy, four-step sequence cards. (You will find some examples to copy on page 92.) Try making sequence cards from photos taken at school or at home. Put the cards out in order, from left to right. Point to the pictures as you tell your Fours what is happening. Then see if the children can tell you the story. Ask questions and point to a card to see if the children can show you the card that comes next.

The boy is brushing his teeth.
What does he do next?

Put the cards in the Book Center for the children to use. Many Fours will want to put the cards in a different order. Enjoy the special way young children see things.

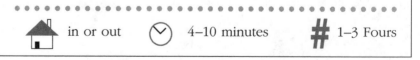

🏠 in or out   🕐 4–10 minutes   # 1–3 Fours

7

Fours can

- recognize some familiar things by touch
- show interest in printed words

Feelie Box Picture Game

Put a plastic margarine tub into a large, stretchy sock to make a feelie box. Have some familiar items that will fit into the box, such as a crayon, paintbrush, or spoon. Make picture cards that show these things. Write the word for each thing on the card, too.

Put one of the things into the feelie box while the child looks away. Then show the child two cards, one of which is a picture of the thing in the box. Read the words on the cards to the child. Let the child reach into the box and feel. See if he can choose the picture of the thing he feels.

Encourage children to play this game with friends. Add challenge by showing more than two pictures or by using things that have a similar feel, such as a crayon and a pencil.

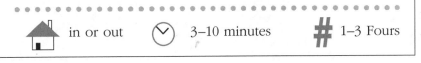

🏠 in or out 🕐 3–10 minutes # 1–3 Fours

8

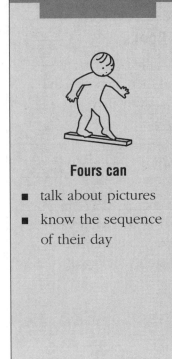

Fours can

- talk about pictures
- know the sequence of their day

Picture Schedule

Make a set of pictures that show things on your schedule. Use pictures you have found or those you draw yourself. Add words to the pictures. Include pictures of washing hands, picking up toys, eating, or going outside. Look at the pictures with the children. See what they can tell you about each one. When it's almost time for a change from one activity to the next, see if anyone can point out the picture of what comes next. Have the child tell what is going to happen next.

Can you find the picture that shows what we do next? Right, Valerie, we wash hands after snack.

Put up pictures with words that show a day's schedule for your Fours to look at and talk about.

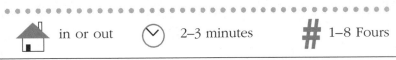

🏠 in or out 🕐 2–3 minutes # 1–8 Fours

Activities for Listening and Talking

9

Fours can

■ help tell a story

Story with Puppets

Have a few Fours use <u>hand puppets</u> to help you tell a very familiar story, such as "The Three Bears." Give each child a puppet to hold. Help the children decide who each puppet will be in the story. Have the children listen carefully so that they will know when to make their puppet talk. Begin telling the story. When the time comes for a child's puppet to say something, give help if needed.

The Mama Bear looked at her bowl.
And what did she say, Latoya?

If you don't have hand puppets, try this activity using toy animals or homemade stick puppets. (See directions for making stick puppets on page 89.)

● ●

🏠 in or out   🕐 5–10 minutes   **#** 2–4 Fours

10

Fours can

■ make up a silly story
■ learn that what they say can be written and read

Making Silly Story Books

Have children help as you make a new <u>silly book</u> for the book center. You can start the story and then have the children continue it. Write down what the children say.

Once upon a time there was a big monster.
This monster had a name. What was his name?
Silly Willy? O.K., His name was Silly Willy.
What silly things did Silly Willy do?

Ask the children to draw <u>pictures</u> for the story. Cover pages with <u>clear contact paper</u>. Tie the pages together with <u>yarn</u> or string. Write the book's title on the front. Make lots of silly books with your Fours. Read them the stories they helped to write.

● ●

🏠 indoors   🕐 5–20 minutes   **#** 1–5 Fours

11

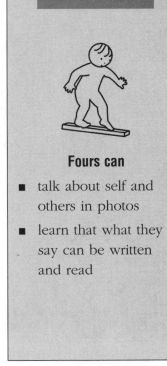

Fours can

- retell a simple story

Retell a Simple Story

Read a simple, familiar story to a small group of Fours. (See Story Times Ideas, page 84.) Leave out a few words on each page and let the children fill them in.

And the Big Bad Wolf said, "_____."
Right! He said, "Little Pig, Little
Pig, Let me come in."
Then the first little pig said, "_____."

Put the book in the Book Center so that children can look at it by themselves or with friends.

....

🏠 indoors   🕐 5–10 minutes   # 1–9 Fours

12

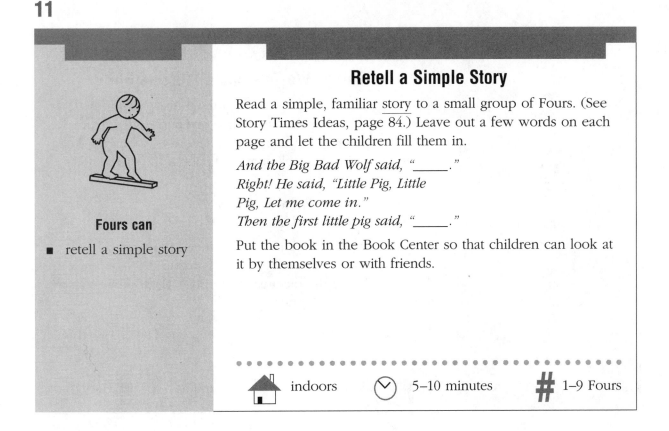

Fours can

- talk about self and others in photos
- learn that what they say can be written and read

Kids' Photo Album

Take photos of the children and other familiar people often. Take pictures on special occasions, such as birthdays, but be sure to have many pictures of your Fours doing everyday things, too. Put the photos into a sturdy photo album with plastic pages.

Have children talk about the pictures. Write down some of the things they say and put their words next to the photos. Put the album in the Book Center for the children to use. Talk with the children about the pictures and read their words to them.

Do you remember where this photo was taken, Marlys?
That's right, we visited the pumpkin patch in the fall.
Why did we visit the pumpkin patch?

....

🏠 indoors   🕐 2–20 minutes   # 1–6 Fours

13

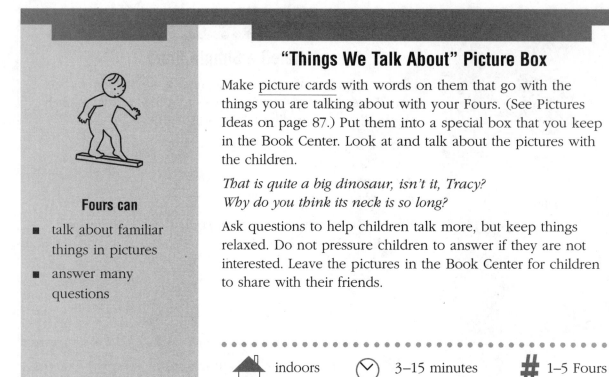

Fours can

- talk about familiar things in pictures
- answer many questions

"Things We Talk About" Picture Box

Make picture cards with words on them that go with the things you are talking about with your Fours. (See Pictures Ideas on page 87.) Put them into a special box that you keep in the Book Center. Look at and talk about the pictures with the children.

That is quite a big dinosaur, isn't it, Tracy?
Why do you think its neck is so long?

Ask questions to help children talk more, but keep things relaxed. Do not pressure children to answer if they are not interested. Leave the pictures in the Book Center for children to share with their friends.

🏠 indoors   🕐 3–15 minutes   # 1–5 Fours

14

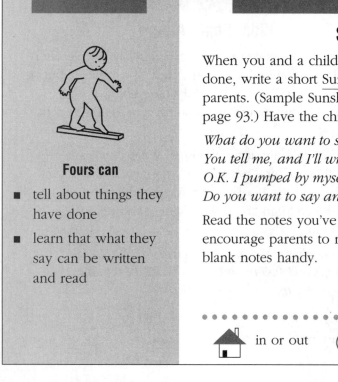

Fours can

- tell about things they have done
- learn that what they say can be written and read

Sunshine Notes

When you and a child are happy about something she has done, write a short Sunshine Note for the child to give to her parents. (Sample Sunshine Notes that you can copy are on page 93.) Have the child tell you what to write.

What do you want to say in this sunshine note, Hiromasa?
You tell me, and I'll write.
O.K. I pumped by myself on the swing.
Do you want to say anything else?

Read the notes you've written back to the children and encourage parents to read them aloud, too. Keep plenty of blank notes handy.

🏠 in or out   🕐 2–5 minutes   # 1 child at a time

15

Fours can

■ sort familiar things by category

Sorting Board Fun

Make some picture sorting games for your Fours to use with a sorting board. (See How to Make Sorting Boards on page 396.) Have sets of pictures, such as toys, animals, clothes, foods, or dinosaurs, that the children can sort. Put out a sorting board with two sets of the cards. Show the child how to sort the cards by what they are.

Can you put all the trucks into this row and all the dinosaurs into this row, Kyle?
What's this picture? Right, it's a tyrannosaur.
Does it go here with the dinosaurs or with the trucks?

You may put out boxes for the children to sort into rather than sorting boards. Make the game more challenging by putting out more than two sets of cards.

indoors   5–15 minutes   # 1–3 Fours

16

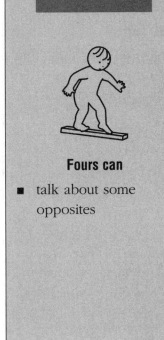

Fours can

■ talk about some opposites

Opposite Pictures

Look at a book or a set of pictures that show opposites. (Ask your public librarian for ideas on books.) Look at the book or pictures with the children and see what they can tell you about all the opposites. Ask questions to encourage children to say more.

That's right, Shizuko. One picture shows night and the other shows day.
What do you do at night when it is dark?

Leave the books or pictures in the Book Center for children to look at on their own.

in or out   2–12 minutes   # 1–6 Fours

17

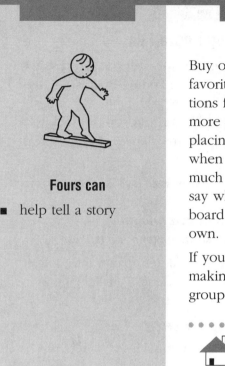

Fours can

- help tell a story

Flannelboard Stories

Buy or make flannelboard pictures to use as you tell a favorite story with a small group of your Fours. (See directions for making a flannelboard on page 94.) Give one or more pictures to each child. Let the child be in charge of placing those pictures on the flannelboard and moving them when needed. Have your Fours take part in the telling as much of the story as they can. Use questions to help them say what is going on. Leave the pictures with the flannelboard in the Book Center for the children to use on their own.

If your Fours are able to work well as a large group, try making up a story that has enough felt pictures for the whole group to use.

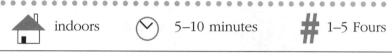

🏠 indoors   🕐 5–10 minutes   # 1–5 Fours

18

Fours can

- enjoy stories
- follow directions

Books with Records or Tapes

Play a record or tape that goes with a picture book. Show the children how to listen to the story and turn the pages at the right times. The record or tape should have a special sound, such as a bell ringing, to tell when to turn the page. Help your Fours listen for the sound. You will probably have to work the record or tape player at first. Your Fours will enjoy taking turns holding the books and turning the pages.

Show your Fours how to use headphones so that they can listen without disturbing other children.

Try making your own tapes of favorite books. Read slowly, ring a bell as you turn the page, and wait ten seconds before starting the next page. Ask some fathers, mothers, or other relatives if they would read and record a story.

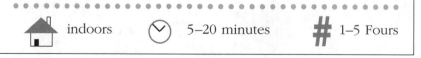

🏠 indoors   🕐 5–20 minutes   # 1–5 Fours

19

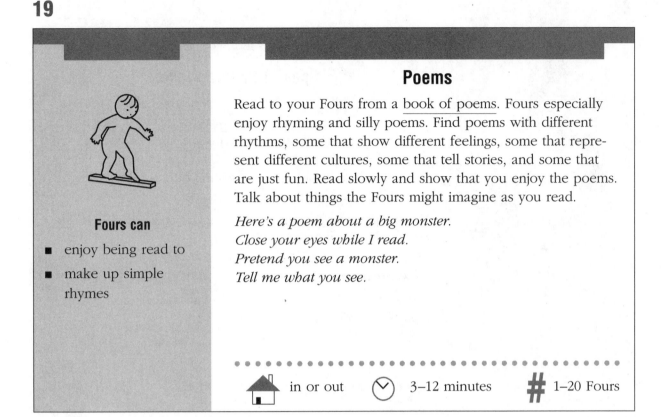

Fours can

- enjoy being read to
- make up simple rhymes

Poems

Read to your Fours from a <u>book of poems</u>. Fours especially enjoy rhyming and silly poems. Find poems with different rhythms, some that show different feelings, some that represent different cultures, some that tell stories, and some that are just fun. Read slowly and show that you enjoy the poems. Talk about things the Fours might imagine as you read.

Here's a poem about a big monster.
Close your eyes while I read.
Pretend you see a monster.
Tell me what you see.

in or out   3–12 minutes   # 1–20 Fours

20

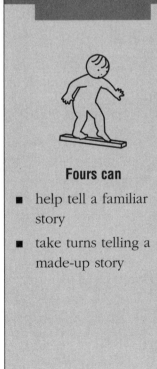

Fours can

- help tell a familiar story
- take turns telling a made-up story

What Will Happen?

Begin to tell a familiar story to your Fours. Do this without a book so that the children listen without looking at pictures. Once you are into the story, choose places where the children might be able to help you tell what happens. Be ready to hear lots of different ideas besides the ones you expect. Show the children how happy you are with whatever they say.

Peter Rabbit hid under the flower pot.
And then what happened?

Try to make up a story with your Fours. See if they can help you make up what happens as the story grows. This can get pretty silly, so be ready to laugh.

in or out   3–10 minutes   # 1–5 Fours

21

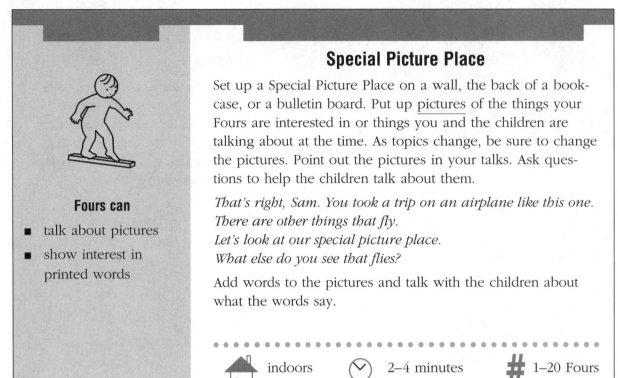

Fours can

- talk about pictures
- show interest in printed words

Special Picture Place

Set up a Special Picture Place on a wall, the back of a book-case, or a bulletin board. Put up pictures of the things your Fours are interested in or things you and the children are talking about at the time. As topics change, be sure to change the pictures. Point out the pictures in your talks. Ask questions to help the children talk about them.

That's right, Sam. You took a trip on an airplane like this one. There are other things that fly. Let's look at our special picture place. What else do you see that flies?

Add words to the pictures and talk with the children about what the words say.

indoors　　2–4 minutes　　# 1–20 Fours

22

Fours can

- enjoy books
- follow some directions

Library or Bookmobile Visit

Take your Fours on a visit to the library. First, plan your visit with the librarian. Then get the children ready. Talk about the library before you go. Explain library rules and talk about how to handle the books there. Make sure you have one adult along for every four children. Then go on your visit.

Let the children look at books for a while. If there's time, read a short story or do another fun library activity. If possible, let each child choose a book to check out. Keep the books in a special place so that they don't get mixed up with other books.

If you cannot make library visits often, see if a Bookmobile will visit. Encourage parents to take their children to the library frequently.

in or out　　45–90 minutes　　# 1–4 Fours per adult

23

Fours can

- print name and a few letters but not perfectly

- show interest in printed words

The Writing Center

Set up a Writing Center for Fours to use if they wish. Put a small table with two or three chairs and a small shelf in a quiet part of the room. On the shelf put neatly organized pencils, colorful watercolor markers of different sizes, and white paper (some with lines and some without). Have an example of the alphabet for children to look at if they want to.

Explain to the children that this is a place where they can write. Tell them that you will write words for them to see or to copy.

Ranika, here's how you spell your name.
You can copy it onto the picture you drew if you want.

. . . .

🏠 indoors   🕐 2–20 minutes   # 1–3 Fours

24

Fours can

- print name and a few letters but not perfectly

The Name Box

Neatly print each child's name onto a sturdy card that is 8" wide and 4" tall. Have each child watch as you print his or her name. Talk about the letters as you write them. See if the child knows what the letters are. Put these cards into a box in the Writing Center.

When a child wants to write her name, have her find her card in the box. Then she can copy the letters from the card.

Look at all the names in the box with a small group of children. See if they can tell which names belong to the different children in the group.

. . . .

🏠 indoors   🕐 1–15 minutes   # 1–5 Fours

25

Fours can

- tell simple stories
- learn that what they say can be written and read

Creating Picture/Word Stories

Use large sheets of <u>paper</u> for children to draw on. Fold the paper in half so that the child makes the picture on one half, while the other half is folded underneath. When the child is finished drawing, ask if he wants to tell a story to go with the picture. Explain that you will write the story for him.

Unfold the paper so that you can write the child's story under the picture. Write exactly what the child tells you, and say the words as you write. Use another piece of paper if you run out of space and the child wants to continue. When the child is done, read the story back to him.

Put up a <u>bulletin board</u> at child height so that you can post children's stories for others to see. You can make a book of all the stories, too.

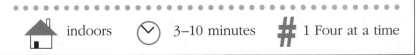

🏠 indoors   🕐 3–10 minutes   # 1 Four at a time

26

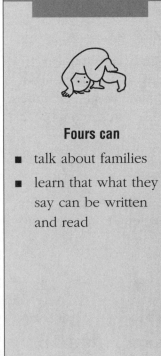

Fours can

- talk about families
- learn that what they say can be written and read

Making Family Posters

Have your Fours find lots of <u>pictures</u> of families in <u>magazines</u> and <u>catalogs</u>. Be sure the children can find families of all races. Let the children cut out the pictures and glue them to large sheets of <u>paper</u>. Look at the pictures and talk with the Fours about the different families.

Ask the children to tell about a family. Write their words near the pictures. Hang the posters with the children's words where your Fours can see them. Look at the posters with the children and read what they told you.

Which family did you talk about, Alicia?
Do you want me to read what you said? See, I wrote it down right here.

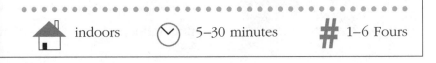

🏠 indoors   🕐 5–30 minutes   # 1–6 Fours

27

Fours can

- sort by shape and size
- recognize their printed names

Letters of the Alphabet

Buy or make alphabet letters in metal, felt, plastic, wood, sandpaper, or cardboard. Put baskets of letters in the Book Center and the Writing Center. Encourage your Fours to have fun touching the shapes of the letters, sorting them in many ways, and finding the letters of their names. Help them use the letters to spell out words they want to see.

Hang a cookie sheet (not aluminum) on the side or back of a shelf. Put a basket or box of magnetic letters on the shelf. Show children how they can stick the letters onto the cookie sheet. Then let them use the letters with the metal sheet in their own creative way.

🏠 indoors   🕐 1–5 minutes   # 1–3 Fours

28

Fours can

- enjoy listening to stories
- begin to recognize the first letter in their names

Alphabet Books

Read your Fours some alphabet books. Point out the letters of the alphabet as you read. Try to find rhyming stories, silly stories, and stories with new words.

When you come to the beginning letter in one of your Four's names, play a guessing game to see if anyone in the group knows whose name starts with that letter.

I see the letter A.
Does anybody here have a name that starts with A?
Yes, Alex. Your name starts with A.
That's right, Aaron. Your name has two A's right next to each other!

🏠 in or out   🕐 3–10 minutes   # 1–20 Fours

29

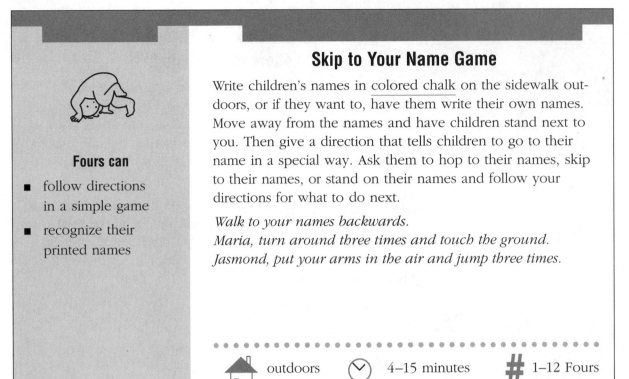

Fours can

- follow directions in a simple game
- recognize their printed names

Skip to Your Name Game

Write children's names in colored chalk on the sidewalk outdoors, or if they want to, have them write their own names. Move away from the names and have children stand next to you. Then give a direction that tells children to go to their name in a special way. Ask them to hop to their names, skip to their names, or stand on their names and follow your directions for what to do next.

Walk to your names backwards.
Maria, turn around three times and touch the ground.
Jasmond, put your arms in the air and jump three times.

outdoors   4–15 minutes   # 1–12 Fours

30

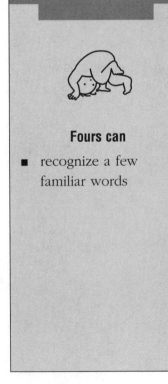

Fours can

- recognize a few familiar words

Word Field Trip

Take a field trip with your Fours to look for words.

Point out the words on stores, street signs, trucks, gas stations, and fast-food restaurants. Note any words your Fours recognize by themselves. When you return from the field trip, ask your Fours if they remember some of the words they saw.

What words did you see, Jesse?
You saw STOP on the sign.
What do drivers do when they see that word?

Later, clearly print the words your Fours knew. Then show them the words. See if they still know any of the words when they are not in their normal place.

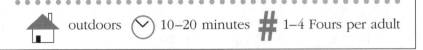

outdoors   10–20 minutes   # 1–4 Fours per adult

31

Fours can

- talk about families
- learn that what they say can be written and read

Family Photo Album

Ask children's parents to bring in family photos for you to put into a Family Photo Album. Put the photos in an album that has clear plastic pages that protect the photos. Have one page for each child's family. Have a page for your family and the families of other important adults, too.

Have each child talk about the people in her photo. Write down the words the child says. Add what the child said to her page in the album. (You may need more than one page if the child has a lot to tell you.)

Look at the photo album often with your Fours. Read what the children said about their families and talk about all the favorite people.

🏠 in or out　　🕐 3–20 minutes　　# 1–6 Fours

32

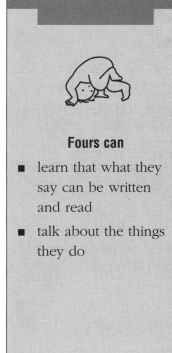

Fours can

- learn that what they say can be written and read
- talk about the things they do

Stories About Classroom Activities

Sit in the Writing Center with a four-year-old who wants to write a story about activities he has done. Ask the child what he would like to say, and write down his words exactly as he says them. Be sure the child is sitting right next to you so that he can see you print the letters. Read back what he said. See if he would like to add a picture to the story. Read what children have said to other children if they are interested. Talk some more about the activities.

*Here's Margaretta's story about what she did this morning.
"I played with David in the little house. Then I made an airplane in carpentry."
I saw you in carpentry, too, Mamie. What did you do?*

🏠 in or out　　🕐 5–10 minutes　　# 1 Four at a time

33

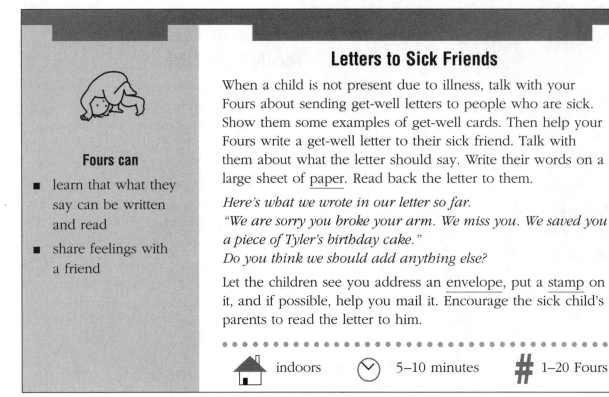

Fours can

- learn that what they say can be written and read

- share feelings with a friend

Letters to Sick Friends

When a child is not present due to illness, talk with your Fours about sending get-well letters to people who are sick. Show them some examples of get-well cards. Then help your Fours write a get-well letter to their sick friend. Talk with them about what the letter should say. Write their words on a large sheet of paper. Read back the letter to them.

Here's what we wrote in our letter so far.
"We are sorry you broke your arm. We miss you. We saved you a piece of Tyler's birthday cake."
Do you think we should add anything else?

Let the children see you address an envelope, put a stamp on it, and if possible, help you mail it. Encourage the sick child's parents to read the letter to him.

🏠 indoors   🕐 5–10 minutes   # 1–20 Fours

34

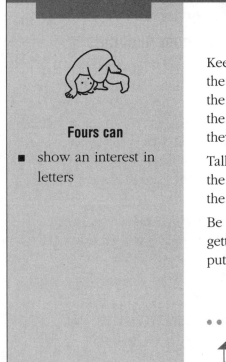

Fours can

- show an interest in letters

Letter Stamps

Keep colorful stamp pads, unlined paper, and letter stamps in the Writing Center. Encourage children to have fun stamping the letters in their names or making their own designs with the letters. See if the children say any of the letter names as they use the stamps. Add some picture stamps, too.

Talk with the children about the designs they made. Point out the letters they used. See if they can see another letter that is the same as the one you are pointing to.

Be sure your Fours know how to use the stamp pads without getting ink on their clothing and how to close the pad before putting it away so that the ink will not dry out.

🏠 indoors   🕐 1–5 minutes   # 1–4 Fours

35

Fours can

- enjoy and use easy computer games

- show interest in printed words

"Getting Ready to Read" Computer Games

Set up a computer with an easy-to-use computer game that helps children learn about letters in the alphabet and simple words. Be sure the game is not violent and is right for the children's abilities.

Show children how to play the game. Make sure they know how to use the computer safely. Have an adult nearby who can supervise.

Limit the time the children spend on computer activities. Remember that computer activities are not necessary to a good preschool program but can be added if you wish.

indoors   3–15 minutes   1–2 Fours at a time

36

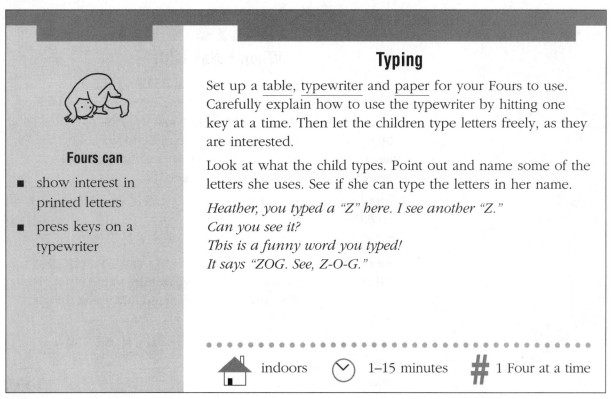

Fours can

- show interest in printed letters

- press keys on a typewriter

Typing

Set up a table, typewriter and paper for your Fours to use. Carefully explain how to use the typewriter by hitting one key at a time. Then let the children type letters freely, as they are interested.

Look at what the child types. Point out and name some of the letters she uses. See if she can type the letters in her name.

Heather, you typed a "Z" here. I see another "Z."
Can you see it?
This is a funny word you typed!
It says "ZOG. See, Z-O-G."

indoors   1–15 minutes   1 Four at a time

37

Fours can

- show interest in print materials

The Reading Classroom

Make your classroom a reading classroom. Add children's magazines and more children's books for the Book Center. Put the daily newspaper, magazines, catalogs, menus, and coupons in the Dramatic Play Center so that children can pretend with these. Post the menu for meals and snacks where children can see it and point it out as you read about what they will be eating each day. Read a variety of stories, poetry, jokes, and riddles. Put children's stories and descriptions on a bulletin board at child height and read them to your Fours at least once a week.

Help children learn to read by watching others read for work and play. Set an example for your Fours in the classroom and talk with parents about the importance of home reading, too.

🏠 indoors   🕐 3–8 minutes   # 1–20 Fours

38

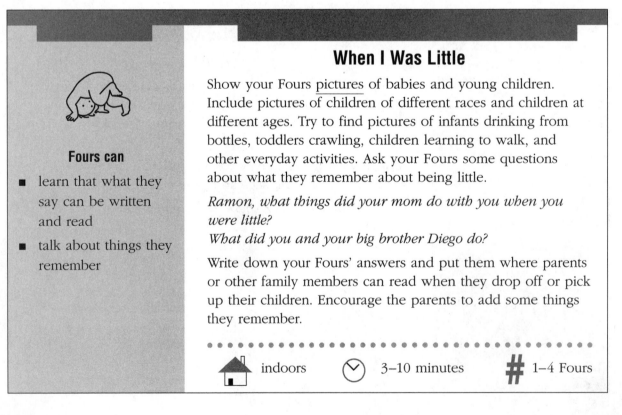

Fours can

- learn that what they say can be written and read
- talk about things they remember

When I Was Little

Show your Fours pictures of babies and young children. Include pictures of children of different races and children at different ages. Try to find pictures of infants drinking from bottles, toddlers crawling, children learning to walk, and other everyday activities. Ask your Fours some questions about what they remember about being little.

Ramon, what things did your mom do with you when you were little?
What did you and your big brother Diego do?

Write down your Fours' answers and put them where parents or other family members can read when they drop off or pick up their children. Encourage the parents to add some things they remember.

🏠 indoors   🕐 3–10 minutes   # 1–4 Fours

39

Fours can

- learn that what they say can be written and read

- talk about things they remember

Writing Outdoor Stories

Bring paper, pencils and washable markers outdoors on a nice day, when you plan to spend lots of time outdoors with your Fours. When a child has run off lots of energy and wants something new to do, see if he would like to tell you a story about what he likes to do outdoors. Write down what he says and read his words back to him.

Here's what you wrote about playing outdoors, Kenneth.
"I chased Lisa and Mei.
I went down the slide forty nineteen times."
Do you want to add anything else to your story?

See if children want to add pictures to their stories. Show them a good place to draw outdoors. Encourage parents to read these outdoor stories to their children at home.

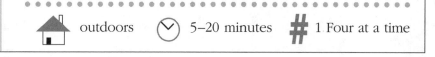

🏠 outdoors 🕐 5–20 minutes # 1 Four at a time

40

Fours can

- pretend to write

- learn about sending mail

Sending Letters

Put out envelopes, pencils, washable markers, and paper so children can write letters to other children, teachers, or parents. Encourage children to draw pictures for their letters. Or they can tell you something that you can write out for them to go into a letter. (Encourage children who are interested to write themselves by scribbling or printing letters).

Have each child fold the paper and put it into an envelope. You can help children write the names they want on the envelope or let them scribble or print themselves.

🏠 indoors 🕐 5–8 minutes # 1–4 Fours

41

Fours can

- follow a simple sequence
- enjoy cooking and eating

Using Picture/Word Recipes to Cook

When cooking with children, have a recipe that uses pictures with words to show what to do. For example, have each child make a fruit kabob for snack time by using the picture recipe on page 95. Before cooking, show the recipe cards and talk about what the picture/words say to do. After cooking, look at the recipe cards again and see what the children can tell you about how to make fruit kabobs.

This picture shows what to put on your skewer, Vinetta.
Can you tell what it is?
Yes, and this word is "orange."

(Look for many other picture/word recipes for children in the book *Cook and Learn* by Beverly Veitch and Thelma Harms, published by Addison-Wesley Publishing Company.)

indoors   5–10 minutes   # 1–6 Fours

42

Fours can

- remember simple rhymes
- act out a simple play

Acting Out Poetry

Help children act out simple poetry. You can show them movements to make, or they can make up their own. Ask your public library for books with lots of other poems for acting out. Act out this silly rhyme with your Fours.

Nobody loves me. (Hang your head.)
Everybody hates me. (Pretend to cry.)
I'm going out to eat some worms. (Pretend to eat slimy, wiggly worms.)
Short ones (crouch down), tall ones (up on tiptoes),
Fat ones (arms out to the side), skinny ones
(arms close together).
I'm going out to eat some worms! (Pretend to eat worms again.)

in or out   3–8 minutes   # 1–20 Fours

43

Fours can

- pretend to read a book
- cooperate in pretend play

Reading to a Pal

Find some small <u>books</u> with photographs or simple pictures. Put them in the housekeeping area next to the dolls. If you have the space, you can make a tiny reading area, using soft pillows or a child-sized rocking chair. Encourage your Fours to read to the <u>dolls, stuffed animals</u>, and friends.

Michelle, can you read this book to Baby Sam?
That's right. Point to the pictures and tell him about them.

🏠 indoors   🕐 1–6 minutes   # 1–3 Fours

44

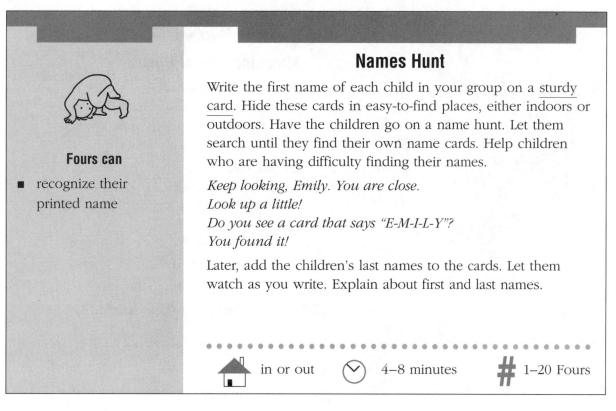

Fours can

- recognize their printed name

Names Hunt

Write the first name of each child in your group on a <u>sturdy card</u>. Hide these cards in easy-to-find places, either indoors or outdoors. Have the children go on a name hunt. Let them search until they find their own name cards. Help children who are having difficulty finding their names.

Keep looking, Emily. You are close.
Look up a little!
Do you see a card that says "E-M-I-L-Y"?
You found it!

Later, add the children's last names to the cards. Let them watch as you write. Explain about first and last names.

🏠 in or out   🕐 4–8 minutes   # 1–20 Fours

45

Fours can

■ try to read books by talking about pictures and/or remembering the story

Children "Read" to You

Sit with a very small group of Fours. Ask one of the children to choose a favorite picture book to use as he tells you the story. Listen with interest as he goes through the book and tells the story in his own way. See if he pretends to read or makes up a new story to go with the pictures. Whatever he does, show delight with the way the story is told.

Encourage children to read to each other in this way often.

in or out   4–10 minutes   # 1–4 Fours

46

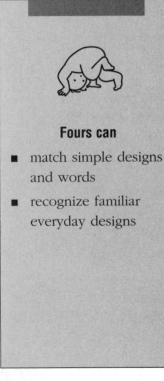

Fours can

■ match simple designs and words

■ recognize familiar everyday designs

Matching Cereal Boxes

Collect empty cereal boxes. Include two boxes each of the children's favorite cereals. Cut out the boxtops from one of each pair of boxes. Cover the boxtop with clear contact paper. Put the boxes and boxtops in an activity box.

When you are ready, take the activity box to the Writing or Book Center. Choose two cereal boxes and put them out for the child to see. Show the children a boxtop that matches one of the boxes.

Which cereal is this?
Yes, Ramon, it's Cheerios.
You found the word Cheerios.

Let the child play until all the boxtops are matched to their boxes.

indoors   1–5 minutes   # 1–5 Fours

47

Fours can

- play matching games
- recognize many objects that go together

Go Together Matching Game

Cut out pictures of things that go together, such as cereal and milk, peanut butter and bread, and a ball and bat. Cover half of each pair with clear contact paper. Mount all the other pictures between two large pieces of contact paper to make a matching board. Make several different cards. Introduce the matching game to one or two children at a time. Show children how to place each picture card onto the pictures they match on the board.

Thelma, what did you pick? You picked the peanut butter. Can you find something you eat with peanut butter?

Children may choose other matches, like peanut butter and milk, or silly matches like hot dogs and jelly. Let them enjoy the game and talk about the choices they make!

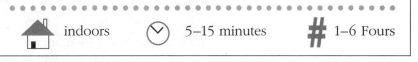

indoors   5–15 minutes   # 1–6 Fours

Book Center

- Keep the Book Center area small, for about four children to use at a time. Make it comfortable and well-lighted. Have a low bookshelf with plenty of children's books. Add pillows, carpet, and a small chair or two near a little table.

- Change many of the books in the Book Center often, but always keep children's favorites. Add books with pictures and information about topics you are discussing with your Fours.

- Place most books so that children can see the front covers.

- Be sure the books show people of many cultures, races, ages, and abilities in a positive way.

- Add some other Book Center materials. Put out soft puppets in a container, a flannelboard with shapes or pictures, and some sets of picture cards. Have a clear place in the center where children can use these things.

- Keep the Book Center organized and neat. Replace books that are not in good shape. Talk with the children about careful use of books and other materials.

Story Times

- Plan at least one special time in your schedule for stories with your Fours. If the time works well, have a story or other talking activity at that time every day. Stories work well at the table after snack is cleared away or before lunch preparation begins. A story as children wake up from nap or rest also is good.

- Be patient. Begin with a 10-minute story time. As children learn to listen with interest, have a longer story time. Stop as soon as interest is gone.

- Use a fingerplay, riddle, song, or puppet to catch children's attention. Then read a book. Also use pictures, books the children have written themselves, and flannelboard stories at this time.

Place

- Plan a place for your story time. Choose a large enough space so that no one will be crowded. A rug helps tell children where they should be.

- Choose an out-of-the way place where you won't be disturbed.

- Find a place where children will pay attention; for example, away from toys on open shelves.

- Give each child his own special space to sit. You can put chairs with names on them in a circle or names on labels around a table if you wish. You can also try putting names on a masking tape circle that you have put down on a rug. Or try giving each child his own carpet square or pillow to sit on.

- Make sure every child can see and hear.

- Keep the story place the same every day unless it does not work well. Changing children's places, making story times shorter, or having stories with fewer children might help.

Group Size

- Begin with a small group. Encourage children to take part, but don't force them.

- If there are two adults, have two groups if you can. Or have one person read while the other sits with the children and helps them listen.

- Plan other quiet activities for children who are not ready to listen to stories in a group.

- Read to children individually or in a very small group during the day whenever you can. Be sure you read to the children who cannot listen to stories in a larger group.

Reading

- Choose the book you will read ahead of time.

- Use books with big, clear, colorful pictures. If there are too many words, tell the story in your own words instead of reading it.

- Hold the book up facing the children so that all of them can see the pictures.

- Point out things on the pages that interest the children. Help them talk about what they see.

- Give the children a chance to help tell the story with you. For example, if the story is a familiar one, see if they can say what is coming next. If the story is a new one, have them guess what will happen.

- Show interest with your face and voice. Change your voice to match the story.

- Use a quiet voice when you want children to listen. Children pay more attention to a quiet voice than to a loud one.

- Look into each child's eyes often as you read or talk.

- Pick books that go with the ideas you are talking about at the time. For example, if it's fall and children bring in pretty leaves from outside, read a book about fall leaves.

- Read books the children have chosen from the library or bookmobile. Try to read all the books they have chosen before they have to be returned. If you can't read each book in a group, try to read to the child individually or with a friend.

- Put books you read in the Book Center for children to look at by themselves. Remind the children how to turn the pages carefully.

- Read a variety of written materials, including poems, stories, magazines, comic strips, and letters.

- Read favorite books often.

Other Ideas

- Use puppets, a flannelboard, pictures, or real objects as you tell a story.

- Add to your book collection by using your public library. Ask if a bookmobile will visit you and your Fours.

- Help children act out a very short, simple story that they know well.

Pictures

Choosing Pictures

- Choose clear photographs or colorful pictures that show things Fours know about—families, food, clothes, animals.

- Choose clear pictures of new things you will be talking about and teaching your Fours—holidays, community helpers, things that go together, people working.

- Make picture collections of different subjects: toys, different kinds of buildings, shapes and numbers, animals, birds.

- Have big pictures and small ones.

- Have pictures that show one thing at a time and pictures that show many things.

- Choose pictures that show people of all ages and races doing many positive things, alone or together.

- Include many nonsexist pictures that show men doing jobs traditionally done by women, such as giving baby a bath, and women doing jobs traditionally done by men, such as fighting fires.

Adding Words to the Pictures

- Print simple words on the cards to label the pictures.

- Print clearly and be sure words are spelled correctly. If you wish, use computer-printed words, but be sure the print is large and easy to read.

- Ask the children to help you think of the words to go on the cards. Write down the words they say.

- Point out the words that are on the picture cards, but do not expect children to read or write these words yet.

Storing Pictures

- Make picture cards with the pictures you want children to use a lot. Glue the pictures onto sturdy cardboard. Cover with clear contact paper. Keep card sets together.

- Put picture cards into separate, labeled boxes or use a picture file box.

- Make a file box for your pictures. Use a large, sturdy cardboard box with folders labeled by topic. It helps to have plastic pages or contact paper over the pictures to protect them.

- Add topics based on the interests of your Fours.

Finding Pictures

- School supply catalogs
- Department store catalogs
- Colorful newspaper ads
- Junk mail
- Photographs, postcards
- Old calendars, magazines, picture books, newspapers, coloring books
- Pictures that parents and friends provide. Tell parents why you need pictures so that they can use some of your ideas at home.
- Free photos you can send for from groups such as the Dairy Association or dental health groups.
- Free posters used as ads in stores, car showrooms, and supermarkets. Ask managers if you can have the pictures when they are no longer needed.

Displaying Pictures

- Hang pictures where Fours can see, reach, and touch them. Hang them on furniture, on walls or doors, or on bulletin boards.
- Change pictures often.
- Use three-ring binders with clear vinyl pages to make a book of pictures. Change the pictures in the pages often.
- Put sturdy picture cards you have made into a box or on a tray. Put these on a shelf in the Book Center for Fours.

Making Your Own Picture Books

1. Glue pictures onto sturdy cardboard.
2. Add your own words or the children's if you wish.
3. Cover with clear contact paper.
4. Punch two or three holes on the left side or across the top of each page.
5. Tie pages together with strong string or narrow ribbon. Do not tie too tightly. Leave pages a bit loose so that they can easily be turned.

Activities for Listening and Talking

Directions for Making Stick Puppets

1. Find or draw a picture of what you want to use as the puppet. Try faces, animals, or anything else you or a child wants to make talk.

2. Cut out the picture, glue it to a larger piece of cardboard, and cover it with clear contact paper, or simply draw the picture onto the cardboard.

3. Make a holder for the picture. Try these ideas:

   Glue smaller pictures to ice cream sticks. Make them more secure with tape.

   Use one-inch brass brads or paper fasteners to hold the picture onto an empty paper towel or toilet paper roll. Poke two brads through the picture and into the roll. Then open the brads so they stay in place.

   Glue pictures to tongue depressors. Make them more secure with tape.

   Cut out a cardboard holder as part of the cardboard you use to mount the picture. Make it sturdier by attaching a stick or some extra cardboard where it might bend.

Sequence Cards

What They Are

- Sequence cards are picture cards that show the steps in a story. They show what happens at the beginning, middle, and end of the story.

- There is often no one right answer when using the cards with young children. Use the cards only to help children talk about what they see and think.

How to Use Them

- Use only easy sequence cards with your four-year-olds. Begin with cards that show four clear, familiar steps for what is happening.

- Fours may not put the cards in the same order you do. They should use the cards in their own creative ways. Listen to how they tell the story and enjoy it together.

- You can put the cards in order and tell the children how you see the story. Use the words *first, second, third,* and *last* or *first, then,* and *finally* as you talk.

How to Make Them

1. Find or draw pictures of the steps in the story you want to show.

2. Cut out the pictures.

3. Glue them to sturdy cardboard squares.

4. Cover them with clear contact paper.

5. Store the cards in a box or container. Keep each set separate with a rubber band or in its own plastic sandwich bag.

Topics for Cards

Getting Up in the Morning

- Child sleeping in bed
- Child getting dressed
- Child all dressed and walking away from bed
- Child eating breakfast cereal

Cooking and Eating

- Putting food in pot
- Stirring food on stove
- Serving food onto plate
- Eating food

Getting Dressed

- Child with shirt and underclothes on, putting on pants
- Child putting on socks
- Child putting on shoes
- Child dressed

Taking a Bath or Getting Washed and Dressed

- Child with clothes on
- Child in bath
- Child drying off with towel
- Child putting on shirt

Sweeping the Floor

- Person looking at dirty floor
- Person with broom, floor partly swept
- Person with dustpan, sweeping trash
- Person with broom, floor clean

Grocery Shopping

- Person with empty shopping cart
- Person with full cart
- Person paying at register
- Person with bags of groceries

Sequence Cards to Use with Fours

- Cut these out. Color them if you wish.
- Glue the cards to cardboard squares.
- Cover them with clear contact paper.
- Have children put them in the order they see, or you can arrange them.
- Talk about the pictures.

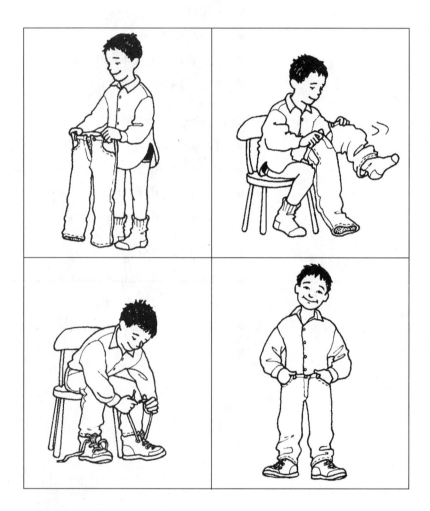

Activities for Listening and Talking

Sunshine Note

Sunshine Note

Directions for Making a Flannelboard

1. Cover a board with a large, wide piece of felt or flannel cloth. For the board, use wood, very sturdy cardboard, or an old bulletin board. A rectangle of 2' by 2½' works well, but you can make a larger or smaller board if you wish. You can even make individual flannelboards, 11" by 14".

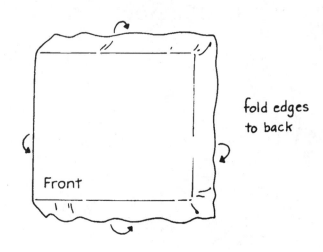

fold edges
to back

Front

2. Fold the cloth over the back of the board, making sure the front is pulled smooth. Sew the ends together, or staple and cover securely with heavy tape.

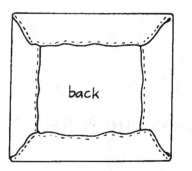

back

3. When you use the board, lean it at an angle against a wall or bookcase. Then the flannel pictures will stay on better. When your Fours use the board, have them place it flat on a table or floor so that the pictures will not fall off.

4. To make pictures, cut out ones you want to use. Cover the front with clear contact paper and glue felt material or sandpaper on the back. Or use pens to draw on felt material. You can buy pictures for use with flannelboards. Check school supply catalogs for prices and ideas.

Picture Word Recipe for Fruit Kabobs

① skewer

② banana

③ strawberry

④ orange

Directions for the teacher:

1. Copy the recipe cards shown above onto sturdy posterboard. Protect with clear contact paper or laminate if you wish.

2. Slice bananas and strawberries, and separate oranges into slices. Children can help with this. Put each fruit into a separate bowl.

3. Cut the points off wooden skewers.

4. Set up the cards on a long table, with the first card on the left and the last card on the right.

5. Put the skewers in front of the first card, the bananas in front of the next, and so on, so that each real thing is in front of the card it matches.

6. Show children how to follow the recipe from left to right to make a fruit kabob.

7. Make the first kabob with your Fours. Put on a slice of banana, a slice of orange, a strawberry, and a slice of orange. Point to the recipe as you work.

8. Eat the kabobs for snack and allow children to make more if they want to.

Materials and Notes

Conversation and Group Talk

things children bring in

Jimmy

things children make

group discussion

talker's turn

- Fours enjoy talking—to you and to each other. Try to keep the happy, busy sound of talking going on most of the day.

- Show children how much you enjoy their talk. Look at children as you listen to things they tell you. Ask many questions to get them to say more. (See page 128 for ideas about different kinds of questions.)

- Include parents in the talks you have with your Fours. Ask them about things the child does at home. Ask questions to help the child add to what they say.

- Keep talking-time groups small so that everyone can have several turns to talk and share ideas.

- Gently help your Fours to understand that a conversation means that people listen when someone talks. Then it is the listener's turn to talk and someone else listens.

Activity Checklist

Conversation and Group Talk

Conversation and Group Talk activities with Fours make use of the informal talking times that happen throughout the day, as well as the planned group time many programs include. By four, most children can talk quite well, using many words and short sentences. They enjoy talking to adults and other children who will listen to them. They ask plenty of questions and answer easy questions you ask. With your help, Fours can use words to solve problems and avoid fights. Most conversations don't have to be planned. They will happen when children find out that what they do is important to you and that listening and talking are ways of sharing ideas and feelings.

Check for each age group

	48–54 months	54–60 months
1. Children are free to talk to adults and each other during most of the day. There are *very few times* when no talking is allowed.	❏	❏
2. Adult talks often with every child about the child's interests.	❏	❏
3. Adult speaks clearly and uses appropriate tone of voice.	❏	❏
4. Adult shows interest when children begin conversations or ask questions.	❏	❏
5. Adult asks different types of questions to encourage children to talk and listens to children's answers.	❏	❏
6. Adult makes eye contact when talking with child.	❏	❏
7. Adult talks with children about the routines and play they experience.	❏	❏
8. Adult adds more information to what children say.	❏	❏
9. Adult encourages children to talk and listen to each other in small groups so that each one can have a turn.	❏	❏
10. Adult encourages children to use talking to solve problems with each other and supplies words when needed.	❏	❏
11. Adult plays rhyming games and provides other playful language experiences.	❏	❏

48

Fours can

- tell about things they have done
- use many words

Early Morning Talks

Show children how happy you are to see them each morning. Plan time to greet each child with a good morning hug and have a little chat. Make time to do this even when you are busy or when everyone seems rushed.

Include parents in the little talks. See if they will help their children remember some nice things they did the night before or what they plan to do over a weekend. Make sure you, the parents, and the children all take turns talking and listening to each other at this time.

How exciting that you have a kitten, Petra.
What color is it?
Have you chosen a name yet?
Socks? It must have white feet.

in or out   1–5 minutes   # 1–2 Fours

49

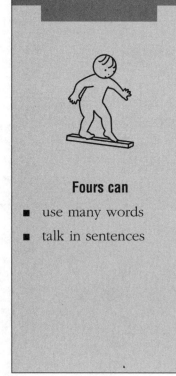

Fours can

- use many words
- talk in sentences

New Information for Fours

Think of a special idea you want your Fours to know more about. (A list of some special ideas for units that you might like to work on with your Fours is in the Planning Section, pages 36–38.) Choose an idea that you and the children will find fun and interesting. An example might be "things with wheels." Then write down many ways to talk about the idea. Use real things, books, pictures, field trips, and anything else you can think of to help the children learn about the idea. Ask easy questions to help Fours talk and think about what they know.

What playthings have wheels? That's right, Juan. The tricycles have wheels. What else? Yes, Patrick. A lawn mower has wheels, too. What other playthings at home have wheels?

in or out   3–10 minutes   # 1–10 Fours

50

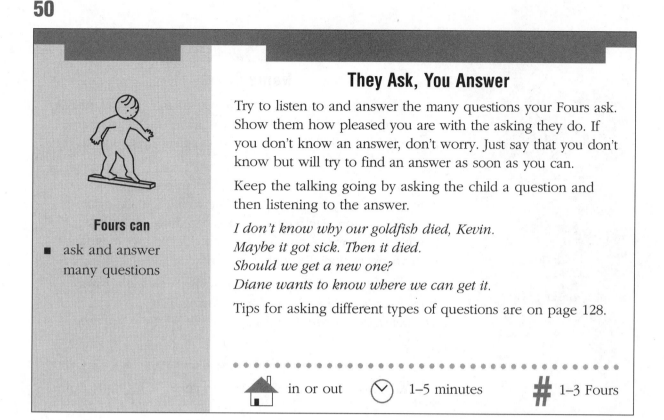

They Ask, You Answer

Try to listen to and answer the many questions your Fours ask. Show them how pleased you are with the asking they do. If you don't know an answer, don't worry. Just say that you don't know but will try to find an answer as soon as you can.

Keep the talking going by asking the child a question and then listening to the answer.

I don't know why our goldfish died, Kevin.
Maybe it got sick. Then it died.
Should we get a new one?
Diane wants to know where we can get it.

Tips for asking different types of questions are on page 128.

Fours can

■ ask and answer many questions

🏠 in or out　🕐 1–5 minutes　# 1–3 Fours

51

Pretend Play Talk

When children are playing in the Dramatic Play Center, ask questions so that they will tell about what they are doing. Choose the right time to ask questions so that you don't spoil the play. Add your own ideas to the children's answers to help the play go better.

Is that your baby, Sandra?
What are you doing with her?
Maybe you and Aretha can take your babies for a walk after their nap.

Ask about children's play in other areas, too.

Fours can

■ tell a little about what they are doing

🏠 in or out　🕐 1–3 minutes　# 1–3 Fours

52

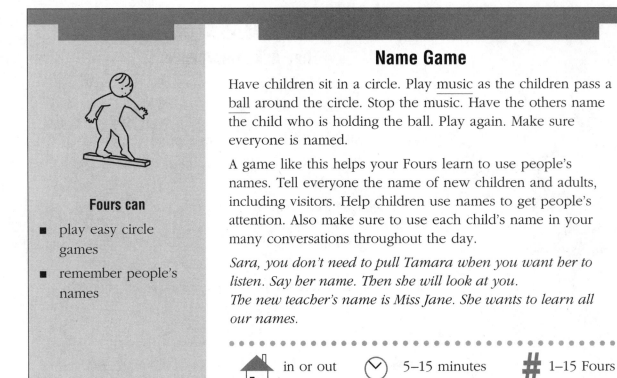

Fours can

- play easy circle games
- remember people's names

Name Game

Have children sit in a circle. Play <u>music</u> as the children pass a <u>ball</u> around the circle. Stop the music. Have the others name the child who is holding the ball. Play again. Make sure everyone is named.

A game like this helps your Fours learn to use people's names. Tell everyone the name of new children and adults, including visitors. Help children use names to get people's attention. Also make sure to use each child's name in your many conversations throughout the day.

Sara, you don't need to pull Tamara when you want her to listen. Say her name. Then she will look at you.
The new teacher's name is Miss Jane. She wants to learn all our names.

🏠 in or out   🕐 5–15 minutes   # 1–15 Fours

53

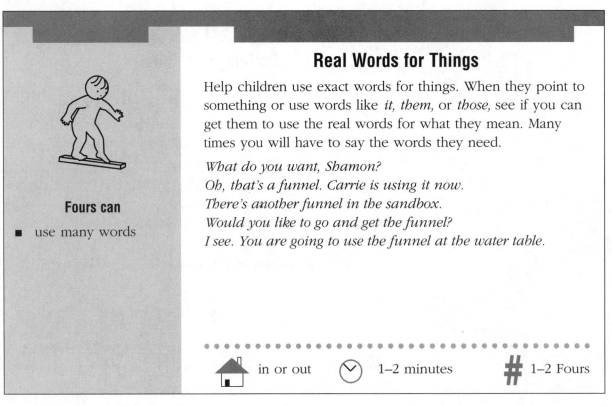

Fours can

- use many words

Real Words for Things

Help children use exact words for things. When they point to something or use words like *it, them,* or *those,* see if you can get them to use the real words for what they mean. Many times you will have to say the words they need.

What do you want, Shamon?
Oh, that's a funnel. Carrie is using it now.
There's another funnel in the sandbox.
Would you like to go and get the funnel?
I see. You are going to use the funnel at the water table.

🏠 in or out   🕐 1–2 minutes   # 1–2 Fours

54

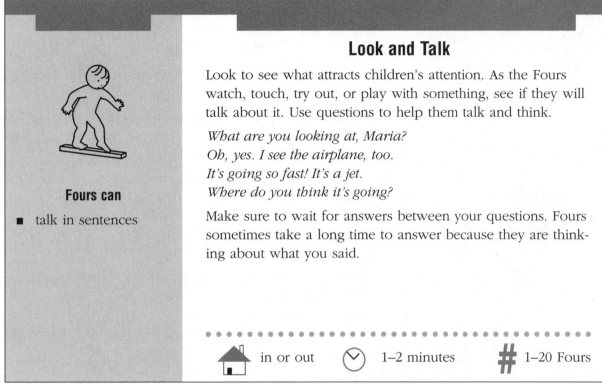

Look and Talk

Look to see what attracts children's attention. As the Fours watch, touch, try out, or play with something, see if they will talk about it. Use questions to help them talk and think.

What are you looking at, Maria?
Oh, yes. I see the airplane, too.
It's going so fast! It's a jet.
Where do you think it's going?

Make sure to wait for answers between your questions. Fours sometimes take a long time to answer because they are thinking about what you said.

Fours can

■ talk in sentences

🏠 in or out   🕐 1–2 minutes   # 1–20 Fours

55

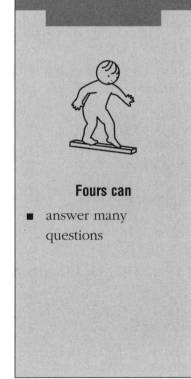

Questions, Questions

Think about the questions you ask the children. Plan questions that need more than just a "yes" or "no" answer. Use your questions to help the children tell what, where, or who. Add easy questions that ask why, when, or how. Be ready to give answers to the harder questions when the children don't know what to say.

Try writing down a few questions you can use each day. Ask them at the right time. See what answers you get.

What's new in our play yard?
Yes, there's new sand in the sandbox.
Where do you think it came from?
How did they get it into the yard?

More tips for asking good questions are on page 128.

Fours can

■ answer many questions

🏠 in or out   🕐 1–5 minutes   # 1–5 Fours

56

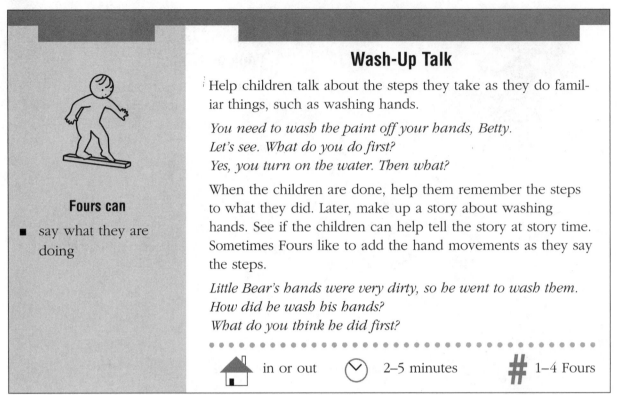

Fours can

- say what they are doing

Wash-Up Talk

Help children talk about the steps they take as they do familiar things, such as washing hands.

You need to wash the paint off your hands, Betty.
Let's see. What do you do first?
Yes, you turn on the water. Then what?

When the children are done, help them remember the steps to what they did. Later, make up a story about washing hands. See if the children can help tell the story at story time. Sometimes Fours like to add the hand movements as they say the steps.

Little Bear's hands were very dirty, so he went to wash them.
How did he wash his hands?
What do you think he did first?

🏠 in or out   🕐 2–5 minutes   # 1–4 Fours

57

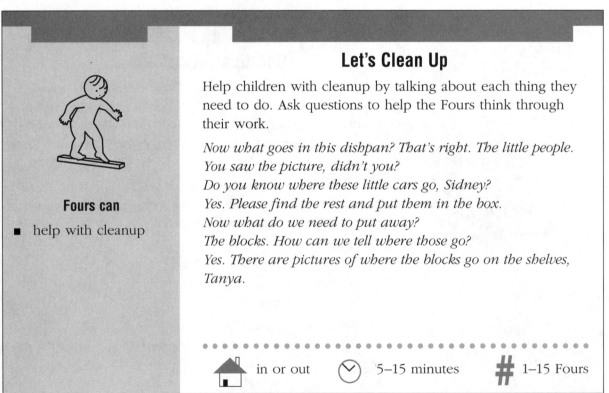

Fours can

- help with cleanup

Let's Clean Up

Help children with cleanup by talking about each thing they need to do. Ask questions to help the Fours think through their work.

Now what goes in this dishpan? That's right. The little people.
You saw the picture, didn't you?
Do you know where these little cars go, Sidney?
Yes. Please find the rest and put them in the box.
Now what do we need to put away?
The blocks. How can we tell where those go?
Yes. There are pictures of where the blocks go on the shelves, Tanya.

🏠 in or out   🕐 5–15 minutes   # 1–15 Fours

58

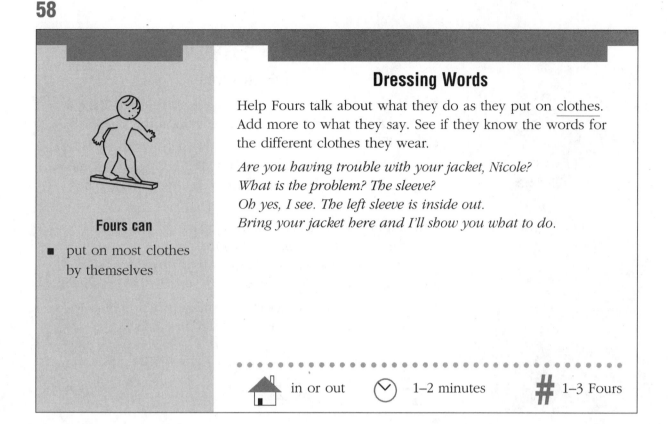

Fours can

■ put on most clothes by themselves

Dressing Words

Help Fours talk about what they do as they put on clothes. Add more to what they say. See if they know the words for the different clothes they wear.

Are you having trouble with your jacket, Nicole?
What is the problem? The sleeve?
Oh yes, I see. The left sleeve is inside out.
Bring your jacket here and I'll show you what to do.

🏠 in or out   🕐 1–2 minutes   # 1–3 Fours

59

Fours can

■ answer many questions

Talk About Treasures

Pay attention to any "treasures" your Fours find or bring in. A treasure may be anything: a new pair of shoes, a favorite toy, or a pretty rock. Notice these things. Ask questions to help the children talk about their treasures.

That's a pretty box, Ginny.
Is there anything in the box? Can you open it?
There's some cotton. It's soft and white.
That looks like a little jewelry box.
Where did you get it?
Was there anything else in the box?

Later, see if children want to tell about their treasures at group time. Keep these group discussions short so that others do not become bored.

🏠 in or out   🕐 1–3 minutes   # 1–4 Fours

60

Fours can

- take turns with friends

Taking Turns

Talk about taking turns as your Fours learn to do it. Make a "waiting list" for the most popular activities to be sure each child will get a chance.

Show the child her name on the list. Tell her that her name keeps her place in line for her. Help children choose other fun things to do while they wait.

I know you want to work with the play dough, Isabella.
Let's put your name on the waiting list.
I'll be sure to call you as soon as it is your turn.
How many children have turns before you? Yes. There are three.

Make sure each child checks off his name when he finishes his turn and goes to call the next child on the list.

 in or out   1–2 minutes   # 1–20 Fours

61

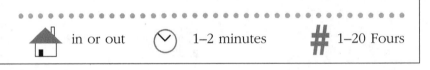

Fours can

- understand many common dangers

Why Be Careful?

Remind your Fours to be careful about things that may be dangerous as it relates to what is happening. Help the children talk about why they need to be careful.

Sammy brought balloons for his birthday today.
Balloons are fun, but we have to be careful with them.
Do you remember our rule about balloons?
Don't put balloons in your _____?
That's right, Andy. Don't put balloons in your mouth.
Why don't you put balloons in your mouth?

Being careful is a good topic for group discussions. You could talk about care in climbing, building, cutting, and so on.

in or out   2–10 minutes   # 1–20 Fours

62

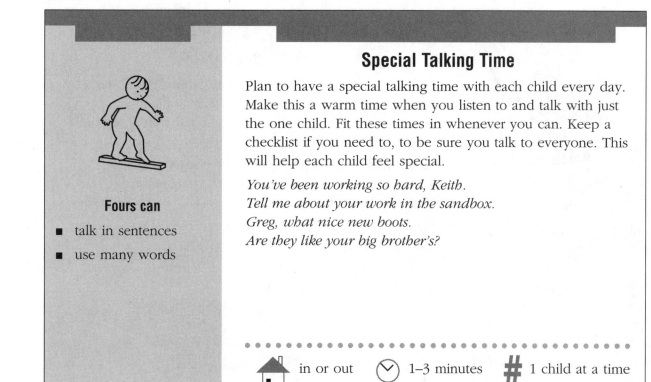

Special Talking Time

Plan to have a special talking time with each child every day. Make this a warm time when you listen to and talk with just the one child. Fit these times in whenever you can. Keep a checklist if you need to, to be sure you talk to everyone. This will help each child feel special.

You've been working so hard, Keith.
Tell me about your work in the sandbox.
Greg, what nice new boots.
Are they like your big brother's?

Fours can

- talk in sentences
- use many words

🏠 in or out   🕐 1–3 minutes   # 1 child at a time

63

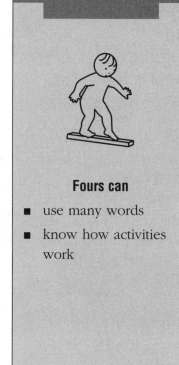

What Are We Going to Do?

At the beginning of the day, tell children about the activities you have planned. Give the Fours clues about what activities they are going to do. Show them some things they will use and see if they can guess what the activities are. This is a good way to help children learn to plan their day.

What's am I holding? Yes. It's string.
And what's this? That's right. These are some beads.
Guess what you can do today.
Let's make a waiting list for the bead-stringing table.

Fours can

- use many words
- know how activities work

🏠 indoors   🕐 2–5 minutes   # 1–20 Fours

64

Fours can

■ share with a friend

Talk About Sharing

Give your Fours chances to share. For example, put one container of crayons between two friends. Talk about sharing, taking turns, and cooperating. Show the children how proud you are when they share.

I like the way you two are sharing the crayons.
It's hard when you both want to use the red crayon.
It's nice that Sherry gave you the red as soon as she was done.

Help children see how sharing helps everyone. Make sure to point out times when children are sharing.

Jonathan brought in this big watermelon from his garden. He wants to share it with all of us!

🏠 in or out   🕐 1–2 minutes   # 1–4 Fours

65

Fours can

■ talk in sentences
■ enjoy playing with others

Talk—Don't Hit

Help Fours learn words to solve problems they have with others. Tell them to use words to say what they do not like. You will often have to help them find the words they need and make them feel safe as they work things out.

What's the matter, Andrew?
Benjamin is taking the blocks you are using?
Tell him you need them. Tell him to get his own.
Show him the blocks on the shelf he can use.

Be sure that when children do "use their words" you are right there to see that the words work to solve the problem. The children may need you to help them listen and solve the problem.

🏠 in or out   🕐 2–5 minutes   # 1–3 Fours

66

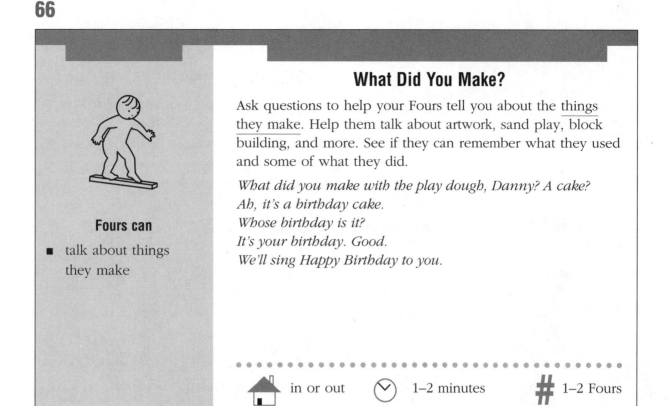

Fours can

- talk about things they make

What Did You Make?

Ask questions to help your Fours tell you about the things they make. Help them talk about artwork, sand play, block building, and more. See if they can remember what they used and some of what they did.

What did you make with the play dough, Danny? A cake?
Ah, it's a birthday cake.
Whose birthday is it?
It's your birthday. Good.
We'll sing Happy Birthday to you.

in or out   1–2 minutes   # 1–2 Fours

67

Fours can

- talk about things they have done

Remember Play Time

Ask questions to help the children remember things they did at play time. Make notes if you need to about who did what so that you can ask the right questions.

I saw you with the baby stroller, Terry.
Who was in the stroller? Yes, the bear.
Where were you going with the bear?

Help children remember other things that happened during the day, such as what snack they ate or what story you read. The remember game can also be played with a group.

Who was playing firefighters outside today?
Who got hurt in the jungle gym?

indoors   2–4 minutes   # 1–20 Fours

68

Fours can

■ enjoy word play

Silly-Nilly Words

Have fun enjoying silly word play with your Fours. Use your imagination to add funny rhymes or sounds to words that all of you use every day.

We're having carrot sticks for lunch today.
This is a munchie crunchie lunchie!

Let's zip up your zipper.
Here it goes. Zipper zapper zip!

🏠 in or out   🕐 45–90 minutes   # 1–4 Fours per adult

69

Fours can

■ name actions

Guess What I'm Doing

Act out some very familiar, easy-to-guess things your Fours do often. Act out getting dressed, drinking, eating, going to sleep, or taking a bath. Do the actions without words. See if the children can say what you're doing.

If they have trouble guessing, then add words to your actions.

First I put on my underwear. Then my shirt.
Then my pants and socks and shoes.
Can you guess what I am doing?

After you act out one or two things, give children a chance to be the actor.

🏠 in or out   🕐 3–10 minutes   # 1–15 Fours

70

Fours can

■ repeat rhymes

Rhyming Words

Point out and repeat words the children say or hear that rhyme. Be excited about these words and show that rhymes can be fun.

Listen, Paul. You made a rhyme! You said, "My coat is new. It's blue."
New. Blue. They rhyme. That was a little poem you made up!

Some of your Fours may be able to do rhyming on purpose. But for others, this will come later and be easier if they have enjoyed rhymes with you. It helps to read simple poems and point out the rhymes, too.

🏠 in or out   🕐 1–2 minutes   # 1–3 Fours

71

Fours can

■ notice changes
■ use short sentences

Words for Changes

Help the four-year-olds talk about simple changes they see. Ask questions to help them out.

Our room looks different this morning.
What's changed in our room? That's right!
The chairs are on top of the tables.
Look at how shiny the floors are!
What do you think happened to the floors?

Changes that are easy to see, such as new materials on the bulletin board or a new activity center, make good topics for guessing games during group time.

🏠 in or out   🕐 1–6 minutes   # 1–20 Fours

72

Fours can

■ tell how to do some things

Child as Teacher

Whenever possible, let children who know how to do something teach others who don't know how. Encourage the children to use words as they show what to do.

Lottie, please tell Debbie how to hang up her painting.
Show her and use words to tell her.

Children can be very helpful in teaching one another playground skills, such as pumping on the swing. You may sometimes need to supply some words to help get the main points across.

in or out   1–3 minutes   # 1–3 Fours

73

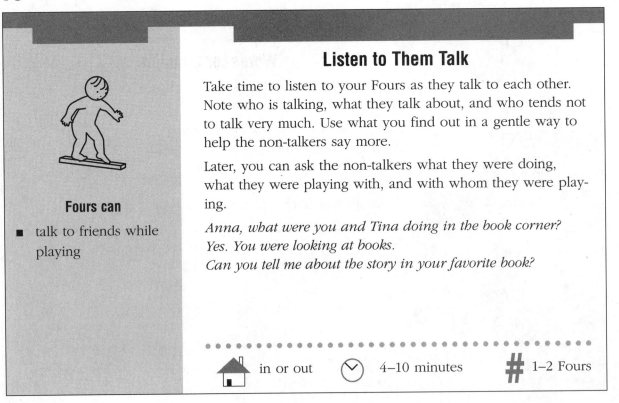

Fours can

■ talk to friends while playing

Listen to Them Talk

Take time to listen to your Fours as they talk to each other. Note who is talking, what they talk about, and who tends not to talk very much. Use what you find out in a gentle way to help the non-talkers say more.

Later, you can ask the non-talkers what they were doing, what they were playing with, and with whom they were playing.

Anna, what were you and Tina doing in the book corner?
Yes. You were looking at books.
Can you tell me about the story in your favorite book?

in or out   4–10 minutes   # 1–2 Fours

Activities for Listening and Talking

74

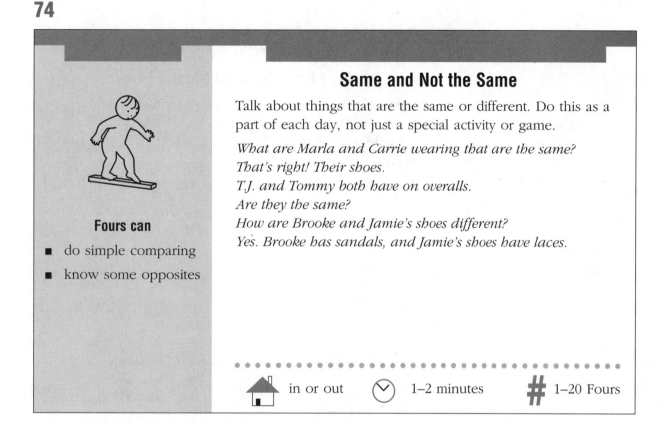

Fours can

■ do simple comparing

■ know some opposites

Same and Not the Same

Talk about things that are the same or different. Do this as a part of each day, not just a special activity or game.

What are Marla and Carrie wearing that are the same?
That's right! Their shoes.
T.J. and Tommy both have on overalls.
Are they the same?
How are Brooke and Jamie's shoes different?
Yes. Brooke has sandals, and Jamie's shoes have laces.

🏠 in or out   🕐 1–2 minutes   # 1–20 Fours

75

Fours can

■ talk in sentences

Talk-About Table

Set aside a little table where you and your Fours can put new objects to talk about every day. You can put something that goes with the special things you and the children are talking about. For example, if you're doing a unit on fruits, put a new fruit on the table to taste and talk about each day.

The children can add whatever interests them. Make sure that things on the Talk-About Table are safe to touch and hold.

As the Fours stop by the table, talk about the name of each thing, what you do with it, and how it looks or feels. Be sure the children know that the things on the table need to stay on the table. Change the things every day.

🏠 in or out   🕐 3–5 minutes   # 1–6 Fours

76

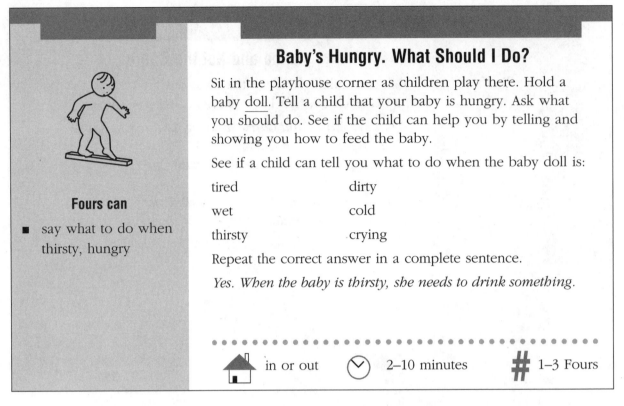

Fours can

- say what to do when thirsty, hungry

Baby's Hungry. What Should I Do?

Sit in the playhouse corner as children play there. Hold a baby <u>doll</u>. Tell a child that your baby is hungry. Ask what you should do. See if the child can help you by telling and showing you how to feed the baby.

See if a child can tell you what to do when the baby doll is:

tired	dirty
wet	cold
thirsty	crying

Repeat the correct answer in a complete sentence.

Yes. When the baby is thirsty, she needs to drink something.

🏠 in or out   🕐 2–10 minutes   # 1–3 Fours

77

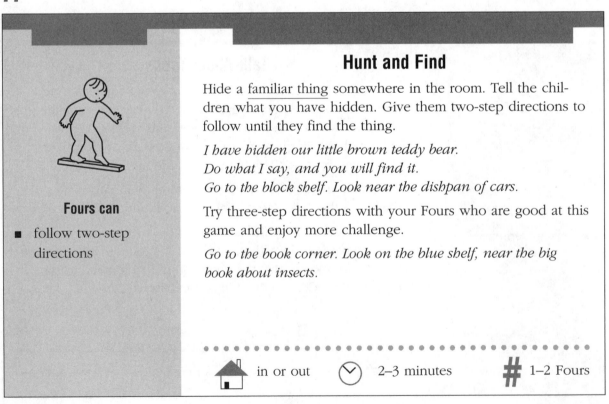

Fours can

- follow two-step directions

Hunt and Find

Hide a <u>familiar thing</u> somewhere in the room. Tell the children what you have hidden. Give them two-step directions to follow until they find the thing.

I have hidden our little brown teddy bear.
Do what I say, and you will find it.
Go to the block shelf. Look near the dishpan of cars.

Try three-step directions with your Fours who are good at this game and enjoy more challenge.

Go to the book corner. Look on the blue shelf, near the big book about insects.

🏠 in or out   🕐 2–3 minutes   # 1–2 Fours

78

Fours can

■ say "please" and "thank you"

Polite Words

Use *please, thank you, excuse me, I'm sorry,* and other polite words in everything you do with the children. In a gentle way, help them remember to use these words.

Don't force the words if a child doesn't mean them. Show how happy you are when they use these words on their own.

Jana, I like the way you said "I'm sorry" when you bumped B.J.'s blocks.
Lauren, you need to say "Excuse me, Rodney" if you want to get past.

At group time you can discuss polite words and how good they make people feel.

🏠 in or out   🕐 1–10 minutes   # 1–20 Fours

79

Fours can

■ answer the telephone

Telephone Words

Practice talking on the telephone with a four-year-old. Use two toy telephones. Have questions ready to ask the child before you play so that the talk will go better. You may have to guide the child in what to say and do.

Ring, ring. Your telephone is ringing, Nina.
Hello, Nina.
This is your teacher, Miss Anna.
What did you make in the art center this morning?

Remind children not to nod "yes" or shake their heads "no" on the phone. They need to use words.

 in or out   🕐 2–3 minutes   # 1 child at a time

80

Fours can

■ talk about things that will happen

Goodbye Talk

As children get ready to go home, talk with each child about what she has done that day. Look at and talk about things children are taking home. Have parents help tell about what the children will do when they get home. Say something about the plans for the next day.

What are you going to do at home, Kristin? Play with your puppy?
Is there anything else Kristin will do, Mrs. Brown?
Wow, Kristin! I bet you like helping your mom feed the chickens! I'll see you tomorrow, Kristin.
Do you remember what we will do tomorrow?

in or out   2–5 minutes   # 1 Four at a time

81

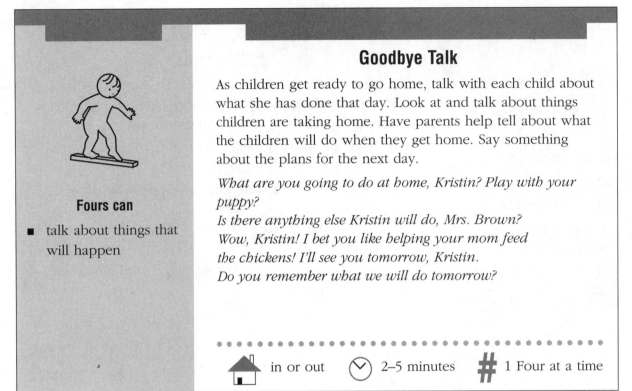

Fours can

■ tell what to do

What Do We Do?

At story time, tell your Fours a little story that ends with someone who is cold, hungry, thirsty, tired, muddy, or too hot. Ask the children what the person in the story should do.

Once there was a little boy named Winston. He woke up and saw that it was a snowy day. So he got dressed and ran out to play in the snow. After a while he said, "Brrrr! I'm cold!" What do you think Winston should do?

Enjoy the many creative answers your Fours might give.

in or out   2–10 minutes   # 1–15 Fours

82

Fours can

- understand what things are used for

- pretend in their play

What Are They Used For?

Collect some common items in a <u>box</u>: <u>spoon</u>, <u>cup</u>, <u>paintbrush</u>, <u>hairbrush</u>, <u>soap</u>, safe scissors, plastic <u>hammer</u>, and <u>crayon</u>. Look at these with your Fours. Have them name each and say how it is used.

Then play this guessing game. Do actions to pretend you are using one of the things. Have the children name and point to what they think it is. Let the children take turns pretending, too. Then you can help with the guessing.

🏠 in or out   🕐 3–7 minutes   # 3–6 Fours

83

Fours can

- whisper

Whisper Game

Play a fun whisper game with several children. Whisper something into the first child's ear. Have that child whisper it to the next child and so on. See if the last child can tell you what you said.

Play over and over. Each player can take a turn being first. Remind Fours not to talk loudly into each other's ears because it hurts.

This game may tickle and words get mixed up, so be ready to laugh at a lot of nonsense.

Brett knows how to whisper in a soft voice.
So do you, Robin.
You have to listen carefully to hear a whisper.

🏠 in or out   🕐 1–5 minutes   # 2–4 Fours

84

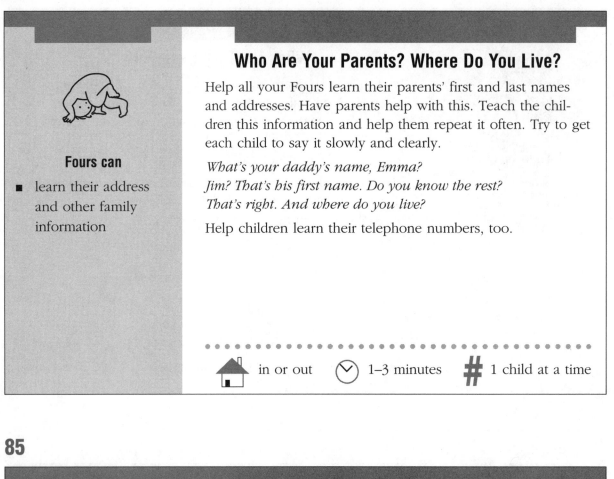

Fours can

- learn their address and other family information

Who Are Your Parents? Where Do You Live?

Help all your Fours learn their parents' first and last names and addresses. Have parents help with this. Teach the children this information and help them repeat it often. Try to get each child to say it slowly and clearly.

What's your daddy's name, Emma?
Jim? That's his first name. Do you know the rest?
That's right. And where do you live?

Help children learn their telephone numbers, too.

● ●

🏠 in or out   🕐 1–3 minutes   # 1 child at a time

85

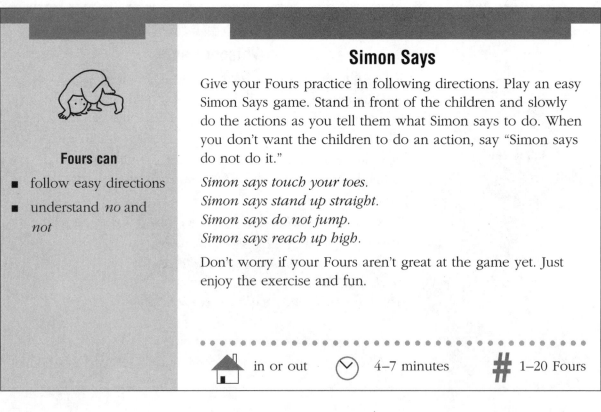

Fours can

- follow easy directions
- understand *no* and *not*

Simon Says

Give your Fours practice in following directions. Play an easy Simon Says game. Stand in front of the children and slowly do the actions as you tell them what Simon says to do. When you don't want the children to do an action, say "Simon says do not do it."

Simon says touch your toes.
Simon says stand up straight.
Simon says do not jump.
Simon says reach up high.

Don't worry if your Fours aren't great at the game yet. Just enjoy the exercise and fun.

● ●

🏠 in or out   🕐 4–7 minutes   # 1–20 Fours

86

Fours can

- take part in a short group time
- tell about something they did

Gathering-Time Talk

Gather your Fours together for a short talking and sharing time. You may want to do this as part of a story time.

Have one child at a time tell things to the group. Ask questions to help the children think of things to say. Have the children talk about what they did at play time, something they made or brought in, or things that go with what they have been working on.

To call attention to the talker, have the talker hold something special, like a yarn ball or a pretend microphone, which is passed from talker to talker. Help the others look at and listen to the one who is speaking.

Thank you, Sam.
Now you can pass the ball to Peter because it's his turn.

🏠 indoors   🕐 3–7 minutes   # 5–15 Fours

87

Fours can

- guess easy words

Guess the Word

Play a word-guessing game with your Fours. Give them easy clues until they guess the familiar thing you are talking about.

Guess what animal I'm thinking about.
It has four legs.
No, it's not a dog. Listen to all the clues.
It has long ears. It goes hop, hop, hop.
We saw one yesterday. It can live in a hutch.

Encourage your Fours to give the clues and have others guess the answers. Be ready for some pretty silly clues and hard-to-discover answers.

🏠 in or out   🕐 2–10 minutes   # 1–15 Fours

88

Fours can

- ask permission to use things
- know about sharing

The Sharing Table

At group time, ask your Fours to bring some <u>toys</u> they want to share. Explain that you will put their toys on a sharing table. When someone wants to play with their toys, the person will ask their permission. Set up a table near the entry door with a felt pen, some slips of <u>paper</u>, and <u>tape</u>. As children bring in their sharing toys, print the child's name and the toy on a slip of paper and tape it near the toy on the table. You may also want to label the toy, too.

This is Blake's car, Rachel. You can ask him if it's OK to play with it. Remember to bring it back to the table when you're through.

Yes, Craig. You need a waiting list for your toy. So many people want to play with it.

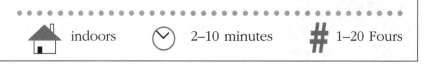

🏠 indoors   🕐 2–10 minutes   # 1–20 Fours

89

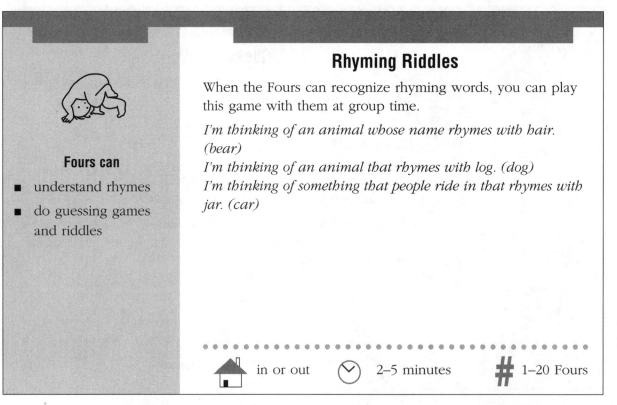

Fours can

- understand rhymes
- do guessing games and riddles

Rhyming Riddles

When the Fours can recognize rhyming words, you can play this game with them at group time.

I'm thinking of an animal whose name rhymes with hair. (bear)

I'm thinking of an animal that rhymes with log. (dog)

I'm thinking of something that people ride in that rhymes with jar. (car)

🏠 in or out   🕐 2–5 minutes   # 1–20 Fours

90

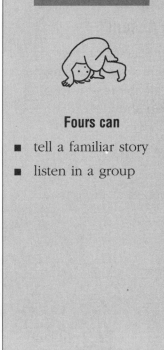

Fours can

- follow directions
- understand *close/closer* and *farther/far away*

Giving Hints

Pick one child to be the hunter. The hunter has to hide his eyes so he can't see where one of the children hides a toy. Help everyone in the group to pay close attention to where the toy is hidden. Tell the hunter what he is hunting for and the side of the room where it is hidden. As the hunter tries to find the toy, have the children tell him if he is getting closer or farther away.

Is she close now? Let's help by telling her.
Closer, closer. Very close! Very close!
Ellen, you're a good hunter. You found the red block Nathan hid. How did you know where to look?

🏠 indoors 🕐 2–6 minutes # 1–20 Fours

91

Fours can

- tell a familiar story
- listen in a group

A Group Story

Explain to the children that they will make up a story together, with each one adding one thing. Start the story and give each child a chance to add one idea. Use simple, everyday subjects, such as getting up and getting dressed to go to school or setting the table and eating dinner. You can also use familiar stories. When the story is completed, repeat the story for the group using the words *first, then,* and *finally* to help the children remember the whole story. Later you can tell funny stories, too.

Early one morning, Heather got up.
Then what did she do, Patty? She stretched and got out of bed.
And then? Good, Adam. She had breakfast. And then?

🏠 indoors 🕐 2–5 minutes # 1–8 Fours

92

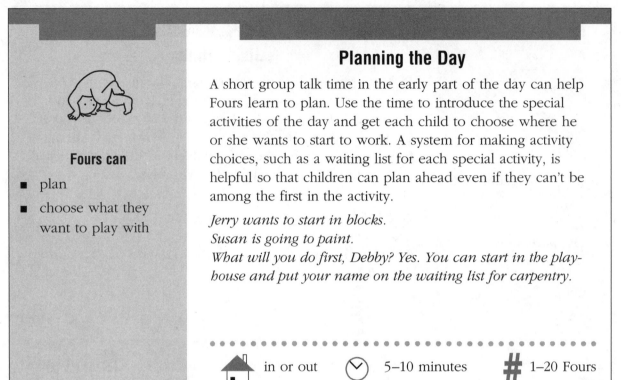

Fours can

- plan
- choose what they want to play with

Planning the Day

A short group talk time in the early part of the day can help Fours learn to plan. Use the time to introduce the special activities of the day and get each child to choose where he or she wants to start to work. A system for making activity choices, such as a waiting list for each special activity, is helpful so that children can plan ahead even if they can't be among the first in the activity.

Jerry wants to start in blocks.
Susan is going to paint.
What will you do first, Debby? Yes. You can start in the play-house and put your name on the waiting list for carpentry.

in or out　　5–10 minutes　　# 1–20 Fours

93

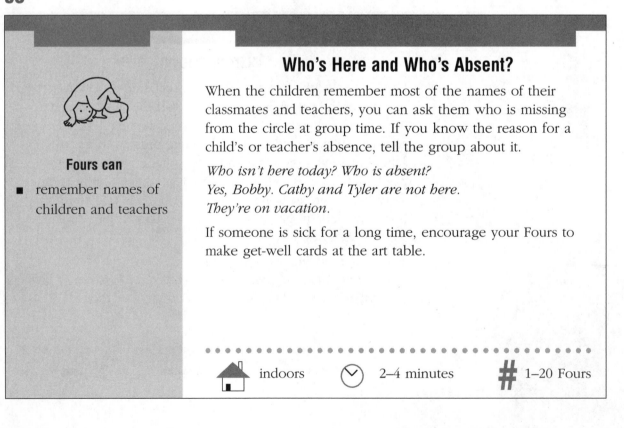

Fours can

- remember names of children and teachers

Who's Here and Who's Absent?

When the children remember most of the names of their classmates and teachers, you can ask them who is missing from the circle at group time. If you know the reason for a child's or teacher's absence, tell the group about it.

Who isn't here today? Who is absent?
Yes, Bobby. Cathy and Tyler are not here.
They're on vacation.

If someone is sick for a long time, encourage your Fours to make get-well cards at the art table.

indoors　　2–4 minutes　　# 1–20 Fours

94

Fours can

- know that holidays are special

Talk about Holidays

Make sure to talk about everybody's holidays and make this a time to learn about many different cultures and traditions. Parents can help the group learn about the holidays their families celebrate.

What is the name of the holiday?
What do people do to make it special?
Are there special foods, gifts, songs?

If the holiday celebrates a famous person, be sure to tell the children something about that person and show them a picture.

🏠 indoors   🕐 2–10 minutes   # 1–20 Fours

95

Fours can

- remember rules
- behave well in public

Preparing for a Field Trip

Before a field trip, gather the children in small groups to discuss where you are going and rules for how to behave.

If parents are coming along, tell the children who they are. Talk about how they will travel. Will they walk, ride in someone's car, or go on a bus? Will they have partners to walk with or will a small group stay together with one adult?

Remind the children that they need to stay close to their leader, a teacher, or a parent. They must also remember the safety rules for riding in a car and for crossing the street.

And, of course, spend time talking about what you will see and do on the trip. If possible, bring in pictures so that the children can start to think about things that will help them get the most out of the trip.

🏠 indoors   🕐 5–10 minutes   # 1–8 Fours

96

Fours can

- tell about what they did

Remembering a Trip

Take a camera along on trips you take with your Fours. Include the children, their parents, and the teachers in your photos. Take pictures of anything of interest that you and the children see. Photos help children remember the details of their trip.

After you return, talk about what you remember about he trip. Let the children draw pictures, tell stories, ask questions, talk about the photos, and write many books about the trip.

🏠 indoors   🕐 5–30 minutes   **#** 1–20 Fours

97

Fours can

- follow two-step directions

Follow the Leader

Play a follow-the-leader game with your Fours. Instead of having them follow you, have them follow directions you give.

Run to the fence and hop up and down.
Now run to the climber and go down the slide.

Try to give two directions in one sentence. When children can remember easily, give three directions. Encourage your Fours to take turns giving directions for their friends to follow, too.

🏠 in or out   🕐 3–8 minutes   **#** 1–10 Fours

98

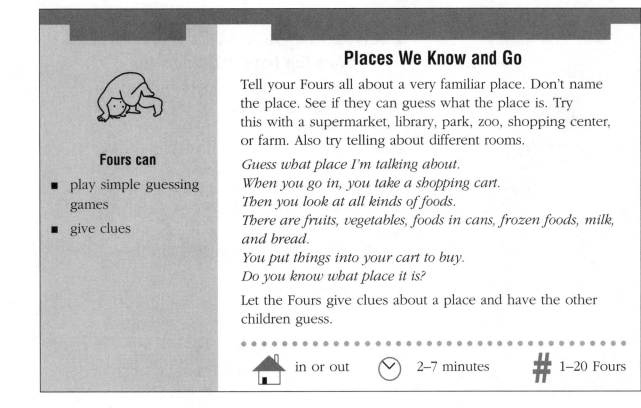

Fours can

- play simple guessing games
- give clues

Places We Know and Go

Tell your Fours all about a very familiar place. Don't name the place. See if they can guess what the place is. Try this with a supermarket, library, park, zoo, shopping center, or farm. Also try telling about different rooms.

Guess what place I'm talking about.
When you go in, you take a shopping cart.
Then you look at all kinds of foods.
There are fruits, vegetables, foods in cans, frozen foods, milk, and bread.
You put things into your cart to buy.
Do you know what place it is?

Let the Fours give clues about a place and have the other children guess.

🏠 in or out   🕑 2–7 minutes   # 1–20 Fours

99

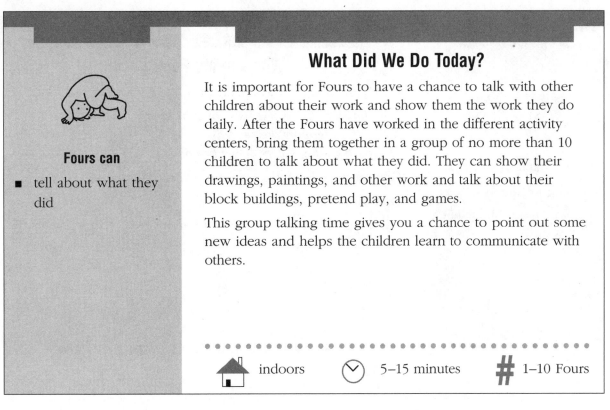

Fours can

- tell about what they did

What Did We Do Today?

It is important for Fours to have a chance to talk with other children about their work and show them the work they do daily. After the Fours have worked in the different activity centers, bring them together in a group of no more than 10 children to talk about what they did. They can show their drawings, paintings, and other work and talk about their block buildings, pretend play, and games.

This group talking time gives you a chance to point out some new ideas and helps the children learn to communicate with others.

🏠 indoors   🕑 5–15 minutes   # 1–10 Fours

100

Fours can

- talk in sentences
- tell about things they know

Work Our Dads and Moms Do

Start a conversation about the work the Fours' dads and moms do. See if they can take turns telling what they know about their parents' work.

Peg's mom is a doctor. Have you been to see her at work, Peg?
Kevin's dad drives a bus, and he gives Kevin a ride sometimes.
Your dad does lots of work at home, Emma.
Can you tell us about some of the things he does?

You can invite some of the parents to tell about their work, too. Remind them to bring along things to show the children if possible.

🏠 indoors   🕐 5–15 minutes   # 1–20 Fours

101

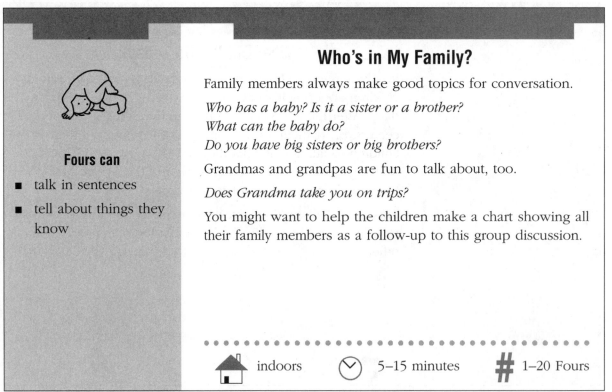

Fours can

- talk in sentences
- tell about things they know

Who's in My Family?

Family members always make good topics for conversation.

Who has a baby? Is it a sister or a brother?
What can the baby do?
Do you have big sisters or big brothers?

Grandmas and grandpas are fun to talk about, too.

Does Grandma take you on trips?

You might want to help the children make a chart showing all their family members as a follow-up to this group discussion.

🏠 indoors   🕐 5–15 minutes   # 1–20 Fours

102

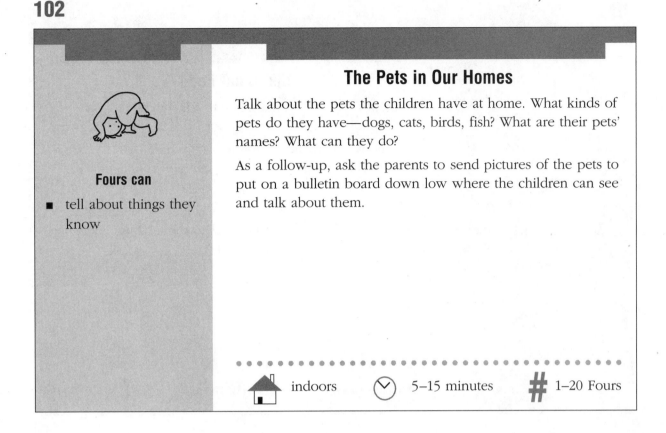

Fours can

- tell about things they know

The Pets in Our Homes

Talk about the pets the children have at home. What kinds of pets do they have—dogs, cats, birds, fish? What are their pets' names? What can they do?

As a follow-up, ask the parents to send pictures of the pets to put on a bulletin board down low where the children can see and talk about them.

🏠 indoors   🕐 5–15 minutes   # 1–20 Fours

103

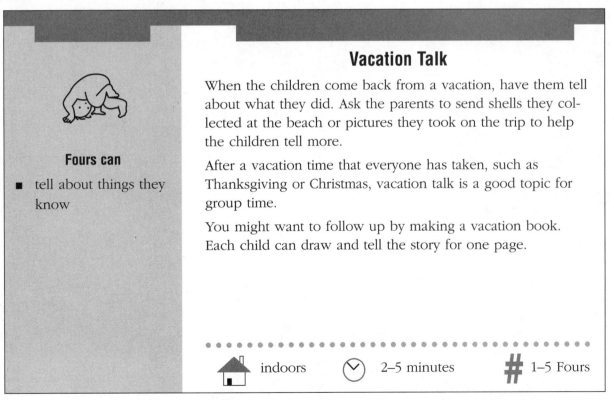

Fours can

- tell about things they know

Vacation Talk

When the children come back from a vacation, have them tell about what they did. Ask the parents to send shells they collected at the beach or pictures they took on the trip to help the children tell more.

After a vacation time that everyone has taken, such as Thanksgiving or Christmas, vacation talk is a good topic for group time.

You might want to follow up by making a vacation book. Each child can draw and tell the story for one page.

🏠 indoors   🕐 2–5 minutes   # 1–5 Fours

Fours can

- tell what they like

- understand *same* and *different*

Talk About Food

Talk about foods the children like to eat. What are their favorite foods? What do they like for breakfast, lunch, dinner?

Have any of the children eaten in a restaurant? What was it like? How is eating in a restaurant different from eating at home?

Do any of the children have jobs at home like setting the table? Who cooks and who helps clear the table at home? Who does those jobs in a restaurant?

in or out   5–10 minutes   # 1–20 Fours

- Keep the group small (under 10 Fours) so that each child can have a chance to ask and answer questions and make comments several times during the meeting.

- Sit in a circle so that the children can see one another. If children sit on a rug, it is not as disruptive as wiggling in chairs.

- Decide on a signal to give when someone wants a turn to talk. Putting up the index (pointer) finger is a good quiet signal.

- When the children are learning that only one person speaks at a time while the others listen, have the speaker hold something to show that it is his turn to speak. A yarn ball, a toy microphone, or anything else that is easy to pass around will do.

- Keep the group time short because it is hard for young children to sit still and listen for a long time. When children are allowed to get bored or restless in group time, they learn to dislike large groups.

- Talk about things the Fours are interested in—what they did, what they want to do, what happened to them.

- Bring in things to look at and touch to make the topics more lively.

- Remember that a group can't learn, only individual children can learn. Make eye contact and talk to each child in the group.

Hints About Asking Questions

- Use different types of questions to help children think about their activities in many different ways.

- Always be sure that your questions sound friendly and that they do not cause stress and pressure.

- Count to ten while you calmly wait for an answer. Remember it takes time for children to think of an answer.

- If a child can't find an answer to your question, then you can answer the question for him and share the information that way.

- In order to help young children think, you'll need to practice asking different types of questions.

An *open-ended question* has no right answer. It is a good type of question to start with because it gives the child a chance to show the adult how he organizes his ideas and expresses himself in words. An example of an open-ended question is "Can you tell me all about your painting?"

Open-ended questions can be used in many situations. When you are reading a story, you can stop and let children tell about one of the pictures by asking, "Can you tell me all about what is happening here?"

An open-ended question may get very different answers depending on the child's level of understanding. One child may be able to pull together all the details and tell you what the whole picture means. Another child may only be able to name the different parts of the picture. The adult can help this child by asking questions that focus his attention on the details. After the child has told about the details, the general question can be asked again: "Now can you tell me what's happening here?" so that the child can give the main idea of the picture.

"How" questions give the child a chance to describe a process or tell about a sequence. "How did you make your pancake when we did cooking today?" "How did you build this tall building?" This is very different from asking a child "What did you build?" *"What" questions* usually get short answers: "What did you build?" "A big tower." A "how" question helps the child remember and organize a lot of information about the process.

"How" questions can also help children recognize relationships, such as same and different, more and less, big and little. "How are these blocks different from one another?" "How are they the same?"

"Why" questions ask children to try to find reasons for the things they see happening. "Why do you think the ice cream became hard in the freezer?" "Why did it melt outside on the table?"

"What if" questions help children think about what might happen next, to predict. "What might happen if you spill water and children walk on the wet floor?"

- In order to build skills in asking questions, it helps to plan the questions you want to ask. Story time is a good time to plan for asking a few questions. You might ask an open-ended question about one of the exciting pictures that has a lot going on in it. You might ask a "how" or a "why" question that is right for the story. The children can also be asked to say what is going to happen next before you turn the page and read the rest of the story.

- After children have been involved in an activity, a question can help them tell about what they have done.

- Planning can help you learn to ask a variety of questions. With practice, questions will become a comfortable way to encourage your Fours to talk more.

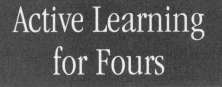

Active Learning for Fours

Activities for Physical Development

Index

of Activities for Physical Development

Here's Why

Fours enjoy physical activity. While they are indoors, they usually want to move about as they play. They always rush outdoors and race around after being indoors for any amount of time. When Fours are moving, they usually seem happy and involved. We know that they need plenty of time for physical activity to build strong bodies. Daily active play both indoors and outdoors in a safe space is important for a group of Fours.

While they are using their muscles, Fours can learn more than physical skills. They learn about how things move and balance in space. They are open to learning the words they need in order to think and talk about what they are doing. The ideas in this section give children many safe and enjoyable large-muscle activities.

Four-year-olds also need lots of practice in using their fingers and hands. Activities with materials that use these small muscles, such as pegboards, beads, and small building toys give Fours the chance to solve problems and use their eyes and hands together. You will find that most of the art activities in the Creative Activities section of this book also encourage Fours to develop small-muscle skills, too.

Each activity in the sections for large- and small-muscle development includes some ideas for you to help children learn words and other thinking skills as they enjoy physical activity. Physical activities are learning activities, and you have to plan for them as carefully as you do for other learning. Every new thing Fours learn to do with their large and small muscles builds their feelings of confidence and pride in what they can do for themselves.

Materials and Notes

Large Muscles

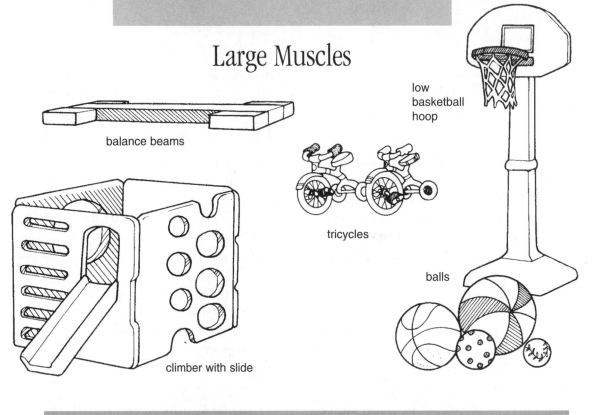

balance beams

low basketball hoop

tricycles

balls

climber with slide

- Younger Fours and older Fours do not differ greatly in the large-muscle activities they enjoy. You will probably be able to use many of the activities in this section for both age groups. When you try any activity, watch carefully to see if the activity is fun for the children and challenges but does not frustrate them. If these things are true, then the activity is right for the children.

- Fours will practice running, climbing, balancing, jumping, and many other large-muscle skills on their own. Just give them lots of time and space to do this in their own special way. Then you can add the activities in this book to what they do by themselves.

- Avoid having Fours compete with one another. Instead, encourage each child to do his or her own best and to face the challenge of getting just a little better.

- To ensure safe large-muscle activities for your Fours, read "Outdoor Play" in the Planning for Fours section of this book.

- Give parents ideas for safe large-muscle activities for children to do at home. Talk about how things in the home, such as grocery store boxes, blankets, and balls can be used in many fun ways.

- Remember that Fours need lots of supervision when doing active play. Remind parents that although their children may seem to be very competent, they still need a safe place to play and good supervision.

Activity Checklist

Large Muscles

Large-muscle activities with Fours include experiences in which the arm, leg, and body muscles are used and strengthened. Large-muscle activities for four-year-olds include climbing, running, throwing, balancing, pedaling wheel toys, pumping on a swing, and many others. Equipment should encourage these skills so that Fours are safely challenged.

Check for each age group

	48–54 months	54–60 months
1. Adult carefully supervises large-muscle activities both indoors and outdoors.	❐	❐
2. Safe, fenced, open space is provided for large-muscle play outdoors every day, except when weather is bad.	❐	❐
3. Safe open space is provided indoors for large-muscle play with some suitable equipment, especially during bad weather.	❐	❐
4. Safe, sturdy, age-appropriate large-muscle equipment (riding toys, wagons, slides, balls, a climber, swings) is available for children's daily use outdoors.	❐	❐
5. Duplicates of popular large-muscle toys are available. When sharing is a problem, a waiting list or other system is used so that the problem is handled fairly.	❐	❐
6. Equipment encourages a variety of skills, such as climbing, balancing, walking, running, swinging, and pedaling.	❐	❐
7. Safe, fenced, open space is provided for large-muscle play outdoors every day, except when weather is bad.	❐	❐
8. A safe area for riding pedal toys is available, separated from swings and other equipment.	❐	❐
9. Adult talks to children about the large-muscle activities they do.	❐	❐
10. Adult encourages independence and new skills, such as pumping on the swings, when children seem ready.	❐	❐
11. Organized group games, such as "How Many Ways Can We Cross the Playground?" or "Easy Simon Says," are suggested for any interested Fours.	❐	❐

105

Fours can

- catch a ball tossed from a short distance
- play with three or four other children

Catching Balls

Stand four or five feet away from your four-year-old. Tell him you are going to throw him the ball, and ask if he can catch it. Gently toss a lightweight ball that is about six inches across. After he catches the ball, ask him to throw it back to you. Encourage a few other Fours to join in the catching game. Have them stand in a circle or square to take turns catching and throwing.

You caught the ball, Jimmy.
Now throw it to Leah.
Whoops! You threw it so high.

Use balls of different sizes and weights with this activity. Keep them in a balls activity box to take outdoors.

in or out   5–20 minutes   # 1–8 Fours

106

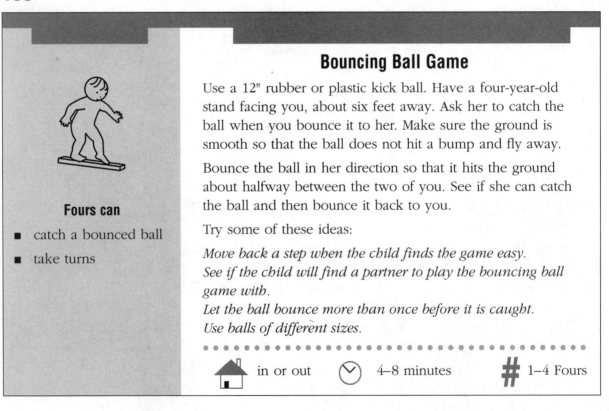

Fours can

- catch a bounced ball
- take turns

Bouncing Ball Game

Use a 12" rubber or plastic kick ball. Have a four-year-old stand facing you, about six feet away. Ask her to catch the ball when you bounce it to her. Make sure the ground is smooth so that the ball does not hit a bump and fly away.

Bounce the ball in her direction so that it hits the ground about halfway between the two of you. See if she can catch the ball and then bounce it back to you.

Try some of these ideas:

Move back a step when the child finds the game easy.
See if the child will find a partner to play the bouncing ball game with.
Let the ball bounce more than once before it is caught.
Use balls of different sizes.

in or out   4–8 minutes   # 1–4 Fours

107

Fours can

- run well
- kick a ball
- follow directions

Kick and Run

Take your Fours outdoors to a big fenced open space and give them each a big <u>ball</u> to kick and chase. Have them kick the balls as hard as they can and then run to kick them again. Let the children enjoy darting in between each other, as well as around playground equipment and then back to you.

You kicked that ball hard, Emma. Where did it go?

Try some of these ideas:

- Tell the children to use only feet, not hands, as they play.
- Set up some special places to be goals that the children can kick their balls into.
- Ask two children to kick one ball back and forth to each other.

🏠 outdoors   🕐 5–20 minutes   # 2–20 Fours

108

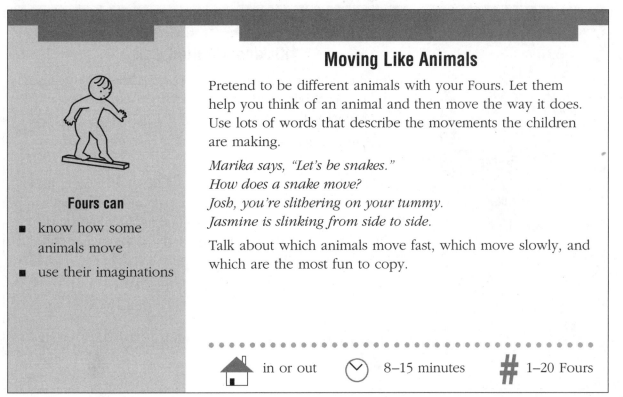

Fours can

- know how some animals move
- use their imaginations

Moving Like Animals

Pretend to be different animals with your Fours. Let them help you think of an animal and then move the way it does. Use lots of words that describe the movements the children are making.

Marika says, "Let's be snakes."
How does a snake move?
Josh, you're slithering on your tummy.
Jasmine is slinking from side to side.

Talk about which animals move fast, which move slowly, and which are the most fun to copy.

🏠 in or out   🕐 8–15 minutes   # 1–20 Fours

109

Fours can

- move in many ways
- know words for different movements

How Many Ways Can We Cross the Playground?

Ask an interested child to show you how many ways he can move across the playground. Watch as he shows you his different ways and talk about what he is doing. Join in and copy how he moves if you wish. Invite other children to join the game.

Wow! Edmund raced across the playground.
Catia, you're going so slowly that I can hardly see you move.

Encourage lots of ideas by making suggestions about moving fast or slowly, high or low, frontward or backward, noisily or quietly.

Try this game inside and see how many ways the children can think of to move across the room or down a hallway.

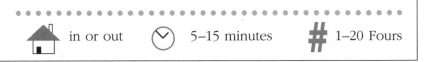

🏠 in or out   🕐 5–15 minutes   # 1–20 Fours

110

Fours can

- kick a ball

Kicking a Rolled Ball

Tell the child that you are going to play a ball-kicking game with her. Have her stand facing you on smooth ground and tell her what will happen.

Lisa, I am going to roll the ball to you. Try to kick it back to me.

Gently roll a big ball toward her feet and see if she can kick it as it moves. Have fun catching the ball and trying again. Invite other children to roll balls to one another and practice kicking. Make sure there is plenty of space for each group that is playing together.

🏠 outdoors   🕐 3–15 minutes   # 1–6 Fours

111

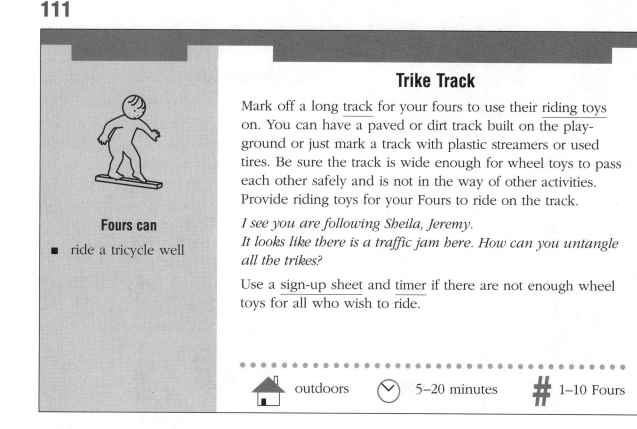

Fours can

- ride a tricycle well

Trike Track

Mark off a long <u>track</u> for your fours to use their <u>riding toys</u> on. You can have a paved or dirt track built on the playground or just mark a track with plastic streamers or used tires. Be sure the track is wide enough for wheel toys to pass each other safely and is not in the way of other activities. Provide riding toys for your Fours to ride on the track.

I see you are following Sheila, Jeremy.
It looks like there is a traffic jam here. How can you untangle all the trikes?

Use a <u>sign-up sheet</u> and <u>timer</u> if there are not enough wheel toys for all who wish to ride.

🏠 outdoors   🕐 5–20 minutes   # 1–10 Fours

112

Fours can

- run well
- begin to understand what time is and what clocks are for

Laps on the Track

On some days, use the <u>trike track</u> for a running track. Do not bring out the wheel toys. Instead, encourage children to run along the track. You can use a <u>stopwatch</u> to time how fast each child runs and let them know if they ran faster or slower than the last time they ran.

You ran the track in 55 seconds, Jinsy. That's five seconds faster than you ran the last time.

Encourage children to figure out many ways to get around the track and talk about which ways are faster/slower, harder/easier.

🏠 outdoors   🕐 5–20 minutes   # 1–10 Fours

113

Fours can

- move in many ways
- follow simple directions

Quiet-Moving Game

Use a whispering voice to invite your Fours to play a quiet-moving game.

The bookmobile is here.
Let's be mice and move so that no one can hear us.
Who can move so that we cannot hear any footsteps or voices?

Remember to move quietly yourself. Then creep or tiptoe quietly with children from one place to another. Use this game when children must move past quiet areas, such as infant rooms, or just for a fun change of pace.

If some children do not play, do not make a fuss. Just continue to enjoy the game with other children.

🏠 in or out   🕐 1–3 minutes   # 1–20 Fours

114

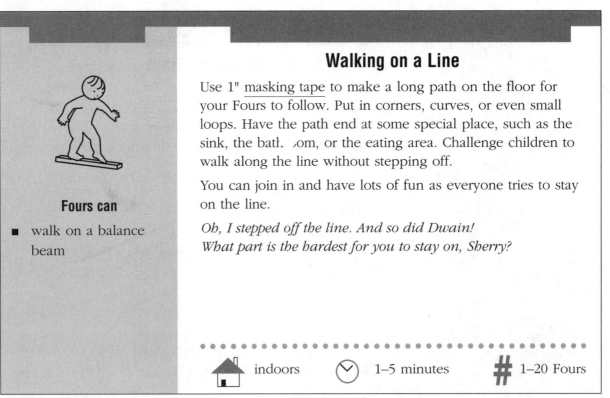

Fours can

- walk on a balance beam

Walking on a Line

Use 1" masking tape to make a long path on the floor for your Fours to follow. Put in corners, curves, or even small loops. Have the path end at some special place, such as the sink, the bathroom, or the eating area. Challenge children to walk along the line without stepping off.

You can join in and have lots of fun as everyone tries to stay on the line.

Oh, I stepped off the line. And so did Dwain!
What part is the hardest for you to stay on, Sherry?

🏠 indoors   🕐 1–5 minutes   # 1–20 Fours

115

Fours can

- enjoy playing with other children
- use their imaginations

Box Play

Bring in a few appliance boxes from a local store. Put these boxes outside on a dry, soft area for free play. Let children have fun using them in their own way. Ask them to tell you about what they are doing.

What are you and Max doing with the boxes, Lois?
Did you build a house? No?
Oh, yes, I see. You made a garage for the bikes.

Be sure to have enough boxes so that children will not be crowded when they play. Talk about rules for taking turns and using boxes safely.

🏠 outdoors   🕐 5–30 minutes   # 1–3 Fours per box

116

Fours can

- follow simple directions
- move in many ways
- know words for different movements

Red Rover

Have all interested Fours stand on one side of the room or playground. Call to them from the other side and say:

Red Rover, Red Rover, everybody run over!

Have them follow your direction and run across the play area. Try some of these ideas: jump, walk backward, hop on one foot, twirl, tiptoe.

Let children take turns thinking of a way for the group to move and then call out their own directions.

🏠 outdoors   🕐 5–20 minutes   # 2–20 Fours

117

Fours can

- walk on a low balance beam

Balancing Acts

Set up very low <u>balance beams</u> of different widths for Fours to use. Have one made of a board that is 12" wide and others that are 6", 4", and 2" wide. Secure these beams to blocks of smooth wood so that they are 3" to 6" off the ground. Place them on a steady surface with grass or mats underneath.

Encourage the children to walk on the balance beams in many ways. See which they can balance on alone. Encourage friends to help one another on the narrow beams.

Enrico, you can walk backward on the wide balance beam! Marissa, can you get to the end of the narrow beam?

🏠 in or out   🕐 2–20 minutes   # 1–10 Fours

118

Fours can

- jump over low obstacles

Hurdles to Jump Over

Set up <u>hurdles</u> for interested Fours to use. First mark off a straight or circular course on a soft surface, such as grass or sand. Then place hurdles (12" or lower) along the course for the children to jump over as they run. You might use vinyl-covered foam blocks as hurdles or low ropes with flags attached so that children can easily see them. Take care not to use a hurdle that might hurt or cause falls. If you make the track indoors for bad-weather play, place carpet or mats around the hurdles.

Show your Fours how to run and jump the hurdles. Help them take turns running so that they do not crowd each other.

Jimmy has jumped over three blocks. See, he is running past the oak tree. Do you think it's safe to start, Dianna?

🏠 in or out   🕐 5–20 minutes   # 1–10 Fours

119

Fours can

- stand on one foot for ten seconds

Standing Like Flamingos

Show your Fours pictures of flamingo birds who are standing on one leg. Talk about how the birds balance. Then pretend to be flamingos with your Fours. Challenge them to stand on one leg for as long as they can balance. Try these flamingo ideas too:

- flap arms to pretend to flap wings
- close eyes and pretend to sleep while on one leg
- change from one leg to another to see which is easiest to balance on
- strut around on two legs and then stop and balance on one leg

🏠 in or out   🕐 2–10 minutes   # 1–20 Fours

120

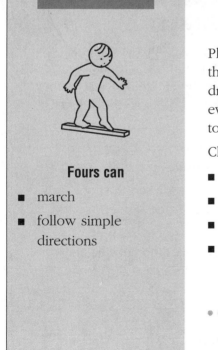

Fours can

- march
- follow simple directions

Move and Stop

Play some lively music for interested Fours to march to. After they have marched a bit, turn the music off and tell the children to stop where they are. Tell them they can march whenever they hear music, but when it stops, they need to stop, too. Make a fun game out of marching and stopping.

Children can move and stop to some of these actions, too:

- clapping
- hopping
- stamping
- shaking hands or whole body

🏠 in or out   🕐 4–20 minutes   # 1–20 Fours

121

Fours can

- move in many ways
- understand some place words, such as *in front of, under, behind, on top of*

Plastic Hoop Places

Give each interested Four a large plastic <u>hoop</u> to use for this game. Tell the children to position themselves by following the directions. Then ask them to

- stand in front of their hoops
- stand inside of their hoops
- run around their hoops
- stand under their hoops
- hop over their hoops

Let the children be creative in the ways they follow your directions. Use other place words, too. Show the children what you mean if they do not understand your directions.

Allow children to give the directions, too. Try the game with other objects, such as soft stuffed animals or blocks.

🏠 in or out 　　🕐 5–20 minutes 　　# 1–20 Fours

122

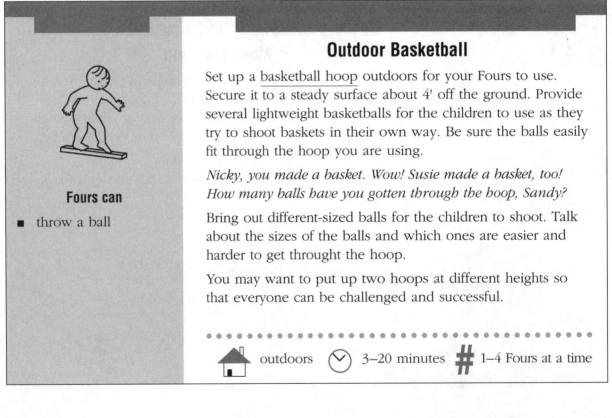

Fours can

- throw a ball

Outdoor Basketball

Set up a basketball <u>hoop</u> outdoors for your Fours to use. Secure it to a steady surface about 4' off the ground. Provide several lightweight basketballs for the children to use as they try to shoot baskets in their own way. Be sure the balls easily fit through the hoop you are using.

Nicky, you made a basket. Wow! Susie made a basket, too! How many balls have you gotten through the hoop, Sandy?

Bring out different-sized balls for the children to shoot. Talk about the sizes of the balls and which ones are easier and harder to get throught the hoop.

You may want to put up two hoops at different heights so that everyone can be challenged and successful.

🏠 outdoors 　　🕐 3–20 minutes 　　# 1–4 Fours at a time

123

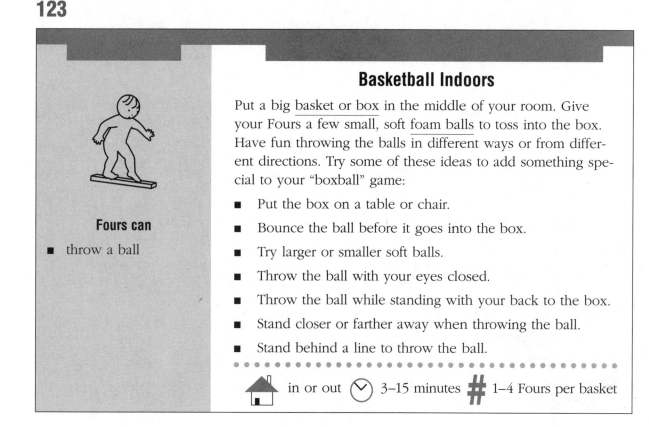

Fours can

- throw a ball

Basketball Indoors

Put a big basket or box in the middle of your room. Give your Fours a few small, soft foam balls to toss into the box. Have fun throwing the balls in different ways or from different directions. Try some of these ideas to add something special to your "boxball" game:

- Put the box on a table or chair.
- Bounce the ball before it goes into the box.
- Try larger or smaller soft balls.
- Throw the ball with your eyes closed.
- Throw the ball while standing with your back to the box.
- Stand closer or farther away when throwing the ball.
- Stand behind a line to throw the ball.

in or out   3–15 minutes   1–4 Fours per basket

124

Fours can

- jump over things
- pretend

Jumping on Stepping Stones

Use masking tape to make a path of "stepping stones" that your Fours can follow by jumping from stone to stone. Just make tape squares on the floor that are large enough and spaced so that children can safely jump from one to the other.

Explain safety rules for using the stones, such as "Only jump to an empty space." Have just a few children use the stones at a time. Avoid lining up all the children to wait a turn.

Have fun as you and your Fours pretend that there is water all around the stones and you are trying not to fall in. Encourage the children to think of their own pretend reasons for staying on the stones as they move.

indoors   2–6 minutes   1–4 Fours

125

Fours can

- move easily in many ways

Tents

Make tents for the children to crawl in and play under. (You'll find tent ideas on page 158.) Allow children to use soft toys, dolls, blankets, and books under each tent to add to their play. If the tents are popular, have several set up or use a waiting list so that each child can get a turn to play.

Deedee, you and Sam want to play in this tent, too. But look how crowded it is. How can we solve your problem? We have another big blanket here. Will that help?

You can also make a covered crawling course by lining up several tents in a row and allowing children to move through as if crawling through tunnels.

Store tent-making materials in a tents activity box for the Fours to use on their own.

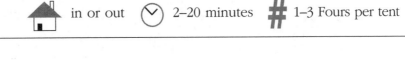

🏠 in or out   🕐 2–20 minutes   # 1–3 Fours per tent

126

Fours can

- copy movements
- know about many animals

Copying Animal Movements

Put pictures of several familiar animals into a feelie box or bag. Have a child close her eyes, reach in, and pick one out. Ask her to tell you about the animal she chose. Then see if the child can show you how it moves.

Everyone can move the way the child does. See if someone else can show you a different way that same animal moves and copy that child's movements, too.

Andre showed us how the lion puts his paws out to swipe and claw. Can anyone think of another movement the lion does? Yes. Marissa knows that lions stretch and yawn!

Leave the feelie box and animal pictures out for children to use on their own.

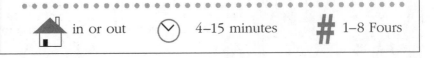

🏠 in or out   🕐 4–15 minutes   # 1–8 Fours

127

Fours can

- cooperate with a small group of friends

Creating Obstacle Courses

Provide <u>materials</u> for your Fours to use to make their own <u>obstacle course</u>. You might have to help the children make the course follow a set path. Include some of these things:

- tunnels or tents to crawl through
- masking tape to mark stepping stones or lines to move along
- mats or big pillows to roll over
- hoops to jump through or in and out of
- boxes or milk crates to step over
- smooth boards to make into low slides

Allow a small group of two or three children to arrange the obstacles in their own way, and then everyone who wishes can try out the challenge.

🏠 in or out   🕐 5–30 minutes   # 1–10 Fours

128

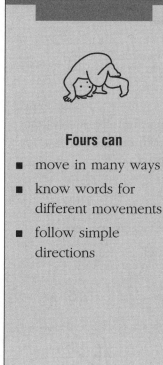

Fours can

- move in many ways
- know words for different movements
- follow simple directions

Movement Path

Allow each child or a small group of friends to use <u>1" masking tape</u> to create different movement paths on the floor. Their paths can be straight, zigzagged, full of loops, or any other shape they can think of. When a path is finished, ask the child to tell others how to move along it. For example, one path might be for hopping on one foot, while another might be for walking backward.

Tell me about your path, James.
How should we move on your curvy path? Can you show us?
Oh, you want us to hop on our left foot.

Outside, children can use chalk to make movement paths on sidewalks, or they can use a stick to make a path in the dirt.

🏠 in or out   🕐 2–15 minutes   # 1–20 Fours

129

Fours can

- throw a ball

Beanbag Toss

Cut out different-sized shapes from the sides of a big cardboard box. For example, cut a 10" circle, a smaller square, and a larger triangle. Trace around each hole with bright markers or paints so that children can easily see them. Be sure that each hole is big enough so a beanbag can go through. Put out a basket or dishpan of beanbags for children to toss through the holes.

You got the beanbag into the big circle, Chris. You missed the triangle. What can you do to get the beanbag through that hole?

You can also use masking tape to make one or more lines on the floor where the children can stand when they toss, or use beanbags of different sizes.

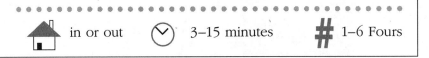

in or out   3–15 minutes   1–6 Fours

130

Fours can

- hop on one foot at least five times

Bunny Hop

Have all interested Fours line up with you to do a Bunny Hop. Hop for a while on one foot, and then on the other. Hop on two feet, too. Hop all over the room or outdoor area. Hop fast and hop slowly. Laugh and have fun as you pretend to be bunnies who are hopping away from danger or bunnies who are tired from eating too much lettuce.

Oh, no! Here comes Farmer Brown!
Quick! Hop fast so he doesn't catch us!

Make time for children to lead the line of hoppers, too.

Pretend to be other types of hoppers, such as grasshoppers or frogs.

in or out   2–5 minutes   1–20 Fours

131

Fours can

- do a forward somersault

Tumbling Time

Take a small group of Fours to a clear, soft area, such as a grassy area on the playground or some mats. Be sure that each child is well away from the others. Then help the children one at a time to do a forward somersault. Help them to remember to keep neck and knees tucked into their chest. Help the child push up with her arms to keep the weight off her neck.

Do you have your chin tucked in, Alice? Great! Now push and go over!

As children become able, let them somersault on their own. Allow them to tumble and roll in their own creative ways, as long as everything is safe.

Always watch tumbling very carefully.

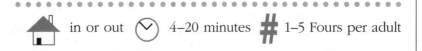

🏠 in or out 🕐 4–20 minutes # 1–5 Fours per adult

132

Fours can

- walk and jump backwards

Backward Times

Have a very short backward time when everyone moves backward. Tell children when the time will start, and remind them to move carefully so that no one gets hurt. Then for about 3 minutes see how much fun it is to change the way you move. Try a backward time during an activity time or during outdoor play. If children must move as a group sometimes, have a backward time then.

Are you going to the art center, Mary?
Watch out for the table as you move.

Talk with the children about how walking backward is different from walking forward. You can also try a sideways walking time.

🏠 in or out 🕐 1–3 minutes # 1–20 Fours

133

Fours can

- build with blocks and other materials
- walk on a balance beam

Creative Playground Equipment

Put out things Fours can use to build their own movable playground equipment. Try long, smooth wooden <u>boards</u>, sturdy cardboard <u>boxes</u>, milk <u>crates</u>, sturdy <u>blocks</u>, a small ladder, wooden or metal <u>triangles</u> to make ramps. Include some <u>mats</u> to put under parts that are off the ground. Let the children set them up in their own creative ways. Supervise carefully to be sure everything they build is safe to use. When things are not safe, have the children figure out what they can do to build something safer.

Amos, do you think this is safe? Let's check it out to see if your bridge is sturdy enough to walk on.
Uh-oh. It's wobbly here. How can you make it steadier?

 outdoors   3–30 minutes   # 1–6 Fours

134

Fours can

- remember several simple directions at once
- move in many ways

Do This, Then Do That

Play a game with any interested Fours where you give them a sequence of two movements to do. For example say:

First hop, then sit on the floor.
First jump, then twirl.
First wave your arms, then stand on one foot.
First squat down, then jump up high.

Make the game more challenging by giving the children three things to do. See how many directions the children can remember at one time without getting frustrated.

Encourage children to give the directions for what to do, too.

in or out   3–10 minutes   # 1–20 Fours

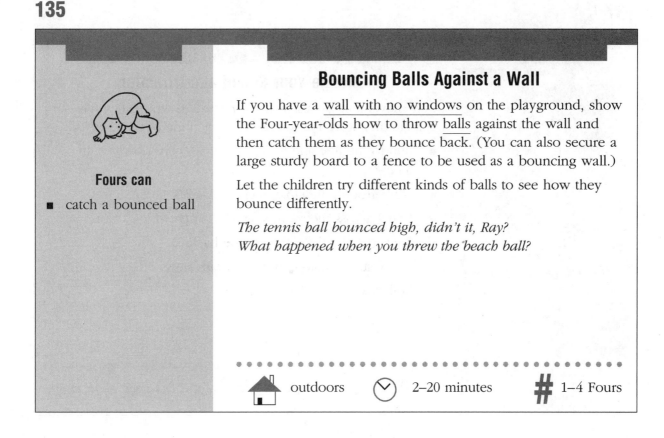

Fours can

- catch a bounced ball

Bouncing Balls Against a Wall

If you have a wall with no windows on the playground, show the Four-year-olds how to throw balls against the wall and then catch them as they bounce back. (You can also secure a large sturdy board to a fence to be used as a bouncing wall.)

Let the children try different kinds of balls to see how they bounce differently.

The tennis ball bounced high, didn't it, Ray?
What happened when you threw the beach ball?

🏠 outdoors   🕐 2–20 minutes   # 1–4 Fours

136

Fours can

- begin to pump on a swing by themselves

Swinging

Have a swing set with low, safe swings for your Fours to use. Be sure the swings are out of the way of other activities. If there are no swings on the playground, take the children to a park where there are safe swings. (Swings should have sling seats, not wooden seats.)

Allow the children to use the swings freely, as long as their swinging is safe. Watch to see which children can manage swinging all by themselves.

Encourage children to swing using their own power rather than being pushed.

Get started by pushing off with your feet, Leroy.
Now swing your legs back and forth.
Watch how Andrew does it. Back and forth, back and forth.

🏠 outdoors   🕐 3–10 minutes   # 1 child per swing

137

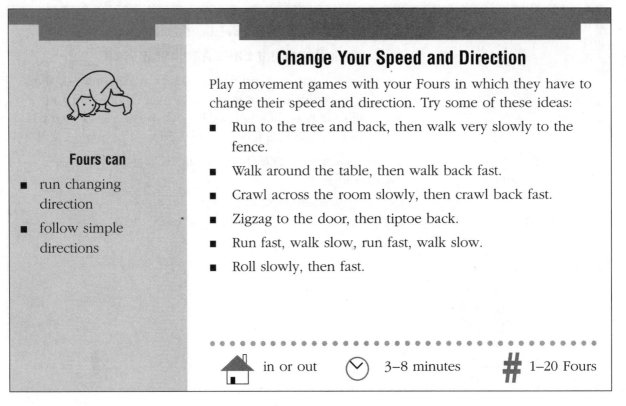

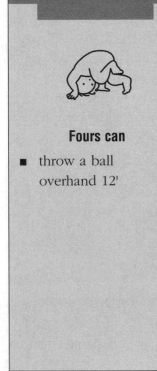

Fours can

- run changing direction
- follow simple directions

Change Your Speed and Direction

Play movement games with your Fours in which they have to change their speed and direction. Try some of these ideas:

- Run to the tree and back, then walk very slowly to the fence.
- Walk around the table, then walk back fast.
- Crawl across the room slowly, then crawl back fast.
- Zigzag to the door, then tiptoe back.
- Run fast, walk slow, run fast, walk slow.
- Roll slowly, then fast.

🏠 in or out   🕐 3–8 minutes   # 1–20 Fours

138

Fours can

- throw a ball overhand 12'

Throw at the Target

Set out a basket of bright tennis balls. Put up a big circle or rectangle or a target for children to throw at and see if they can hit. You can make a target on a big sheet of easel paper or cardboard and hang it outdoors on a wall without windows or doors, on a fence, or on a tree.

Use chalk to mark where children can stand when they throw—at about 3', 5', 8', 10', 12', and 15' from the target. Allow the children to begin at the closest line and move back each time hitting the target is too easy.

The children can help you measure where the lines should go, and you can even label them with the distance from the target. Talk with the children about distances as they play.

🏠 outdoors   🕐 2–15 minutes   # 1–4 Fours

139

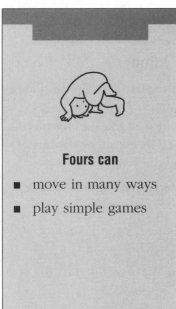

Fours can

- move in many ways
- play simple games

How Many Ways Can You Go Over and Under?

Have two children or adults hold the ends of a jump rope so that it is about waist high for the other children. Place one or more big mats under the rope so that if children trip or fall while playing this game, they will not be hurt. Challenge the Fours to go over or under the rope in as many ways as they can.

Move the rope to higher and lower levels every so often to give the children different challenges as they play.

Encourage the children to describe the ways they moved.

Jerry, you went over the rope when it was really high. How did you do it? Yes. You did fly like Superman!

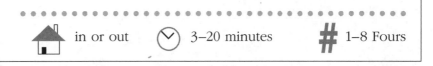

🏠 in or out   🕐 3–20 minutes   # 1–8 Fours

140

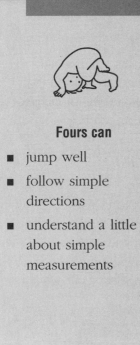

Fours can

- jump well
- follow simple directions
- understand a little about simple measurements

Standing Broad Jump

Make a 6' ruler out of strips of cardboard. Mark off every foot and inch. Place this ruler along a grassy area outdoors or a carpeted area indoors where it will be safe for children to jump. Show the children how to stand next to the beginning of the long ruler and then jump as far as they can. Let the children try. You can point out how far each child was able to jump. Encourage children to compete with themselves, not against others.

Laura, you jumped a whole foot further this time than last time. Do you think you can do it again?

Children may not be very exact about using the correct jumping-off place. That's OK as long as children are stretching and using their muscles.

🏠 in or out   🕐 1–20 minutes   # 1–6 Fours

141

Fours can

- jump well
- follow simple directions
- understand a little about simple measurements

Running Broad Jump

Have the children try running up to the starting point on the 6' ruler used for the standing broad jump and then jump as far as they can. Don't worry if they run past the starting place and then jump. It's hard for children to be exact when they are running. Just laugh and enjoy how they try.

Show the children how far they jumped by using the ruler as a measure.

Help the children figure out which kind of jump (standing or running) helps them go farther.

Do you jump farther with the standing jump or the running jump? Let's try both and measure to see, Daniel.

🏠 outdoors   🕐 2–15 minutes   # 1–6 Fours

142

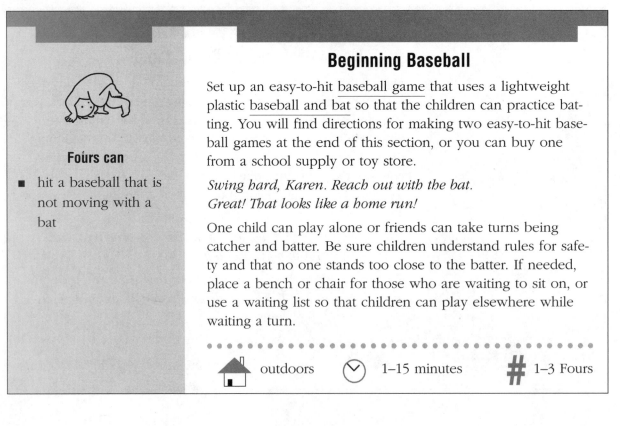

Fours can

- hit a baseball that is not moving with a bat

Beginning Baseball

Set up an easy-to-hit baseball game that uses a lightweight plastic baseball and bat so that the children can practice batting. You will find directions for making two easy-to-hit baseball games at the end of this section, or you can buy one from a school supply or toy store.

Swing hard, Karen. Reach out with the bat.
Great! That looks like a home run!

One child can play alone or friends can take turns being catcher and batter. Be sure children understand rules for safety and that no one stands too close to the batter. If needed, place a bench or chair for those who are waiting to sit on, or use a waiting list so that children can play elsewhere while waiting a turn.

🏠 outdoors   🕐 1–15 minutes   # 1–3 Fours

143

Fours can

- roll a ball
- cooperate with a friend

Bowling

Make a Bowling Activity Box with a set of plastic <u>bowling pins</u> and a lightweight <u>bowling ball</u> for your Fours to use. Have the Fours use these in a narrow area (bowling lane) that you can separate from the rest of the room with bookcases, cubbies, or other room dividers. Then the ball will not escape.

Have several <u>masking tape</u> lines where the children can stand to bowl. Allow them to choose the place where they can bowl most comfortably.

Show the children how one person can bowl while a friend catches the ball, returns it to the bowler, and resets the pins. Children can change places.

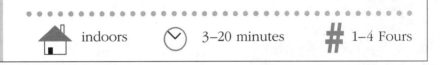

🏠 indoors   🕐 3–20 minutes   # 1–4 Fours

144

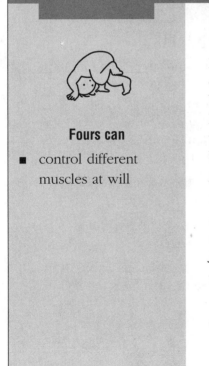

Fours can

- control different muscles at will

Relax!

Have Fours lie down on their backs, with each child in his own space. Ask the children to think about the part of their body that you name. First have them tighten that body part as hard as they can. Watch to see if they can do this. Then tell them to relax that part of their body. Do this for hands, feet, back, legs, neck, face, and arms. See if the children can suggest which parts of the body to do next.

Tighten your hand. Make a hard, hard fist.
Now relax your hand. Make it as floppy as you can.
Shake it around and see if it flops.
Just let your hand hang and take a big rest.

This activity is great after very active play.

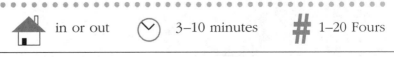

🏠 in or out   🕐 3–10 minutes   # 1–20 Fours

145

Fours can

- jump and hop
- play simple games

Leapfrog

Explain the way to play leapfrog to any Fours who are interested. Tell them to make a line and then squat down on their hands and knees. Be sure they tuck their heads into their arms so that they are like small balls.

Help the child at the end of the line to place her hands on the back of the child in front of her and then to leap over, like a frog. She should continue until she is at the front of the line. Then the next child at the end becomes the leaper, and so on, until all children have had a chance.

It helps if children have their shoes off for this game so that no one gets kicked by hard shoes. Guide the children so that they jump carefully and do not hurt each other.

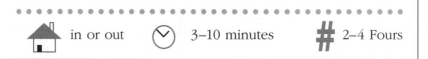

🏠 in or out   🕐 3–10 minutes   # 2–4 Fours

146

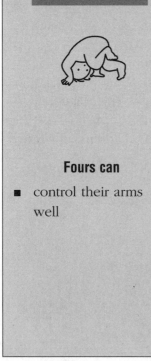

Fours can

- control their arms well

Beginning Golf

Make a golf hole for the children to practice hitting a golf ball into. Place a small <u>pail</u> in a hole in the ground so that its rim is at ground level. Provide <u>golf balls</u> and sturdy child-sized plastic <u>golf clubs</u> for the children to use. Show them how to hold the golf club, face the ball, and gently hit it toward the hole. Mark a place for them to start with a rope or stick.

Have them count how many times they hit the ball before getting it in the hole.

Wow, Jamaal! You got a hole-in-one! How many times do you have to hit the ball if you begin at the fence?

You can make holes of different sizes by using larger and smaller containers for the holes. See which ones the children think are easiest to make.

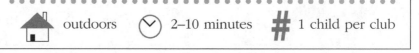

🏠 outdoors   🕐 2–10 minutes   # 1 child per club

Fours can

- jump over knee-high obstacle with both feet together

- cooperate with a few friends

The High Jump

Have a very lightweight <u>dowel</u> (1/4" in diameter and 4' long) for your Fours to jump over. Place <u>mats</u> on one side of the dowel where the children can land without getting hurt. Hold the dowel out at different heights for the children to jump over. If you wish, you can measure the height of the dowel with a <u>yardstick</u> and tell children how high they jumped.

Show the children how to hold the dowel steady for their friends to jump over.

You held the dowel so still for Sabrina to jump over, Matthew. Let's measure to see how high she jumped.

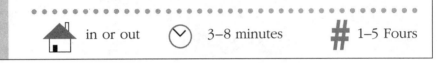

🏠 in or out   🕐 3–8 minutes   # 1–5 Fours

Ways to Make Tents

- Put a blanket or sheet over a table.

- Set up a child's bed-tent on an old mattress in a corner of the room.

- String a rope between two trees outdoors and then throw a sheet or blanket over the rope.

- Get a real tent at a yard sale or at a thrift shop and set it up for the children to use.

- Cut large openings in the ends of a large box and lay it on its side. Throw a blanket or sheet over it.

- Make a house shape with large snap-together plastic panels. Put a blanket over the top.

- Throw two or three blankets over a small climber.

- Tack old blankets or sheets around the platform of a climber so that children can hide and play underneath.

- Ask the children for more ideas on how to make tents.

Easy-To-Hit Baseball Games

Hit the Ball Off the Pipe

1. Attach a plastic plumber's pipe that is 24" high and 2" wide to the middle of a sturdy board that is about 8" wide by 4' long. Use screws to attach the pipe securely.

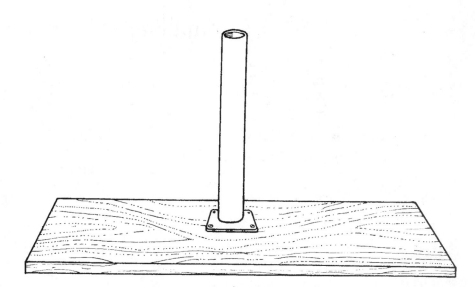

2. Child can place a lightweight plastic baseball on top of the pipe, stand on the opposite end of the board, and then hit the ball off the pipe with the bat.

3. Use in an out-of-the-way place.

Hit the Hanging Ball

1. Thread some sturdy cord through a lightweight plastic baseball with holes in it. Make a knot in the cord so that the ball will not fall off.

2. Hang the ball in an out-of-the-way place so that it is about 2½' from the ground, or waist-high for most of the children. For example, hang it from the limb of a tree in a corner of the playground, or from an overhang of the building where not many people play.

3. Children can take turns trying to hit the ball with the bat.

4. Supervise carefully and remove the cord when not being used, to avoid accidents.

Materials and Notes

Small Muscles

beads to string

marbles of different sizes

puzzles

pegs and pegboards

Pegs

put-together toys

- A Small-Muscle Center should be set up so Fours can use the toys and materials on their own. Be sure to read "Making Activity Centers" in the Planning for Fours section.

- Store each toy with many pieces in its own sturdy box, dishpan, or plastic container. Put a picture/word label showing the toy and its name on the box. Put out four or five different sets at a time on a low shelf and change them often.

- Avoid problems with sharing. Have more than one set of the most popular small-muscle toys. Do not store the materials as one very big set. Instead, store them as two or more sets so that one or two children can play with each.

- Check often for broken or lost pieces. Lost pieces frustrate children and keep them from finishing an activity with success.

- Make careful cleanup of the Small-Muscle Center an important part of your daily schedule with the children. Challenge children to find every small piece of the various materials and put them into the proper container. Turn this clean-up time into a fun activity by showing delight with each small piece they find.

- Give parents ideas about how they can help their children practice using their small muscles at home (putting tops back onto jars, breaking eggs while helping to cook, putting pillow cases on pillows, folding laundry).

Activities for Physical Development

Activity Checklist

Small Muscles

Small-muscle activities with Fours include experiences in which children learn to control hand and finger movements. As eye-hand coordination improves, Fours enjoy being more independent as they dress themselves, buttoning their own buttons and zipping zippers. As children near their fifth birthday, they can draw some figures we can recognize, including people that have more and more parts. Fours build with toys that have small pieces, are able to use scissors to cut out some simple shapes, and have often begun to print a few letters by the end of the year.

Check for each age group

	48–54 months	54–60 months
1. A variety of safe small-muscle toys for children to explore with fingers and hands is available for children to use by themselves.	❏	❏
2. Safe small-muscle toys are organized by type and stored on low, open shelves for children's free use.	❏	❏
3. Small-muscle toys are changed regularly.	❏	❏
4. Duplicates of popular toys are available.	❏	❏
5. Adult shows children how to use small-muscle toys as needed.	❏	❏
6. Toys are clean and in good condition.	❏	❏
7. Protected space is set aside for play with small-muscle toys.	❏	❏
8. Children are encouraged to serve and feed themselves.	❏	❏
9. Safe scissors are available for use, and children are helped to learn to cut.	❏	❏
10. Pencils, paper, and other writing materials are freely available for Fours to choose to use every day. No pressure is placed on the children to print or write.	❏	❏

148

Fours can

- use toys with many small pieces

Lots of Put-Together Toys

Have many different types of put-together/pull-apart toys. Store all sets in their own labeled containers. Put four or five sets out on a low shelf in the Small-Muscle Center for your Fours to choose when they are interested. Change some of the sets that are out on the shelves every week. Leave the most popular sets for children to use every day.

Some put-together/pull-apart small-muscle toys that Fours enjoy are:

- Lego® or other put-together building bricks
- blocks that stick together with plastic bristles
- small wooden or plastic table blocks
- blocks that snap together

in or out   5–30 minutes   # 1–2 Fours per set

149

Fours can

- use toys with many small pieces

Pegs and Pegboards

Have several different types of pegboards with pegs. For example, have big wooden pegs, thin wooden pegs, and brightly colored plastic pegs, too. Use a separate plastic container to store the pegs for each type of board.

Place two types of pegboards on the shelves of the Small-Muscle Center for your Fours to use when they are interested. Talk with the children about the colors of pegs they use, the number of pegs, and the designs they create.

Tell me about your peg design, Martin.
Oh, yes. I can see that you are sorting the different colors into different rows.

Keep changing the types of pegs that are out on the shelf.

indoors   5–20 minutes   # 1 child per board

150

Fours can

■ use their fingers and thumbs together very well

Geoboards

Make a few geoboards for your Fours to use. (Directions for making geoboards are on page 184.) Put the boards out on a low shelf in the Small-Muscle Center. Place a container full of colorful rubber bands next to each board.

Show interested children how to stretch a rubber band around a few nails to make a shape. Then let each child use the board and rubber bands in creative ways.

Talk with the children about the shapes they make.

You really had to stretch that rubber band to make it go around all those nails, Jasmine! Let's count to see how many nails you stretched the rubber band around.

● ●

🏠 indoors　　🕐 4–20 minutes　　# 1 child per board

151

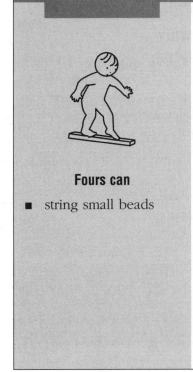

Fours can

■ string small beads

Stringing Buttons

Collect many colorful buttons of different sizes and shapes. Ask the children's parents to help add buttons to your collection. Store the buttons in one or more plastic containers with lids so they do not spill out. Add some sturdy shoelaces that will fit through the holes in the buttons. Allow children to string them in their own creative ways.

See if children discover that the buttons can be strung so that they look different on the string. For example, if a button is strung using two of its holes, it will lie flat.

Which buttons do you like the best, Charles?
Why do you like them?

Keep these materials in a Stringing Buttons Activity Box.

● ●

🏠 indoors　　🕐 3–15 minutes　　# 1–6 Fours

Activities for Physical Development　　　　**163**

152

Fours can

■ do simple folding

Folding Blankets and Napkins

Encourage Fours to help you with the folding tasks that you do each day. Show them how to place the object on a flat surface, put the corners and edges together to fold, then smooth, then put the new edges together, and continue folding. Talk the child through the folding steps.

Now put the edges together, Cathy.
Great! You really smoothed the bumps away.

Fours can also help fold

■ napkins as they set the table
■ notes to parents
■ dry easel paintings to fit into cubbies
■ extra clothes
■ doll clothes and blankets

🏠 in or out   🕐 2–6 minutes   # 1–20 Fours

153

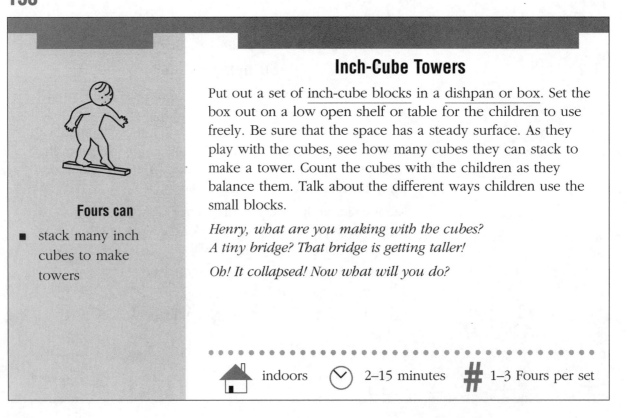

Fours can

■ stack many inch cubes to make towers

Inch-Cube Towers

Put out a set of inch-cube blocks in a dishpan or box. Set the box out on a low open shelf or table for the children to use freely. Be sure that the space has a steady surface. As they play with the cubes, see how many cubes they can stack to make a tower. Count the cubes with the children as they balance them. Talk about the different ways children use the small blocks.

Henry, what are you making with the cubes?
A tiny bridge? That bridge is getting taller!

Oh! It collapsed! Now what will you do?

🏠 indoors   🕐 2–15 minutes   # 1–3 Fours per set

154

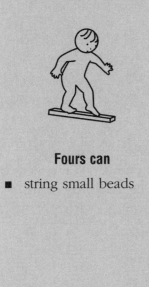

Fours can

■ string small beads

Stringing Beads

Place plenty of small colorful stringing beads into several plastic containers so that one or two children can use each container. Add sturdy shoestrings with plastic tips at the ends. Tie a knot in one end of each string. Place the containers on low, open shelves for the children to choose. You can add new interest to the beads by changing the way they are stored in their containers. For example:

■ sort and store the beads by color and have one container of each color for the children to choose from

■ sort the beads into containers of two colors each

■ sort the beads by shape

■ have big beads in one container and small beads in another

indoors 2–20 minutes # 1–2 Fours per container

155

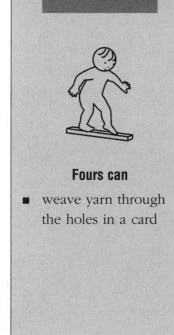

Fours can

■ weave yarn through the holes in a card

Lacing Cards

Cut out pictures of things your Fours will be interested in. Glue the pictures onto sturdy cardboard and cover with clear contact paper. Punch several holes around the outline of each picture with a paper punch. Tie a long shoestring or colored yarn through one of the holes. Be sure the string has a firm tip. Use tightly wrapped masking tape to make a firm tip if needed.

Show the children how to outline the picture with the string by "sewing" through the holes. Remind children to go under and over as they sew, but do not worry if they do not follow the lines well or loop the string around the card. Just enjoy the amazing patterns they make with the string.

in or out 2–10 minutes # 1 child per card

156

Fours can

- do puzzles with more than four pieces

Puzzle Place

Set up a place in the Small-Muscle Center just for puzzles. (You'll find ideas for the puzzle place on page 185.) Put out a few easier puzzles and a few harder ones on a low shelf. Keep the rest stored away. Change the puzzles often.

Keep an eye on children doing puzzles and give help if a child wishes. You can use words to help the child see the next step, move a piece just a little until the child sees the answer, or work as partners to finish the puzzle. Do not make a fuss if children do not finish a puzzle. Be sure puzzles are put away properly.

I bet we can work together to finish this puzzle, Aaron. I'll do a piece and then you do a piece.

🏠 in or out   🕐 2–20 minutes   # 1–7 Fours

157

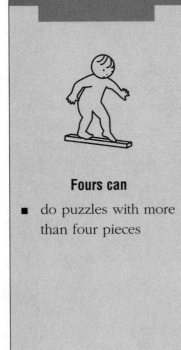

Fours can

- do puzzles with more than four pieces

Floor Puzzles

Place one or two large floor puzzles on the puzzle shelf for Fours to choose. Show children a clear floor space nearby that is out of traffic so that they can work on these big puzzles by themselves or with a friend.

You can make your own floor puzzles by gluing or drawing big pictures onto large sheets of cardboard and then cutting each one into five or six pieces.

Try outlining your Fours onto sheets of cardboard. They can color the outline the way they want. Then you can cut these pictures into a puzzle. (Be sure to let each child choose whether to cut the picture up into a puzzle or to leave it whole.) Add these puzzles to the puzzle place.

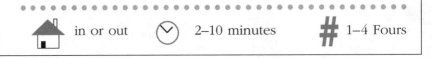

🏠 in or out   🕐 2–10 minutes   # 1–4 Fours

158

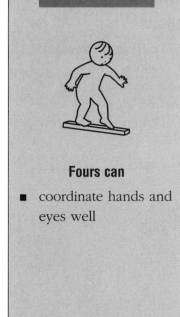

Fours can

- coordinate hands and eyes well

Lock Boards

Make several <u>lock boards</u> for your Fours to use. (You will find directions for making lock boards on pages 186.) Have different-sized locks with their keys on the boards. Be sure the keys to the locks are securely attached to the boards. Also try easy-to-use combination locks with numbers or letters that must be lined up. Write the combinations on the board next to the lock.

Show children how to work the different kinds of locks and then let them try on their own. Talk about why people use locks and give help as children ask.

You can't find the right key for that lock, can you, Brian?
Try each key, one at a time, until you find the right one.
Which one do you want to try first?

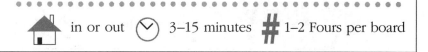

🏠 in or out 🕐 3–15 minutes # 1–2 Fours per board

159

Fours can

- eat well with a fork
- cut easy foods with a knife

Practice with Knives and Forks

Give children the chance to use use safe <u>knives</u> and <u>forks</u> whenever possible. Serve easy-to-cut-up <u>foods</u>, such as cooked carrots or potatoes, in larger pieces at meals so that children can practice using their knives and forks together.

Give help when children can't manage, but let them try on their own. Be sure children do not put large pieces of food in their mouths. Encourage them to cut the food into small pieces instead.

Wow, Sheila! That piece of potato is really big!
I'm afraid you might choke.
Can you cut it into smaller pieces?

🏠 indoors 🕐 1–15 minutes # 1–20 Fours

Activities for Physical Development

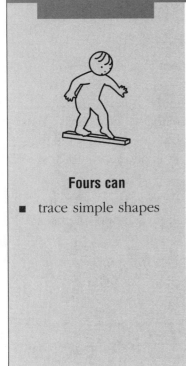

Tracing with Stencils

Provide <u>stencils</u> of simple shapes for your Fours to trace. Have <u>paper</u> and <u>pencils</u> or watercolor <u>markers</u> for the children to use as they trace. Keep these things together in a stencil activity box or in a container on a low shelf in the Writing or Art Center. Then the children can choose this activity when they wish.

Talk with the children about the patterns and designs they make using the stencils.

You traced lots of different shapes, all on top of each other, didn't you, Jeremy? What did you trace first?

Fours can

- trace simple shapes

🏠 in or out   🕐 2–15 minutes   # 1–6 Fours

161

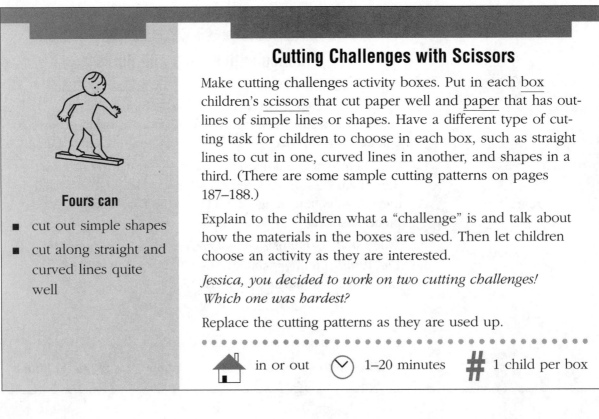

Cutting Challenges with Scissors

Make cutting challenges activity boxes. Put in each <u>box</u> children's <u>scissors</u> that cut paper well and <u>paper</u> that has outlines of simple lines or shapes. Have a different type of cutting task for children to choose in each box, such as straight lines to cut in one, curved lines in another, and shapes in a third. (There are some sample cutting patterns on pages 187–188.)

Explain to the children what a "challenge" is and talk about how the materials in the boxes are used. Then let children choose an activity as they are interested.

Jessica, you decided to work on two cutting challenges! Which one was hardest?

Replace the cutting patterns as they are used up.

Fours can

- cut out simple shapes
- cut along straight and curved lines quite well

🏠 in or out   🕐 1–20 minutes   # 1 child per box

162

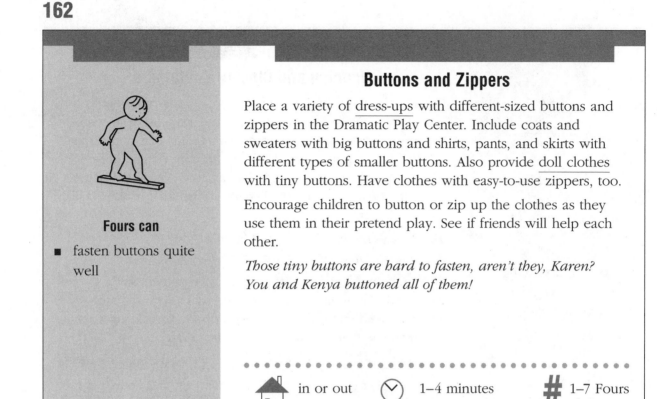

Buttons and Zippers

Place a variety of dress-ups with different-sized buttons and zippers in the Dramatic Play Center. Include coats and sweaters with big buttons and shirts, pants, and skirts with different types of smaller buttons. Also provide doll clothes with tiny buttons. Have clothes with easy-to-use zippers, too.

Encourage children to button or zip up the clothes as they use them in their pretend play. See if friends will help each other.

Those tiny buttons are hard to fasten, aren't they, Karen? You and Kenya buttoned all of them!

Fours can

- fasten buttons quite well

🏠 in or out   ◷ 1–4 minutes   # 1–7 Fours

163

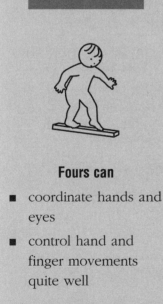

Fours can

- coordinate hands and eyes

- control hand and finger movements quite well

Marble-Rolling Game

Place eight to ten large marbles into a plastic container or box with a large cutout paper or cloth circle. Put the circle out on a flat surface. Show children how to roll the marble gently so it rolls onto the circle and then stops before it goes out. Let the children play to see how many marbles they can get onto the circle. Children can play this game with a friend. One child can roll the marble, and the friend can catch those that go too far.

How gently can you roll the marble, LaMont? Great! It stopped so near the circle!

It's best for children to play the marble rolling game in a corner so that the marbles that go too far can be stopped by the walls or furniture.

🏠 in or out   ◷ 2–15 minutes   # 1–4 Fours

Fours can

- screw lids onto jars
- control hand and finger movements quite well

Opening and Closing Containers

Make a containers-and-lids activity box so that your Fours can practice different kinds of opening and closing. Include plastic jars with screw-on lids, as well as lids that pop on and off. Be sure to put in a thermos like the ones children bring to school in their lunchboxes. Explain how to use the materials in the box. Then put the box on a low shelf in the Small-Muscle Center.

You're working hard to get that lid to fit, Leroy. Are you sure that you have the right lid?

Encourage children to open and close containers as they work and play in the classroom every day. For example, allow your Fours to open and close plastic jars of finger paint or containers that contain toys with many pieces.

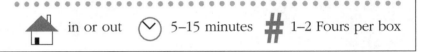

in or out   5–15 minutes   1–2 Fours per box

Fours can

- control hand and finger movements quite well

Clothespin Work

Give your Fours chances to use clothespins as they work and play each day. For example, show them how to use clothespins to hang up artwork to dry, to hold paper in place on the easel, or to hang up doll clothes that have been washed. Keep a box of clothespins in the Dramatic Play Center so children can use them when they play.

Encourage children to work together to be successful.

Matt, see if Andrew will help you put the paper on the easel. One of you can hold the paper while the other puts on the clothespins.

in or out   1–2 minutes   1–20 Fours

166

Fours can

- control hand and finger movements quite well
- play well with another child

Rolling Small Cars

Have a box of small toy cars on a shelf in the Small-Muscle Center for the children to use to play a rolling game. Show them how they can sit at a table and gently roll a car across the table so that it goes close to the opposite edge without rolling off.

Encourage friends to play together, taking turns rolling and catching.

Your Fours can try these games too:

- roll the cars into different-sized boxes
- roll the cars so that they stop close to a masking-tape line
- roll the cars so that they stop on a paper "parking lot"

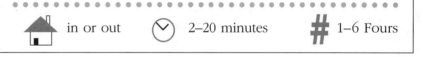

in or out   2–20 minutes   # 1–6 Fours

167

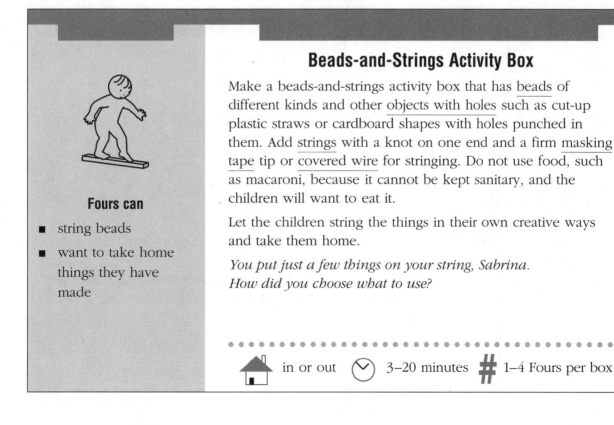

Fours can

- string beads
- want to take home things they have made

Beads-and-Strings Activity Box

Make a beads-and-strings activity box that has beads of different kinds and other objects with holes such as cut-up plastic straws or cardboard shapes with holes punched in them. Add strings with a knot on one end and a firm masking tape tip or covered wire for stringing. Do not use food, such as macaroni, because it cannot be kept sanitary, and the children will want to eat it.

Let the children string the things in their own creative ways and take them home.

You put just a few things on your string, Sabrina. How did you choose what to use?

in or out   3–20 minutes   # 1–4 Fours per box

168

Fours can

- control hand and finger movements quite well

- experiment and talk about their discoveries

Tweezers-and-Tongs Activity Box

Collect different-sized <u>tweezers</u> and <u>tongs</u>, from small to quite large. Place them in a container with many <u>objects</u> of different sizes. Include tiny dried beans, small plastic toys, wooden 1" blocks, and beads of various sizes. Let the children experiment with picking up the things with the tweezers and tongs. Talk about which tools are easiest to use to pick up the different things.

Dick, what things are easiest to pick up with the biggest tongs?

Let children use these tools for real activities, too. For example, have children serve some foods at mealtimes with tongs, and have tweezers in the Science and Nature Center to pick up small pebbles or leaves.

🏠 in or out   🕐 3–20 minutes   # 1–3 Fours

169

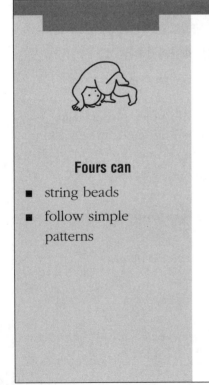

Fours can

- string beads
- follow simple patterns

Bead Patterns

Make some easy <u>bead patterns</u> that your Fours can follow as they string beads. (You will find some sample patterns on page 189.) Show your Fours how they can follow the pattern by matching the bead colors and shapes and then stringing them in the right order.

Leave a few bead patterns out with the beads for any interested children to use. Show delight in the many different ways children choose to string beads.

Aurora, you followed the red-green pattern. How many times did you repeat the pattern?
Bryan, you did your own creative bead stringing. It looks like you used all the colors and shapes. Did you leave any colors out?

🏠 in or out   🕐 2–30 minutes   # 1–8 Fours

170

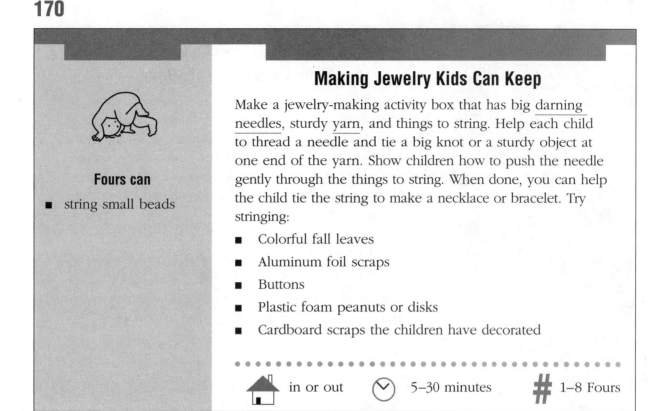

Fours can

- string small beads

Making Jewelry Kids Can Keep

Make a jewelry-making activity box that has big darning needles, sturdy yarn, and things to string. Help each child to thread a needle and tie a big knot or a sturdy object at one end of the yarn. Show children how to push the needle gently through the things to string. When done, you can help the child tie the string to make a necklace or bracelet. Try stringing:

- Colorful fall leaves
- Aluminum foil scraps
- Buttons
- Plastic foam peanuts or disks
- Cardboard scraps the children have decorated

🏠 in or out   🕐 5–30 minutes   # 1–8 Fours

171

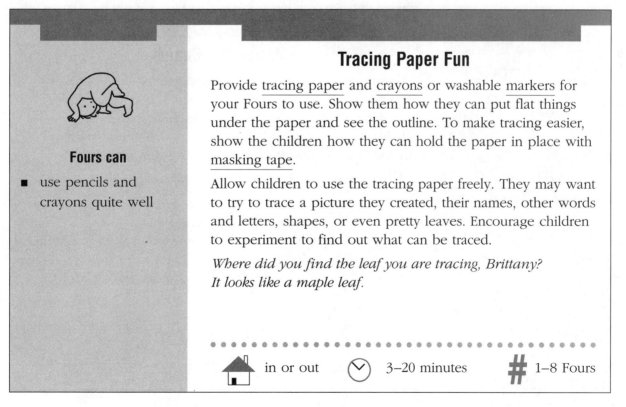

Fours can

- use pencils and crayons quite well

Tracing Paper Fun

Provide tracing paper and crayons or washable markers for your Fours to use. Show them how they can put flat things under the paper and see the outline. To make tracing easier, show the children how they can hold the paper in place with masking tape.

Allow children to use the tracing paper freely. They may want to try to trace a picture they created, their names, other words and letters, shapes, or even pretty leaves. Encourage children to experiment to find out what can be traced.

*Where did you find the leaf you are tracing, Brittany?
It looks like a maple leaf.*

🏠 in or out   🕐 3–20 minutes   # 1–8 Fours

172

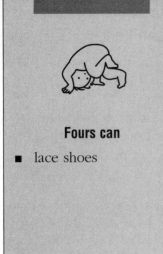

Fours can

- lace shoes

Shoe-Lacing Activity Box

Make a shoe-lacing activity box that has one or two pair of clean, low-cost sneakers and lots of brightly colored shoelaces. In each box you might have one adult's and one child's shoe. Have all kinds of laces for the children to use: gold and silver sparkles, pretty designs, and ribbons. You can find fancy laces in many shoe stores. Be sure all have sturdy tips to make lacing easier.

Show your Fours how to lace the shoes and then let them practice on their own. Leave the activity box on a low, open shelf for children to choose when they wish.

You used the short shoelace with stars for the baby shoe, Bryanna. Which lace will you use for the adult's shoe?

· ·

🏠 in or out   🕐 3–15 minutes   # 1–2 Fours per box

173

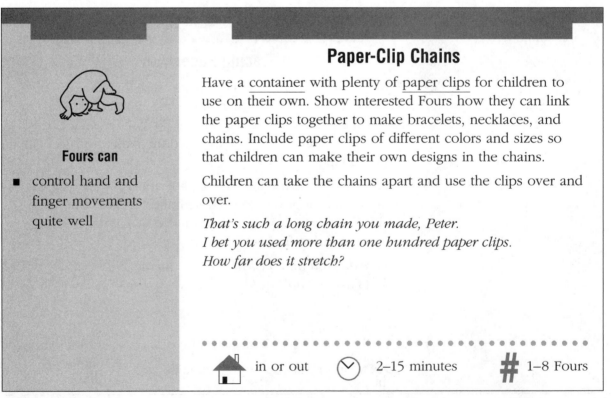

Fours can

- control hand and finger movements quite well

Paper-Clip Chains

Have a container with plenty of paper clips for children to use on their own. Show interested Fours how they can link the paper clips together to make bracelets, necklaces, and chains. Include paper clips of different colors and sizes so that children can make their own designs in the chains.

Children can take the chains apart and use the clips over and over.

That's such a long chain you made, Peter.
I bet you used more than one hundred paper clips.
How far does it stretch?

· ·

🏠 in or out   🕐 2–15 minutes   # 1–8 Fours

174

174

Fours can

- control hand and finger movements quite well

Fishing Game

Make a magnetic fishing game with several fishing rods and lots of pretend fish. Tie a sturdy 18" string to the end of a 12" dowel. Attach a magnet to the other end of the string. Cut out large fish from colorful construction paper or cardboard and attach a metal paper clip for the mouth.

Show your Fours how to put the fish on the floor, hold the rod steady, move it gently until the magnet attracts the paper clip, and then bring in the fish. Allow the children to experiment in their own ways to fish successfully. Talk about the different things they do to catch the fish.

Emma caught a fish! She held the line with her hand to keep it steady.
Show me how you caught so many fish, Paul.

in or out   2–15 minutes   # 1 child per rod

175

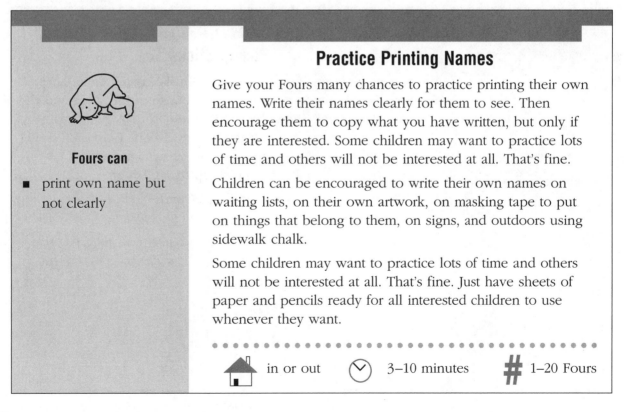

Fours can

- print own name but not clearly

Practice Printing Names

Give your Fours many chances to practice printing their own names. Write their names clearly for them to see. Then encourage them to copy what you have written, but only if they are interested. Some children may want to practice lots of time and others will not be interested at all. That's fine.

Children can be encouraged to write their own names on waiting lists, on their own artwork, on masking tape to put on things that belong to them, on signs, and outdoors using sidewalk chalk.

Some children may want to practice lots of time and others will not be interested at all. That's fine. Just have sheets of paper and pencils ready for all interested children to use whenever they want.

in or out   3–10 minutes   # 1–20 Fours

Fours can

■ brush teeth quite
well

Toothbrushing

Be sure to have toothbrushing after meals as a daily part of
your Fours' schedule. Have a toothbrush for each child that is
clearly labeled with the child's name. Teach children how to
squeeze a small amount of toothpaste onto their own brush
and then brush all of their teeth carefully. Watch and guide
the children to be sure they brush well.

Now how do your teeth feel, Virginia?
*Do your back molars feel as smooth and clean as your front
teeth feel?*

indoors   3–7 minutes   # 1–4 Fours

177

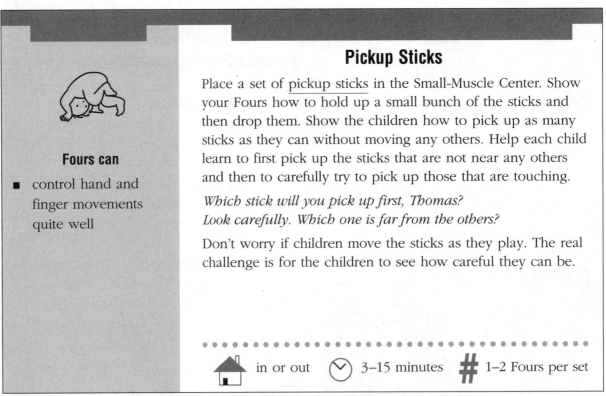

Fours can

■ control hand and
finger movements
quite well

Pickup Sticks

Place a set of pickup sticks in the Small-Muscle Center. Show
your Fours how to hold up a small bunch of the sticks and
then drop them. Show the children how to pick up as many
sticks as they can without moving any others. Help each child
learn to first pick up the sticks that are not near any others
and then to carefully try to pick up those that are touching.

Which stick will you pick up first, Thomas?
Look carefully. Which one is far from the others?

Don't worry if children move the sticks as they play. The real
challenge is for the children to see how careful they can be.

in or out   3–15 minutes   # 1–2 Fours per set

178

Fours can

- use and enjoy simple computer or video games

Computer Games

Computer or video games are not required in good preschool classrooms. You can provide plenty of other more valuable ways for your Fours to learn. However, almost all computer or video games will allow your Fours to work on small-muscle skills, and many children enjoy this type of activity. Computer and video games are fine for Fours, as long as they are not violent, are challenging but not too difficult, and do not take up a lot of a child's time.

If you wish to have computer or video games, set them up in a quiet, out-of-the-way space where one or two children can play. Teach children how to use the equipment carefully. If needed, use a timer to remind children to move on to another activity.

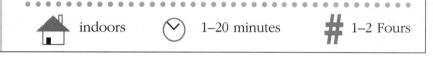

indoors   1–20 minutes   # 1–2 Fours

179

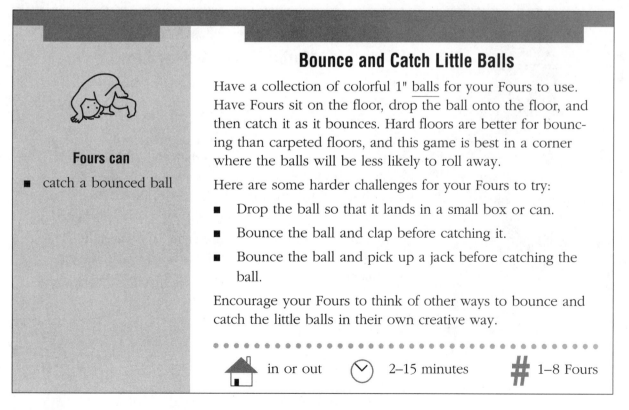

Fours can

- catch a bounced ball

Bounce and Catch Little Balls

Have a collection of colorful 1" balls for your Fours to use. Have Fours sit on the floor, drop the ball onto the floor, and then catch it as it bounces. Hard floors are better for bouncing than carpeted floors, and this game is best in a corner where the balls will be less likely to roll away.

Here are some harder challenges for your Fours to try:

- Drop the ball so that it lands in a small box or can.

- Bounce the ball and clap before catching it.

- Bounce the ball and pick up a jack before catching the ball.

Encourage your Fours to think of other ways to bounce and catch the little balls in their own creative way.

in or out   2–15 minutes   # 1–8 Fours

180

Fours can

- control hand and finger movements quite well

Spinning Tops

Make a tops activity box for the Small-Muscle Center. Place tops of different sizes and colors, tops made of wood and of plastic, and dreidels in a labeled container. Show interested Fours how to hold the top and give it a spin while releasing it onto a smooth surface. Allow children to practice as much as they like. Explain that it takes lots of practice to make the top spin.

Show delight as the children think of their own ways to use the tops.

Amos, you are spinning the top on its side.
It went around very fast.
Zina, you lined all the tops up from big to small.

🏠 in or out   🕐 1–15 minutes   # 1–3 Fours

181

Fours can

- control hand and finger movements quite well
- play simple games with others

Marble Game Activity Box

Make a marble game activity box for your Fours to use. Include 3 big marbles, 12 smaller marbles, and a circle (2 feet across) cut out of plain fabric. Show your Fours how to spread the circle out on the floor in a quiet corner, place the smaller marbles in the center, and then roll a large marble into the group of smaller ones to scatter them. Then they can try to knock all the smaller marbles out of the circle.

One child can play alone, or two friends can take turns. Point out that the way to do well at the game is to carefully aim the big marble, rather than just to roll hard. Then let children experiment with rolling and aiming in their own ways.

You hit it, Adele! You aimed very carefully.
Which will you try for next?

🏠 in or out   🕐 2–15 minutes   # 1–2 Fours

182

Fours can

- control hand and finger movements quite well

Peel-and-Stick Sticker Fun

Have lots of different, colorful peel-and-stick stickers that your Fours can peel off by themselves and stick onto things they want to decorate. Keep these in a container with paper for the children to use when they are interested.

Show them how to bend the backing of the sticker so that an edge of the sticker comes loose. Then they can grasp the sticker and pull it off.

Marcia, what are you making with these bird stickers?

You can look for free stickers that come in junk mail. Ask parents to bring in any stickers they find, too.

in or out   2–12 minutes   # 1–6 Fours

183

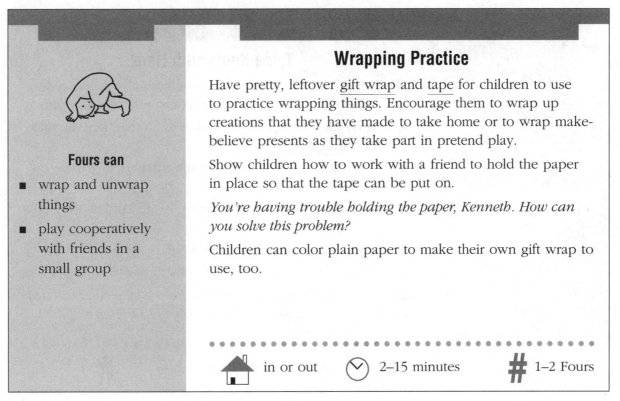

Fours can

- wrap and unwrap things
- play cooperatively with friends in a small group

Wrapping Practice

Have pretty, leftover gift wrap and tape for children to use to practice wrapping things. Encourage them to wrap up creations that they have made to take home or to wrap make-believe presents as they take part in pretend play.

Show children how to work with a friend to hold the paper in place so that the tape can be put on.

You're having trouble holding the paper, Kenneth. How can you solve this problem?

Children can color plain paper to make their own gift wrap to use, too.

in or out   2–15 minutes   # 1–2 Fours

Activities for Physical Development

184

Fours can

- control hand and finger movements quite well
- follow easy directions

Telephone-Wire Jewelry

Ask your local telephone company for leftover colorful strands of plastic-covered wire. They are usually in a big cable. Just cut off the plastic covering of the cable and pull out the brightly colored wires. Cut the wires into 6" to 12" pieces and place them in a container for the children to use. Show your Fours how to twist the wires together to make rings, bracelets for wrists and ankles, necklaces, and anything else they can think of.

Daniel, you have blue wire with white stripes and some yellow wire. What do you plan to make with it?

You can also provide pipe cleaners for children to twist into amazing creations.

🏠 in or out   🕐 2–20 minutes   # 1–8 Fours

185

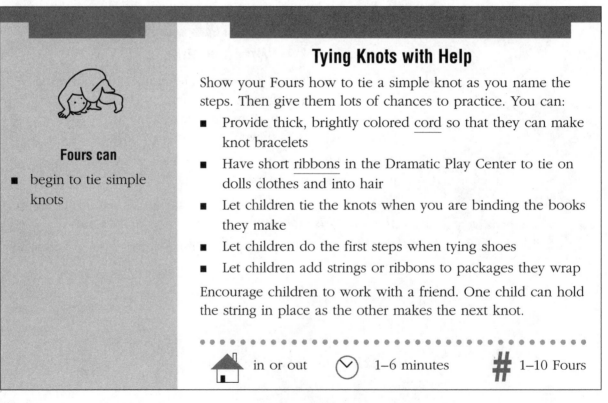

Fours can

- begin to tie simple knots

Tying Knots with Help

Show your Fours how to tie a simple knot as you name the steps. Then give them lots of chances to practice. You can:

- Provide thick, brightly colored cord so that they can make knot bracelets
- Have short ribbons in the Dramatic Play Center to tie on dolls clothes and into hair
- Let children tie the knots when you are binding the books they make
- Let children do the first steps when tying shoes
- Let children add strings or ribbons to packages they wrap

Encourage children to work with a friend. One child can hold the string in place as the other makes the next knot.

🏠 in or out   🕐 1–6 minutes   # 1–10 Fours

186

Fours can

- cut easy foods with a knife

Using Real Knives for Cooking

Give children chances to use real <u>knives</u> when cooking. Help the children understand that they <u>must</u> be very careful when using knives. Explain the rules to follow when cutting, such as "Keep your eyes on your work," and "Stand away from anyone who is cutting."

Set up cutting so that the activity will be safe. Make sure the children are sitting at a table and are not crowded. Use cutting boards. Precut larger foods so children can handle them easily. Show the children how to cut, and supervise carefully.

Some foods children can cook that give them lots of practice cutting are vegetable soup, fruit salad, and applesauce.

indoors 2–20 minutes # 1–2 Fours at a time

187

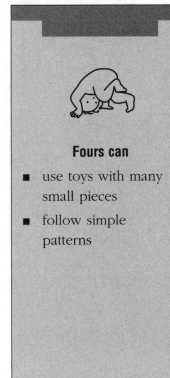

Fours can

- use toys with many small pieces
- follow simple patterns

Pegboard Patterns

Make simple pegboard patterns for interested children to follow. Trace an outline of the <u>pegboard</u> on a piece of <u>paper</u>. Then draw little circles where all of the holes are. Make ten copies of your pegboard drawing so that you can make ten different patterns. Color in the little circles to make simple patterns. For example, on one sheet color in a straight line of yellow circles and a line of blue ones. On another sheet color in circles with red to make a red X across the board.

Keep the patterns very easy until you see how the children do. Then make harder patterns for them to follow if the first are too easy. Cover the patterns with clear contact paper or laminate them. Keep the patterns in a container with the pegboards and pegs.

in or out 3–30 minutes # 1 child per board

Fours can

- begin tying simple knots

Knot-Tying Place

Set up a knot-tying place where the children can practice tying lots of knots. (There is a picture of a knot-tying place on page 183.) Screw a few sturdy cup hooks into a wall or onto the back of a low shelf within easy reach. Tie a 24" rope or ribbon to each hook so that there are two 12" pieces hanging from each hook.

Show children how to tie simple knots. They can practice over and over until the ropes are full of knots. Keep extra rope handy so that the tied-up ropes can be replaced. Encourage children to untie the knots, too.

Jason, you have really been working on tying knots! I think you tied more than ten. Look how tight they are!

in or out   1–10 minutes   1–2 Fours per rope

Knot-Tying Place

Here is what a knot-tying place should look like.

How to Make Geoboards

1. Cut a piece of 1" thick plywood into 7" squares. Sand all edges and corners until they are smooth.
2. Follow the pattern below and hammer 25 nails 1/2" deep into each plywood square. Use sturdy 2" nails with smooth, flat heads.

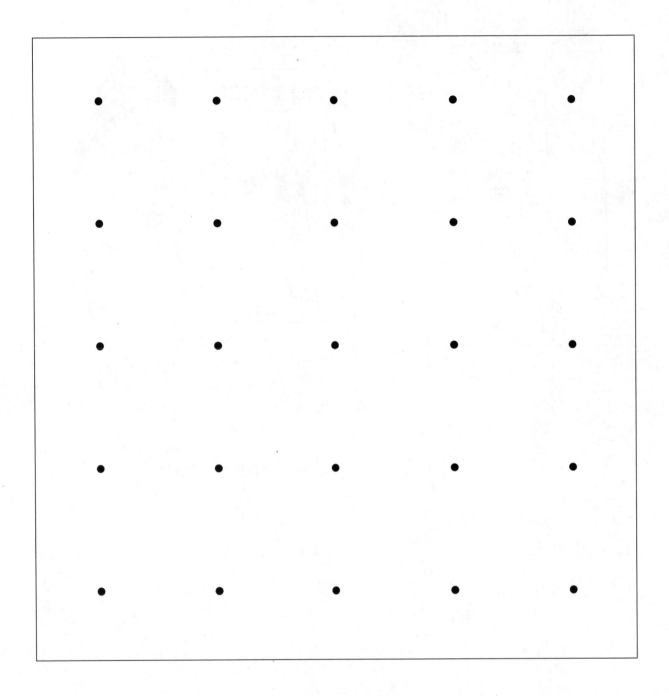

If you don't have any plywood, hammer a few nails into a stump or big log outside. Have fun making designs on it with rubber bands.

Puzzle Place Ideas

- Before you put puzzles out on the shelf, mark the back of each piece with the puzzle's name. Then you can tell which pieces go with each puzzle.

- Set puzzles out on a low, open shelf. Make sure the shelf is not cluttered with other toys and that the puzzles are not piled on top of each other.

- If you have problems with pieces getting mixed up a lot or lost, store each puzzle on its own tray. Be sure the tray is big enough to hold the puzzle frame and all the pieces when they have been dumped out. Show the children how to keep the pieces on the tray as they work.

- Be sure to have a flat, open space near the open shelf where the children can work on their puzzles. A low table or rug out of traffic works best.

- Have several different kinds of puzzles for the children to do. Choose ones that have different textures and numbers of pieces and are different colors and sizes.

- Do not keep all the puzzles out at the same time and change the selection often.

- Encourage children to finish one puzzle before starting another, but do not make a fuss if a child becomes frustrated and does not want to go on. Instead, work as a partner to put the puzzle away, helping the child do as much as he can by himself.

- Help children learn how to do harder puzzles. Do not start by dumping all the pieces out at once. Instead, begin by helping the child look at the whole puzzle. Talk with the child about what is in the picture. Then take out one piece and let the child put it back. Next, take out two pieces and let her replace them. Continue this way until the child can handle the whole puzzle on her own.

- Puzzle racks make it hard for children to see and choose puzzles. Use them for storing extra puzzles that are not out for the children to use. Separate easy from hard puzzles and label each rack.

- Puzzles for Fours should
  - have seven to twenty pieces
  - be colorful
  - be interesting for children to look at
  - be sturdy
  - be of different textures (wood, rubber, plastic)
  - not be too hard or too easy

Lock Board Ideas

1. Hammer two or three very large, sturdy staples into a board. You can get these at a hardware store. Or use hasps that open and close.

2. Put pictures under the hasps so that the children will see them if they get the lock open. A small unbreakable mirror under one flap is also fun.

3. Put different-sized padlocks on the staples or hasps.

4. Put the keys to the padlocks on a key ring. Attach the ring to a sturdy string and fasten it to the board so that the keys won't get lost.

Put the Lock Board in a safe place where it can't tip over, or nail it to the end of a bookcase or cabinet where the children can easily reach and play with it.

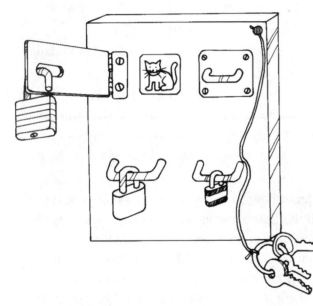
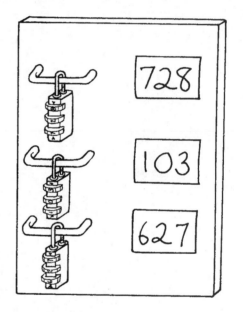

Activities for Physical Development

Cutting Challenges
for Fours

_____

_____

_____

_____

Cut along these curved lines.

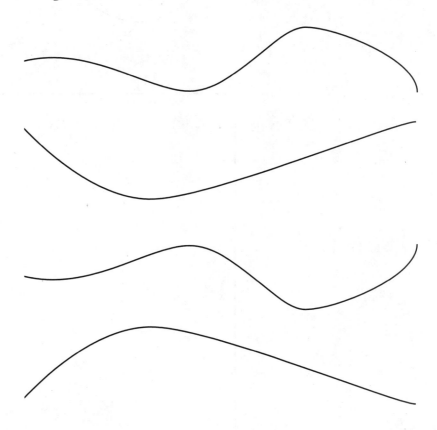

Cut along these shapes.

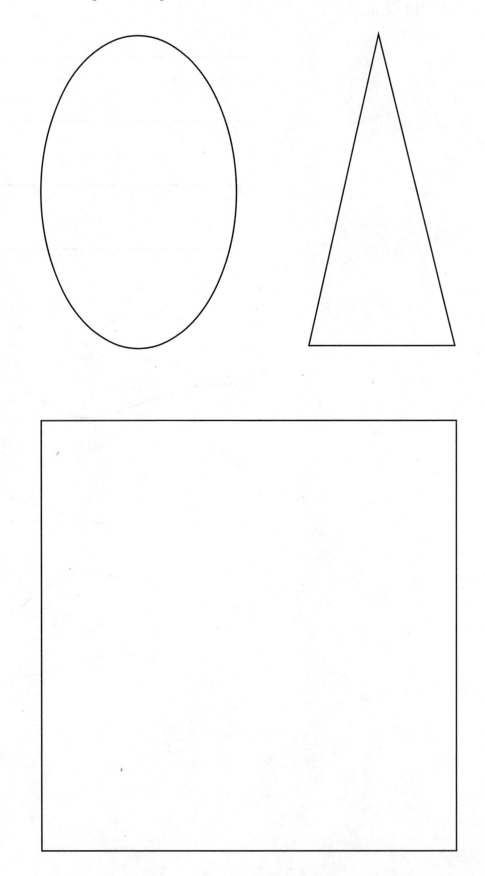

Bead Patterns

1. Copy bead patterns onto cardboard cards. Use the real beads you have as a guide for drawing.

2. Color beads to match the beads you have. Use only two, three, or four colors in one pattern. Have some patterns with just one color, too.

3. Show children how to copy the pattern by first putting beads on the cards, then stringing them in the right order.

4. Show children how to string the pattern again.

5. Try making your own patterns, too.

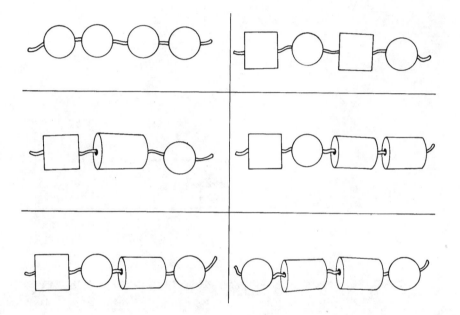

Active Learning
for Fours

Creative Activities

Index

of Creative Activities

Here's Why

Art and carpentry, blocks, dramatic or pretend play, and music give Fours chances to do interesting things by themselves that show clear results. Fours need to have many creative materials every day to use in their own ways.

Drawing helps young children learn to understand things in their lives. Fours' drawings begin to show what they know and are interested in. It takes a lot of practice before a child learns to control his hands and focus his ideas well enough to draw a face we can all see. When children are allowed plenty of time to practice drawing, they benefit most. Many Fours will be able to draw recognizable things or will be trying to do so. They will also want to tell you about their pictures. When you display the drawings Fours make, they know how proud you are of what they can do by themselves. Fours are also able to use other materials to create their own designs. Play dough, artwork with scrap materials, and carpentry encourage children to create work that is not on a flat surface, but can fill space in many ways.

The other creative activities are also important. Both music and dramatic play help to build memory for words and ideas. Fours love to sing along with familiar songs. They also enjoy pretending about the things they see happening around them, as well as things they hear and read about. Fours begin to understand their lives as they pretend. Pretend play materials are needed both indoors and outdoors for active Fours.

When Fours play with blocks, they become aware of differences in shape, size, and weight. They learn about balance as they build a big tower. Block play can also be a form of pretend play. Block play is a good way to learn how to share and how to play near others without bothering them.

Fours enjoy all the creative activities. They like the fact that they can do things themselves. They also enjoy the messy, active, noisy way the arts work. You can help them learn many skills as they work with the activities in this section.

Materials and Notes

Art and Carpentry

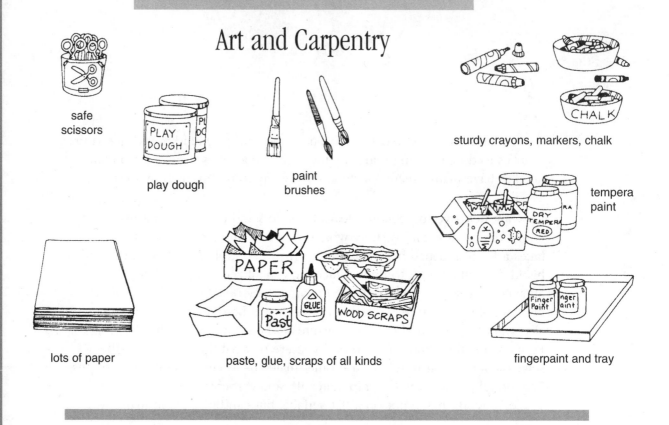

safe scissors

play dough

paint brushes

sturdy crayons, markers, chalk

CHALK

tempera paint

DRY TEMPERA RED

lots of paper

PAPER

GLUE

Past

WOOD SCRAPS

paste, glue, scraps of all kinds

Finger Paint

fingerpaint and tray

- Most of the activities in this section can be done by either younger or older Fours. This is because the activities are open-ended and can be done in many ways by children with different abilities.

- Make sure all the art materials you use are nontoxic.

- Have sturdy art equipment and supplies out for long periods of time for Fours to use every day as a free-choice activity.

- Put up lots of the children's artwork to look at. Change the things often.

- Encourage parents to enjoy and hang up their children's work at home.

- Let the children use art materials in their own way. Do not have Fours copy things you have made.

- Do not have Fours color in coloring books. Coloring does not help them develop creative drawing skills.

- Protect art tables with newspaper or heavy plastic.

- Note that beginning carpentry activities are a part of this section.

Activity Checklist

Art and Carpentry

Art for Fours includes providing things for them to look at as well as art materials for them to use. By the time children are four years old, they are usually interested and able to use art materials independently. This is the time the child can use drawing materials, finger paints, and play dough with quite a bit of control. Fours enjoy scribbling and making designs but also start to draw recognizable faces, shapes, and pictures of other things they are interested in. They also enjoy new challenges and new materials such as sewing, carpentry, and wood/glue sculpture.

Check for each age group

	48–54 months	54–60 months
1. An Art Center is set up with a variety of nontoxic art materials for children to choose freely and is available daily for long periods of time.	❏	❏
2. Art materials include pencils, watercolor markers, crayons, and other drawing materials, as well as a variety of paper, paste, and play dough.	❏	❏
3. Several colors of paint with brushes are offered to the children to use on paper. Finger paint is also provided.	❏	❏
4. Art materials are organized for easy independent use by the children.	❏	❏
5. A low, sturdy table or easel is used for art activities.	❏	❏
6. Children are offered art as a free-choice activity. Other activities are available at the same time.	❏	❏
7. Children are encouraged to feel, handle, and explore materials and create what they want to.	❏	❏
8. Adults and children talk about shape, color, and textures of things and about what the child is doing as he uses art materials.	❏	❏
9. Children help with easy cleanup.	❏	❏
10. Children's drawings and other artwork are displayed where children can see them.	❏	❏
11. Artwork is sent home with each child.	❏	❏

189

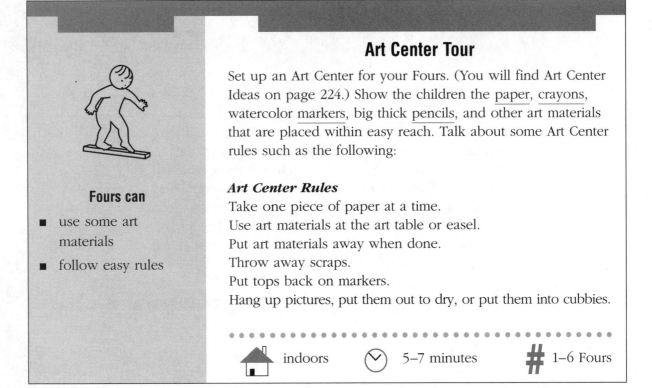

Fours can

- use some art materials
- follow easy rules

Art Center Tour

Set up an Art Center for your Fours. (You will find Art Center Ideas on page 224.) Show the children the paper, crayons, watercolor markers, big thick pencils, and other art materials that are placed within easy reach. Talk about some Art Center rules such as the following:

Art Center Rules

Take one piece of paper at a time.
Use art materials at the art table or easel.
Put art materials away when done.
Throw away scraps.
Put tops back on markers.
Hang up pictures, put them out to dry, or put them into cubbies.

indoors   5–7 minutes   # 1–6 Fours

190

Fours can

- scribble or draw simple forms

My Art Book

Save some of the drawings made by each child in folders with their names. Put the date on each drawing. When a child has ten drawings, staple the drawings into the folder for the child to take home to share with parents. Go through each child's drawings with her and talk about them. Ask the parents to do the same. Talk about how the child's drawings have changed.

This is the first picture you made, Germaine.
See the colors you used?
And here's the next one.
You made long and short lines, and lots of shapes.
Can you tell me about this picture?

in or out   5–15 minutes   # 1–2 Fours

191

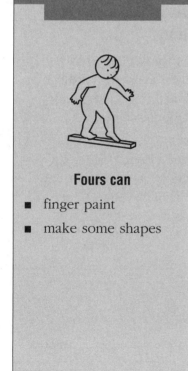

Fours can

- scribble and draw simple shapes
- begin to share

Crayon Art

Put several small <u>containers</u> of sturdy <u>crayons</u> on a low shelf, along with lots of <u>paper</u> for your Fours to use freely. Have a small container for every one or two children. Add variety to crayon art by putting crayons out on a table with different colors or shapes of paper. Or put crayons and paper on the easel for a change of pace. Talk with the children about the colors they use as they draw.

I like all the blue shapes you made, Charlene.
Tell me about this part over here.
What other colors did you use?

🏠 in or out   🕐 2–20 minutes   # 1–6 Fours

192

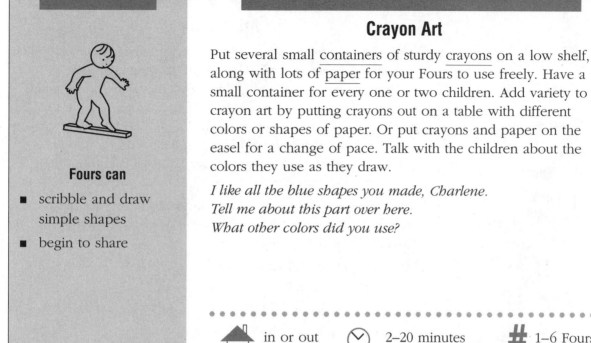

Fours can

- finger paint
- make some shapes

Finger Paint on a Tray

Set some large plastic <u>trays</u> on a low table. Help the children who want to finger paint put waterproof <u>aprons</u> on. Be sure there is a sink nearby so that children can wash their hands. Offer the children three colors to choose from. Use bright colors such as red, yellow, and blue. Let each child choose two colors. Then put one tablespoon of each color of paint on each tray. (You'll find finger paint recipes on page 234.) Let the child finger paint in his own way. Talk about the different kinds of designs the children make and the colors the paints make when they mix.

You made big swirls here, Jimmy.
And you made squiggles and tiny dots, Jay.

🏠 in or out   🕐 3–20 minutes   # 1–4 Fours

193

Fours can

- do lots of artwork
- enjoy seeing their work

Art Gallery

Make special display spaces (art galleries) where Fours can put their favorite artwork. Use a wall, the backs of toy shelves, or doors. Tell the children that they can choose what they want to hang up. Have enough space for everyone to use. Have a shelf or windowsill to display play dough or carpentry art. Let children help hang up their work or choose where it should go. Encourage your Fours to talk about their creations.

Moira, do you want to hang this in our art gallery or take it home?
Great! Can you help with the tape?

Also hang children's work in other places in the room where they can easily see it.

🏠 indoors   🕐 1–3 minutes   # 1–2 Fours

194

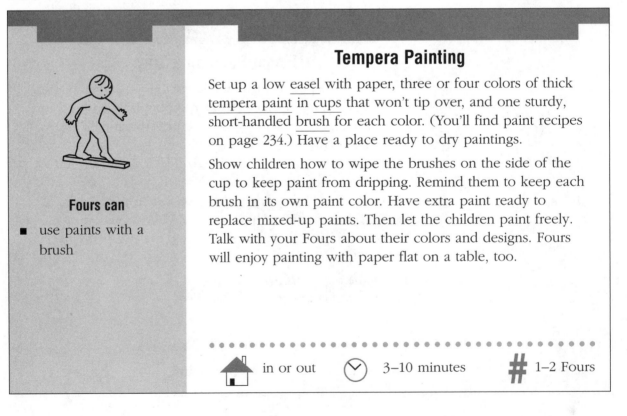

Fours can

- use paints with a brush

Tempera Painting

Set up a low easel with paper, three or four colors of thick tempera paint in cups that won't tip over, and one sturdy, short-handled brush for each color. (You'll find paint recipes on page 234.) Have a place ready to dry paintings.

Show children how to wipe the brushes on the side of the cup to keep paint from dripping. Remind them to keep each brush in its own paint color. Have extra paint ready to replace mixed-up paints. Then let the children paint freely. Talk with your Fours about their colors and designs. Fours will enjoy painting with paper flat on a table, too.

🏠 in or out   🕐 3–10 minutes   # 1–2 Fours

195

Play-Dough Fun

Have the children help you mix play dough. (See Play Dough recipe on page 235.) Before children help, get all the things you will need: flour, salt, oil, tempera paint powder, water, measuring cups, and a big unbreakable bowl. Have the Fours help you measure, pour, and mix. Make one color at a time. When it is done, give each child some dough to use at a table in his own way. See how many things the Fours do with the play dough using just their hands. Help the children remember how they made the play dough. A picture recipe can help them remember.

How did you make your play dough, Fred?
Yes, you measured and stirred. How much flour did you use?

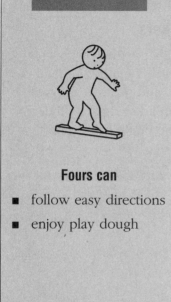

Fours can

- follow easy directions
- enjoy play dough

in or out   10–30 minutes   # 1–5 Fours

196

Hanging Pictures to Dry

Put up a low clothesline or fishnet where Fours can hang their artwork to dry. Have lots of clothespins ready. Show children how to bring wet pictures to the hanging place and get a clothespin. Then you can help them squeeze the clothespins open to hold the pictures in place. Be sure that children's names are on their pictures and that there is plenty of room so that pictures don't stick together. A wooden clothes-drying rack can also be used.

Is your name on the painting, Nathan?
You can help me write it on.
Tomorrow this will be dry enough to bring it home or put in the art gallery.

Fours can

- remember where things go
- squeeze with thumb and fingers

indoors   1–2 minutes   # 1–2 Fours

197

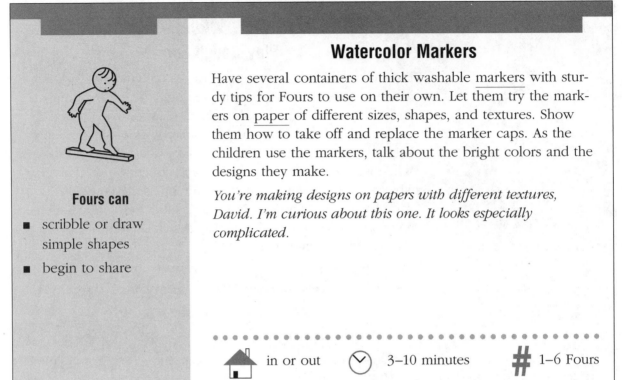

Watercolor Markers

Have several containers of thick washable <u>markers</u> with sturdy tips for Fours to use on their own. Let them try the markers on <u>paper</u> of different sizes, shapes, and textures. Show them how to take off and replace the marker caps. As the children use the markers, talk about the bright colors and the designs they make.

You're making designs on papers with different textures, David. I'm curious about this one. It looks especially complicated.

Fours can

- scribble or draw simple shapes
- begin to share

🏠 in or out   🕐 3–10 minutes   # 1–6 Fours

198

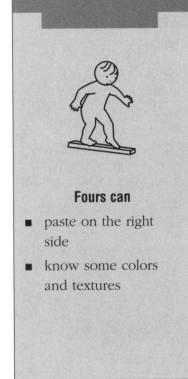

Paper Scraps Collage

Collect pretty <u>paper scraps</u> for your Fours to <u>paste</u> onto pieces of <u>paper</u>. Include scraps of construction paper, wallpaper, and gift wrapping. Give each child a little paste in a paper cup to use with an <u>ice cream stick</u>. Remind Fours to put paste on the correct side of each scrap and then to put the scrap on the bigger paper, paste side down. Let them paste the scraps they like and make their own designs. Talk about the scraps they used when they are finished.

This is a scrap of birthday paper here, Maria. What other types of paper did you use?

Try collages made of pretty fabric scraps or even different grades of sandpaper for a change of pace.

Fours can

- paste on the right side
- know some colors and textures

🏠 indoors   🕐 5–15 minutes   # 1–6 Fours

199

Fours can

- scribble and draw some shapes we can recognize

Chalk Art

Cover a low table with newspaper. Put each child's name on the back of a piece of black or dark-colored construction paper. To keep chalk from rubbing off, show your Fours how to use a brush to wet the paper with a mixture of half liquid starch and half water. Give each child a bowl with some large, brightly colored nontoxic chalks. Let the children draw on the wet paper. They may need to press hard to see their lines. Use a piece of sandpaper to clean the ends of the chalk when done. At other times, let your Fours use chalk on a chalkboard, or take chalk outside for drawing on the sidewalk.

Are you making a nighttime picture, Jana?
Yes, I see the stars you drew.

indoors   5–15 minutes   # 1–6 Fours

200

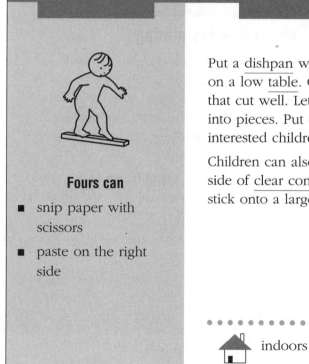

Fours can

- snip paper with scissors
- paste on the right side

Paper Bits Collage

Put a dishpan with colored paper strips about ½" to 1½" wide on a low table. Give each child a pair of small, safe scissors that cut well. Let your Fours pick paper strips and cut them into pieces. Put out paste and larger sheets of paper so that interested children can make a collage with their pieces.

Children can also place the pieces they cut onto the sticky side of clear contact paper. Turn the contact paper over to stick onto a larger piece of black paper and smooth it down.

indoors   3–15 minutes   # 1–6 Fours

201

Fours can

■ peel and stick
stickers onto paper

Sticker Pictures

Collect free or inexpensive stickers for children to use. Have parents bring in the ones they get in junk mail. Also save scraps of contact paper to use as stickers. Keep all of these in a box. Show your Fours how to peel the stickers away from the paper backing. Then they can put the stickers onto a larger piece of paper to make a design. When the children are done, talk with them about the colors and shapes of the stickers they used, and the pictures on them.

At another time, use free junk mail stamps the children can wet with a sponge and stick to half sheets of paper.

Your stickers have animals on them, Jesse.
Can you tell what they are?
What pictures are on your stickers, Susan?

🏠 indoors   🕐 2–10 minutes   # 1–6 Fours

202

Fours can

■ finger paint

Mural Finger Painting

Cut a very large sheet of paper from a big roll of butcher paper or printer's newsprint. Hang this on the wall of a building or put it on a floor that can easily be cleaned. Put out several trays that have finger paint on them. Encourage children to use finger paint on their hands or fingers to make hand prints and other designs on the paper.

You can do this on a hot day, when the children can wear swimsuits. Then you can rinse the paint off the children with a hose when they are finished with their designs.

What did you finger paint, Kevin? It looks like ocean waves or clouds.

🏠 outdoors   🕐 2–10 minutes   # 1–4 Fours at a time

203

Stringing Things

Put out a tray with things to string that have big holes, such as buttons, spools, washers, and cut-up straws. Give each child a bowl in which to keep his stringing things and a string that has one taped end. You will have to help the children tie one thing to the end of the string so that the other things stay on. Let the children string the many kinds of stringing things in their own way. Let them keep their work. Talk with each child about the things he used.

Do you know what this is? It's a circle. It's called a washer. What other things with holes could we string?

Do not use food, such as macaroni or cereal, to string because it will get dirty, and children may eat it.

Fours can

- string beads

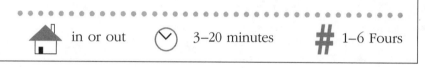

🏠 in or out   🕐 3–20 minutes   # 1–6 Fours

204

Painting Little Pictures

Put onto a low table cups of tempera paint in a paint cup holder. Also put out some thin paintbrushes and small pieces of paper. Let your Fours use these things to paint little pictures in their own way. Talk about the size of the brushes, paper, and the designs they make.

If you wish, have an easel set up nearby and let children choose to paint big or small.

You're using the little brush in the purple paint, aren't you, Susie? Which do you like better, painting on big paper or on little paper? Why?

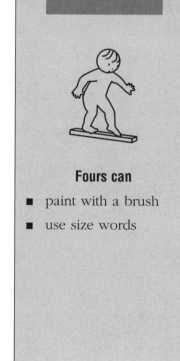

Fours can

- paint with a brush
- use size words

🏠 in or out   🕐 5–15 minutes   # 1–6 Fours

205

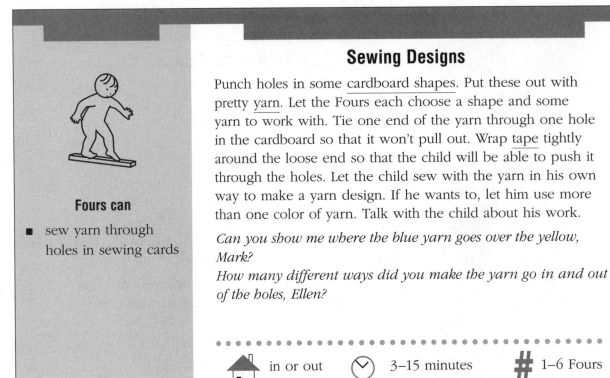

Fours can

- sew yarn through holes in sewing cards

Sewing Designs

Punch holes in some cardboard shapes. Put these out with pretty yarn. Let the Fours each choose a shape and some yarn to work with. Tie one end of the yarn through one hole in the cardboard so that it won't pull out. Wrap tape tightly around the loose end so that the child will be able to push it through the holes. Let the child sew with the yarn in his own way to make a yarn design. If he wants to, let him use more than one color of yarn. Talk with the child about his work.

Can you show me where the blue yarn goes over the yellow, Mark?

How many different ways did you make the yarn go in and out of the holes, Ellen?

🏠 in or out   🕐 3–15 minutes   # 1–6 Fours

206

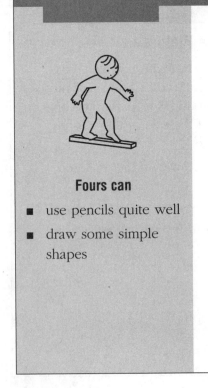

Fours can

- use pencils quite well
- draw some simple shapes

Pencil Pictures

Put out soft lead pencils for your Fours to use freely. Keep these in a container on the art shelf with plenty of paper nearby for children to use with the pencils. Make pencil art a special activity by putting pencils out with different shapes of paper. For example, put out pencils to use with long, narrow paper, heart or star paper shapes, or with very tiny paper.

That is a tall person you made on the long paper, Justin.

You outlined the shape of the star paper, didn't you, Karen?

🏠 in or out   🕐 2–10 minutes   # 1–6 Fours

207

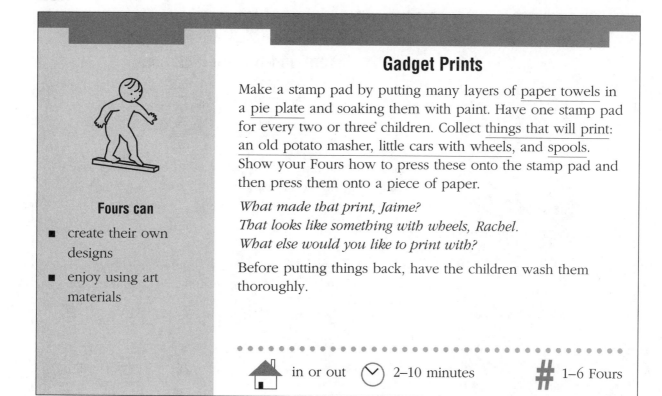

Fours can

- create their own designs
- enjoy using art materials

Gadget Prints

Make a stamp pad by putting many layers of paper towels in a pie plate and soaking them with paint. Have one stamp pad for every two or three children. Collect things that will print: an old potato masher, little cars with wheels, and spools. Show your Fours how to press these onto the stamp pad and then press them onto a piece of paper.

What made that print, Jaime?
That looks like something with wheels, Rachel.
What else would you like to print with?

Before putting things back, have the children wash them thoroughly.

🏠 in or out   🕑 2–10 minutes   # 1–6 Fours

208

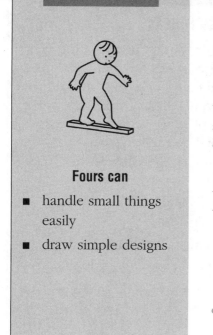

Fours can

- handle small things easily
- draw simple designs

Thin Markers

Bring out some sturdy thin washable markers for your Fours to use with small pieces of paper. Look at the markers with the children before they use them. Talk about not pressing too hard and putting the tops back on when done. Also talk about the thin lines the markers will make. Let the children draw with the markers in their own way.

You made a face with the markers, Karen.
I see it has a blue nose.
Do you want to tell me more about the face you made?

🏠 in or out   🕑 2–10 minutes   # 1–6 Fours

209

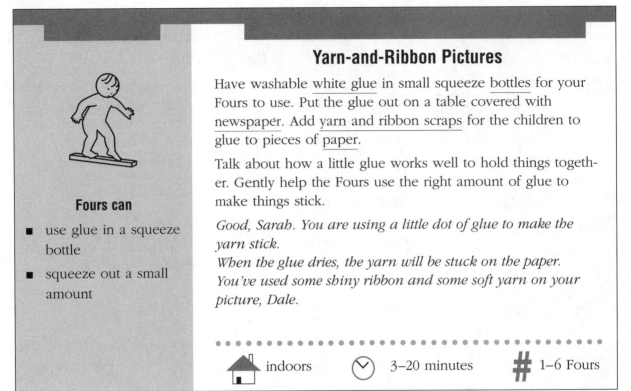

Yarn-and-Ribbon Pictures

Have washable white glue in small squeeze bottles for your Fours to use. Put the glue out on a table covered with newspaper. Add yarn and ribbon scraps for the children to glue to pieces of paper.

Talk about how a little glue works well to hold things together. Gently help the Fours use the right amount of glue to make things stick.

Good, Sarah. You are using a little dot of glue to make the yarn stick.
When the glue dries, the yarn will be stuck on the paper.
You've used some shiny ribbon and some soft yarn on your picture, Dale.

Fours can

■ use glue in a squeeze bottle

■ squeeze out a small amount

🏠 indoors 🕐 3–20 minutes # 1–6 Fours

210

Paper-Plate Masks

Look at some pictures of masks or some real masks with your Fours. Then cut eye holes in paper plates for your Fours to make into masks. Have the children use washable markers to color their masks in their own way. Let each child help you staple yarn or cloth strips to the plate so that it can be tied. Have a mirror nearby so that children can see themselves in the masks they made. Talk about the different ways the Fours decorated their masks.

Matthew, you drew a nose on your mask.
Why do you think people use masks?

Do mask activities at Halloween and at other times, too. If children wish, let them staple yarn for hair, and help them cut out nose and mouth holes.

Fours can

■ begin to draw a face

■ create their own designs

■ enjoy using art materials

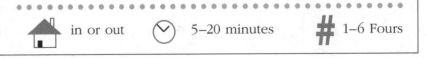

🏠 in or out 🕐 5–20 minutes # 1–6 Fours

211

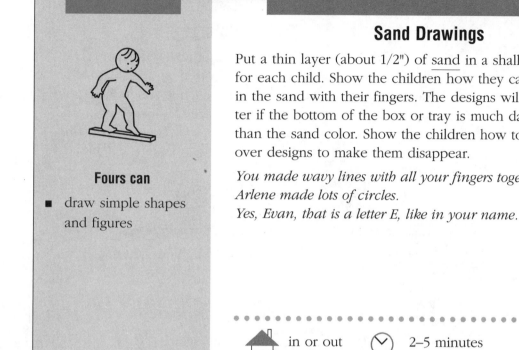

Fours can

- draw simple shapes and figures

Sand Drawings

Put a thin layer (about 1/2") of sand in a shallow box or tray for each child. Show the children how they can make designs in the sand with their fingers. The designs will show up better if the bottom of the box or tray is much darker or lighter than the sand color. Show the children how to smooth sand over designs to make them disappear.

You made wavy lines with all your fingers together.
Arlene made lots of circles.
Yes, Evan, that is a letter E, like in your name.

🏠 in or out　　🕐 2–5 minutes　　# 1–4 Fours

212

Fours can

- tell about their art
- be proud of things they make

Show-and-Tell Artwork

Give Fours a chance to tell their friends about the artwork they have done. Have one child at a time show his work to a small group. Ask questions to help the child say a little about the artwork.

Tell us about your painting, Tim.
What did you use to make this picture?
Did anyone else paint today?
Cathy wants to show us her clay work.

Then help the children put their work up in the art gallery.

🏠 in or out　　🕐 2–5 minutes　　# 3–6 Fours

213

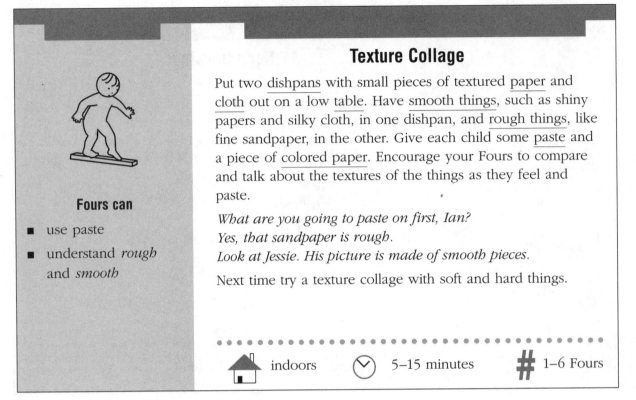

Fours can

- use paste
- understand *rough* and *smooth*

Texture Collage

Put two dishpans with small pieces of textured paper and cloth out on a low table. Have smooth things, such as shiny papers and silky cloth, in one dishpan, and rough things, like fine sandpaper, in the other. Give each child some paste and a piece of colored paper. Encourage your Fours to compare and talk about the textures of the things as they feel and paste.

What are you going to paste on first, Ian?
Yes, that sandpaper is rough.
Look at Jessie. His picture is made of smooth pieces.

Next time try a texture collage with soft and hard things.

indoors   5–15 minutes   # 1–6 Fours

214

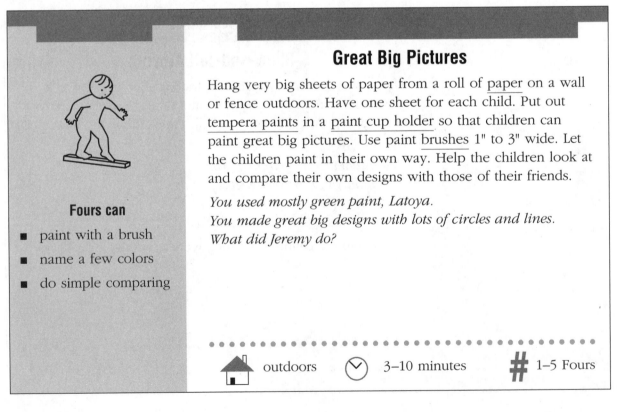

Fours can

- paint with a brush
- name a few colors
- do simple comparing

Great Big Pictures

Hang very big sheets of paper from a roll of paper on a wall or fence outdoors. Have one sheet for each child. Put out tempera paints in a paint cup holder so that children can paint great big pictures. Use paint brushes 1" to 3" wide. Let the children paint in their own way. Help the children look at and compare their own designs with those of their friends.

You used mostly green paint, Latoya.
You made great big designs with lots of circles and lines.
What did Jeremy do?

outdoors   3–10 minutes   # 1–5 Fours

215

Fours can

- follow clear directions
- paint with a brush

Watercolor Paintings

Put out watercolor paints with small, sturdy brushes for your Fours to use. Begin with two of the three primary paint colors (red, yellow, or blue). Have margarine tubs filled with clean water and paper towels ready.

First show the children how to wet a piece of white paper to paint on. Then show them how to dip a brush into water, swirl it in a color, and paint on paper. Remind children to clean brushes in water as they change colors. Children can use paper towels to blot too-wet papers or brushes. Talk about how the colors spread out on the paper and what happens when colors mix together. Rinse and blot paints dry when done to keep colors clean. Add other colors one at a time when the children are able to manage the process.

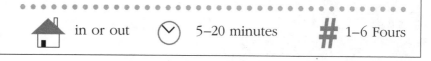

🏠 in or out   🕐 5–20 minutes   # 1–6 Fours

216

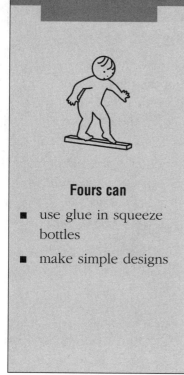

Fours can

- use glue in squeeze bottles
- make simple designs

Sand-and-Glue Pictures

Show your Fours how to place a piece of paper into a shallow box. Let them squeeze a little line of white glue onto the paper in a design. Then have them sprinkle sand over the glue and carefully lift the paper so that the extra sand falls into the box.

Make this more fun by putting out colored sand in empty spice bottles that have covers with holes big enough for the fine sand to pass through. Color sand by mixing it with a little dry tempera paint powder.

You are letting the extra sand roll off the paper now. What made the sand stick on the paper?

🏠 in or out   🕐 5–10 minutes   # 1–2 Fours

217

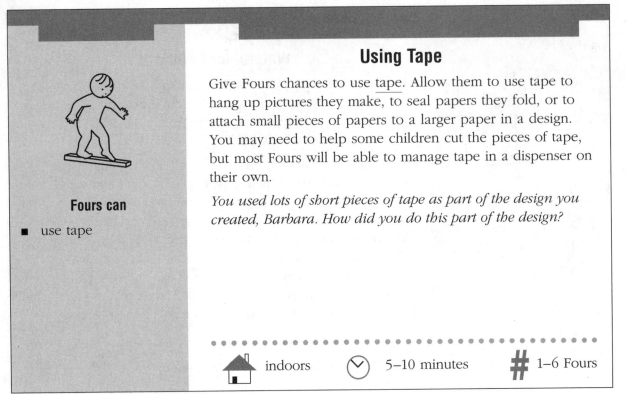

Fours can

■ use tape

Using Tape

Give Fours chances to use <u>tape</u>. Allow them to use tape to hang up pictures they make, to seal papers they fold, or to attach small pieces of papers to a larger paper in a design. You may need to help some children cut the pieces of tape, but most Fours will be able to manage tape in a dispenser on their own.

You used lots of short pieces of tape as part of the design you created, Barbara. How did you do this part of the design?

🏠 indoors   🕐 5–10 minutes   # 1–6 Fours

218

Fours can

■ tell about their artwork

Picture Stories

Give children pieces of <u>paper</u> to draw on with <u>markers</u> or to <u>paint</u> on. Fold under the bottom part of the paper about two or three inches from the bottom edge, so that they do not draw or paint on that part. Let the children do a picture on the part of the paper that is left.

When a child is done, ask her to tell you about her picture. Unfold the bottom of the paper and use that space to print what the child says. Read the child's words back to her.

Let me read what you said about your picture, Lashawna. It says, "This is mommy, and this is me. We are going to the store."

🏠 in or out   🕐 5–15 minutes   # 1–5 Fours

219

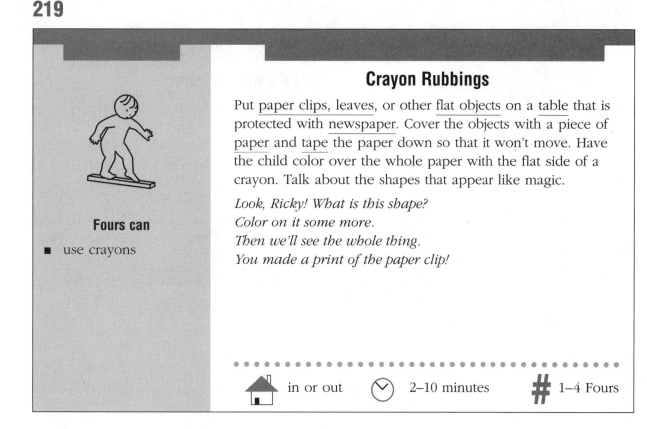

Crayon Rubbings

Put paper clips, leaves, or other flat objects on a table that is protected with newspaper. Cover the objects with a piece of paper and tape the paper down so that it won't move. Have the child color over the whole paper with the flat side of a crayon. Talk about the shapes that appear like magic.

Look, Ricky! What is this shape?
Color on it some more.
Then we'll see the whole thing.
You made a print of the paper clip!

Fours can

■ use crayons

🏠 in or out   🕐 2–10 minutes   **#** 1–4 Fours

220

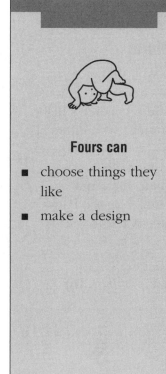

Sand Casting

Put one or two inches of sand in the bottom of a small, flat cardboard box. Have one box for each child. Make the sand damp with a little water. Put out a tray of pebbles, shells, and other nature things that the children have collected on walks outside. Let each child choose what he likes and place the things on the sand.

For every box, have the child help you mix plaster of Paris with water in a cottage cheese container until it is as thick as sour cream. Help the child pour it over the sand. While it is still wet, press into the plaster a piece of paper with the child's name and a loop of string to use as a hanger. When the plaster is dry, have the child lift it out and brush off the extra sand.

Fours can

■ choose things they like

■ make a design

🏠 in or out   🕐 5–20 minutes   **#** 1–4 Fours

221

Fours can

- make forms with play dough
- create their own designs

Play-Dough Pictures

Give each child a piece of wood or heavy stiff cardboard about 8" × 10". Put out small lumps of play dough of different colors. (The recipe for Self-Hardening Play Dough is on page 235.) Let the Fours take the colors they need to make a picture. Show them how to flatten out the play dough on the board to cover a big space—green for grass, blue for the sky—and how to press the play-dough pieces close together to make one big picture. When the play dough dries, the picture will stick to the backing.

When you take a walk with your Fours, talk about the things and the colors you see. This will help them get ideas to put in their play-dough pictures.

🏠 in or out　　🕐 5–15 minutes　　# 1–6 Fours

222

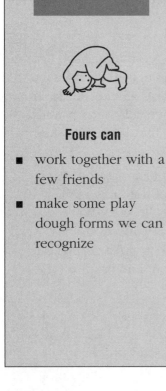

Fours can

- work together with a few friends
- make some play dough forms we can recognize

Play-Dough Group Mural

After taking a walking trip, plan a mural with the interested Fours. Plan what will be on the mural, such as a road, houses, stores, trees, people, and so on. With the children's help, take a large piece of plywood and cover areas with different colors of self-hardening play dough to make the background. (Recipe is on page 235.) Let the children make their own buildings, people, and other forms to add to the mural. Remind them to press their parts of the mural on the background so that things will stick. Use a little water to make things stick if the play dough gets dry.

You're making a flag on the post office, Denise.
Norman is making a blue lake in the middle of the grass.
What can we put in the lake?

🏠 in or out　　🕐 10–30 minutes　　# 1–4 Fours

223

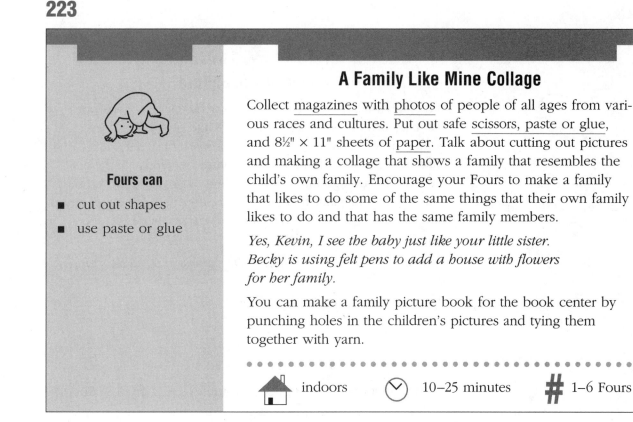

Fours can

- cut out shapes
- use paste or glue

A Family Like Mine Collage

Collect magazines with photos of people of all ages from various races and cultures. Put out safe scissors, paste or glue, and 8½" × 11" sheets of paper. Talk about cutting out pictures and making a collage that shows a family that resembles the child's own family. Encourage your Fours to make a family that likes to do some of the same things that their own family likes to do and that has the same family members.

Yes, Kevin, I see the baby just like your little sister. Becky is using felt pens to add a house with flowers for her family.

You can make a family picture book for the book center by punching holes in the children's pictures and tying them together with yarn.

🏠 indoors   🕐 10–25 minutes   # 1–6 Fours

224

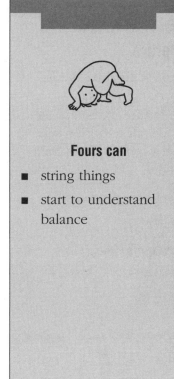

Fours can

- string things
- start to understand balance

Make a Mobile

Hang up a wire coat hanger for each child. Put out a tray of stringing things with holes in them—small unbreakable Christmas tree ornaments, buttons with big holes, shapes made of pipe cleaners. Use easy-to-bend covered wire or 12" string to attach the shapes to the bottom of the coat hanger. Let your Fours choose what they like and hang them on the hanger. Then encourage them to move things back and forth until the hanger is balanced. Use tape to make things stay in one place. Take the mobiles outside and watch them blow and move in the wind.

Juan, the mobile tips down on this side. Can you make your mobile balance so that it is straight?

🏠 in or out   🕐 5–20 minutes   # 1–4 Fours

225

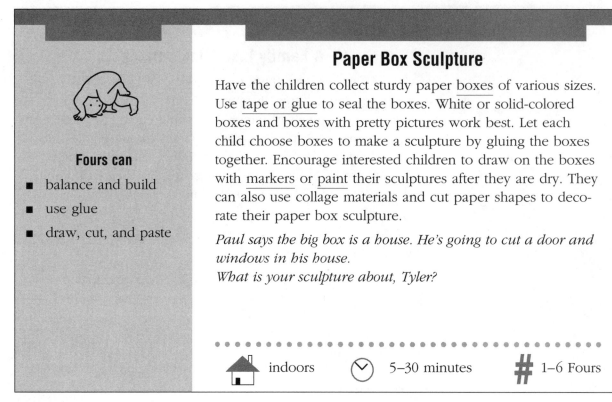

Fours can

- balance and build
- use glue
- draw, cut, and paste

Paper Box Sculpture

Have the children collect sturdy paper boxes of various sizes. Use tape or glue to seal the boxes. White or solid-colored boxes and boxes with pretty pictures work best. Let each child choose boxes to make a sculpture by gluing the boxes together. Encourage interested children to draw on the boxes with markers or paint their sculptures after they are dry. They can also use collage materials and cut paper shapes to decorate their paper box sculpture.

Paul says the big box is a house. He's going to cut a door and windows in his house.
What is your sculpture about, Tyler?

🏠 indoors   🕐 5–30 minutes   # 1–6 Fours

226

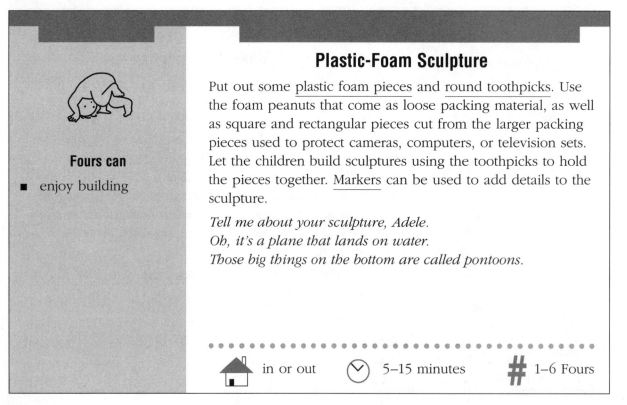

Fours can

- enjoy building

Plastic-Foam Sculpture

Put out some plastic foam pieces and round toothpicks. Use the foam peanuts that come as loose packing material, as well as square and rectangular pieces cut from the larger packing pieces used to protect cameras, computers, or television sets. Let the children build sculptures using the toothpicks to hold the pieces together. Markers can be used to add details to the sculpture.

Tell me about your sculpture, Adele.
Oh, it's a plane that lands on water.
Those big things on the bottom are called pontoons.

🏠 in or out   🕐 5–15 minutes   # 1–6 Fours

227

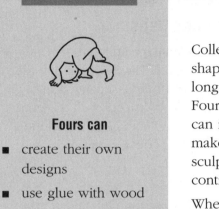

Fours can

- create their own designs
- use glue with wood

Wood-Scrap Sculpture

Collect small wood scraps, spools, and other small wooden shapes. Give each child a flat piece of wood about 8" to 10" long to use as a base, and a small bottle of glue. Let your Fours choose the shapes they need to build whatever they can imagine. Remind them that they need only a little glue to make the wood stick. Children may need to work on their sculptures a little at a time, wait for the glue to dry, and then continue work if they wish.

When the glue is dry, the children may want to rub the sculpture with some cooking oil on a cloth to bring out the grain of the wood.

 in or out   10–20 minutes   # 1–6 Fours

228

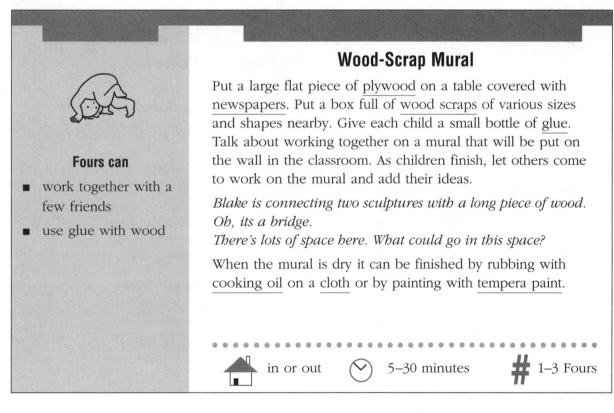

Fours can

- work together with a few friends
- use glue with wood

Wood-Scrap Mural

Put a large flat piece of plywood on a table covered with newspapers. Put a box full of wood scraps of various sizes and shapes nearby. Give each child a small bottle of glue. Talk about working together on a mural that will be put on the wall in the classroom. As children finish, let others come to work on the mural and add their ideas.

Blake is connecting two sculptures with a long piece of wood. Oh, its a bridge.
There's lots of space here. What could go in this space?

When the mural is dry it can be finished by rubbing with cooking oil on a cloth or by painting with tempera paint.

 in or out   5–30 minutes   # 1–3 Fours

229

Fours can

- follow simple safety rules
- hammer nails with adult supervision

Hammer and Nails

Put out two medium-sized claw hammers, about 10–13 ounces in weight, on a carpentry table. Have several different lengths and thicknesses of nails with heads, separated in different small boxes. Collect soft wood pieces with the grain running the length of the piece to prevent splitting. Include a tray of things that are easy to hammer onto wood such as bottle caps and leather and fabric scraps. Then help the children learn to hammer safely.

Jesse, you made an airplane. Walter wants to know how you did it. Can you tell him?

More carpentry ideas are on page 225. Always watch carpentry carefully, and make sure children follow the carpentry safety rules on page 225.

🏠 in or out   🕐 5–15 minutes   # 1–2 Fours

230

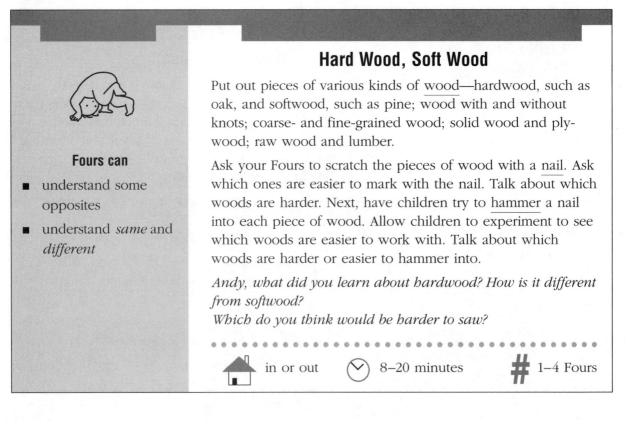

Fours can

- understand some opposites
- understand *same* and *different*

Hard Wood, Soft Wood

Put out pieces of various kinds of wood—hardwood, such as oak, and softwood, such as pine; wood with and without knots; coarse- and fine-grained wood; solid wood and plywood; raw wood and lumber.

Ask your Fours to scratch the pieces of wood with a nail. Ask which ones are easier to mark with the nail. Talk about which woods are harder. Next, have children try to hammer a nail into each piece of wood. Allow children to experiment to see which woods are easier to work with. Talk about which woods are harder or easier to hammer into.

Andy, what did you learn about hardwood? How is it different from softwood?
Which do you think would be harder to saw?

🏠 in or out   🕐 8–20 minutes   # 1–4 Fours

231

Fours can

- follow simple safety rules
- enjoy a challenge
- use a saw with adult supervision

Sawing Wood

Put out a box of soft wood pieces about 6" long and no more than 2" wide for sawing. Have a C-clamp or a vise on the carpentry table to hold the wood for sawing. Have a crosscut saw about 12" to 15" long for the Four who is going to saw. After the child chooses his wood, help him fix it tightly in the vise or C-clamp and show him how to keep his other hand far from the saw. Help get the sawing started so that there is a little groove in the wood. If the saw sticks, you can rub it lightly with soap.

You're working hard, Thomas. You're making the saw go back and forth smoothly. That's sawdust on the ground. Where did it come from?

🏠 in or out 🕐 10–20 minutes # 1 Four at a time

232

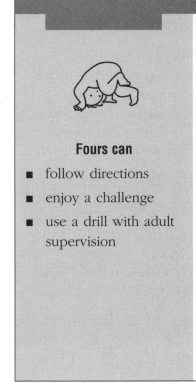

Fours can

- follow directions
- enjoy a challenge
- use a drill with adult supervision

Drilling Holes in Wood

With a C-clamp, attach a piece of soft wood so that it sticks out away from the carpentry table. Have a brace and bit drill or a hand drill for the child to use that makes a hole about 1/4" to 1/2" in diameter. Have the child mark the wood where she wants to drill the hole. Tap a nail in that place to make a dent. This little dent keeps the drill steady. Now the child can turn the drill. If you use a brace and bit, hold the brace steady as the child turns it.

What do you see coming up? Yes, its sawdust. You drilled a hole clear through, Catherine.

🏠 in or out 🕐 5–15 minutes # 1 Four at a time

233

Fours can

- follow clear directions
- hammer nails with adult supervision

Making a Sanding Block

Select small blocks of wood that fit in a child's hand. Cut pieces of three grades of sandpaper—fine, medium, and coarse, into lengths that can fit around the block with a 1" overlap where the two ends meet. Have your Fours try each grade of sandpaper and choose the one they want. Then help them wrap the piece around the block tightly and nail the sandpaper in place with short nails. Show the children how to sand wood pieces smooth with their sanding blocks.

Let's see if your wood is smooth on the edges, Ray.
Good, Julie. You remembered to sand with the side that has no nails!
What would happen if we left wood rough? Yes, you could get splinters.

🏠 in or out   🕐 10–20 minutes   # 1–4 Fours

234

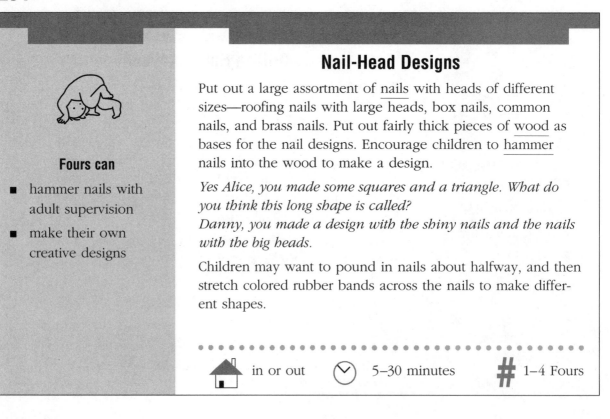

Fours can

- hammer nails with adult supervision
- make their own creative designs

Nail-Head Designs

Put out a large assortment of nails with heads of different sizes—roofing nails with large heads, box nails, common nails, and brass nails. Put out fairly thick pieces of wood as bases for the nail designs. Encourage children to hammer nails into the wood to make a design.

Yes Alice, you made some squares and a triangle. What do you think this long shape is called?
Danny, you made a design with the shiny nails and the nails with the big heads.

Children may want to pound in nails about halfway, and then stretch colored rubber bands across the nails to make different shapes.

🏠 in or out   🕐 5–30 minutes   # 1–4 Fours

235

Fours can

- hammer, saw, and drill with adult supervision

- create with wood

Carpentry Display

After a carpentry piece is finished, encourage the child to tell you about it. Print what he says on a piece of paper and either you or the child can add his name. Ask the child to put the carpentry piece on the display table with the story about it nearby. Let everybody know about the carpentry display. Read the children's stories often.

Here is Aaron's story about what he made in carpentry.
Do you want me to tell you what it says? It says, "I made an airplane. It does not really fly. I hammered in a nail to hold the wings on."

🏠 in or out 🕐 5–20 minutes # 1–10 Fours

236

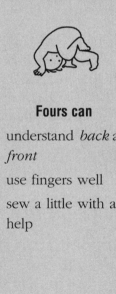

Fours can

- understand *back* and *front*

- use fingers well

- sew a little with adult help

Sewing on Cloth

Stretch loosely woven cloth such as burlap in a small round embroidery hoop or tack it onto a wooden picture frame. Thread large needles that are not sharp with brightly colored yarn. Put a big knot at the end of the yarn. Show your Fours the back and the front of the cloth in the hoop. Explain that the needle goes in one side, then back out to the other side, not around the hoop.

You made lots of stitches with yellow yarn, Peggy. What color will you use next?
Noah is threading the needle with blue yarn. If you twist the yarn, it fits in the eye of the needle better.

🏠 in or out 🕐 5–30 minutes # 1–4 Fours

237

Fours can

- tell colors of many things

- draw some things we can recognize

Pictures with Seasonal Colors

As the seasons change, have your Fours collect natural things such as leaves in fall, budding branches and bright flowers in spring. Put up a display of these things and of pictures showing what people like to do in that season. Help the children tune into the colors they see around them. Include these seasonal colors as paints at the easel and as the crayons or markers at the drawing table. Add the children's pictures using the special colors to the seasonal display.

What colors should we have for spring?
Light green like the buds, and yellow, like the flowers? And some light brown for the mud after it rains? You've really been watching what happens to colors in the spring.

🏠 indoors   🕐 5–15 minutes   # 1–6 Fours

238

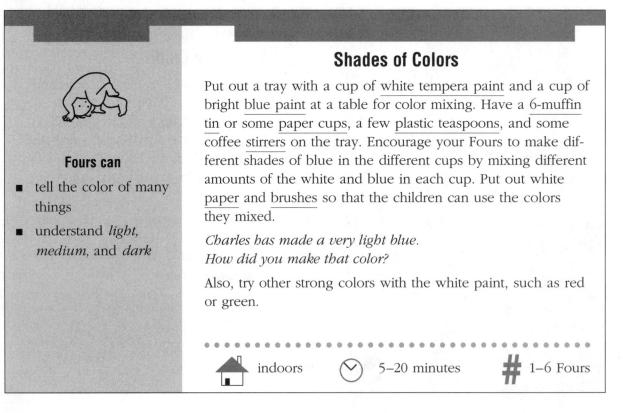

Fours can

- tell the color of many things

- understand *light, medium,* and *dark*

Shades of Colors

Put out a tray with a cup of white tempera paint and a cup of bright blue paint at a table for color mixing. Have a 6-muffin tin or some paper cups, a few plastic teaspoons, and some coffee stirrers on the tray. Encourage your Fours to make different shades of blue in the different cups by mixing different amounts of the white and blue in each cup. Put out white paper and brushes so that the children can use the colors they mixed.

Charles has made a very light blue.
How did you make that color?

Also, try other strong colors with the white paint, such as red or green.

🏠 indoors   🕐 5–20 minutes   # 1–6 Fours

239

Fours can

- draw some pictures we can recognize
- tell about their artwork

Picture Story Books

Put out thick and thin washable <u>markers</u> and light-colored <u>construction paper</u> that has holes punched on the left-hand side. Encourage your Fours to draw pages for a book to go into the Book Center. Suggest book topics such as: What I Like to Do in Spring, Summer, Fall, or Winter; What I Was for Halloween; My Family; My House. Any topic that interests children may become the subject for a class book. Remember to read the class books in the Book Center and at story time, too.

I'd be glad to read our book about Halloween, Jonathan. It's fun to see what everyone pretended to be.

🏠 indoors 🕐 5–20 minutes # 1–6 Fours

240

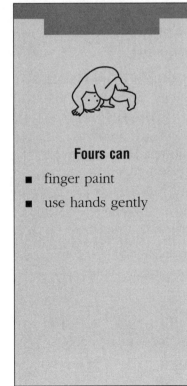

Fours can

- finger paint
- use hands gently

Finger Paint Prints

Have your Fours <u>finger paint</u> on a <u>tray</u>. Ask each child to tell you when he has made a design in the paint that he wants to keep as a print on paper. When the child is ready, have him wash and dry his hands. Then put his name on the back of a piece of <u>paper</u>. Help him gently smooth the front of the paper onto the paint and carefully lift it off. Talk about the print the child has made. Hang it up, or place it on a flat surface to dry.

Can you feel the bumps of finger paint through the paper?
You are being very gentle, Ricky.
You'll be able to take your print home when it is dry, Charlotte. How long do you think it will take to get dry?

🏠 indoors 🕐 5–20 minutes # 1–6 Fours

241

Fours can

- cut and paste simple shapes
- work carefully with small things

Making a Mosaic

Introduce your Fours to mosaics. Show them some things made of tiles, such as a floor in the bathroom or a kitchen counter top. Ask parents to send in any mosaic objects they might have. Make sure to explain that a mosaic has small pieces glued very close together to make one big design. Then cut paper strips 1" to 1½" wide of different textures and colors. Have children cut these into small squares and rectangles. Put out paste or glue and 5" × 5" construction paper squares. See if the children can make their own mosaic-like designs.

Later, set up an art activity with real mosaic tiles that the children can glue onto pieces of thin plywood.

🏠 indoors   🕐 5–15 minutes   # 1–6 Fours

242

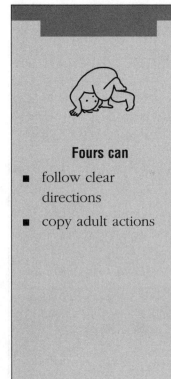

Fours can

- follow clear directions
- copy adult actions

Table Washing after Art

Fill a bucket about 1/3 full of water. Put in a sponge that fits a child's hand. Show the children how to wring the sponge close to the top of the bucket so that the water goes inside and does not spray around. Then show them how to wash spots off the table. After they wash the whole table, show them how to wash, rinse, and wring out the sponge, and then soak up all the excess water with the almost dry, clean sponge. If the children do this carefully with long strokes, the table will look bright and shiny when they are finished.

Table washing can also be done after snack and lunch time. You can follow up with the bleach and water solution to sanitize the table.

🏠 indoors   🕐 3–7 minutes   # 1–2 Fours

243

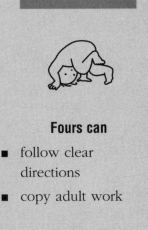

Fours can

- follow clear directions
- copy adult work

Sweeping Up after Art

After an art activity that has left scraps of paper and other art materials on the table and floor, have children help with cleanup. First, have the children put the bigger pieces in the wastepaper basket. To sweep the floor, help them choose a small part of the floor that they want to sweep. Show them a place where they can sweep the dirt into a pile. Have the children work on their own smaller areas while you do the rest. Be sure children use child-sized <u>brooms</u> that are easy for them to handle.

After the dirt is swept into little piles, have children work with a partner to sweep them into a <u>dustpan</u> with a <u>brush</u> and put them into a nearby wastepaper basket.

🏠 indoors　　🕐 3–8 minutes　　# 1–4 Fours

244

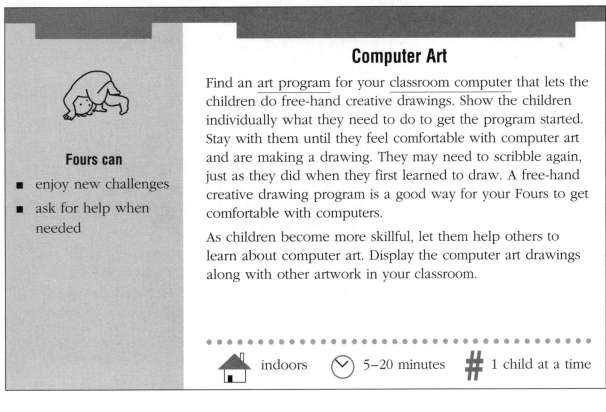

Fours can

- enjoy new challenges
- ask for help when needed

Computer Art

Find an <u>art program</u> for your <u>classroom computer</u> that lets the children do free-hand creative drawings. Show the children individually what they need to do to get the program started. Stay with them until they feel comfortable with computer art and are making a drawing. They may need to scribble again, just as they did when they first learned to draw. A free-hand creative drawing program is a good way for your Fours to get comfortable with computers.

As children become more skillful, let them help others to learn about computer art. Display the computer art drawings along with other artwork in your classroom.

🏠 indoors　　🕐 5–20 minutes　　# 1 child at a time

Art Center

- Set up an Art Center in a space where the floor and walls can be easily cleaned and where there is a sink nearby.

- Put easy-to-use art materials on low shelves for Fours to use freely every day: sturdy crayons, watercolor markers, lots of paper, safe scissors, collage materials, and paste or glue. Keep the materials in good shape.

- Show children where art materials are stored by putting picture labels on the shelf. Then encourage children to put things back in their proper places.

- Store art materials in many small containers instead of one big one. Giving one or two children a small container of art materials to use cuts down on fighting.

- Let children use art materials in their own way. Don't show children something you have made for them to copy.

- Let Fours use play dough without cookie cutters. Then they will be able to see the many original shapes they can make with their own hands and imaginations.

- Bring out art materials that need more help from you when you are free to watch them. Don't have all the children work with them at one time. Add these activities to the many other child-directed activities children can choose to do.

- Make sure that everyone who is interested gets a chance to do artwork. Keep the same special art activity out for more than one day if it is popular.

- Encourage children to talk about what they have made. Show them you enjoy their artwork. Mention colors, shapes, and materials they used in their work.

- Protect the floor, tables, and walls in the art area. Art materials are messy, and accidents can easily happen.

- Teach your Fours how to use clean-up things, such as sponges, paper towels, and water, and have them ready.

- Cut the handles of paintbrushes to about 6" so that they are easier for Fours to control. Smooth the rough edges. Cut down legs on easels if easels are too high and can't be lowered.

- Use art materials outdoors as well as indoors, especially for messy activities such as finger painting or noisy activities such as carpentry.

- Put the children's artwork on display low on the walls or on the backs of bookshelves where the children can easily see their work. Change the display often.

Carpentry Center

- If possible, set up the Carpentry Center in a corner of the outdoor playground, where the noise is not so noticeable.

- If you have to do carpentry indoors, cover the woodworking table with thick carpeting to cut down the noise of hammering.

- You will need a sturdy woodworking table and a cabinet for storing tools, nails, wood scraps, and accessories to use for building.

- The tools you buy should be real tools of the right size for children, not play tools. A Carpentry Center should have the following tools:
  - 2 claw hammers, 10 to 13 ounces in weight
  - 1 10-point crosscut saw about 12" to 15" long and less than 12 ounces in weight
  - 1 brace and bit drill that can make holes 3/16" to 1" in diameter
  - 1 hand drill that makes small holes up to 1/2" in diameter
  - 1 C-clamp and a wood vise to hold wood for sawing and drilling

  You will also need:
  - Nails of different lengths with flat heads, including common nails and box nails
  - A box of soft wood pieces, such as pine, with the grain running the length of the wood to prevent splitting
  - A box of carpentry accessories to use in building, such as small rug scraps, covered wire, rubber bands, linoleum scraps, spools, and bottle caps

- Start a waiting list for each tool if necessary.

- Make sure that the Carpentry Center is closely supervised and never without an adult nearby.

- Make sure that the children know the *safety rules:*
  - Work far from other children.
  - Watch where you are hammering, sawing, or drilling.
  - Use a C-clamp to hold the wood to protect your hands.
  - Keep your other hand (the hand that is not hammering or sawing) as far as possible from the hammer or saw.

The carpentry cards on the following pages can be used as you do carpentry activities with the children.

Carpentry Tools

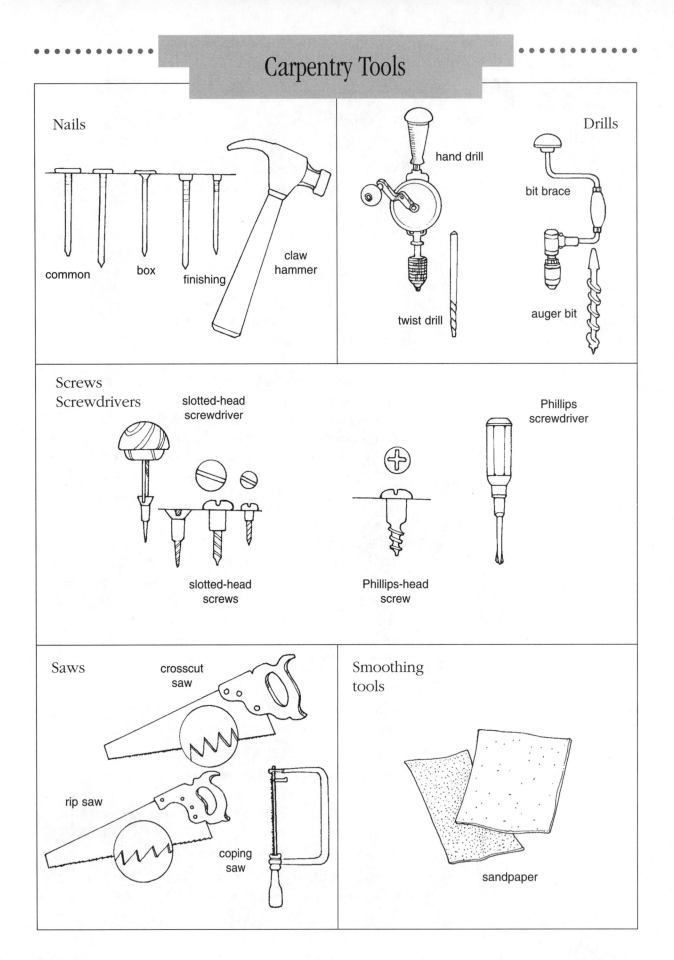

Nails

common   box   finishing   claw hammer

Drills

hand drill
bit brace
twist drill
auger bit

**Screws
Screwdrivers**

slotted-head screwdriver
Phillips screwdriver

slotted-head screws
Phillips-head screw

Saws

crosscut saw
rip saw
coping saw

Smoothing tools

sandpaper

HAMMERING	
1. DeShon	7. Chris
2. Gloria	8. Kim
3. Carlos	9. Andre
4. Brett	10.
5. Danielle	11.
6. Billy	12.

SAFETY RULES
1. Give yourself room.
2. Watch where you work.
3. Keep your other hand far from the hammer or saw.

Sign-Up Lists   Safety Rules

Tool Storage Pegboard

Outline hanging tools to make clean-up easier.

Low Shelves for Nails and Accessories

Accessories

WOOD SCRAPS

Wood Storage

Carpentry Center

Exploring Kinds of Wood

1 Scratch wood with nail.

softwood

hardwood

2 Rub vegetable oil into surface.

fine-grained

coarse-grained

OIL

3 Look at sides.

plywood

solid

4 Look at surface—see grain.

straight

whorled

5 Find knots, markings.

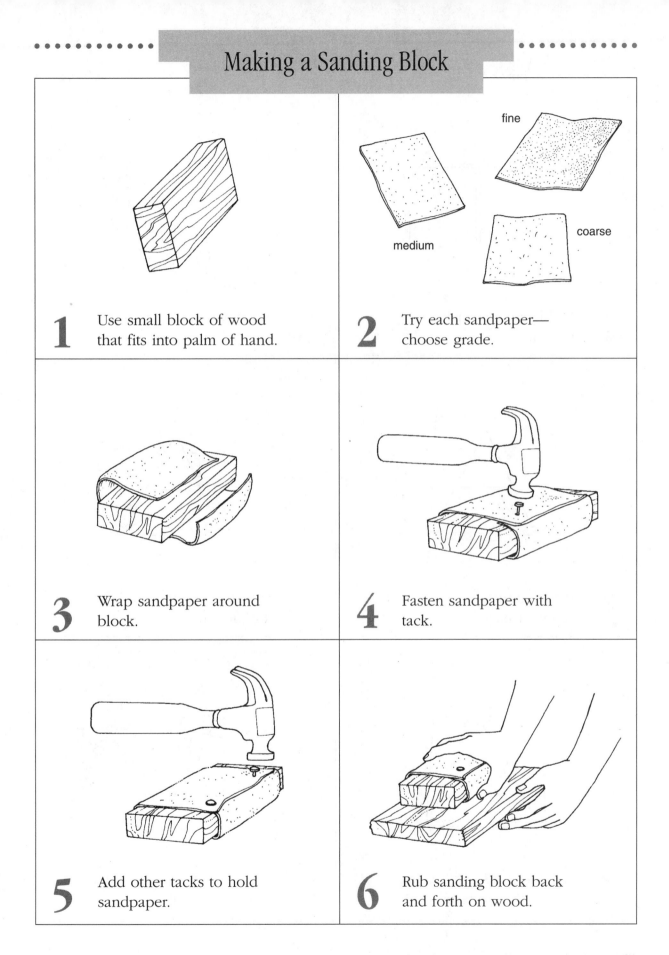

1 Use small block of wood that fits into palm of hand.

2 Try each sandpaper—choose grade.

fine

medium

coarse

3 Wrap sandpaper around block.

4 Fasten sandpaper with tack.

5 Add other tacks to hold sandpaper.

6 Rub sanding block back and forth on wood.

Making Patterns with Nails

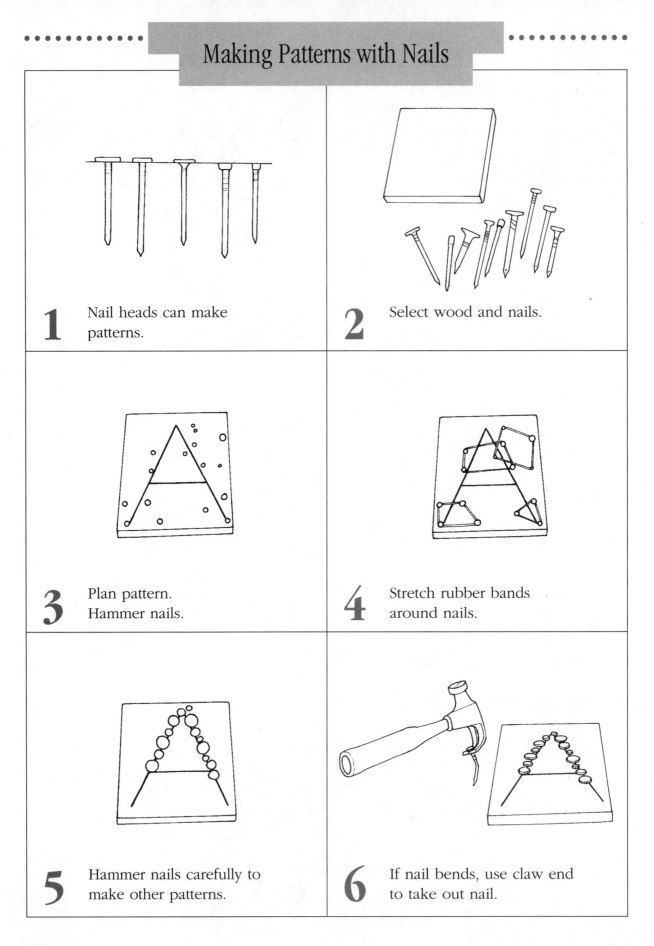

1 Nail heads can make patterns.

2 Select wood and nails.

3 Plan pattern. Hammer nails.

4 Stretch rubber bands around nails.

5 Hammer nails carefully to make other patterns.

6 If nail bends, use claw end to take out nail.

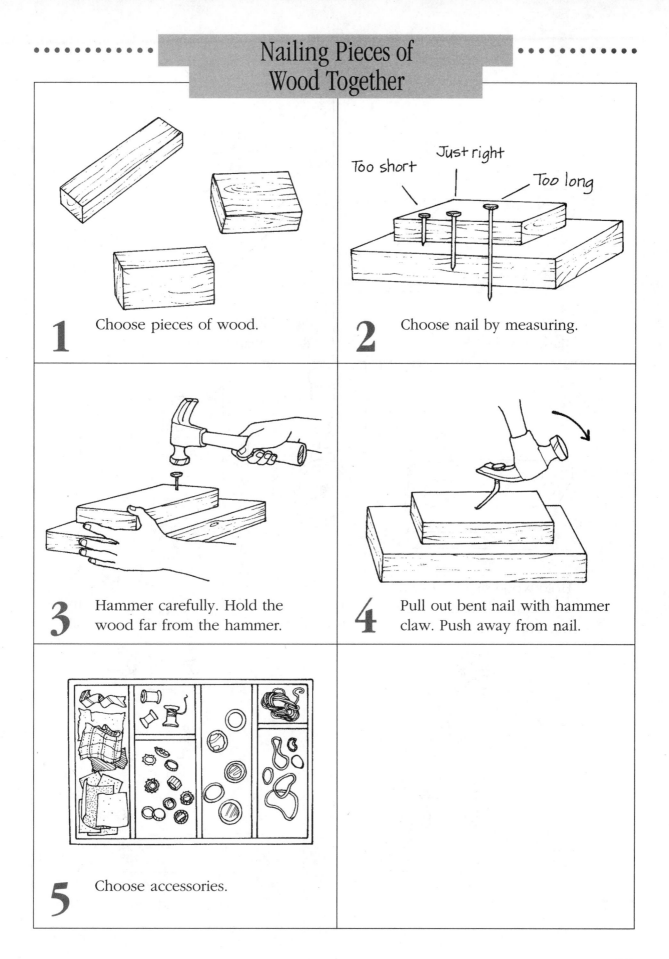

1 Choose pieces of wood.

2 Choose nail by measuring.

Too short · Just right · Too long

3 Hammer carefully. Hold the wood far from the hammer.

4 Pull out bent nail with hammer claw. Push away from nail.

5 Choose accessories.

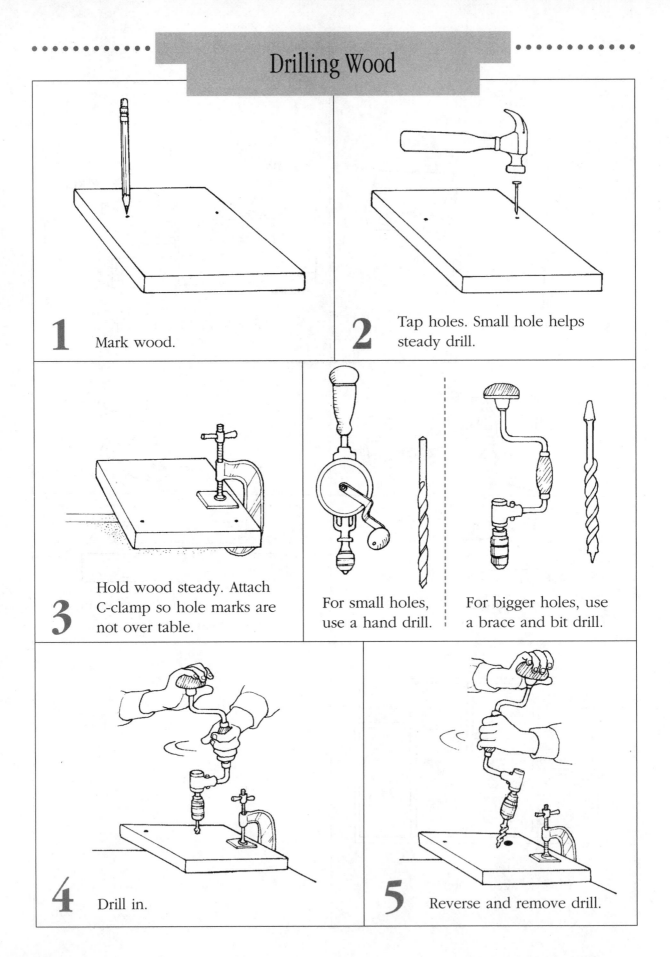

1 Mark wood.

2 Tap holes. Small hole helps steady drill.

3 Hold wood steady. Attach C-clamp so hole marks are not over table.

For small holes, use a hand drill.

For bigger holes, use a brace and bit drill.

4 Drill in.

5 Reverse and remove drill.

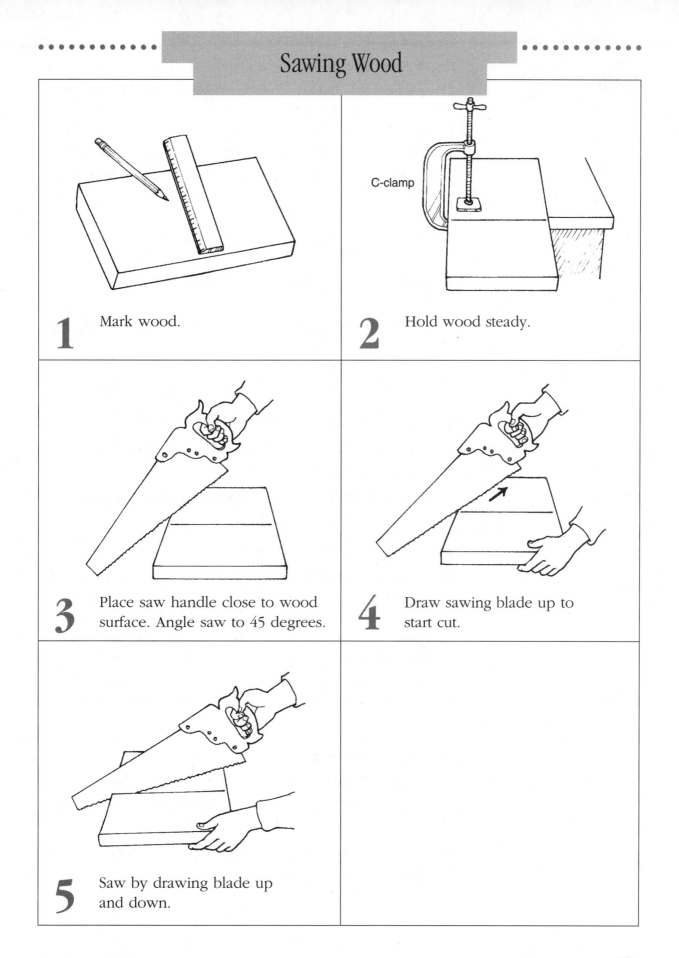

1 Mark wood.

2 Hold wood steady.

C-clamp

3 Place saw handle close to wood surface. Angle saw to 45 degrees.

4 Draw sawing blade up to start cut.

5 Saw by drawing blade up and down.

Recipes

Brush Paint Recipe

This recipe will help keep down your painting costs because it uses very little dry tempera paint.

1. Mix 1 cup bentonite (an inexpensive clay product that you can get at a pottery supply company) with 2 quarts hot water.

2. Let the mixture stand in a large container with a lid for two or three days. Stir each day. It will be sticky and lumpy to begin with.

3. When the bentonite is smooth and thick, pour it into smaller jars.

4. Add 3 or more tablespoons of dry tempera paint to each jar. Stir.

5. Add more paint if the color is not bright enough. Add more water if the paint is too thick.

6. Keep jars covered so paint won't dry out.

7. Pour paint into smaller unbreakable cups for children to use.

Soap Finger Paint

1. Mix 3 cups of Ivory Snow® Soap Flakes with one cup of water.

2. Beat with an eggbeater until it's thick.

3. Color with a few drops of food coloring. (You can also try shaving cream as finger paint.)

Easy Finger Paint

1. Mix 2 cups of flour with 1/4 cup of water. Add more water if needed and stir until the mixture is as thick as white glue.

2. Add a few drops of food coloring or 1/2 teaspoon of tempera paint powder and mix. For a deeper color, add more food coloring or powder.

3. Let each child finger paint with 2 or 3 tablespoons of the mixture on large, sturdy paper; a plastic tray; a cookie sheet; or a tabletop.

Cooked Finger Paint

1. Mix 1/2 cup flour with 1 cup water. Stir until smooth.

2. Bring to a boil, still stirring. Cook until it is thick as pudding.

3. Cool.

4. Thin with dishwashing liquid until it is right for finger painting.

5. Add a few drops of food coloring.

Creative Activities

Play Dough

1. Mix 1½ cups of flour, 1/2 cup salt, 1/4 cup vegetable oil, about 1/4 cup water, and a few drops of food coloring. (The color mixes most easily when added to the water.)

2. Knead until the dough is smooth and the color is well mixed.

3. Add more flour if the mixture is too wet. Add more water if the mixture is too dry.

Self-Hardening Play Dough

1. Mix 2 cups of flour, 1/2 cup salt, and 1 teaspoon of powdered color.

2. Gradually add 3/4 cup of water.

3. Mix well and knead till smooth.

4. Add more flour if wet or more water if dry.

Jewelry Modeling Clay

1. Mix 3/4 cup flour, 1/2 cup salt, and 1/2 cup cornstarch in a bowl.

2. Add warm water slowly and gradually until mixture can be kneaded into stiff dough.

3. Dust with flour to reduce stickiness. Roll into balls for beads, pierce with toothpick, allow to dry (2–4 days), and paint if desired.

4. Food coloring may also be added with water or paint powder with flour as the mixture is being made.

Materials and Notes

Blocks

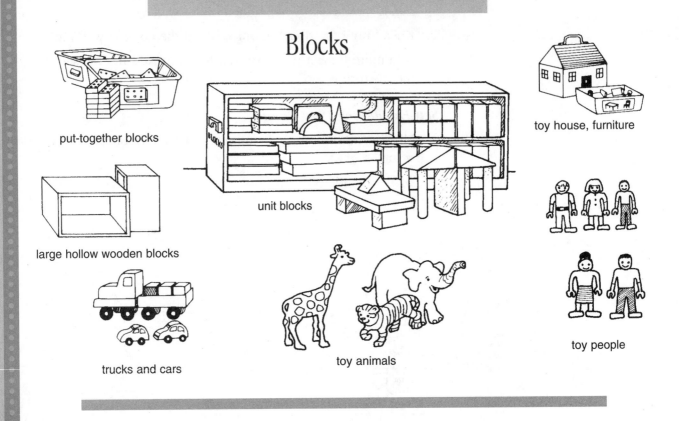

put-together blocks

large hollow wooden blocks

trucks and cars

unit blocks

toy animals

toy house, furniture

toy people

- Encourage both boys and girls to play in the Block Center.

- Show interest in what your Fours do with blocks. Sit with them as they play with the blocks and talk with them about their block-building ideas.

- Make sure children understand a few simple rules for using the blocks:

  - Build in the Block Center but not too close to the shelves.

  - Use blocks gently so that nobody gets hurt.

  - Move carefully to protect buildings.

  - Use blocks that are not being used by others. Ask if you are not sure.

  - Put a "Please Save" sign on any building that is not to be cleaned up.

  - Clean up by putting blocks and toys back in their places on the shelves.

- Keep the area interesting by frequently changing some of the toys to use with the blocks.

- Check blocks and block toys often for sharp edges, rust, or splinters.

- Many of the activity ideas for younger and older Fours can be used with either age group. This is because they are open-ended and can be challenging to children with a wide range of abilities.

- See Block Center Ideas on page 255.

Activity Checklist

Blocks

Block play for Fours includes creating, building, and experimenting with wooden or plastic unit blocks and larger hollow wooden, plastic, or cardboard blocks. Fours use blocks to make tall buildings, roadways, and other patterns, and to build structures for pretend play.

Check for each age group

	48–54 months	*54–60 months*
1. Special Block Center is set up for block play with low open shelves, flat carpet, and a variety of blocks.	❑	❑
2. Accessories for block play are used, such as toy animals and people and trucks, cars, and other vehicles.	❑	❑
3. Blocks and accessories are safe and in good repair.	❑	❑
4. Block Center is not shared with other activities while blocks are being used.	❑	❑
5. Block Center is large enough for at least four children to play without being crowded.	❑	❑
6. Blocks and accessories are available to children for at least two hours daily.	❑	❑
7. Block Center is out of traffic so that children can work without interruptions.	❑	❑
8. Blocks and accessories are organized by type and stored on shelves and in containers that are clearly labeled.	❑	❑
9. Plenty of wooden unit blocks are available so that children can build large, complex structures if they wish.	❑	❑
10. Adult watches and talks with children about their block play when they are interested.	❑	❑
11. Some block play is available outdoors with larger blocks and more space.	❑	❑

245

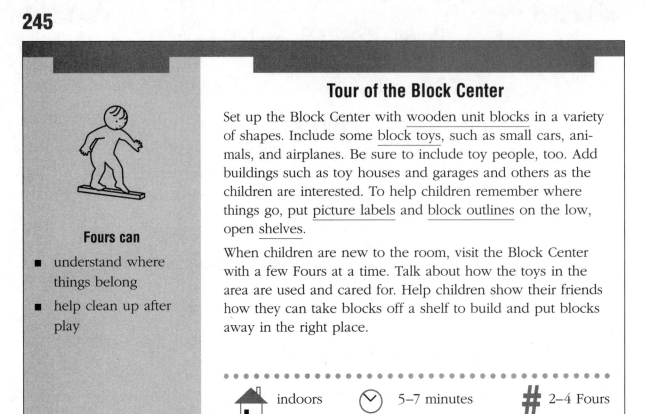

Fours can

- understand where things belong
- help clean up after play

Tour of the Block Center

Set up the Block Center with wooden unit blocks in a variety of shapes. Include some block toys, such as small cars, animals, and airplanes. Be sure to include toy people, too. Add buildings such as toy houses and garages and others as the children are interested. To help children remember where things go, put picture labels and block outlines on the low, open shelves.

When children are new to the room, visit the Block Center with a few Fours at a time. Talk about how the toys in the area are used and cared for. Help children show their friends how they can take blocks off a shelf to build and put blocks away in the right place.

⌂ indoors   ⊘ 5–7 minutes   # 2–4 Fours

246

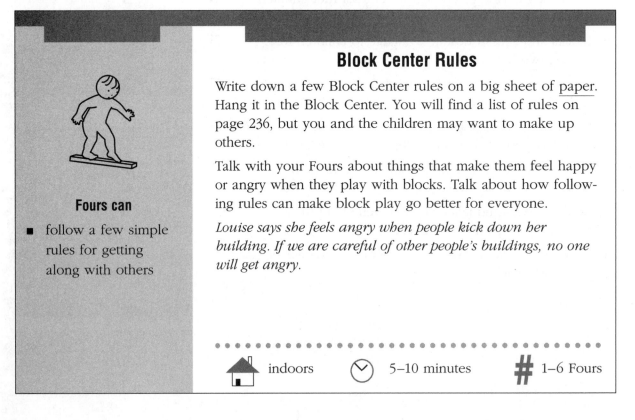

Fours can

- follow a few simple rules for getting along with others

Block Center Rules

Write down a few Block Center rules on a big sheet of paper. Hang it in the Block Center. You will find a list of rules on page 236, but you and the children may want to make up others.

Talk with your Fours about things that make them feel happy or angry when they play with blocks. Talk about how following rules can make block play go better for everyone.

Louise says she feels angry when people kick down her building. If we are careful of other people's buildings, no one will get angry.

⌂ indoors   ⊘ 5–10 minutes   # 1–6 Fours

247

Fours can

- build with a friend
- try to get along well with others

Friendly Building

Watch your Fours as they build with blocks. Whenever you see cooperation, being careful of other's buildings, sharing, or other thoughtful acts, let the children know that you noticed how they handled things.

Talk about what they did and how it made others feel.

Nicky, you walked so carefully.
You really watched out for Robin's tower.

Peter, did you hear Robin say "Excuse me" so that you would let her reach the shelf?

🏠 indoors   🕐 4–10 minutes   # 1–6 Fours

248

Fours can

- share and cooperate sometimes

Spaces to Build

When you have several Fours who want to work in the Block Center, make sure no one builds too near the shelves. Help the Fours leave a clear path to the blocks so that everyone can get the blocks they need.

Since Fours need lots of room for building, give each child or small group its own space. Use masking tape on the floor to mark spaces if you wish. Remind children to get blocks and toys from the shelves and to be careful of each others' buildings. Encourage children to combine spaces when they want to work together.

You and Rosie are sharing a big space, Brooke.
That's right. You can really build something big now!

🏠 indoors   🕐 2–6 minutes   # 2–4 Fours

249

Talk About Block Shapes

As Fours play with blocks, talk about the shapes they are using. Tell the names of the shapes, use words for the block sizes, and say more about how the shapes look.

You used two squares and one triangle to make your house, Jenna. See how the triangle fits on top?

Ask questions to see what the children can say about the blocks.

Can you tell me about your building? What kinds of blocks did you use?

Fours can

■ use some size and number words

🏠 in or out   🕐 1–2 minutes   # 1–4 Fours

250

Sorting Game at Clean-Up Time

Make cleaning up blocks into a sorting game. Ask your Fours to find all of each shape and put them on the shelves in their own labeled spaces. For example, first ask the children to find all the small square blocks and put them away. Then ask them to find the cylinders. Children can pick up each block shape until all the blocks have been found.

Show how delighted you are as the children find the blocks. Give them chances to decide which blocks to find. You can help find the blocks and put them away, too.

That's great, Juan. You and Henry found all the squares. Now which shape block should we work on?
OK, let's find all the long rectangles. Here's one! I put three away.

Fours can

■ sort by shape
■ clean up with help

🏠 indoors   🕐 5–10 minutes   # 1–4 Fours

251

Fours can

- match block shapes
- copy simple designs

Making Buildings That Are the Same

As a child begins building with blocks, ask if you can try to copy what she is doing. If she says OK, then match each block she uses. Do this for a little while, talking together about the shapes and where they are placed.

Oh, oh! I do not know if I can get my rectangle to balance on top of the cylinder like you did, Theresa.
Wow! I did it!
Now what are you planning to do with that triangle?

Make a game of copying. See if children want to play the block-copying game with each other. But make sure the child who is being copied is asked first and says OK.

🏠 in or out 🕐 7–15 minutes # 1–4 Fours

252

Fours can

- tell you about their families
- pretend play as they use blocks and accessories

Families

Talk with your Fours about the people in their families. Then put out a dishpan of toy people and a large play house in the Block Center. Be sure to include enough figures to make families of different races with many brothers and sisters, grandmothers, grandfathers, or other relatives. Include figures of people with disabilities, too.

Who is in your family, Annie?
I see you have two grown-ups here.
Is this your Mommy?

Encourage the children to use all the toy people in their block play.

🏠 indoors 🕐 3–20 minutes # 1–4 Fours

253

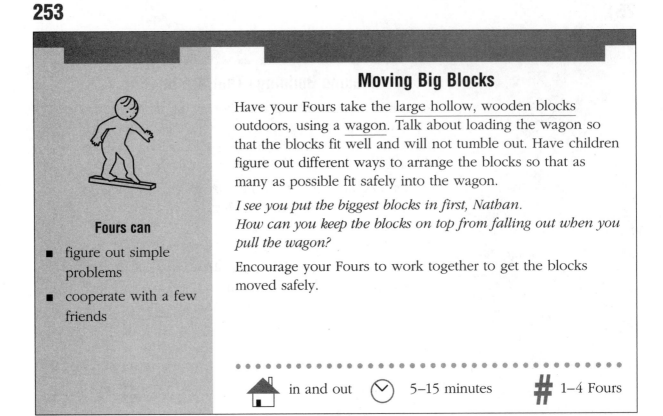

Moving Big Blocks

Have your Fours take the large hollow, wooden blocks outdoors, using a wagon. Talk about loading the wagon so that the blocks fit well and will not tumble out. Have children figure out different ways to arrange the blocks so that as many as possible fit safely into the wagon.

I see you put the biggest blocks in first, Nathan.
How can you keep the blocks on top from falling out when you pull the wagon?

Encourage your Fours to work together to get the blocks moved safely.

Fours can

- figure out simple problems
- cooperate with a few friends

in and out   5–15 minutes   # 1–4 Fours

254

Road Building

Look at a picture book about building roads with your Fours. Then add toy road-building vehicles such as bulldozers and dump trucks to the Block Center. Have plastic hardhats for children to wear if they wish. Encourage children to build roads with blocks and to use the vehicles as they work.

Be sure to have a dishpan of little cars and plenty of other blocks so that the children can add to their road-building play.

Did the four of you build all these roads?
Where does this road go?
Is this a house? Who lives here?

Fours can

- enjoy building with blocks
- pretend in their block play

indoors   10–20 minutes   # 1–4 Fours

255

Fours can

- use their imaginations
- build with many types of blocks

Shoe Boxes as Blocks

Bring in some empty shoe boxes and place them in the Block Center. Watch to see how children use them as they play. Encourage your Fours to use the boxes in many ways—to stack, to use as cars or trucks, to load blocks into.

If children are interested, they can decorate the boxes to turn them into accessories for the Block Center. For example, they might want to make a house for small dolls or a car. Help them take the boxes to the Art Center where they can use art materials and then return the finished box to the Block Center if they wish.

Remove the boxes when children lose interest and bring something else that is new into the Block Center.

🏠 indoors   🕐 5–30 minutes   # 1–6 Fours

256

Fours can

- pretend in their block play
- count from 1 to 10 but not perfectly

The Longest Train

Read *The Little Engine That Could* with a small group of Fours. Talk about how long the train is. Count as many cars as the children can count together.

Denise and Cathy, you counted 10 cars in that train. If you count the caboose, there are 11 cars. That must have been a very heavy train to pull up the mountain!

Encourage interested Fours to use big cardboard blocks to make "little engines that could." Help them count out blocks and put them in a row to make a train. Let them make trains of any length. Show them how to push the trains from the back to see if they will move. Allow your Fours to add dolls and stuffed animals to put on each car.

🏠 indoors   🕐 10–20 minutes   # 1–8 Fours

257

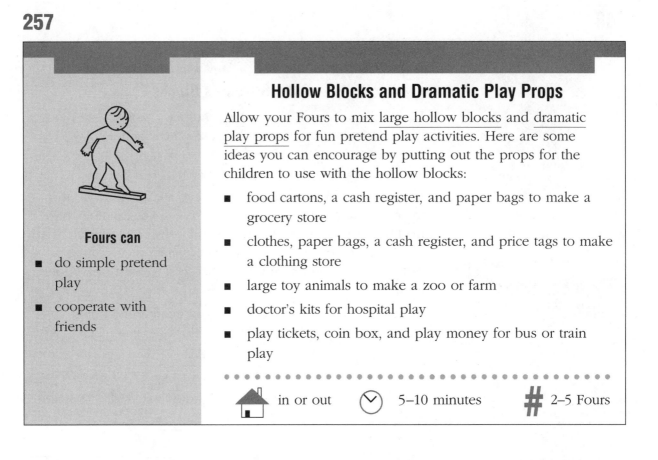

Fours can

- do simple pretend play
- cooperate with friends

Hollow Blocks and Dramatic Play Props

Allow your Fours to mix large hollow blocks and dramatic play props for fun pretend play activities. Here are some ideas you can encourage by putting out the props for the children to use with the hollow blocks:

- food cartons, a cash register, and paper bags to make a grocery store
- clothes, paper bags, a cash register, and price tags to make a clothing store
- large toy animals to make a zoo or farm
- doctor's kits for hospital play
- play tickets, coin box, and play money for bus or train play

🏠 in or out   🕐 5–10 minutes   # 2–5 Fours

258

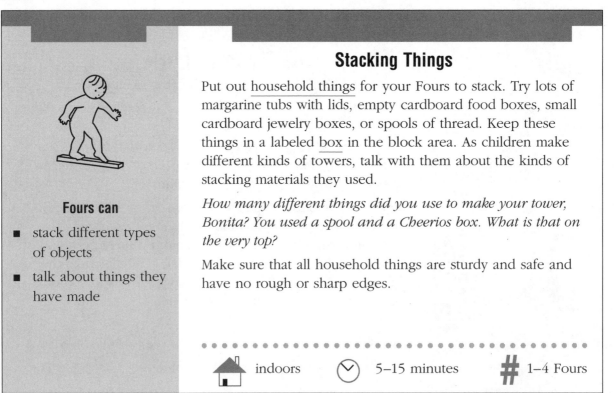

Fours can

- stack different types of objects
- talk about things they have made

Stacking Things

Put out household things for your Fours to stack. Try lots of margarine tubs with lids, empty cardboard food boxes, small cardboard jewelry boxes, or spools of thread. Keep these things in a labeled box in the block area. As children make different kinds of towers, talk with them about the kinds of stacking materials they used.

How many different things did you use to make your tower, Bonita? You used a spool and a Cheerios box. What is that on the very top?

Make sure that all household things are sturdy and safe and have no rough or sharp edges.

🏠 indoors   🕐 5–15 minutes   # 1–4 Fours

259

Building a Big House

Work with any interested Fours to build a house that they can pretend to live in. Make an outline with long wooden blocks for the outside walls. Leave an opening for the door. Have the children build up the walls. Help them think of what they need inside the house.

Where is the door to your house?
How many bedrooms do you need?
Elena, you made a corner all by yourself.

At another time, try building an airport for airplanes or a parking lot for cars as a group project.

Fours can

- pretend in their block play
- share and cooperate sometimes

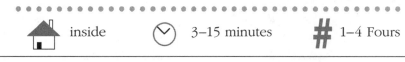

🏠 in or out   🕐 10–20 minutes   # 1–4 Fours

260

Animal Cages

Look with your Fours at books and pictures of animals in cages, pens, or other fenced-in areas. Talk about the pictures with the children. Put up some of the pictures in the Block Center so that children can look as they build. Put out some toy farm or zoo animals like the ones in the pictures. Add some toy fences, too. See how the children use all these things as they build. Talk with the children about what they are building.

Rasheed, I see you fenced in some lions.
What are you building?

Try this activity after children have visited a zoo or farm.

Fours can

- show things they know about as they build with blocks

🏠 inside   🕐 3–15 minutes   # 1–4 Fours

261

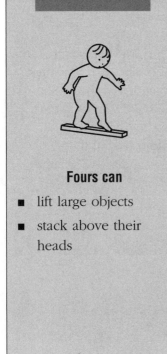

Fours can

- say how some things are same and different

Same-and-Different Blocks

Show two different blocks to your Fours. For example, show a short red rectangle and a long red rectangle. Ask them to tell you all they can about each shape. Then ask them questions to help them tell how the blocks are the same or different from each other.

Are they the same color?
Are they the same size?
Are they the same shape?
Do they both have corners or curves?

Help the Fours compare several different kinds of blocks: cylinder and square, big and little rectangles, and so on.

🏠 in or out   🕐 4–8 minutes   # 1–5 Fours

262

Fours can

- lift large objects
- stack above their heads

Big Boxes as Outdoor Blocks

Bring in eight or ten big sturdy cardboard cartons or storage boxes for your Fours to use as blocks outdoors on a dry day (or indoors in a large space). Tape the boxes closed with masking tape. Let the children stack them and build with them in many ways. Talk with them about the ways they use the boxes. They can also use these boxes as houses, cars, or boats.

You've stacked five boxes, Carlos.
What can you do to make the tower more steady?

Check all boxes to be sure they are safe and have no sharp staples. Throw away boxes when they become worn out.

🏠 in or out   🕐 3–20 minutes   # 1–6 Fours

263

Fours can

- use their bodies to lift, stretch, and crawl
- know some words for how they move

How We Move as We Build

Watch Fours as they build with wooden unit blocks in the Block Center. See how they stretch to stack blocks up high or reach out as far as they can. Talk with the children about the many different ways they move their bodies as they build.

Alicia, you stacked those blocks up high.
How are you going to take them down?
You really had to control your arm to keep from knocking down the tower.

Play a game with the children where everyone acts out familiar movements they make while using blocks, such as taking a block from a shelf, balancing a block on top of a tower, or taking a building apart.

🏠 indoors   🕐 3–15 minutes   # 1–4 Fours

264

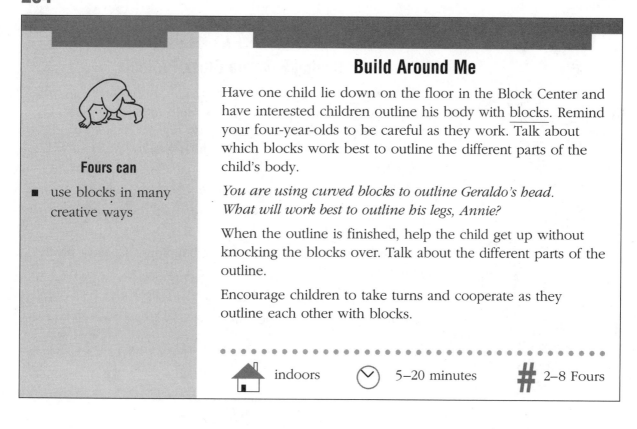

Fours can

- use blocks in many creative ways

Build Around Me

Have one child lie down on the floor in the Block Center and have interested children outline his body with blocks. Remind your four-year-olds to be careful as they work. Talk about which blocks work best to outline the different parts of the child's body.

You are using curved blocks to outline Geraldo's head.
What will work best to outline his legs, Annie?

When the outline is finished, help the child get up without knocking the blocks over. Talk about the different parts of the outline.

Encourage children to take turns and cooperate as they outline each other with blocks.

🏠 indoors   🕐 5–20 minutes   # 2–8 Fours

265

Fours can

- write a few letters
- know familiar things in their neighborhood

Making Signs for the Block Area

Display pictures of signs for your Fours to look at in the Block Center. Talk about the signs with the children. See which ones they know.

You know this sign is a stop sign, don't you, Kirsty?
Do you want to make one to put on your road?

Encourage children to make signs for their block buildings. They can use materials in the Art Center, such as sturdy paper, washable markers, ice cream sticks, and masking tape. Help them to write words if they wish.

What name do you want to put on your road, Mari?
That's your address! I can help you write it.

indoors   3–15 minutes   # 1–8 Fours

266

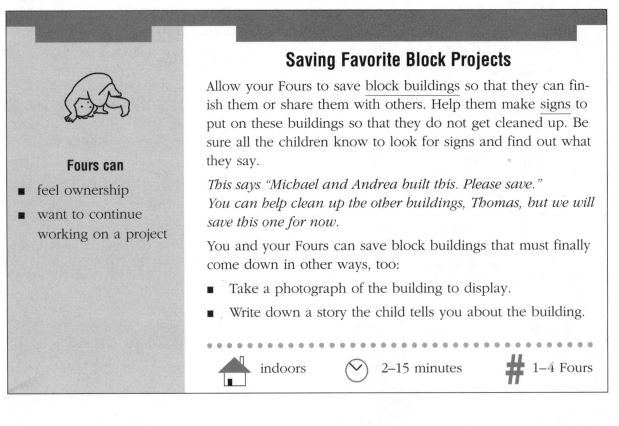

Fours can

- feel ownership
- want to continue working on a project

Saving Favorite Block Projects

Allow your Fours to save block buildings so that they can finish them or share them with others. Help them make signs to put on these buildings so that they do not get cleaned up. Be sure all the children know to look for signs and find out what they say.

This says "Michael and Andrea built this. Please save."
You can help clean up the other buildings, Thomas, but we will save this one for now.

You and your Fours can save block buildings that must finally come down in other ways, too:

- Take a photograph of the building to display.
- Write down a story the child tells you about the building.

indoors   2–15 minutes   # 1–4 Fours

267

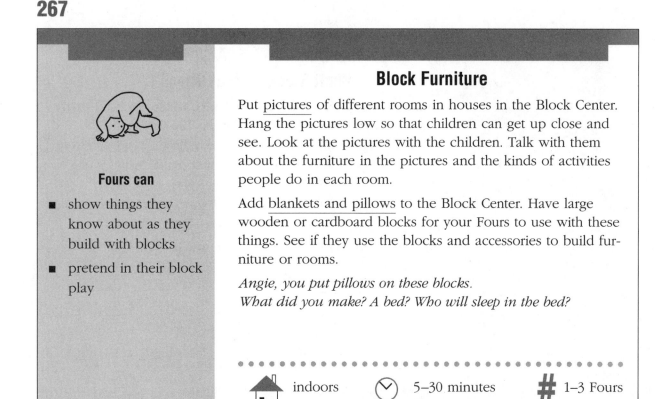

Fours can

- show things they know about as they build with blocks
- pretend in their block play

Block Furniture

Put pictures of different rooms in houses in the Block Center. Hang the pictures low so that children can get up close and see. Look at the pictures with the children. Talk with them about the furniture in the pictures and the kinds of activities people do in each room.

Add blankets and pillows to the Block Center. Have large wooden or cardboard blocks for your Fours to use with these things. See if they use the blocks and accessories to build furniture or rooms.

Angie, you put pillows on these blocks.
What did you make? A bed? Who will sleep in the bed?

indoors   5–30 minutes   # 1–3 Fours

268

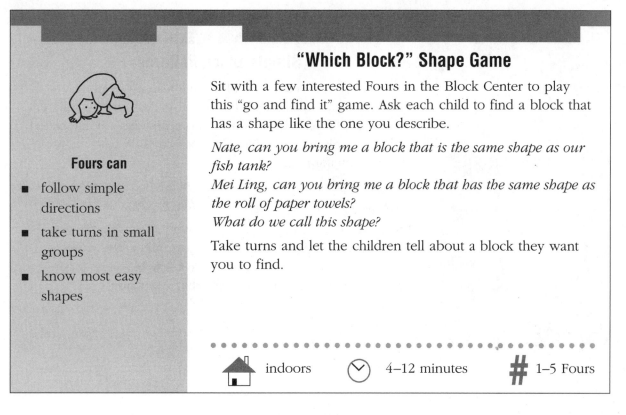

Fours can

- follow simple directions
- take turns in small groups
- know most easy shapes

"Which Block?" Shape Game

Sit with a few interested Fours in the Block Center to play this "go and find it" game. Ask each child to find a block that has a shape like the one you describe.

Nate, can you bring me a block that is the same shape as our fish tank?
Mei Ling, can you bring me a block that has the same shape as the roll of paper towels?
What do we call this shape?

Take turns and let the children tell about a block they want you to find.

indoors   4–12 minutes   # 1–5 Fours

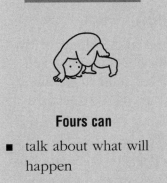

Fours can

- talk about what will happen
- balance blocks while building
- take turns in small groups

What Stacks, What Doesn't?

Build a tower with a few of your Fours, using blocks of many shapes. As you add each block, look at the tower and the block you are going to add. Talk about the different ways the block could be added. Help the children guess when a block will balance and when it won't.

Jamal, do you think this cylinder will stay on top of this triangle or will it fall? Let's try and see. Oh! What happened?

Take turns adding blocks and guessing what will balance.

indoors   3–12 minutes   # 1–4 Fours

270

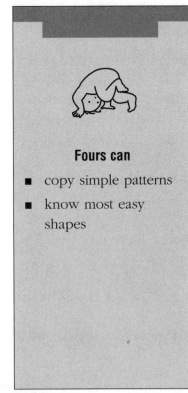

Fours can

- copy simple patterns
- know most easy shapes

Simple Block Patterns

Sort square and rectangular block shapes into several dishpans with your Fours. Then put a pattern of one square, one rectangle, one square on the floor and ask any interested children to place blocks just like you did. Talk with them about following patterns.

Emily, I'm putting a square, a rectangle and a square on the floor. Can you make a pattern just like mine?

Encourage children to make their own patterns that you and their friends can follow. See if they can repeat the patterns they have made. You can also stack a few blocks in a pattern and see if the children can copy what you made.

inside   3–5 minutes   # 1–4 Fours

271

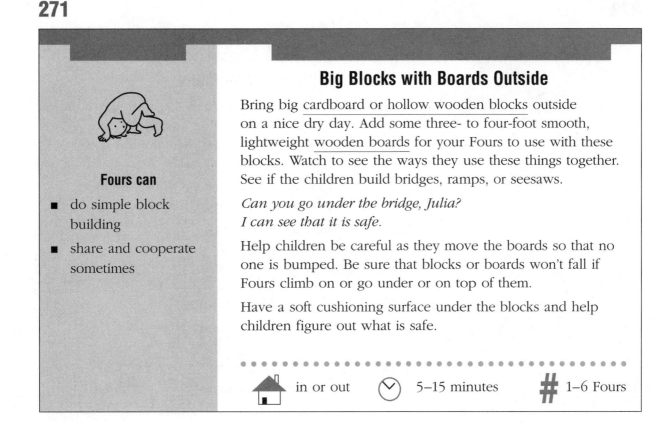

Fours can

- do simple block building
- share and cooperate sometimes

Big Blocks with Boards Outside

Bring big cardboard or hollow wooden blocks outside on a nice dry day. Add some three- to four-foot smooth, lightweight wooden boards for your Fours to use with these blocks. Watch to see the ways they use these things together. See if the children build bridges, ramps, or seesaws.

Can you go under the bridge, Julia?
I can see that it is safe.

Help children be careful as they move the boards so that no one is bumped. Be sure that blocks or boards won't fall if Fours climb on or go under or on top of them.

Have a soft cushioning surface under the blocks and help children figure out what is safe.

in or out   5–15 minutes   # 1–6 Fours

272

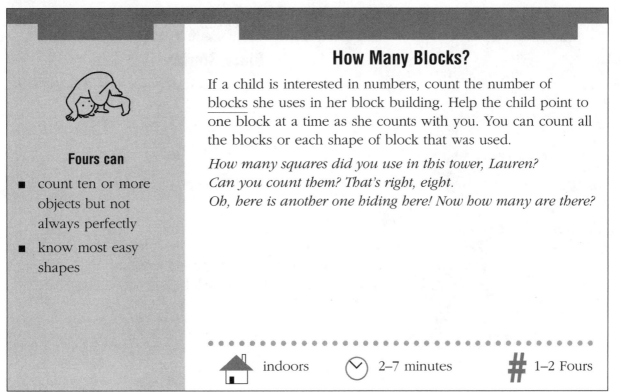

Fours can

- count ten or more objects but not always perfectly
- know most easy shapes

How Many Blocks?

If a child is interested in numbers, count the number of blocks she uses in her block building. Help the child point to one block at a time as she counts with you. You can count all the blocks or each shape of block that was used.

How many squares did you use in this tower, Lauren?
Can you count them? That's right, eight.
Oh, here is another one hiding here! Now how many are there?

indoors   2–7 minutes   # 1–2 Fours

273

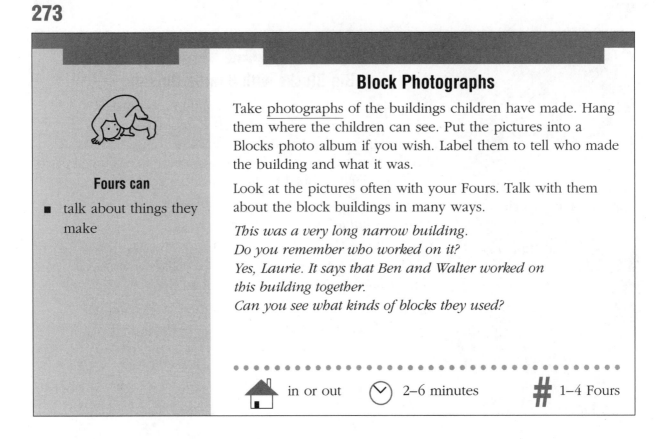

Fours can

- talk about things they make

Block Photographs

Take <u>photographs</u> of the buildings children have made. Hang them where the children can see. Put the pictures into a Blocks photo album if you wish. Label them to tell who made the building and what it was.

Look at the pictures often with your Fours. Talk with them about the block buildings in many ways.

This was a very long narrow building.
Do you remember who worked on it?
Yes, Laurie. It says that Ben and Walter worked on
this building together.
Can you see what kinds of blocks they used?

🏠 in or out   🕐 2–6 minutes   # 1–4 Fours

274

Fours can

- talk about things they make

- enjoy having you write down and read stories they tell

Block Stories

When a child has built something with <u>blocks</u>, see if he will tell you something about what he did. Ask questions to help him say more.

What did you build, Tyler?
Oh, a house for Daddy and the dog.
What do they like to do in the house?
The dog jumps out?
Show me how he does that.

Try tape recording or writing down the things a child says about his block building. Put them in the Block Center and play them back or read them back for the child to hear.

🏠 inside   🕐 2–4 minutes   # 1–2 Fours

275

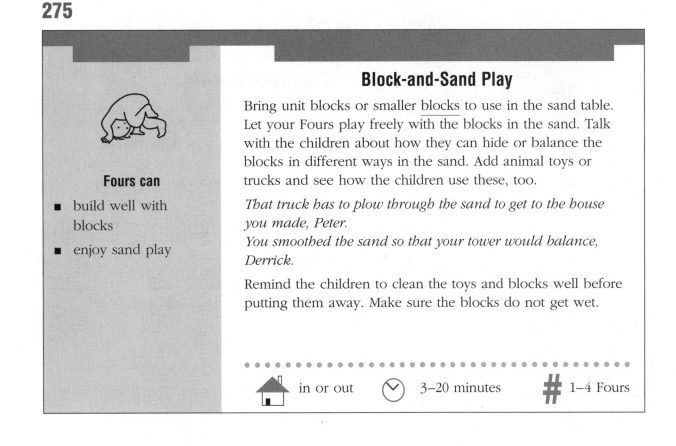

Fours can

- build well with blocks
- enjoy sand play

Block-and-Sand Play

Bring unit blocks or smaller <u>blocks</u> to use in the sand table. Let your Fours play freely with the blocks in the sand. Talk with the children about how they can hide or balance the blocks in different ways in the sand. Add animal toys or trucks and see how the children use these, too.

That truck has to plow through the sand to get to the house you made, Peter.
You smoothed the sand so that your tower would balance, Derrick.

Remind the children to clean the toys and blocks well before putting them away. Make sure the blocks do not get wet.

🏠 in or out   🕐 3–20 minutes   # 1–4 Fours

276

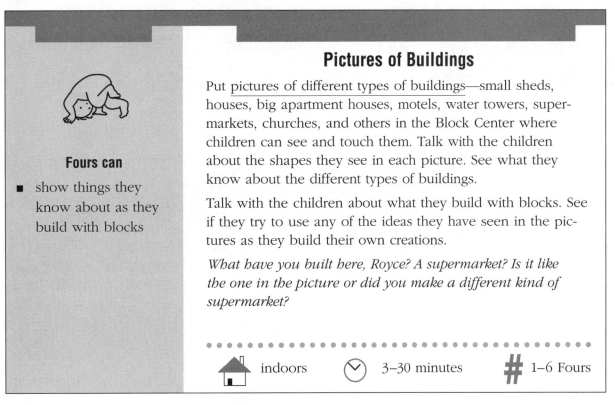

Fours can

- show things they know about as they build with blocks

Pictures of Buildings

Put <u>pictures of different types of buildings</u>—small sheds, houses, big apartment houses, motels, water towers, supermarkets, churches, and others in the Block Center where children can see and touch them. Talk with the children about the shapes they see in each picture. See what they know about the different types of buildings.

Talk with the children about what they build with blocks. See if they try to use any of the ideas they have seen in the pictures as they build their own creations.

What have you built here, Royce? A supermarket? Is it like the one in the picture or did you make a different kind of supermarket?

🏠 indoors   🕐 3–30 minutes   # 1–6 Fours

Fours can

- show things they know about as they build with blocks

Looking at Buildings

Take your Fours on a short "Looking at Buildings" walk. Help them see the different parts of the buildings. Look at and talk about the buildings' floors, steps, windows, walls, and other parts. Encourage children to feel the buildings, too—to run their fingers along the bricks or feel the sharp corners in a wall.

As children build with blocks, talk with them about what they have built. See if they tell you about the parts of the buildings that they have created.

You made a sharp corner here, Glenda. What are you working on now? Oh. Steps are tricky to build, aren't they?

in or out   10–30 minutes   1–20 Fours

Block Center

- Find a corner for blocks away from doorways so people do not have to walk through it to get to other areas.

- Make the Block Center big enough for at least four children to play in with plenty of space to build and move.

- If too many children want to build at the same time, help children sign up on a waiting list to get a turn.

- Store blocks and the toys used with blocks on open shelves no taller than the children.

- Label each place on the shelves with a picture of what goes there. Draw outlines of blocks or paste cutouts of the blocks near the front of the shelf and show the block with the long side to the front.

- At clean-up time, show children where block shapes belong by putting a block in the right place and having them copy you.

- Keep small people, animals, little trucks, and airplanes to use with blocks in separate boxes, each labeled with a picture of the toys. Include enough people for large families and multiracial figures, older adults, and people with disabilities.

- Put the heavier blocks and play buildings on the lower shelves, so that children can take them out and put them back by themselves.

- Have a large flat rug to build on in the block area.

- Have different kinds of blocks: many wooden unit blocks, large cardboard or large wooden hollow blocks, various colorful plastic building blocks. Keep all of these organized in their own spaces.

- Put up pictures of real buildings and buildings under construction to add interest and new ideas. Include men and women construction workers of different ages and races.

- Show children how to take the blocks off the shelves carefully and put them back without knocking the buildings down. Show children how proud you are of them when they are careful.

- Encourage children to come back and finish their buildings later, or to save a favorite project for others to enjoy.

- Have some block play outdoors. Let children help take blocks outdoors in a wagon and later put them back.

Materials and Notes

Dramatic Play

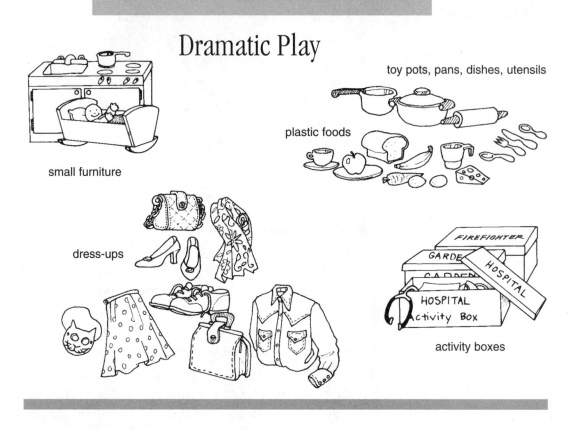

small furniture

toy pots, pans, dishes, utensils

plastic foods

dress-ups

FIREFIGHTER

GARDE

HOSPITAL

HOSPITAL
Activity Box

activity boxes

- Most of the activity ideas for younger and older Fours can be used with either age group. This is because they are open-ended and can be challenging to children with a wide range of abilities.
- Have many props for Fours to use in their pretend play. Add to these often.
- Have more than one of the most popular toys to prevent fights about sharing.
- Use plastic hats whenever possible and wash all dress-ups weekly. If lice is a problem in your group, omit hats from all activities.
- Encourage both girls and boys to enjoy the Dramatic Play Center.
- Make sure that all toys and props in the Dramatic Play Center are clean and safe for children to use. Shorten dress-ups, disinfect shoes, and wash things regularly.
- Add activity boxes to encourage different types of pretend play. You will find ideas for pretend play activity boxes in the activities in this section.
- Use field trips, books, pictures, and visitors to the classroom to give children the information they need to pretend about many topics.
- Ask parents to help in collecting things for use in pretend play. Send home lists of the kinds of things you need, such as dress-ups, old pots and pans, or empty containers from healthful foods.

Activity Checklist

Dramatic Play

Dramatic play for Fours includes pretend play with dolls, stuffed animals, housekeeping toys, community helper props, and other things children use when they act out what they see happening every day. Fours also enjoy props about fantasy or super characters they learn about. Adults can help Fours get new information for play by providing field trips, reading books, inviting visitors to talk with children, and providing props for work roles and adventure. Fours enjoy make-believe play on their own, but sometimes need adult help to solve problems.

Check for each age group

	48–54 months	54–60 months
1. Dramatic Play Center is set up and available for children to choose freely several hours daily.	❐	❐
2. Center has small housekeeping furniture and props for playing house, job and community helper play, and fantasy.	❐	❐
3. Props are clearly organized on low shelves and in storage areas of small play furniture.	❐	❐
4. All materials are sturdy, safe, and clean.	❐	❐
5. All children are encouraged to use pretend play materials in their own ways.	❐	❐
6. Additional toys and props are stored but handy so that they can be taken out often to be used.	❐	❐
7. Dolls are of different races, both male and female. Props from many cultures, such as cooking utensils, pretend foods, dress-ups, and doll clothes, are included for everyday play.	❐	❐
8. Adult helps encourage pretend play by adding new props, reading stories, talking about ideas with children, and providing field trips.	❐	❐
9. Adult supervises pretend play by helping children solve problems and guiding play so it does not become dangerous.	❐	❐
10. Props for pretend play are used outdoors as well as indoors.	❐	❐

278

Fours can

- cooperate with one or two friends in pretend play

- pretend about things they know

Play House

Set up a simple playhouse in a corner of the room. (See Dramatic Play Center Ideas on page 278.) Include small furniture, such as a table and chairs, a low, open shelf, a doll bed, and a pretend stove and sink. Add dolls, pots and pans, and an unbreakable tea set. To help Fours at clean-up time, put picture/word labels of toys on the shelf and on other places where things go.

Let your Fours play freely in this playhouse. Talk with the children about their play and even join in the play if you wish.

You are putting on some fancy clothes, Dennis.
What are you going to do?

Be careful—do not take over the play or interrupt the way it is going unless things are getting out of control.

🏠 indoors 🕐 5–60 minutes # 1–6 Fours

279

Fours can

- enjoy playing dress-up as they pretend

Dress-Up Fun

Collect easy-to-put-on men's and women's clothes for your Fours to use in dress-up play. Include hats, shoes, dresses, skirts, jackets, pants, and purses. Shorten clothes to make them safe. Let children put on these big people's clothes and pretend in their own way. Have a large, unbreakable mirror nearby for children to use.

You and Louise are all dressed up, Kendra.
Did you button those buttons yourself?

Make sure that there are enough clothes for all who want to play, but don't put out too many clothes at once. Then you can add new interest to dress-ups by changing the clothes you add, and by adding the uniforms of community helpers the children are interested in.

🏠 in or out 🕐 5–20 minutes # 1–6 Fours

280

Fours can

- cooperate with one or two friends in pretend play
- pretend about things they know

Telephone Talk

Have several real or toy telephones in the Dramatic Play Center. Let the children play with these freely. Encourage Fours to talk to each other on the telephones. Enjoy their telephone conversations.

Hi, Ramon. Who are you talking with on the phone?
With the doctor? Is it an emergency?
You'll have to tell me about what he says!

Also add toy walkie-talkies to the Dramatic Play Center and show children how they can pretend with them.

🏠 indoors 🕐 1–5 minutes # 1–4 Fours

281

Fours can

- cooperate with one or two friends in pretend play
- use realistic props in their pretend play

Kitchen Play

Make a kitchen play activity box. Include kitchen things, such as sturdy plastic knives, forks, and spoons, a potato masher, a strainer, big cooking spoons, cooks' hats and aprons, measuring cups, and a whisk. Put in pictures of people using some of these things, too.

Look at and talk about the pictures and all the things with your Fours. Then hang up the pictures and put the things into the Dramatic Play Center. Let the children play and have fun.

What do you stir with a whisk, Jana? Peanut butter? I bet that's hard to stir!

🏠 in or out 🕐 5–20 minutes # 1–6 Fours

282

Fours can

- cooperate with one or two friends in pretend play

- use realistic props in their pretend play

Changing Baby

Make a changing baby activity box with squares of cloth that will make doll-sized diapers, a few newborn-sized rubber pants, and empty baby powder and lotion bottles. Look at all the things in the box with your Fours. Talk about what each thing is and what it's for. Show the children how you diaper a baby doll. Then put the box out for the Fours to use on their own. Children can use masking tape to hold diapers on babies.

How often do you need to change your baby, Sandy?
A hundred times? Your baby must wet a lot!

This is a good activity to try when one of your Fours has a new baby brother or sister.

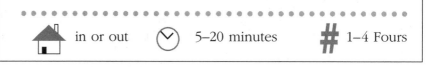

🏠 in or out   🕐 5–20 minutes   # 1–4 Fours

283

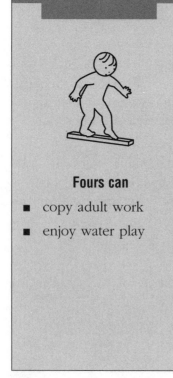

Fours can

- copy adult work
- enjoy water play

Laundry Day

Tie a rope about 2' high between two trees outside. On a warm, sunny day, put buckets of soapy water out in the middle of the play area along with some clean rags or small items of clothing. Let the children wash and then hang things up on the line to dry. Show the children how to wring out the clothes. Also help them use clothespins. Make sure the children wear waterproof aprons if they need to stay dry.

Carl, you're washing the doll's dress. It's so nice and clean.
Now what will you do with it?

Remind the children to check on the clothes several times during the next few hours to see if they are dry.

🏠 outdoors   🕐 5–15 minutes   # 1–6 Fours

284

Fours can

- use realistic props in their pretend play

Sandbox Kitchen

On a nice day, check to see that the sandbox is clean. Then bring out a box of pots, pans, unbreakable dishes, and spoons. Make sure there is a smooth board to place things on in the sandbox.

Let the children play house in the sandbox in their own way. If the sand is damp, show them how to make a cake by patting damp sand into a pan, turning the pan over onto the board, and carefully removing the pan.

After play is over, have the children help you wash the things and put them back in the box.

🏠 outdoors   🕐 10–45 minutes   # 1–6 Fours

285

Fours can

- copy adult work

Cleaning Day

On a nice day, take out some small brooms, rags, sponges, and a bucket of water. Show interested children how to dust and wash equipment, walls, sidewalks, or outdoor furniture, and then let them play freely with the materials.

Tricia, you are really cleaning that slide.
You can dry it with this old towel.

Try this indoors without the water. Or, if you are willing to teach your Fours to clean up a wet floor, add a little water too.

🏠 in or out   🕐 3–15 minutes   # 1–10 Fours

286

Fours can

- pretend about familiar things

Shower Time

Put a cardboard box big enough for a child to stand in into the Dramatic Play Center. Make sure that you leave one side open so that you can supervise.

Add clean old towels, some clean, empty shampoo bottles, and a wooden block that the children can use as a bar of soap.

Talk with the children about how all these things are used at shower or bath time. Then let them make-believe in the house with the shower as part of their play.

Did you take a shower, Aretha? How did you make the water come out? Which do you take at home, a shower or bath?

🏠 indoors   🕐 2–7 minutes   # 1–2 Fours

287

Fours can

- cooperate with one or two friends in pretend play
- copy adult work

Baby's Bath Time

Take some washable dolls outdoors. Also take out some dishpans with warm, soapy water and some washcloths and towels. Make sure your Fours wash their hands before they play in the water.

Let your Four undress a doll and bathe the baby. Give him a towel to dry the baby doll, too.

Encourage children to use these props in their own ways. Let the pretend play take off in the direction the children want. If you have two children using the same dishpan, see that each one has a doll and a washcloth. Remember, waterproof aprons help keep children dry.

🏠 outdoors   🕐 3–14 minutes   # 1–2 Fours per dishpan

288

Car Wash

Take an activity box with cars and trucks outdoors. Put some water, small rags, and dish soap into some dishpans. Make sure that all interested children wash their hands before playing with the water. Let a few children at a time wash the cars. After the cars are washed, the children can let them dry in the sun. Be sure they are dry before putting them away.

Talk about who washes the car when it's dirty. Collect pictures of people washing cars and talk about them with your Fours.

On another day, have Fours help you wash wheel toys that need cleaning.

Fours can

- copy adult work
- pretend about familiar things

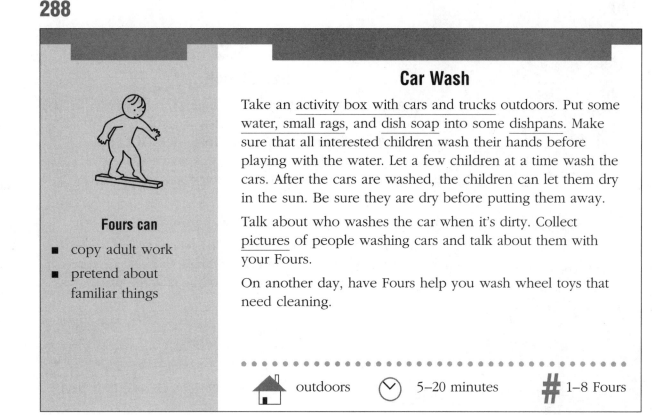

🏠 outdoors   🕐 5–20 minutes   # 1–8 Fours

289

Garbage Truck

Read the children a book that has pictures of a garbage collector's truck. Talk about what garbage collectors do. Then show them how they can make a garbage truck to clean up the yard. Put a cardboard box into a small wagon and have the children help clean up the yard. Have them wear gloves to be garbage collectors, and have them wash their hands after the job is done.

Does this toy go in the trash, Sammy? No? Where should we put it? What about this old paper towel that blew away? That's right. It goes in the trash.

When the children clean up after a snack or meal, tell them they are doing clean-up work like garbage collectors.

Help children pretend to be recyclers, too.

Fours can

- copy adult work

🏠 outdoors   🕐 5–10 minutes   # 1–6 Fours

290

Fours can

- cooperate with one or two friends in pretend play

Gas Station

Put together in an activity box the things your Fours will need to play gas station—pieces of hose 1 to 2 yards long with nozzles attached, and sturdy plastic fix-it-tools. With the children, look at a book that shows things that happen at a gas station. Ask questions to help your Fours say what they know about gas stations.

What else happens at the gas station, Tanya?

Secure one end of several hoses to the fence outside to show the children where they can bring riding toys to be fixed or filled up. Add the other things and let the children play.

🏠 in or out   🕐 5–20 minutes   # 1–6 Fours

291

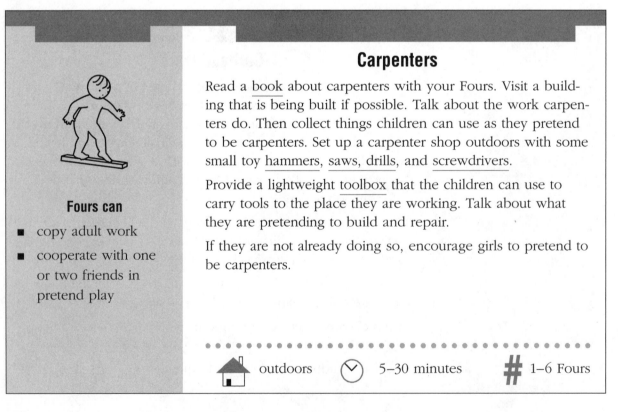

Fours can

- copy adult work
- cooperate with one or two friends in pretend play

Carpenters

Read a book about carpenters with your Fours. Visit a building that is being built if possible. Talk about the work carpenters do. Then collect things children can use as they pretend to be carpenters. Set up a carpenter shop outdoors with some small toy hammers, saws, drills, and screwdrivers.

Provide a lightweight toolbox that the children can use to carry tools to the place they are working. Talk about what they are pretending to build and repair.

If they are not already doing so, encourage girls to pretend to be carpenters.

🏠 outdoors   🕐 5–30 minutes   # 1–6 Fours

292

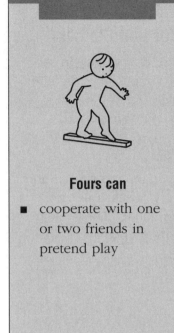

Fours can

- cooperate with one or two friends in pretend play

Take a Trip

Read a story or show a picture about taking a trip by car, bus, or train. Talk with your Fours about any trips they have taken.

Kim, how did you get to Florida? You took the train. Tell us about your trip. Has anyone else ever slept in a bed on a train? Jerome says he sleeps in the car.

Help interested Fours make a car, bus, or train to use when taking pretend trips. Use small chairs or cardboard blocks for seats. Add a steering wheel if you have one. Have purses, tote bags, or old luggage in the dress-up area to pack for the trip. Encourage them to make their own paper tickets and money for the trip. Have the children take turns being the driver. Use a waiting list and have more than one vehicle if there are problems with sharing this role.

🏠 in or out   🕐 10–40 minutes   # 1–8 Fours

293

Fours can

- cooperate with one or two friends in pretend play
- pretend about familiar experiences

Playing Doctors and Nurses

Put out an activity box of doctor and nurse things for your Fours to play with. Use only safe things, such as a toy or real stethoscope, a flashlight, pretend thermometer, short strips of gauze bandage material, plastic bandage strips or tape, and paper with pencils to keep records or write prescriptions. Do not put in bottles of candy pills because you do not want children ever to take medicine alone. Encourage children to remember and talk about visiting the doctor.

Why did you visit the doctor last week, Monique? Did she use a stethoscope like this?

To help your Fours think of more play ideas, read books about going to the doctor with the children.

🏠 in or out   🕐 10–40 minutes   # 1–6 Fours

294

Fours can

- copy adult work
- pretend about familiar experiences

Dressing Dolls and Caring for Doll Clothes

Buy or make simple doll clothes that are easy to put on. Ask parents or volunteers to help with this. Have clothes that are loose or that fasten with buttons or snaps. Keep these in a dishpan on a low shelf for Fours to use. Encourage your Fours to dress babies, but don't be surprised if you find them undressed again very quickly.

Add a toy ironing board with iron. Buy a pretend washer and dryer or make a set out of sturdy grocery boxes. Talk about washing, drying, and folding clothes for babies. Then watch to see how children use these things in their play.

You put all the doll clothes into the laundry basket, Damara? What are you planning to do?

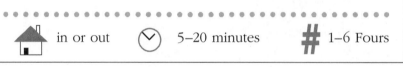 in or out   5–20 minutes   # 1–6 Fours

295

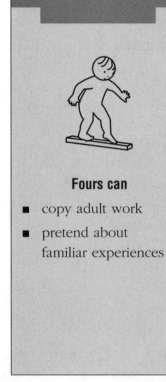

Fours can

- copy adult work
- pretend about familiar experiences

Dentist Play

Make a dentist activity box with some unbreakable hand mirrors, a book about going to the dentist, and pictures of toothbrushing.

Talk with the children about the dentist and what he or she does. Let the children look at your teeth. Have them look at their own teeth in the mirrors. If the children have tooth-brushes, have them brush their teeth and see if their teeth are clean after they brush. When they brush, have them look in the sink to see if anything brushed out of their teeth.

Encourage children to pretend to be dentists for dolls and toy animals. Help them figure out how to make a dentist's chair or a waiting room. Supply rubber gloves, dentist's masks, and other props to use with the dolls.

indoors   5–30 minutes   # 1–6 Fours

296

Fours can

- copy adult work
- pretend about familiar experiences

Painters

Make a painter's activity box, with big brushes, paint rollers with pans, buckets, paint scrapers, and plastic aprons or large men's shirts. Include pictures of people painting houses, furniture, or fences for children to look at. Arrange a field trip to a place where painters are working and let your Fours watch.

Talk with the children about the work painters do. Take the activity box outdoors and let the Fours use water for paint and pretend to be painters.

I see you have a crate to stand on so that you can reach up high to paint, Maria. Do you remember what the painters stood on to paint up high? That's right, It was called a scaffold.

🏠 outdoors   🕐 5–30 minutes   # 1–8 Fours

297

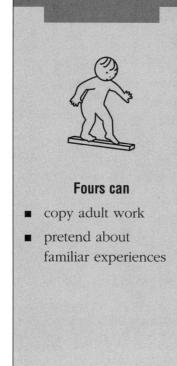

Fours can

- copy adult work
- pretend about familiar experiences

Firefighters

Read a book about firefighters with your Fours. Take a field trip to a fire station, too. Then put out a firefighter activity box for your Fours to use in make-believe play. Have in the box some short pieces of hose, firefighter hats, a lightweight toy plastic hammer to use as an ax, some firefighter badges made of aluminum foil over cardboard, and a bell. The children can use a wagon as the fire truck and put out pretend fires on the playground.

Ring the fire bell, Maura! The big climber is on fire!

Talk about fire safety with your Fours and remind them that real fires are dangerous.

🏠 outdoors   🕐 5–30 minutes   # 1–10 Fours

298

Fours can

- copy adult work
- pretend about familiar experiences
- cooperate with friends

Post Office

Collect used envelopes, post cards, and lots of unopened junk mail. Put these into a post office activity box with bags that can be used for mail bags, smaller boxes to sort mail, and free stamps that come in junk mail. Talk with the children about the post office and what its workers do. Visit the post office and read books about how mail is delivered.

Let the children pretend with the things in the post office box. See if they will put stamps on envelopes, deliver mail to different people in the room, and open the letters they get. Make sure to use post office words, such as *address, deliver,* and *cancel.*

On a special day when cards are sent, such as Valentine's Day, Mother's Day, or Father's Day, have the children use the real post office to mail home a card that they have made.

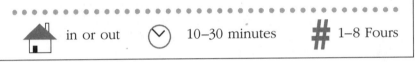

in or out   10–30 minutes   # 1–8 Fours

299

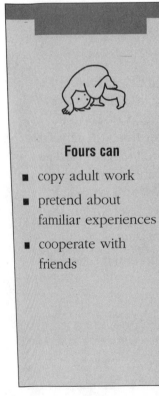

Fours can

- copy adult work
- pretend about familiar experiences
- cooperate with friends

Playing Office

With your Fours, visit someone who works in an office. A short trip can be made to the office in your own building. Help the children see the kinds of equipment people use as they do office work, such as typewriters, pens and paper, calculators, telephones, or computers. Read books with your Fours about what office workers do. See what they know about this kind of work from their own experiences.

Put together an office activity box. Put office envelopes and stationery, a small file box, a rubber stamp and stamp pad, and a pad and pencil in the box. Make a pretend computer out of a cardboard box and add toy or real typewriters.

Encourage your Fours to pretend about working in an office as they play in their own way.

indoors   10–30 minutes   # 1–8 Fours

300

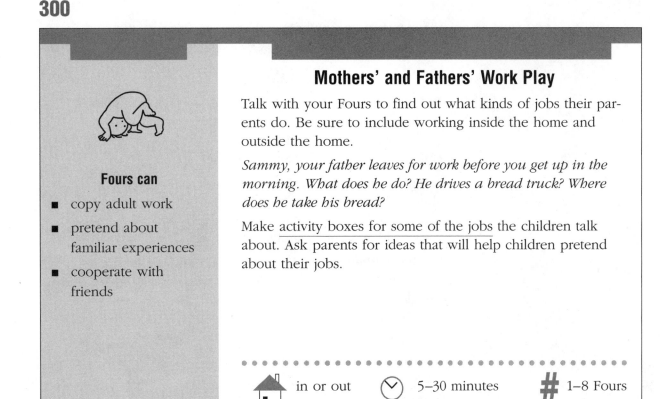

Fours can

- copy adult work
- pretend about familiar experiences
- cooperate with friends

Mothers' and Fathers' Work Play

Talk with your Fours to find out what kinds of jobs their parents do. Be sure to include working inside the home and outside the home.

Sammy, your father leaves for work before you get up in the morning. What does he do? He drives a bread truck? Where does he take his bread?

Make activity boxes for some of the jobs the children talk about. Ask parents for ideas that will help children pretend about their jobs.

🏠 in or out   🕐 5–30 minutes   # 1–8 Fours

301

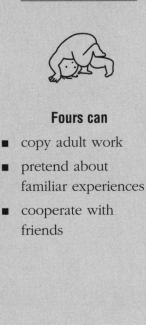

Fours can

- copy adult work
- pretend about familiar experiences
- cooperate with friends

Cleaning House

Put together a house-cleaning activity box with things you use to clean the house. Include dustrags, a spray bottle of water, an apron, rubber gloves, a small broom and a dustpan, a small mop, and a toy vacuum cleaner. Add clean, empty containers that held household cleaners. (Be sure these are completely rinsed.) Let interested Fours pretend about cleaning the housekeeping area and other parts of the room.

Talk with children about the things people clean in their houses. Write down some of the things they say on a big piece of chart paper and read their ideas back to them.

What else do you help your mom and dad with when they are cleaning up, Desmond?

🏠 indoors   🕐 10–30 minutes   # 1–8 Fours

302

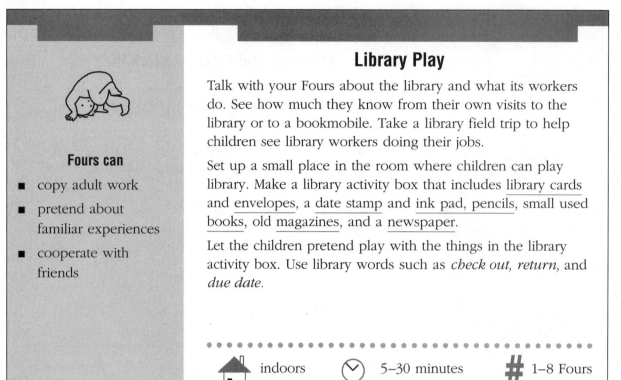

Fours can

- copy adult work
- pretend about familiar experiences
- cooperate with friends

Library Play

Talk with your Fours about the library and what its workers do. See how much they know from their own visits to the library or to a bookmobile. Take a library field trip to help children see library workers doing their jobs.

Set up a small place in the room where children can play library. Make a library activity box that includes library cards and envelopes, a date stamp and ink pad, pencils, small used books, old magazines, and a newspaper.

Let the children pretend play with the things in the library activity box. Use library words such as *check out, return,* and *due date.*

🏠 indoors   🕐 5–30 minutes   # 1–8 Fours

303

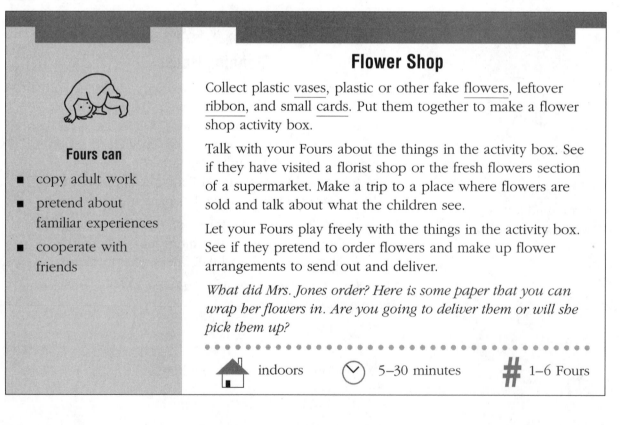

Fours can

- copy adult work
- pretend about familiar experiences
- cooperate with friends

Flower Shop

Collect plastic vases, plastic or other fake flowers, leftover ribbon, and small cards. Put them together to make a flower shop activity box.

Talk with your Fours about the things in the activity box. See if they have visited a florist shop or the fresh flowers section of a supermarket. Make a trip to a place where flowers are sold and talk about what the children see.

Let your Fours play freely with the things in the activity box. See if they pretend to order flowers and make up flower arrangements to send out and deliver.

What did Mrs. Jones order? Here is some paper that you can wrap her flowers in. Are you going to deliver them or will she pick them up?

🏠 indoors   🕐 5–30 minutes   # 1–6 Fours

304

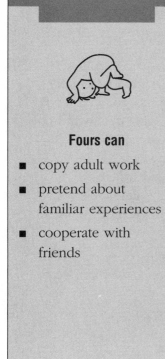

Fours can

- pretend about fantasy
- cooperate in play with friends

Masks

Save masks from Halloween costumes to put into a masks activity box. Make sure the masks aren't scary ones. Bring the masks out a few months after Halloween time. Talk about Halloween memories and what the mask faces are supposed to be.

Who wore this rabbit face at Halloween?
That's right, Jonah, you did.

Let your Fours pretend in their own ways with the masks. Have an unbreakable mirror nearby so that children can see how they look. When the play is done, help the children put the masks away to save for another day.

Try painting faces for pretend play, too. Use face paints or special Halloween makeup that washes off easily.

🏠 in or out   🕐 5–20 minutes   # 1–15 Fours

305

Fours can

- copy adult work
- pretend about familiar experiences
- cooperate with friends

Rescue Squad Play

Put blankets, a first aid kit with plastic bandage strips and gauze bandages, a flashlight, and a toy walkie-talkie in a rescue squad activity box. Read a book to your Fours about the job that rescue squad workers do. Visit your local rescue squad or see if an ambulance will visit your class. Explain about some of the things rescue workers do.

Why do you think they need blankets, Brooke?
Yes, that's right. They want to keep people warm.
Why do you think rescue workers need flashlights?

Encourage the children to pretend in their own way with the things in the rescue squad activity box. Add toy dolls and animals, wagons and a pretend stretcher for the Fours to use.

🏠 in or out   🕐 5–30 minutes   # 1–8 Fours

306

Fours can

- pretend about familiar experiences
- cooperate with friends

Birthday Party Play

Put a collection of paper or plastic party <u>plates</u>, plastic <u>spoons</u>, bright paper <u>napkins</u>, streamers, <u>party hats</u>, and some <u>birthday cards</u> in a birthday party activity box.

Talk with interested children about when and how these things are used. Encourage them to talk about birthday parties they remember. Then let them pretend with the things in the activity box in their own way, either with friends or dolls.

Whose birthday is it today? Elizabeth's? How old are you, Elizabeth? What are all of you planning for Elizabeth's birthday?

🏠 indoors   🕐 5–30 minutes   # 1–6 Fours

307

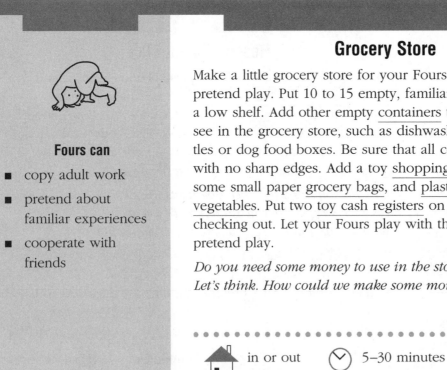

Fours can

- copy adult work
- pretend about familiar experiences
- cooperate with friends

Grocery Store

Make a little grocery store for your Fours to use in their pretend play. Put 10 to 15 empty, familiar <u>food containers</u> on a low shelf. Add other empty <u>containers</u> that children would see in the grocery store, such as dishwashing detergent bottles or dog food boxes. Be sure that all containers are safe, with no sharp edges. Add a toy <u>shopping cart</u>, a <u>wagon</u>, some small paper <u>grocery bags</u>, and <u>plastic fruits</u> and <u>vegetables</u>. Put two <u>toy cash registers</u> on a little table for checking out. Let your Fours play with these props in their pretend play.

Do you need some money to use in the store, Andrew? Let's think. How could we make some money for you to use?

🏠 in or out   🕐 5–30 minutes   # 1–6 Fours

308

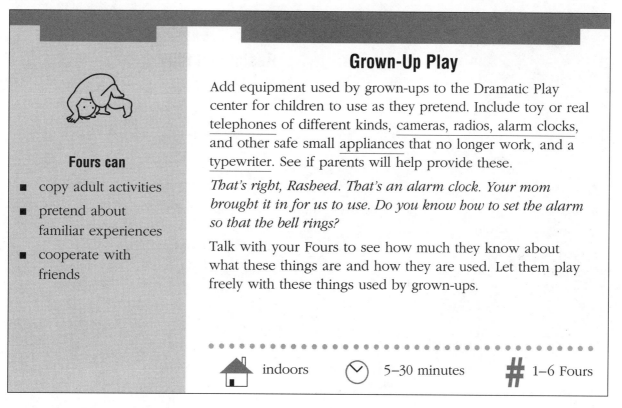

Fours can

- pretend about familiar experiences
- cooperate with friends

Fancy Tea Party Play

Read a picture <u>book</u> about a tea party. Talk about things people use when they have tea parties—teapots, kettles to heat water, teacups and saucers, and so on. Have a real tea party with the children. Use a <u>teapot</u> to serve <u>juice</u>, <u>milk</u>, or even <u>mint tea</u>. Serve <u>sandwiches</u> that are cut up into little shapes.

Make a fancy tea party activity box for your Fours to use. Include a pretty, unbreakable <u>tea set</u>, a toy <u>kettle</u>, fancy <u>place mats</u>, a small <u>vase</u>, and artificial or dry <u>flowers</u>. Encourage children to dress up while they pretend.

Children can make play-dough foods for the party if they wish, or they can use water if messy play is OK.

🏠 indoors 🕐 5–30 minutes # 1–5 Fours

309

Fours can

- copy adult activities
- pretend about familiar experiences
- cooperate with friends

Grown-Up Play

Add equipment used by grown-ups to the Dramatic Play center for children to use as they pretend. Include toy or real <u>telephones</u> of different kinds, <u>cameras</u>, radios, alarm clocks, and other safe small <u>appliances</u> that no longer work, and a <u>typewriter</u>. See if parents will help provide these.

That's right, Rasheed. That's an alarm clock. Your mom brought it in for us to use. Do you know how to set the alarm so that the bell rings?

Talk with your Fours to see how much they know about what these things are and how they are used. Let them play freely with these things used by grown-ups.

🏠 indoors 🕐 5–30 minutes # 1–6 Fours

310

Fours can

- copy adult activities
- pretend about familiar experiences
- cooperate with friends

Many-Cultures-Cooking Activity Box

Ask your local librarian for picture books that show food preparation and eating in stories. Read the books to your Fours. Show them pictures of people using these cooking and eating things. Try to have real cooking and eating activities also so that children use the items.

Make a many-cultures-cooking activity box that has items for food preparation used by various cultural groups. Include items such as bamboo steamers, tortilla presses, clay pots, baskets, and different kinds of dishes and pots or pans.

Put out the activity box for children to use in their own creative pretend play. Add some of these props to the everyday housekeeping center.

indoors   5–30 minutes   # 1–6 Fours

311

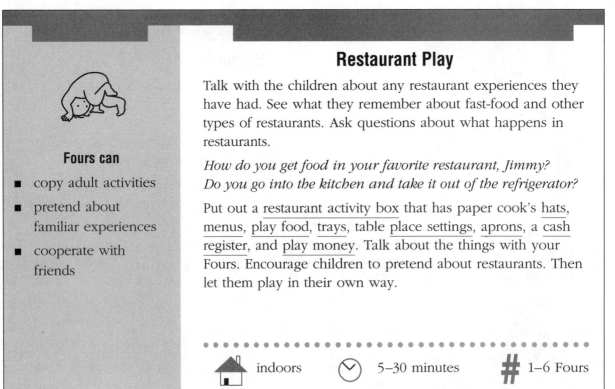

Fours can

- copy adult activities
- pretend about familiar experiences
- cooperate with friends

Restaurant Play

Talk with the children about any restaurant experiences they have had. See what they remember about fast-food and other types of restaurants. Ask questions about what happens in restaurants.

How do you get food in your favorite restaurant, Jimmy?
Do you go into the kitchen and take it out of the refrigerator?

Put out a restaurant activity box that has paper cook's hats, menus, play food, trays, table place settings, aprons, a cash register, and play money. Talk about the things with your Fours. Encourage children to pretend about restaurants. Then let them play in their own way.

indoors   5–30 minutes   # 1–6 Fours

312

Fours can

- copy adult activities
- pretend about familiar experiences
- cooperate with friends

Shoe Store Play

Talk with children about the things they do when they get new shoes. Encourage them to talk about the different things that are found in shoe stores, such as foot measurers and shoe boxes. Talk about how shoe sales clerks help the customers. Take a short field trip to a shoe store so that children can see what happens.

Make a shoe store activity box for your Fours to use to play shoe store, including sandals, high heels, men's shoes, sneakers, and baby shoes. Make sure all the shoes are clean and sprayed inside with disinfectant. Add cardboard foot measurers that you have made, empty shoe boxes, a cash register, play money, paper bags, and shoe horns. Talk about how shoes are displayed in shoe stores.

indoors   5–30 minutes   1–6 Fours

313

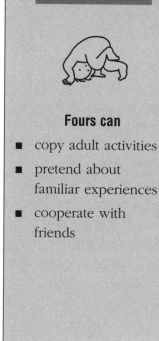

Fours can

- copy adult activities
- pretend about familiar experiences
- cooperate with friends

Dress-Ups from Many Cultures

Make a many-cultures dress-ups activity box with boy's and girl's clothes that are worn by different cultural groups, such as boys' and girls' clothing from Asia, Africa, Central and South America, and Europe. Parents may be able to donate some of these things. Add picture books and pictures that show people using clothes like the ones in the box. Encourage children to use these dress-ups in their play.

Talk with the children about the clothing. Tell them where the clothes come from. See if the clothes are familiar to any of the children. If the clothes have special names, use those words with your Fours.

Yoshiko's mom gave us these tabis and yukata to use for dressing up. Yoshiko, could you show us how to put the tabis on?

in or out   5–30 minutes   1–6 Fours

314

Fours can

- copy adult activities
- pretend about familiar experiences
- cooperate with friends

Pretend to Swim

Make a swimming activity box with things people use at the beach, swimming pool, or other swimming place. Include large towels, sunglasses, sun hats, and clean and empty plastic suntan lotion bottles. Talk with the children about swimming experiences they have had. Read picture books that tell about swimming in different places—pool, lake, beach. Add an empty wading pool for children to use as they pretend.

Bring this activity box out in the winter and talk about summer memories. Let the children use the props in their own make-believe play.

You are sunbathing. I'm glad you have sunglasses to protect your eyes. Did you put on sunscreen to protect your skin?

🏠 in or out   🕐 5–30 minutes   # 1–6 Fours

315

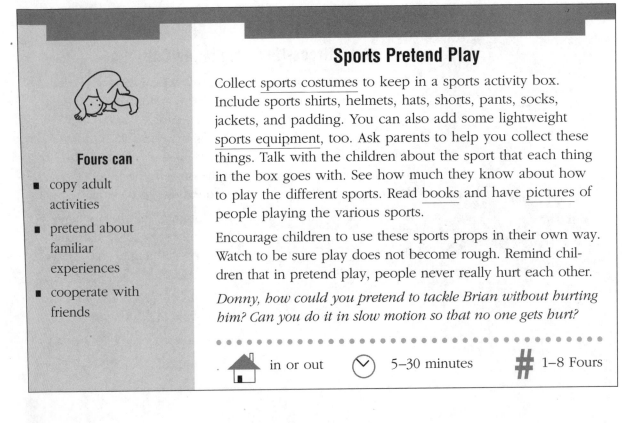

Fours can

- copy adult activities
- pretend about familiar experiences
- cooperate with friends

Sports Pretend Play

Collect sports costumes to keep in a sports activity box. Include sports shirts, helmets, hats, shorts, pants, socks, jackets, and padding. You can also add some lightweight sports equipment, too. Ask parents to help you collect these things. Talk with the children about the sport that each thing in the box goes with. See how much they know about how to play the different sports. Read books and have pictures of people playing the various sports.

Encourage children to use these sports props in their own way. Watch to be sure play does not become rough. Remind children that in pretend play, people never really hurt each other.

Donny, how could you pretend to tackle Brian without hurting him? Can you do it in slow motion so that no one gets hurt?

🏠 in or out   🕐 5–30 minutes   # 1–8 Fours

316

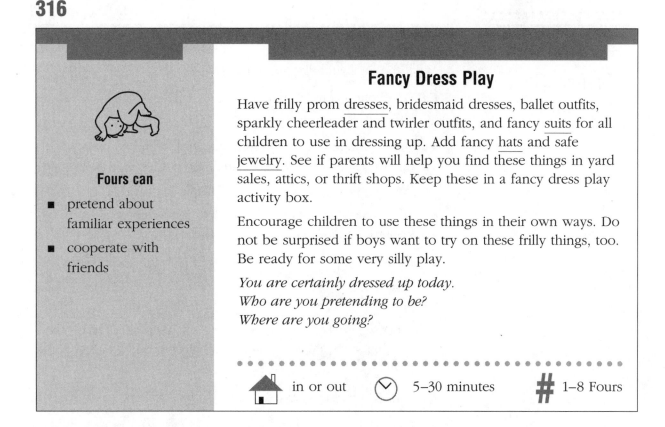

Fours can

- pretend about familiar experiences
- cooperate with friends

Fancy Dress Play

Have frilly prom <u>dresses</u>, bridesmaid dresses, ballet outfits, sparkly cheerleader and twirler outfits, and fancy <u>suits</u> for all children to use in dressing up. Add fancy <u>hats</u> and safe <u>jewelry</u>. See if parents will help you find these things in yard sales, attics, or thrift shops. Keep these in a fancy dress play activity box.

Encourage children to use these things in their own ways. Do not be surprised if boys want to try on these frilly things, too. Be ready for some very silly play.

You are certainly dressed up today.
Who are you pretending to be?
Where are you going?

🏠 in or out   🕐 5–30 minutes   # 1–8 Fours

317

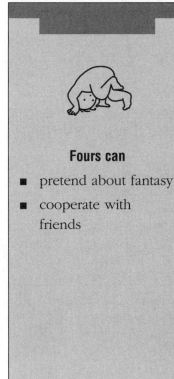

Fours can

- pretend about fantasy
- cooperate with friends

Super Heroes!

Help your Fours do super-hero pretend play without hurting one another. Have a super-hero activity box with props they can use, such as <u>costumes</u> and <u>capes</u>. Ask the children about other things that they need to pretend. Talk with the children about the super heroes that they pretend to be. Talk about how super heroes are not real and their fighting is just pretend. Have children practice the fighting they have seen without really touching or hitting. Emphasize that this is the way actors pretend, too.

Supervise carefully and be ready to help children avoid becoming too rough in this play. When children use capes, watch to see that they do not do play where capes can be caught and cause choking.

🏠 outdoors   🕐 5–30 minutes   # 1–8 Fours

IDEAS

Dramatic Play Center

Make the Dramatic Play Center easy for Fours to use.

- Don't put too much out at once, but have enough so that children do not fight over toys and props.

- Have enough open shelves to separate different kinds of things: dishes in one place, dress-up clothes in another place.

- Don't use a big box or toy chest to keep things in because children can't find things easily.

- Have picture labels of toys or other play things on shelves and storage places. These help children (and adults) know where things go at clean-up time.

- When play has been especially messy, help children clean up a little at a time. Name one thing at a time for them to find and put away.

Make dress-ups fun and safe.

- Have dress-up clothes for girls and boys that are easy to put on and not too long.

- Watch carefully when children are wearing capes or long clothes that they do not climb or get their clothes caught on things.

- Put loops on dress-up clothes so that children can hang them on low, safe hooks.

- Wash dress-ups often and use plastic hats that are easy to clean and sanitize whenever possible to prevent spreading infections.

- Have children wear socks with dress-up shoes and spray shoes often with disinfectant.

- Be sure dress-up shoes are safe: heels are not too high, laces are tied or removed.

Have dramatic play outdoors as well as indoors.

- Put a play stove and sink outdoors where the children can use sand and water. Have one indoors too.

- Bring activity boxes outdoors to encourage many different types of play. Be sure to have children collect and clean all the things that they used from the activity box.

- Use activity boxes outdoors to act out different jobs: painter, firefighter, police.

- Bathe baby dolls and wash doll clothes and dishes outdoors.

Bring in new ideas for pretend play.

- Read stories. Then put out what children need to act out the stories.

- Use pictures or take walking trips for new ideas.

- Set up different pretend play places: a kitchen, bedroom, store, garage.

- Talk about different jobs children have seen adults do and give them what they need to play.

- Give children a chance to practice self-help skills as they play, such as pouring, washing tables, and sweeping.

Talk to children and get them to tell you about their play, but be sure not to interfere.

- Dramatic play lets you give children new words and new ideas. A story before or after dramatic play often works well.

- Talk about taking turns, sharing, playing near and with others. Help children work out problems that come up when they play with each other.

- Use words such as *make-believe* and *pretend* so that children start to understand the difference between real and make-believe.

Materials and Notes

Music

song and rhyme books

musical instruments
homemade and bought

record or tape player
records or tapes

- Plan music times in your daily schedule, but also add informal music to many other things you do with Fours.
- Encourage Fours to sing with the group, but don't force them to. Let a child watch or do another activity when the rest are singing.
- Relax and enjoy the Fours' music, even if it gets noisy. If the noise is too much inside, take the music outside.
- Turn off the record player, tape player, or compact disc player when a music activity is over. Fours will listen better to music if it is not a part of general background noise.
- If you can't sing, you can chant or use records, tapes, and compact discs. Your Fours will love your singing, even if you don't think your voice is good.
- Put up the words to new songs where you can see them when you sing until you know all the words by heart. Be sure children can see the words, too, even though they will not be able to read them yet.
- Teach new songs, but make time for Fours to sing the same songs over and over.
- Share songs with parents. Ask parents to share their children's favorite songs.
- See Music Center Ideas and Songs and Rhymes at the end of this section.

Activity Checklist

Music

Music for Fours includes songs and chants, moving to rhythms, making music with musical toys or instruments, and listening to music made by others. Four-year-olds enjoy all kinds of music experiences: rhythmic movement, singing or chanting, musical instruments. They want to move to music in their own way and can make their own sounds by using everyday objects and simple musical instruments. They remember words and melodies to many songs and can add their own words, too. You will hear Fours making up their own songs, too.

Check for each age group

	48–54 months	54–60 months
1. Adult sings with children daily, at both planned and informal times.	❑	❑
2. New songs are introduced regularly and repeated often so that children can learn them. Old favorites are sung often.	❑	❑
3. Words to songs are displayed on posters or in books where children can see them. Children see how adults use these written words.	❑	❑
4. Children are encouraged but not forced to take part in group music activities.	❑	❑
5. Movement to music is included daily.	❑	❑
6. Dance props are available (wrist bells, ankle bells, pom-poms to shake).	❑	❑
7. Music is on only when it is being used for children's activities or for a quiet listening time, such as before nap.	❑	❑
8. Different types of music are used (special children's songs, classical, rock, music of many cultures).	❑	❑
9. A Music Center is set up for daily free play with simple sound-making toys and instruments, as well as a simple tape player with headphones that children are taught to use by themselves.	❑	❑
10. Adult helps children become aware of sounds and rhythms by planning activities with sounds and talking about them.	❑	❑

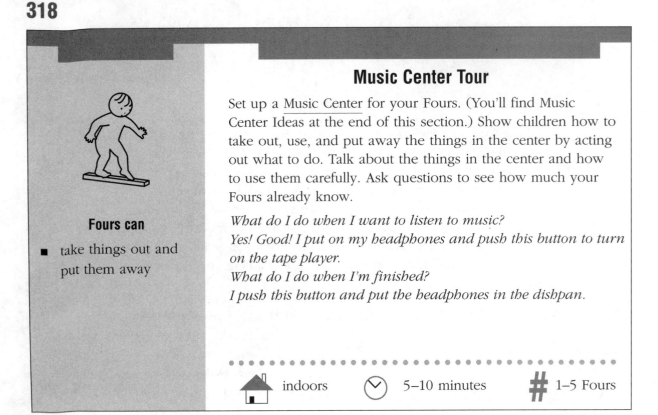

Fours can

- take things out and put them away

Music Center Tour

Set up a <u>Music Center</u> for your Fours. (You'll find Music Center Ideas at the end of this section.) Show children how to take out, use, and put away the things in the center by acting out what to do. Talk about the things in the center and how to use them carefully. Ask questions to see how much your Fours already know.

What do I do when I want to listen to music?
Yes! Good! I put on my headphones and push this button to turn on the tape player.
What do I do when I'm finished?
I push this button and put the headphones in the dishpan.

indoors   5–10 minutes   # 1–5 Fours

319

Fours can

- talk about familiar pictures

Music Pictures

In the Music Center, hang <u>pictures</u> of people singing, dancing, or playing music. Make sure the pictures are down low where your Fours can reach and touch them. Look at the pictures with the children. Talk about them in many ways. Ask questions to see what the children can tell you about the pictures.

What is the girl doing in the picture?
Yes. She's playing the drums. Do we have drums here?
Look, Jonathan sees them!
How are our drums different from the ones she's playing?

indoors   1–5 minutes   # 1–5 Fours

320

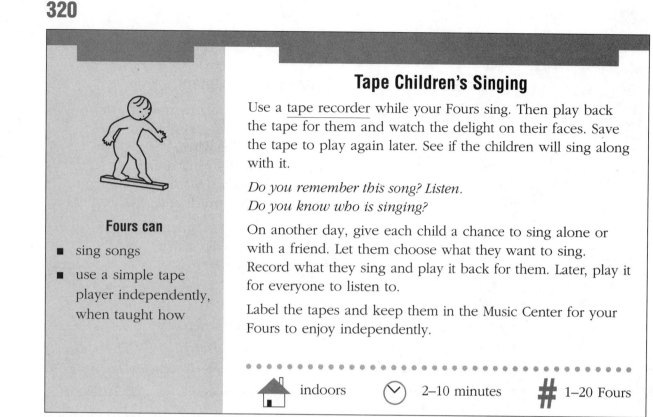

Fours can

- sing songs
- use a simple tape player independently, when taught how

Tape Children's Singing

Use a <u>tape recorder</u> while your Fours sing. Then play back the tape for them and watch the delight on their faces. Save the tape to play again later. See if the children will sing along with it.

Do you remember this song? Listen.
Do you know who is singing?

On another day, give each child a chance to sing alone or with a friend. Let them choose what they want to sing. Record what they sing and play it back for them. Later, play it for everyone to listen to.

Label the tapes and keep them in the Music Center for your Fours to enjoy independently.

⌂ indoors   ⊘ 2–10 minutes   # 1–20 Fours

321

Fours can

- play easy musical instruments

Play to Music

Give your Fours easy-to-play musical <u>instruments</u>, such as drums or wrist bells. Then put on a <u>record</u>, <u>tape</u>, or <u>CD</u> for them to play along with. Try many kinds of music and see if the children play in different ways. Play the background music softly.

Hear comes the music. Do you hear it?
Now play your drums.

Try soul, rap, rock, classical, or any other record you might have, as long as the words are appropriate for young children. Be sure to turn the music off after you have finished the activity.

⌂ in or out   ⊘ 5–10 minutes   # 1–20 Fours

322

Fours can

- match simple sounds

Guess the Instrument

Put three musical instruments on a table in front of a four-year-old. Sit across from the child. Have instruments that match those on the table on your lap where the child can't see them. Let the child try out her three instruments to hear how they sound. Then play one of your instruments so that the child can hear it but cannot see which one it is. See if she can guess which one you played.

Which instrument makes this sound, Nina? That's right!
See, here's mine! Let's play them together.

Begin with instruments that make very different sounds, such as a bell, clacking sticks, and a drum. When that's too easy, use instruments that sound more like each other.

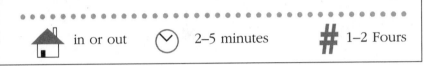

🏠 in or out   🕐 2–5 minutes   # 1–2 Fours

323

Fours can

- make up their own simple songs

Child-Created Songs

Make up short little songs about things the children do in the classroom. Sing them for children to hear.

Jason is building,
Building with the blocks.
Jason is building
One block on top of another.

After your Fours see that you make up songs about familiar things, encourage interested children to make up their own songs.

Look at Harriet swinging, Charlotte.
Do you want to make up a little song about swinging?
I'll listen.

🏠 in or out   🕐 1–5 minutes   # 1 Four at a time

324

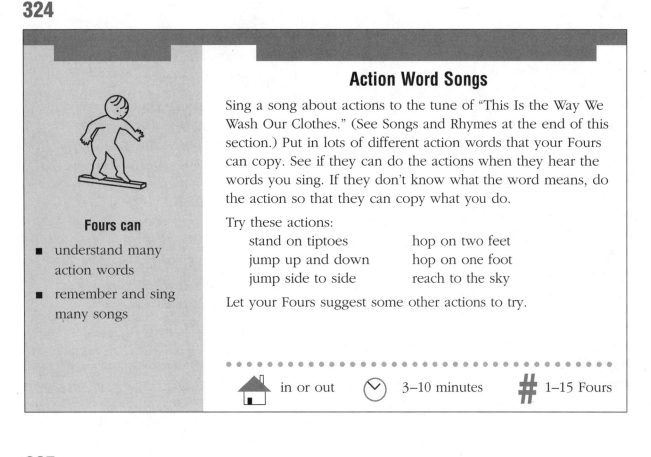

Action Word Songs

Sing a song about actions to the tune of "This Is the Way We Wash Our Clothes." (See Songs and Rhymes at the end of this section.) Put in lots of different action words that your Fours can copy. See if they can do the actions when they hear the words you sing. If they don't know what the word means, do the action so that they can copy what you do.

Try these actions:

stand on tiptoes	hop on two feet
jump up and down	hop on one foot
jump side to side	reach to the sky

Let your Fours suggest some other actions to try.

Fours can

- understand many action words
- remember and sing many songs

🏠 in or out   🕐 3–10 minutes   # 1–15 Fours

325

Fours can

- remember and sing many songs

Cozy Singing Time

Have a special, warm, cozy singing time with just one or two children. Sing a favorite song with them. See if they can sing back to you. Give them a little help if they need it, but they may want to do it all by themselves. Try to do this with every child who is interested, fitting it in whenever you get a chance.

Come here, Ronnie. Sit by me. Let's sing a song. Do you have a song you want to sing?

🏠 in or out   🕐 2–4 minutes   # 1–2 Fours

Fours can

■ say and do
fingerplays

Fingerplay Songs

Sing or chant fingerplays with your Fours. Do them over and over so that your Fours will learn the words and actions. When the children know the fingerplays well, let them sing and do the actions without you. Try some of the following:

"In a Cabin, In the Woods"
"If You're Happy and You Know It"
"The Bee Hive"
"Five Little Monkeys"

Sing or chant other fingerplays, too. Try "I'm a Little Teapot" or "There Was a Duke of York." (See Songs and Rhymes, page 306, and Counting Songs and Rhymes, page 388.)

· ·

🏠 in or out   🕐 5–10 minutes   # 1–15 Fours

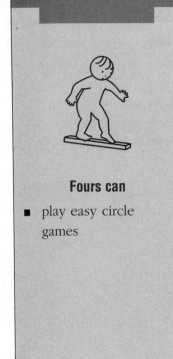

Fours can

■ play easy circle
games

Simple Circle Game Songs

Make a circle with some of your Fours. Begin with a small circle with four or five children. As they learn how to play circle games, you can add more children.

Do easy circle games at first, such as "Ring Around the Rosey" or "Swing Your Hands." Later, add other songs, such as "Hokey Pokey," "The Farmer in the Dell," or "London Bridge."

Soon your Fours will tell you which circle games they want to play.

Let Fours come and go from the circle as they wish.

· ·

🏠 in or out   🕐 5–10 minutes   # 4–15 Fours

328

Fours can

■ move to music

Dance Your Own Way

Choose music on records, tapes, or CDs that your Fours will enjoy moving to. Be sure to have music that will bring out different kinds of movement—fast and slow, music with a hard beat, music with a soft beat, and others.

Tell your Fours to move the way the music tells them. Play one piece for a few minutes as the children dance. Show the children how much you enjoy the ways they dance. Talk about the music with those who just want to watch.

Make sure there is plenty of space for dancing. Have children relax while you change the music.

in or out   3–10 minutes   # 1–20 Fours

329

Fours can

■ move to music

■ recognize familiar animals

Animal Music Games

Choose music on records, tapes, or CDs that reminds you of animals your Fours know about. Before the music starts, ask your Fours what animal they can pretend to be. Talk about how that animal moves.

Isaac, you said this music is about a bear. How do you think a bear moves? He moves slowly and takes BIG steps. Let's try it. You move just like a bear.

Play the music for two or three minutes. Let the children move as they wish. Be sure they have plenty of room.

At another time, try having the children tell you different animals they can be with the same music, or change the music and keep the animal the same.

in or out   3–10 minutes   # 1–20 Fours

330

Dance with Props

Give your Fours props, such as long, colorful <u>scarves</u>, paper streamers, or cheerleading <u>pompoms</u> to dance with. Encourage them to experiment to find out how these things move or swirl in different ways. Play <u>music</u> and let the children dance with the props.

Try props on different parts of the children's bodies: streamers on wrists, waists, knees, and even as headbands. Try a long scarf around a child's head and another around his wrist. As usual, watch carefully when you use long streamers or scarves that might trip or choke children.

Try other props, such as dolls or noise-making toys, to dance with, too.

Fours can

■ move to music

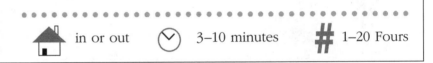 in or out   3–10 minutes   # 1–20 Fours

331

Musical Instruments—Stop and Go

Give your Fours musical <u>instruments</u> to play as they listen to a <u>record</u> that you can stop and start. See if you can make a game of playing only when the music is on and stopping when it stops. It may be easier if you have the children put their instruments down when the music stops.

Do you all have an instrument to play?
Put your instrument down on the floor so that we can all see it.
(Practice each of the instructions.)
When the music plays, pick up your instrument and play it.
When the music stops, put your instrument down on the floor.
Do you think you can do that? I bet you can!

Be patient with your Fours who are excited and want to keep playing. Most of all, enjoy the music together.

Fours can

■ play easy musical instruments

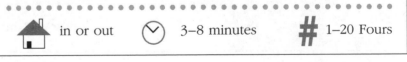 in or out   3–8 minutes   # 1–20 Fours

332

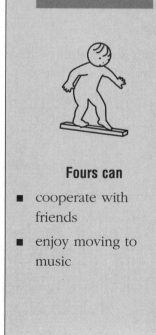

Fours can

- point to their own body parts
- remember and sing many songs

Body Parts Songs

Sing a song or chant a rhyme that names parts of the body. Have your Fours help you sing while they point to their own body parts. Try making up a rhyme of your own, such as this one that you can sing to the tune of "Row, Row, Row Your Boat."

Elbow, elbow, where's your elbow?
Pat your elbow now.
Elbow, elbow, where's your elbow?
Pat your elbow now.

Try other body parts, too:

eyebrow	wrist	knee	thigh
ankle	chest	bicep	forehead
heel	waist	earlobe	lip

🏠 in or out　　🕐 3–5 minutes　　# 1–20 Fours

333

Fours can

- cooperate with friends
- enjoy moving to music

Follow the Leader

Gather a small group of Fours who want to play this movement game with you. Tell them that when you play music, each child will get a turn showing the others how to move. Children can follow the leader and do what he or she does until the music stops. Then it will be another child's turn.

Be sure children have plenty of space to move. Choose the first child to lead, turn on the music, and encourage the others to copy the leader's movements. After a few minutes, stop the music so that a new child can lead.

Johnny is hopping! Hop like Johnny. Watch him. Now he's rolling on the floor. You can roll on the floor, too.

Make sure every child who wants a turn gets one. This is easier when you keep the group small.

🏠 in or out　　🕐 4–20 minutes　　# 1–8 Fours

334

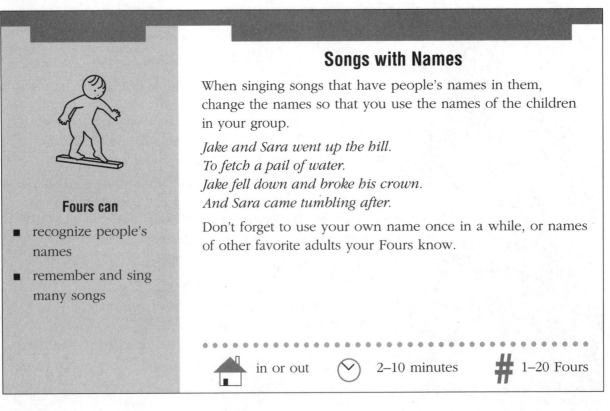

Fast/Slow Singing

Choose a familiar song your Fours enjoy. Try singing the song slowly. Talk about how the song was sung. Then try singing the song fast. Talk about that, too. Be ready for lots of giggles when you sing fast.

Let's sing "Mary Had a Little Lamb."
Let's sing it as slowly as we can.
Listen. I'll show you how.
That was slow singing, wasn't it?
It made me sleepy to sing so slowly.
Can you sing it like that?

Play records, tapes, or CDs of fast and slow music. Talk about each kind.

Fours can

■ remember and sing many songs

■ recognize some opposites

🏠 in or out   🕐 4–7 minutes   # 1–20 Fours

335

Songs with Names

When singing songs that have people's names in them, change the names so that you use the names of the children in your group.

Jake and Sara went up the hill.
To fetch a pail of water.
Jake fell down and broke his crown.
And Sara came tumbling after.

Don't forget to use your own name once in a while, or names of other favorite adults your Fours know.

Fours can

■ recognize people's names

■ remember and sing many songs

🏠 in or out   🕐 2–10 minutes   # 1–20 Fours

336

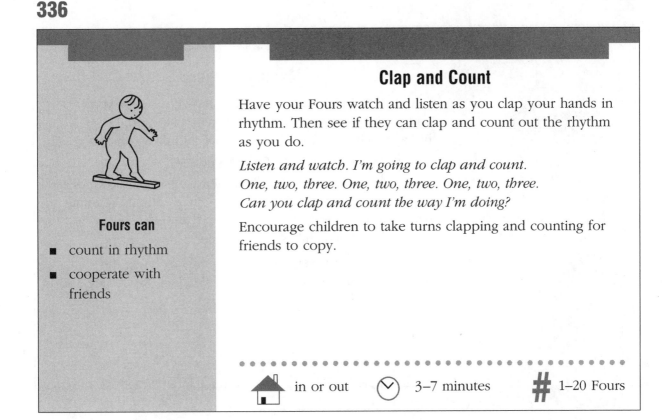

Clap and Count

Have your Fours watch and listen as you clap your hands in rhythm. Then see if they can clap and count out the rhythm as you do.

Listen and watch. I'm going to clap and count.
One, two, three. One, two, three. One, two, three.
Can you clap and count the way I'm doing?

Encourage children to take turns clapping and counting for friends to copy.

Fours can

- count in rhythm
- cooperate with friends

🏠 in or out   🕐 3–7 minutes   # 1–20 Fours

337

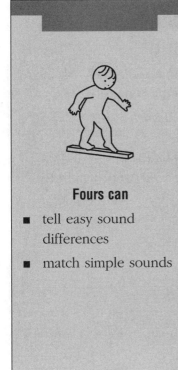

Matching Sounds

Cover empty juice cans or plastic jars with colored contact paper so they all look the same. Then fill two sets of cans with things that make sounds, such as rice, sand, bells, wooden beads, or pebbles. Tape the lids on securely.

Let your Fours shake all the cans and listen. Then pick up one can. Shake it. Give the child three other cans to shake. Make sure that one of them matches the one you are shaking. See if the child can find the one whose sound matches yours.

Listen, Katsuji. Which one sounds like this one?
I'll shake it again. Do you hear the sand in the can?

Begin with cans that make very different sounds. See if two children will play this game without you once they know how.

Fours can

- tell easy sound differences
- match simple sounds

🏠 in or out   🕐 3–10 minutes   # 1–2 Fours

338

Making Shakers

Collect lots of juice cans or plastic jars with lids for your Fours to fill to make their own shakers. Put out different things the children can choose to put into their cans, such as rice, dried beans, sand, stones, or pebbles.

Let the children take turns filling their cans in their own ways. Remind the children to leave lots of space so that the things inside can move to make noise. Secure all lids with strong tape and put each child's name on her or his shakers.

Use the cans at singing time later in the day. Help the children talk about how they made their shakers, what they put in them, and how they sound.

Fours can

- follow clear directions

⌂ in or out   ◔ 5–10 minutes   # 1–5 Fours

339

What Comes Next?

Sing one line of a song your Fours know well. Then ask them to sing the next line, or even to finish the song for you.

Can you help me sing a song? Listen, I'll start.
Twinkle, twinkle, little star...

Also give children a chance to choose words to use in different songs. For example, when singing "Old MacDonald," let the children name the animals to sing about and tell what sounds the animals make.

Fours can

- remember and sing many songs

⌂ in or out   ◔ 2–5 minutes   # 1–20 Fours

340

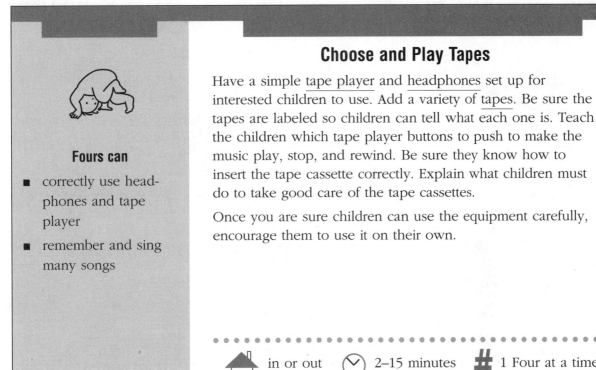

Fours can

- correctly use head-phones and tape player
- remember and sing many songs

Choose and Play Tapes

Have a simple tape player and headphones set up for interested children to use. Add a variety of tapes. Be sure the tapes are labeled so children can tell what each one is. Teach the children which tape player buttons to push to make the music play, stop, and rewind. Be sure they know how to insert the tape cassette correctly. Explain what children must do to take good care of the tape cassettes.

Once you are sure children can use the equipment carefully, encourage them to use it on their own.

in or out   2–15 minutes   # 1 Four at a time

341

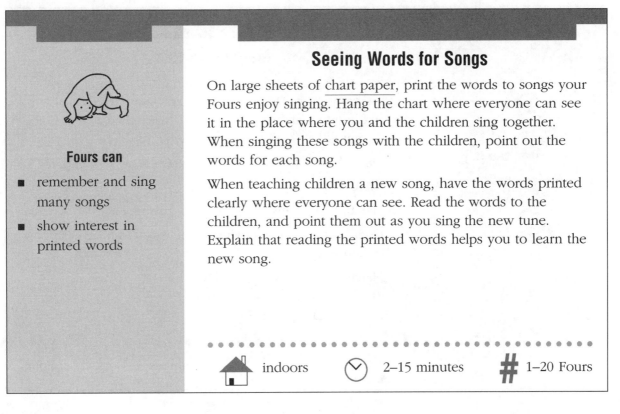

Fours can

- remember and sing many songs
- show interest in printed words

Seeing Words for Songs

On large sheets of chart paper, print the words to songs your Fours enjoy singing. Hang the chart where everyone can see it in the place where you and the children sing together. When singing these songs with the children, point out the words for each song.

When teaching children a new song, have the words printed clearly where everyone can see. Read the words to the children, and point them out as you sing the new tune. Explain that reading the printed words helps you to learn the new song.

indoors   2–15 minutes   # 1–20 Fours

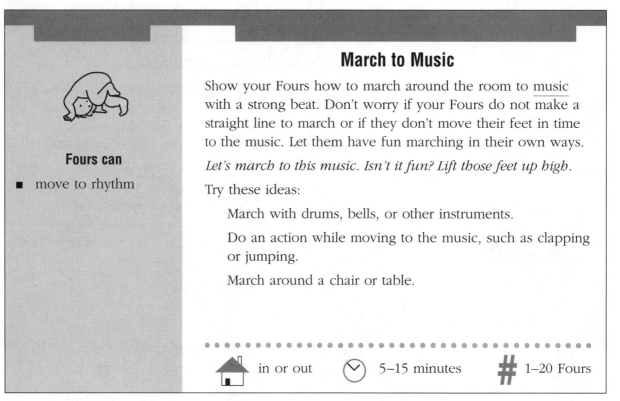

Many Drums

Collect many different kinds of drums for your Fours to try out. Include homemade drums made from oatmeal boxes or coffee cans with lids, as well as different drums you can buy. Talk about the different ways they can be played, the sounds they make, and how they look. See if your Fours can find other things that sound like drums, too.

Can this bucket be a drum, Katerina? Let's turn it upside down and thump on it. Can you find anything else that can be a drum?

Fours can

- play easy musical instruments

in or out   5–15 minutes   # 1–20 Fours

343

March to Music

Show your Fours how to march around the room to music with a strong beat. Don't worry if your Fours do not make a straight line to march or if they don't move their feet in time to the music. Let them have fun marching in their own ways.

Let's march to this music. Isn't it fun? Lift those feet up high.

Try these ideas:

March with drums, bells, or other instruments.

Do an action while moving to the music, such as clapping or jumping.

March around a chair or table.

Fours can

- move to rhythm

in or out   5–15 minutes   # 1–20 Fours

344

Fours can

- follow some directions
- play easy musical instruments

Play Your Kazoo

Make kazoos with four or five Fours at a time. Cover one end of an empty paper towel roll with tissue paper. Secure with tape. Let the children color or put stickers on the rolls and choose the color of tissue paper they wish to use. Put the child's name on his kazoo.

Show the children how to toot into their kazoos. See if they can play a song they know well on their new musical instruments.

Tape them as they play their kazoos. Put the tape in the Music Center so that they can listen to it later.

🏠 in or out   🕐 10–15 minutes   # 1–5 Fours

345

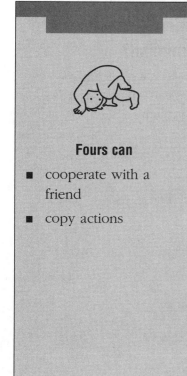

Fours can

- cooperate with a friend
- copy actions

Dance with a Partner

Help a few of your Fours choose a partner. Have the couples look at each other. Chant a little song that tells them ways they can move together. As the children get used to moving with partners, add more couples to the group. Make sure you leave enough room for everyone to move freely.

Clap, clap, clap your hands.
Clap your hands together.
Shake, shake, shake your hands.
Shake your hands together.
Smile, smile, smile, smile.
Smile to each other.

Try other actions the children can do as partners.

🏠 in or out   🕐 4–10 minutes   # 2–12 Fours

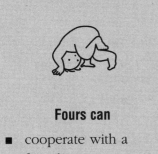

Fours can

- cooperate with a friend
- move to music

Mirror Dance

Have a few Fours stand in front of a large, unbreakable mirror. Put on happy, lively music and encourage the children to dance or move the way the music makes them feel. Point out the children in the mirror so that they will look at themselves and their friends as they dance.

Encourage children to take turns being the leader for others to copy. Have them copy the leader by watching in the mirror to see what she does.

Do you see yourself in the mirror, Dante?
Watch how Katy is moving. Can you copy her?

indoors   3–7 minutes   # 1–4 Fours

347

Fours can

- remember and sing many songs

What Song Am I Humming?

Choose some songs your Fours know very well. Hum one of them to the children. See if your Fours can sing the words to the song with you after you hum it for them.

Listen, I'm going to hum a song. It's a song you know well. That's right, Raul. It is "Twinkle, Twinkle, Little Star." Can you sing the words with me?

Encourage children to hum songs they know, too.

in or out   2–10 minutes   # 1–20 Fours

348

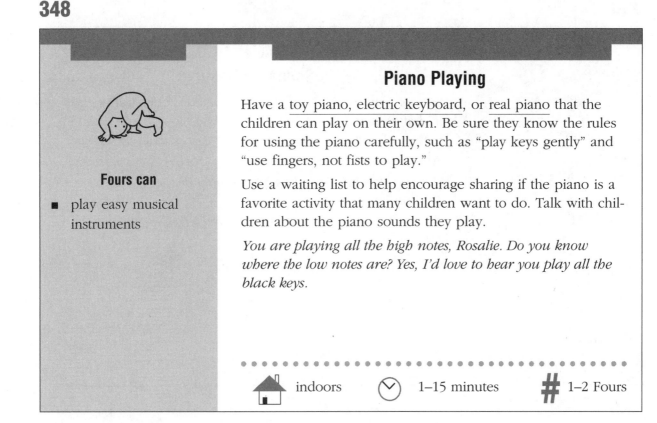

Fours can

■ play easy musical instruments

Piano Playing

Have a toy piano, electric keyboard, or real piano that the children can play on their own. Be sure they know the rules for using the piano carefully, such as "play keys gently" and "use fingers, not fists to play."

Use a waiting list to help encourage sharing if the piano is a favorite activity that many children want to do. Talk with children about the piano sounds they play.

You are playing all the high notes, Rosalie. Do you know where the low notes are? Yes, I'd love to hear you play all the black keys.

indoors   1–15 minutes   # 1–2 Fours

349

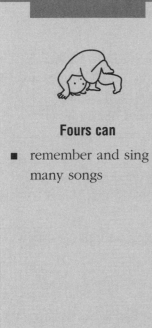

Fours can

■ remember and sing many songs

Holiday Songs

At holiday times, teach the children a song or rhyme to go with the holiday. Make sure to learn songs for the different holidays celebrated by all children in your group. Ask your public librarian or parents to help you with this. Or look for records, tapes, and CDs with holiday songs. For example, at Halloween, sing or chant "Five Little Pumpkins." Don't be surprised if the children want to sing these songs year round, especially "Jingle Bells."

in or out   2–10 minutes   # 1–20 Fours

350

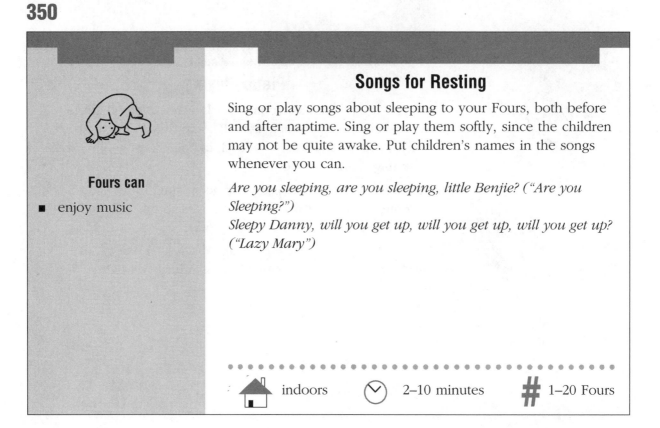

Fours can

■ enjoy music

Songs for Resting

Sing or play songs about sleeping to your Fours, both before and after naptime. Sing or play them softly, since the children may not be quite awake. Put children's names in the songs whenever you can.

Are you sleeping, are you sleeping, little Benjie? ("Are you Sleeping?")
Sleepy Danny, will you get up, will you get up, will you get up? ("Lazy Mary")

🏠 indoors   🕐 2–10 minutes   # 1–20 Fours

351

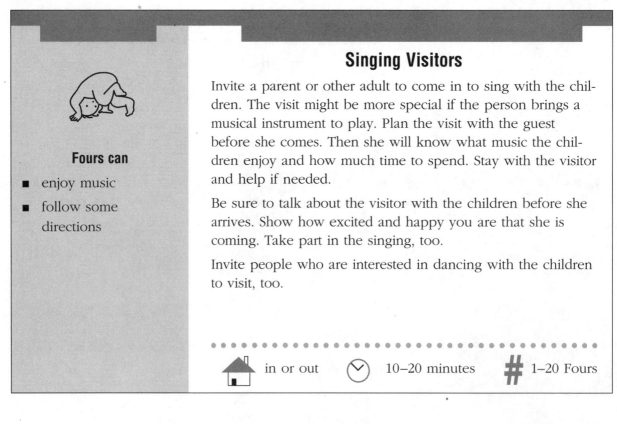

Fours can

■ enjoy music
■ follow some directions

Singing Visitors

Invite a parent or other adult to come in to sing with the children. The visit might be more special if the person brings a musical instrument to play. Plan the visit with the guest before she comes. Then she will know what music the children enjoy and how much time to spend. Stay with the visitor and help if needed.

Be sure to talk about the visitor with the children before she arrives. Show how excited and happy you are that she is coming. Take part in the singing, too.

Invite people who are interested in dancing with the children to visit, too.

🏠 in or out   🕐 10–20 minutes   # 1–20 Fours

352

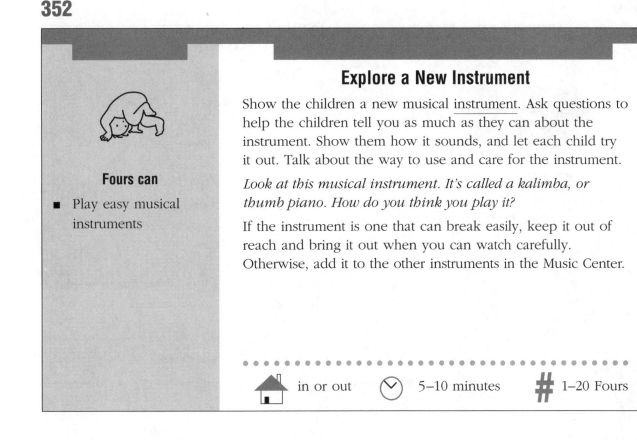

Fours can

■ Play easy musical instruments

Explore a New Instrument

Show the children a new musical instrument. Ask questions to help the children tell you as much as they can about the instrument. Show them how it sounds, and let each child try it out. Talk about the way to use and care for the instrument.

Look at this musical instrument. It's called a kalimba, or thumb piano. How do you think you play it?

If the instrument is one that can break easily, keep it out of reach and bring it out when you can watch carefully. Otherwise, add it to the other instruments in the Music Center.

🏠 in or out   🕐 5–10 minutes   # 1–20 Fours

353

Fours can

■ move to music

Dancing Like the Weather

Have children pretend to move like the wind, the rain, clouds, lightning, or snowflakes. This is especially fun on very windy, rainy, or snowy days. You can do this with or without music. Talk to children as they move.

Lizzie, you're moving just like a snowflake.
First you fall slowly to the ground.
Then you melt away.

On warm, sunny days lie down on the grass with two or three of your Fours. Watch how the clouds move across the sky. When they get up, see if your Fours can move like the clouds.

🏠 outdoors   🕐 1–15 minutes   # 1–20 Fours

Fours can

- help clean up
- follow easy directions

Clean-Up Song

Sing this song at clean-up time to the tune of "London Bridge" or "Here We Go 'Round the Mulberry Bush."

Let's clean up the toys right now, toys right now, toys right now.
Let's clean up the toys right now. We're done playing.

Warn children that clean-up time is coming. Give each child a small clean-up job to do. Be as exact as you can so that the Fours know what to do. Break larger jobs into two or more parts and sing easy directions.

Joey, you clean up the blocks, clean up the blocks, clean up the blocks. Joey, you clean up the blocks, and put them on the shelf.

🏠 in or out   🕐 5–10 minutes   # 1–20 Fours

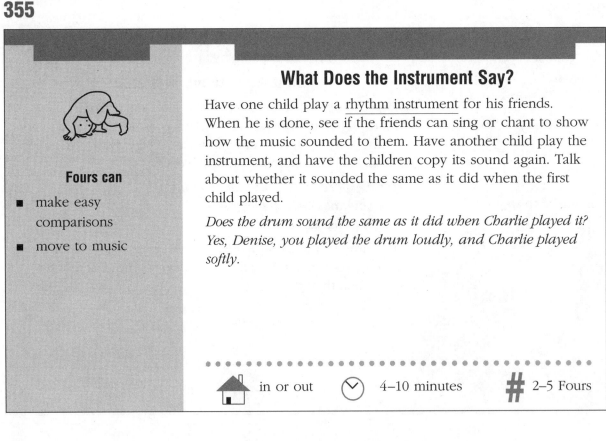

Fours can

- make easy comparisons
- move to music

What Does the Instrument Say?

Have one child play a rhythm instrument for his friends. When he is done, see if the friends can sing or chant to show how the music sounded to them. Have another child play the instrument, and have the children copy its sound again. Talk about whether it sounded the same as it did when the first child played.

Does the drum sound the same as it did when Charlie played it? Yes, Denise, you played the drum loudly, and Charlie played softly.

🏠 in or out   🕐 4–10 minutes   # 2–5 Fours

356

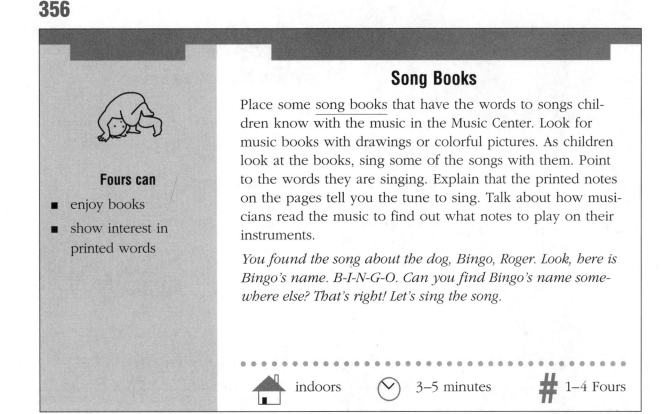

Fours can

- enjoy books
- show interest in printed words

Song Books

Place some song books that have the words to songs children know with the music in the Music Center. Look for music books with drawings or colorful pictures. As children look at the books, sing some of the songs with them. Point to the words they are singing. Explain that the printed notes on the pages tell you the tune to sing. Talk about how musicians read the music to find out what notes to play on their instruments.

You found the song about the dog, Bingo, Roger. Look, here is Bingo's name. B-I-N-G-O. Can you find Bingo's name somewhere else? That's right! Let's sing the song.

indoors   3–5 minutes   1–4 Fours

357

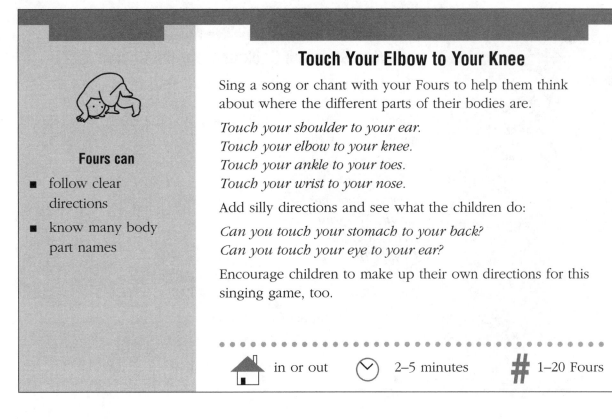

Fours can

- follow clear directions
- know many body part names

Touch Your Elbow to Your Knee

Sing a song or chant with your Fours to help them think about where the different parts of their bodies are.

Touch your shoulder to your ear.
Touch your elbow to your knee.
Touch your ankle to your toes.
Touch your wrist to your nose.

Add silly directions and see what the children do:

Can you touch your stomach to your back?
Can you touch your eye to your ear?

Encourage children to make up their own directions for this singing game, too.

in or out   2–5 minutes   1–20 Fours

358

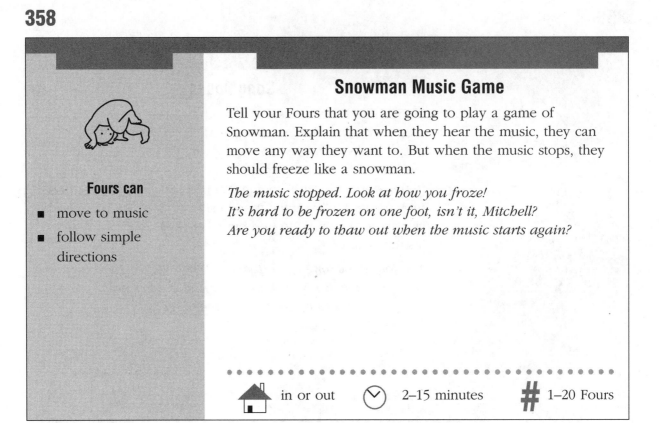

Fours can

- move to music
- follow simple directions

Snowman Music Game

Tell your Fours that you are going to play a game of Snowman. Explain that when they hear the music, they can move any way they want to. But when the music stops, they should freeze like a snowman.

The music stopped. Look at how you froze!
It's hard to be frozen on one foot, isn't it, Mitchell?
Are you ready to thaw out when the music starts again?

in or out   2–15 minutes   # 1–20 Fours

359

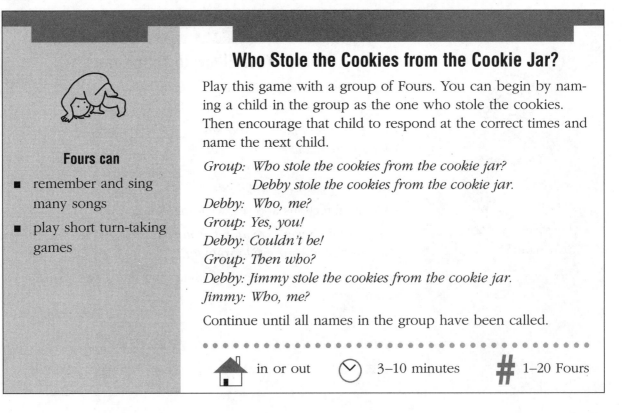

Fours can

- remember and sing many songs
- play short turn-taking games

Who Stole the Cookies from the Cookie Jar?

Play this game with a group of Fours. You can begin by naming a child in the group as the one who stole the cookies. Then encourage that child to respond at the correct times and name the next child.

Group: Who stole the cookies from the cookie jar?
       Debby stole the cookies from the cookie jar.
Debby: Who, me?
Group: Yes, you!
Debby: Couldn't be!
Group: Then who?
Debby: Jimmy stole the cookies from the cookie jar.
Jimmy: Who, me?

Continue until all names in the group have been called.

in or out   3–10 minutes   # 1–20 Fours

360

Fours can

- remember and sing many songs

The Name Chant

Here is a simple name chant that you can use if you take attendance in the morning. Chant the words with a little melody you make up if you wish.

It's morning. It's morning.
Who came to school this morning?
Scott? Yes, Scott!
Marcia, No, not Marcia.
Kerry? Yes, Kerry.

Continue until you have used the names of all your Fours. Add clapping to the song to make it more fun.

in or out   2–7 minutes   # 1–15 Fours

361

Fours can

- remember and sing many songs

Caring Songs

Be sure to include some songs about caring for others in the songs you teach your Fours. Some favorite songs are "Reach Out and Touch Somebody's Hand," "We Are the World," and "It's a Small, Small World."

Write the words to these songs on chart paper and post it where the children can see. Use the chart to help you remember the words.

indoors   3–5 minutes   # 1–15 Fours

Music Center

- Choose a small, out-of-the-way corner for a Music Center. Use low shelves or other sturdy furniture to keep music noises in and other noises out. A carpet on the floor and big soft pillows will cut down on noise, too.

- Put *sturdy* musical instruments and toys neatly on shelves. Use picture and word labels to help Fours remember where things are to be put away. Keep smaller musical instruments in a labeled box or dishpan. If your Music Center must share space with other toys, keep the instruments in an activity box and bring them out often for children to use.

- Have two or more of the instruments children enjoy the most. This will cut down on fights.

- Include a simple tape player with headphones and cassette tapes for children to use.

- Put out only a few musical instruments to begin with. Show children how to use them. Add new things often. Always show and tell your Fours about all of the things you add.

- Buy or make musical instruments and toys such as the following:

  wrist bells, melody bells, cowbells, bells on sticks
  many kinds of drums, with or without sticks
  many kinds of shakers
  sturdy toy piano
  xylophone with mallet
  cymbals (large and finger size)
  clackers, clave tone blocks, castanets, rhythm sticks
  kalimba (thumb piano)
  scraping instruments with sticks, such as guiros
  tambourines
  sandpaper blocks

- If you use harmonicas, whistles, horns, recorders, kazoos, or other mouth instruments, make sure to wash them with bleach solution and air dry them after each use. Keep them in a separate box. Also be sure that instruments have no loose or broken parts that could cut or choke a child.

- Have a children's sturdy tape player for your Fours to use independently. Show them how to handle the tape player and tape cassettes carefully.

- Allow children to use the record player or compact disc player only when you are there to watch closely. This equipment lasts longer when use is supervised.

- Change toys and instruments in the Music Center often.

- Keep children from being crowded in the Music Center. Give them plenty of choices of other interesting things to do if they can't fit in right away. Use a waiting list or other assignment system and make sure children do get a turn after a short wait. Or have music for a larger group outside of the center if there is lots of interest.

- Help Fours keep the center neat and organized. Make sure the center is cleaned up after each day's use.

- Have movement in a large enough area so that Fours will not bump into one another. Give them a chance to calm down with a quiet song after they dance.

- Try music outdoors. This will give you lots of space for movement or dance. If you can't have music outdoors, move furniture and other equipment aside to make a bigger space.

- Add dance props for movement and dance. Try musical instruments, dress-ups, large plastic hoops, and long streamers.

Songs and Rhymes

A Hunting We Will Go

A hunting we will go, a hunting we will go.
Hi-ho the merrio, a hunting we will go.

Are You Sleeping?

Are you sleeping, are you sleeping,
Brother John, Brother John?
Morning bells are ringing,
Morning bells are ringing,
Ding, ding, dong.
Ding, ding, dong.

Clap, Clap, Clap Your Hands

Clap, clap, clap your hands,
Clap your hands together.
Clap, clap, clap your hands,
Clap your hands right now.
Additional verses: (2) Touch your nose; (3) Tap your knees;
(4) Pat your head

Did You Ever See a Lassie (or Laddie)

Did you ever see a lassie, a lassie, a lassie?
Did you ever see a lassie go this way and that?
Go this way and that way, go this way and that way.
Did you ever see a lassie go this way and that?

The Eensy Weensy Spider

The eensy weensy spider went up the water spout.
Down came the rain and washed the spider out.
Out came the sun and dried up all the rain.
And the eensy weensy spider went up the spout again.

The Farmer in the Dell

The farmer in the dell, the farmer in the dell,
Hi Ho the Derry O, the farmer in the dell.
The farmer takes a wife . . .
The wife takes a child . . .
The child takes a nurse . . .
The nurse takes a dog . . .
The dog takes a cat . . .
The cat takes a mouse . . .
The mouse takes the cheese . . .
The cheese stands alone . . .

Creative Activities

Head and Shoulders, Knees and Toes

Head and shoulders, knees and toes, knees and toes.
Head and shoulders, knees and toes, knees and toes.
Eyes and ears and mouth and nose.
Head and shoulders, knees and toes, knees and toes.

Here We Go 'Round the Mulberry Bush

Here we go 'round the mulberry bush, the mulberry bush, the
mulberry bush.
Here we go 'round the mulberry bush, so early in the morning.

Hey Diddle Diddle

Hey diddle diddle, the cat and the fiddle.
The cow jumped over the moon.
The little dog laughed to see such fun.
And the dish ran away with the spoon.

Hickory Dickory Dock

Hickory, dickory, dock!
The mouse ran up the clock.
The clock struck one,
The mouse ran down.
Hickory, dickory, dock!

Hush Little Baby

Hush, little baby, don't say a word, Momma's gonna buy you
a mocking bird.
If that mocking bird won't sing, Momma's gonna buy you
a diamond ring.
If that diamond ring turns brass, Momma's gonna buy you
a looking glass.
If the looking glass gets broke, Momma's gonna buy you
a billy goat.
If that billy goat won't pull, Momma's gonna buy you a cart
and bull.
If that cart and bull turn over, Momma's gonna buy you a dog
named Rover.
If that dog named Rover won't bark, Momma's gonna buy you a
horse and cart.
If that horse and cart fall down, you'll still be the sweetest little baby
in town.

I Am Walking

I am walking, walking, walking,
    I am walking, walking, walking,
I am walking, walking, walking,
    I am walking, walking, walking,
Now I stop.

If You're Happy and You Know It

If you're happy and you know it, clap your hands. (clap, clap)
If you're happy and you know it, clap your hands. (clap, clap)
If you're happy and you know it, then your face will surely show it.
If you're happy and you know it, clap your hands. (clap, clap)
Additional verses: (2) Stamp your feet; (3) Nod your head; (4) Pat
      your knees; (5) Wave good-bye

I'm a Little Teapot

I'm a little teapot short and stout.
Here is my handle, here is my spout.
When I get all steamed up, hear me shout,
"Just tip me over and pour me out."

In a Cabin, In the Woods

In a cabin, in the woods
Little old man by the window stood
Saw a rabbit hopping by,
Knocking at his door.
"Help me, Help me!" the rabbit said,
"Or the hunter will catch me instead!"
Little rabbit, come inside;
Safely you'll abide.

It's Raining, It's Pouring

It's raining, it's pouring,
The old man is snoring.
He went to bed
And bumped his head,
And didn't wake up till morning.

Jack and Jill

Jack and Jill went up the hill to fetch a pail of water.
Jack fell down and broke his crown and Jill came tumbling after.

Jack Be Nimble

Jack be nimble.
Jack be quick.
Jack jump over the candlestick.

Lazy Mary

Lazy Mary will you get up, will you get up, will you get up?
Lazy Mary will you get up, will you get up this morning?

Little Duckie Duddle

Little Duckie Duddle
Went wading in a puddle,
Went wading in a puddle quite small.
Said he, "It doesn't matter
How much I splash and splatter,
I'm only a duckie, after all. Quack, Quack."

Little Green Frog

Ah—ump went the little green frog one day.
Ah—ump went the little green frog.
Ah—ump went the little green frog one day.
And his eyes went blink, blink, blink.

Little Jack Horner

Little Jack Horner sat in a corner,
Eating his Christmas pie.
He stuck in his thumb and pulled out a plum,
And said, "What a good boy am I."

Little Miss Muffet

Little Miss Muffet
Sat on a tuffet
Eating her curds and whey.
Along came a spider
And sat down beside her
And frightened Miss Muffet away.

Little Turtle

There was a little turtle
He lived in a box.
He swam in a puddle,
And he climbed on the rocks.
He snapped at a mosquito,
He snapped at a flea,
He snapped at a minnow
And he snapped at me.
He caught the mosquito.
He caught the flea.
He caught the minnow.
But he didn't catch me.

London Bridge

London bridge is falling down, falling down, falling down,
London bridge is falling down, my fair lady.

Mary Had a Little Lamb

Mary had a little lamb,
Little lamb, little lamb,
Mary had a little lamb
Whose fleece was white as snow.

Miss Lucy Had a Baby

Miss Lucy had a baby,
She named him Tiny Tim,
She put him in the bathtub
To see if he could swim.

He drank up all the water,
He ate up all the soap,
He tried to eat the bathtub,
But it wouldn't go down his throat.

Miss Lucy called the Doctor,
Miss Lucy called the Nurse,
Miss Lucy called the lady
With the alligator purse.

"Little Turtle" reprinted with permission of Macmillan Publishing Company from Collected Poems by Vachel Lindsay. Copyright © 1920 by Macmillan Publishing Company, renewed 1948 by Elizabeth C. Lindsay.

"Mumps," said the Doctor,
"Measles," said the Nurse.
"Nothing," said the lady
With the alligator purse.

Out went the Doctor,
Out went the Nurse,
Out went the lady
With the alligator purse.

Miss Mary Mack

Miss Mary Mack, Mack, Mack,
All dressed in black, black, black,
With silver buttons, buttons, buttons
All down her back, back, back.

She asked her mother, mother, mother,
For fifteen cents, cents, cents,
To see the elephant, elephant, elephant
Jump over the fence, fence, fence.

He jumped so high, high, high,
He touched the sky, sky, sky,
And didn't come back, back, back
Until the Fourth of July, ly, ly.

Miss Polly Had a Dolly

Miss Polly had a dolly that was sick, sick, sick,
So she telephoned the doctor to come quick, quick, quick.
The doctor came with her bag and her cap.
And she knocked on the door with a rat-a-tat-tat.
She looked at the dolly and she shook her head,
"Miss Polly, put that dolly straight to bed, bed, bed."
She wrote on the paper for the pill, pill, pill,
"I'll be back tomorrow with the bill, bill, bill!"

Muffin Man

Do you know the muffin man, the muffin man, the muffin man?
Do you know the muffin man who lives on Drury Lane?

Oats, Peas, Beans

Oats, peas, beans and barley grow;
Oats, peas, beans and barley grow;
Do you or I or anyone know
How oats, peas, beans and barley grow?

Creative Activities

Old King Cole

Old King Cole was a merry old soul,
And a merry old soul was he.
He called for his pipe and he called for his bowl,
And he called for his fiddlers three.

Old MacDonald

Old MacDonald had a farm
E-I - E-I - O
And on his farm he had a cow
E-I - E-I - O
With a moo moo here
And a moo moo there
Here a moo, there a moo
Everywhere a moo moo
Old MacDonald had a farm
E-I - E-I - O.
(Additional verses with other animals)

On Top of Spaghetti

On top of spaghetti, all covered with cheese,
I lost my poor meatball, when somebody sneezed.
It rolled off the table, and onto the floor,
And then my poor meatball rolled out of the door.
It rolled in the garden and under a bush.
And then my poor meatball was nothing but mush.
But the mush was as tasty, as tasty could be,
And early next summer, it grew into a tree.
The tree was all covered with beautiful moss.
It grew lovely meatballs and tomato sauce.
So if you eat spaghetti, all covered with cheese,
Hold onto your meatball and don't ever sneeze!

Open, Shut Them

Open, shut them, open, shut them, give a little clap.
Open, shut them, open, shut them, lay them in your lap.
Creep them, creep them, creep them, creep them right up to your
*   chin.*
Open wide your little mouth, but do not let them in.

Pat-A-Cake

Pat-a-cake, pat-a-cake, baker's man,
Bake me a cake as fast as you can.
Pat it and prick it and mark it with "B,"
And put it in the oven for baby and me.

Creative Activities

Pease Porridge Hot

Pease porridge hot, pease porridge cold,
Pease porridge in the pot, nine days old.
Some like it hot, some like it cold,
Some like it in the pot nine days old.

Pop Goes the Weasel

All around the cobbler's bench the monkey chased the weasel.
The monkey thought 'twas all in fun.
Pop goes the weasel.

Put Your Right Hand In (Hokey Pokey)

Put your right hand in.
Put your right hand out.
Put your right hand in
And you shake it all about.
You do the Hokey Pokey and you turn yourself around;
That's what it's all about.
(Continue with left hand, right foot, left foot, whole self.)

Ring Around the Rosy

Rind around the rosy,
A pocket full of posies.
Ashes, ashes,
We all fall down.

Rock-A-Bye Baby

Rock-a-bye baby, in the tree top,
When the wind blows, the cradle will rock,
When the bough breaks, the cradle will fall.
And down will come baby, cradle and all.

Row, Row, Row, Your Boat

Row, row, row, your boat
Gently down the stream.
Merrily, merrily, merrily, merrily,
Life is but a dream.

Rub-a-Dub-Dub

Rub-a-dub-dub, three men in a tub,
And who do you think they be?
The butcher, the baker, the candlestick maker.
Turn them out, knaves all three.

See Saw, Margery Daw

See saw, Margery Daw, Johnny shall have a new master;
He shall have but a penny a day because he can't work any faster.

Sing A Song of Sixpence

Sing a song of sixpence, a pocket full of rye.
Four and twenty blackbirds baked in a pie.
When the pie was opened the birds began to sing,
Wasn't that a dainty dish to set before the king?

Swing Our Hands

Swing our hands, swing our hands, swing our hands together.
Swing our hands, swing our hands, in our circle now.
Tap our toes, tap our toes, tap our toes together
Tap our toes, tap our toes, in our circle now.
Additional verses: (2) Shake our heads; (3) Move our hips;
(4) Bend our legs; and others

Take Me Riding in Your Airplane

Take me riding in your airplane.
Take me riding in your airplane.
Take me riding in your airplane.
I want to go riding in your airplane.
(Add motions to the song.) Additional verses: (2) Bumpety bus;
(3) Motorcycle; (4) Bicycle; (5) Rowboat; (6) Rocket ship; and others

Teddy Bear

Teddy bear, teddy bear, turn around,
Teddy bear, teddy bear, touch the ground.
Teddy bear, teddy bear, show your shoe,
Teddy bear, teddy bear, that will do!

There Was a Duke of York

There was a Duke of York.
He had ten thousand men.
He marched them up the hill.
And then he marched them down again.
When you're up, you're up.
And when you're down, you're down.
And when you're only halfway up
You're neither up nor down.

Creative Activities

This is the Way We Wash Our Clothes

This is the way we wash our clothes, wash our clothes, wash our
*   clothes.*
This is the way we wash our clothes, so early in the morning.
Additional verses: (2) Hang up our clothes; (3) Iron our clothes;
(4) Fold our clothes; (5) Put on our clothes

This Little Piggy

This little piggy went to market and this little piggy stayed home,
This little piggy had roast beef and this little piggy had none,
And this little piggy went "wee, wee, wee, wee," all the way home.

Twinkle, Twinkle, Little Star

Twinkle, twinkle, little star, how I wonder what you are.
Up above the world so high, like a diamond in the sky,
Twinkle, twinkle, little star, how I wonder what you are.

Wheels on the Bus

The wheels on the bus go round and round, round and round,
*   round and round.*
The wheels on the bus go round and round all through the town.
Additional verses: (2) Baby goes wah wah wah; (3) Lights go blink
blink blink; (4) Driver says move on back; (5) Money goes clink
clink clink; (6) People go up and down; (7) Wipers go swish, swish,
swish

Where is Thumbkin?

Where is thumbkin? Where is thumbkin? Here I am, here I am.
How are you today sir? Very well I thank you. Run away,
*   run away.*
(Continue with pointer, tall man, ring man, and pinky.)

Where Oh Where Is Pretty Little Susie?

Where, oh where is pretty little Susie?
Where, oh where is pretty little Susie?
Where, oh where is pretty little Susie?
Way down yonder in the pawpaw patch.

Yankee Doodle

Oh, Yankee Doodle went to town a riding on a pony,
He stuck a feather in his cap and called it macaroni.
Yankee Doodle keep it up; Yankee Doodle Dandy,
Mind the music and the step and with the girls be handy.

Activities for Learning from the World Around Them

Index

of Activities for Learning from the World Around Them

Here's Why

Fours experience the world with great delight and excitement. You can enjoy this with them in many new ways. They can tell you about why they think things happen and even carry out very simple experiments to come to their own conclusions. Of course, like all young children, they still depend on their senses—hearing, sight, smell, taste, and touch—as they come to understand the world, so some of their conclusions may be a bit puzzling to you.

Real things in the world around us are fun for Fours to watch and learn about. Many of the topics that Fours enjoy the most are about animals, insects, gardens, plants, the weather, rocks, rivers and other bodies of water. It is important for Fours to have lots of time outdoors so that they can roll in grass or snow, feel the wind, let sand fall between their fingers, and experience nature in many ways.

If your Fours have already taken part in lots of fun activities to help them learn about numbers, sizes, and shapes, they will now know many words about these ideas. Fours are beginning to really understand that numbers mean "how many." The children can help you count, and often they can count small numbers of things all by themselves.

There are many activities in this section to help the children continue learning without feeling pressured or bored. In the real-life activities, such as cooking or setting the table, children can learn how numbers are important in our lives. Fours will also enjoy playing number, size, and shape games with real objects that they can move around. All these early experiences about the world help get children ready for much of the learning that will come later.

Materials and Notes

Science and Nature

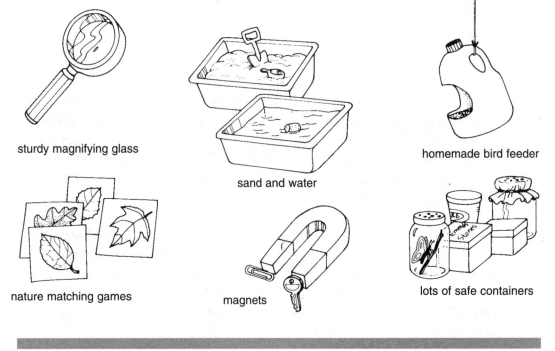

sturdy magnifying glass

sand and water

homemade bird feeder

nature matching games

magnets

lots of safe containers

- Fours learn best about science and nature through their senses. Allow Fours to have many chances to explore nature in their own ways. Give children words for what they experience and listen to their thoughts. Remember that your most important job is to join in, share discoveries, and help children see new things.

- Set up a Science and Nature Center. Fill this area with interesting natural things for the children to explore, as well as games for them to play. Add pictures and books that give more information about things the children explore. Keep the center interesting by changing it often. Encourage children and parents to add to this center, too.

- Make sure to keep things safe. Avoid glass containers. Be sure that plants are not poisonous and that animals and insects will not harm children. If in doubt, be cautious and check things out.

- Fours will ask many questions about science and nature. Try to answer these as simply as you can. Help children use their senses and thinking skills to find answers. Don't be afraid to admit that you do not know an answer. Show Fours how to look in books or ask others to find information.

- Ask parents to help with science and nature activities. They can help on field trips, bring in new and interesting natural things, and find the information you need. At home, they can continue the science and nature activities that you and the children have begun.

Activity Checklist

Science and Nature

Science and Nature for Fours includes experiences in exploring natural things both indoors and out, learning words about natural things, and beginning what can be a lifelong interest in our environment. Learning about what plants and animals need to live, how to protect the environment, different kinds of weather, and even about long-gone dinosaurs are only a few of the science/nature activities Fours enjoy. Playing in sand and water continues to be a favorite activity for Fours.

Check for each age group

	48–54 months	54–60 months
1. Children have a daily outdoor time, weather permitting.	❑	❑
2. Adult points out and talks about natural things, such as birds, insects, plants, animals, the weather.	❑	❑
3. Adult shows appreciation and respect for nature when with children (shows curiosity and interest rather than disgust about insects, worms; has positive attitude about going outside in different kinds of weather).	❑	❑
4. Adult encourages children to explore safe, natural things with their senses.	❑	❑
5. Adult asks interested children questions about their science and nature experiences to encourage talking and thinking things through.	❑	❑
6. Sand and/or water play with a variety of toys is available daily, both indoors and outdoors.	❑	❑
7. A Science and Nature Center is set up for children to use daily, with natural things, books and pictures, and science and nature games. Things in the center are changed often.	❑	❑
8. The interests of the children are considered when adding new things to learn about in science and nature.	❑	❑
9. Safe science and nature materials are provided for experiments, such as magnifying glasses, magnets, sinkers and floaters, and natural objects of many types.	❑	❑
10. Cooking activities in which the children take a meaningful part are provided regularly.	❑	❑

Activities for Learning from the World Around Them

362

Fours can

- show curiosity and delight about natural things
- talk about many things that interest them

Ever-Changing Science and Nature Center

Set up a Science and Nature Center where there are things for the children to explore and experiment with. If possible, place the center near a window and have a table and shelf to hold games, books, and natural things.

Change the things in the center often. Add new games and pictures. Be sure to add things that the children bring in and find interesting. Tell the children about the new things and join them when they show interest.

Kent, I see you and Peter are looking at the wasps' nest that Monique brought in. Did she tell you where she found it? Here is a book that shows what the inside of the nest looks like.

There are more ideas about a Science and Nature Center on page 347.

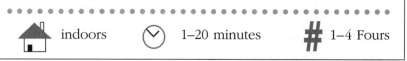

🏠 indoors   🕐 1–20 minutes   # 1–4 Fours

363

Fours can

- talk about things that interest them

Tuning into the Weather

Each day, take a little time to talk with your Fours about what the weather is like. Have them close their eyes and try to remember what it was like when they arrived in the morning. Then let them check by looking out the window or going outdoors to see.

Help the children tune into the signs of the weather, such as the clouds, wind, sun, rain or other precipitation, dryness or humidity. Talk about how the weather looks or feels. Talk about what children wear and do in the different types of weather.

How did the weather feel when you left your house this morning, Jack? It was cold, wasn't it? What did you do to keep warm?

🏠 in or out   🕐 1–5 minutes   # 1–20 Fours

364

Fours can

- enjoy playing with sand

Basic Sand Play

Set up a sand table for your Fours to use. If you do not have a sand table, use sturdy dishpans or other large containers. Add different-sized unbreakable jars, cups, funnels, and digging tools. Allow interested children to play freely with the sand every day. Have sand-toy activity boxes on a nearby shelf for the children to choose. For example, have a box with small trucks and cars, another box with small farm or zoo animals, and so on.

Be sure the children know that sand is to stay in the table, but expect some spills. If the sand table is indoors, put a rug underneath to catch the spills. Have a small brush and dustpan nearby for children to clean up spilled sand. Show them how to work with a friend to clean up.

Be sure to have sand play with lots of toys outdoors, too.

🏠 in or out   🕐 1–20 minutes   # 1–4 Fours

365

Fours can

- enjoy water play

Basic Water Play

Set up a water play area for your Fours to use every day. Use a water table, sturdy dishpans, or other large containers. Add unbreakable cups, funnels, spoons, and other toys. Have a place where children can put things when they take them out of the water. Have smocks, mops and towels handy for children to use as needed. Spread a large towel under the water table to catch spills so children don't slip.

Have water-toy activity boxes on a shelf nearby for the children to use. Different boxes could hold small boats, plastic fish and sea animals, seashells, small rocks, or sponges. Let water-play toys dry out before children put them away.

Have water play outdoors when the weather is nice, too. Use hoses, sprinklers, and water tables with toys.

🏠 in or out   🕐 1–20 minutes   # 1–4 Fours

366

Fours can

- experiment as they play
- enjoy sand and water play

Water and Sand

Give your Fours a fun change by mixing <u>sand</u> and <u>water</u> together for play. Do this in two <u>dishpans</u> if you don't want to get lots of sand wet. Have one pan for sand and the other for water and let the children mix up the two with <u>spoons</u>, <u>cups</u>, and other unbreakable sand and water <u>toys</u>.

You can also add water to the outdoor sand area if you wish.

Talk with the children about how the texture and firmness of the sand changes as water is added. Show them how to mold the damp sand and see if dry sand molds as well.

Press the damp sand into the bucket, Dana. Now turn it over and see if it has the bucket shape. Now try to make a mold with this dry sand. What happened?

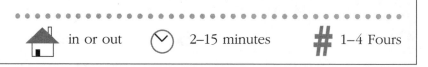

🏠 in or out   🕐 2–15 minutes   # 1–4 Fours

367

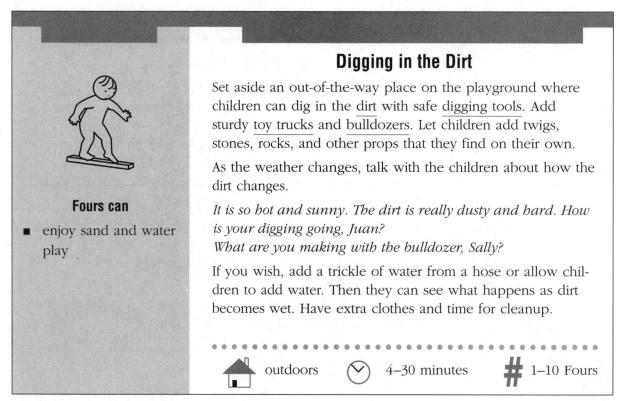

Fours can

- enjoy sand and water play

Digging in the Dirt

Set aside an out-of-the-way place on the playground where children can dig in the <u>dirt</u> with safe <u>digging</u> tools. Add sturdy <u>toy trucks</u> and <u>bulldozers</u>. Let children add twigs, stones, rocks, and other props that they find on their own.

As the weather changes, talk with the children about how the dirt changes.

It is so hot and sunny. The dirt is really dusty and hard. How is your digging going, Juan?
What are you making with the bulldozer, Sally?

If you wish, add a trickle of water from a hose or allow children to add water. Then they can see what happens as dirt becomes wet. Have extra clothes and time for cleanup.

🏠 outdoors   🕐 4–30 minutes   # 1–10 Fours

368

Fours can

■ sort by color, then by other aspects, such as size

Sorting Soft and Hard

Put lots of soft and hard things into a big box. As your Fours take out each thing, help them talk about whether it is soft or hard. See if the children can sort the hard things into one pile and the soft things into another. Talk with the children about what each thing is made of.

Do you know what that is, Victor? Right! It is a blue jay's feather! Do you remember where we found it?

Is the feather hard or soft? Which pile does it go in?

Once the children know how to sort on their own, leave the box on a low shelf so that they can work with it when they want to. Change the things in the box to add new interest.

🏠 in or out   🕐 5–15 minutes   # 1–4 Fours

369

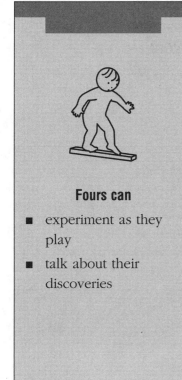

Fours can

■ experiment as they play

■ talk about their discoveries

Spice Packets

Shake a nice smelling spice (ground cloves, cinnamon) or an extract (vanilla, peppermint) onto eight or ten cotton balls. Put the cotton balls into a square of tightly woven scrap material. Pull the edges together and securely tie the spice packets closed with yarn. Make many of these packets, using different smells. Put each packet into a sturdy covered container, labeled with the name of the spice, for your Fours to use. As children take out and sniff the packets, encourage them to talk about the different smells.

What do you think of that smell, Germaine? You really like it, don't you? Do you know the name of that spice? It's mint. See, here's the name, M-I-N-T. Have you ever eaten anything with a mint flavor?

🏠 in or out   🕐 2–10 minutes   # 1–6 Fours

370

Fours can

- tell heavy- from lightweight objects
- do very simple matching or sorting

Heavy/Light Cans

Collect nine empty frozen-juice cans with metal lids. Fill three with sand or pebbles. Fill the next three one-quarter full. Leave the last three empty. Tightly seal the lids on all the cans with strong tape. Have your Fours pick up each of the cans and talk about which ones feel heavy, medium, and light. Then help the children sort the cans into the three weight groups.

Which ones are the heavy ones, Noah?
Which ones are the lightest?
And what about these?

Leave the set of cans in the Science and Nature Center for the children to use on their own once you have shown them how to do the activity.

in or out   5–15 minutes   # 1–3 Fours

371

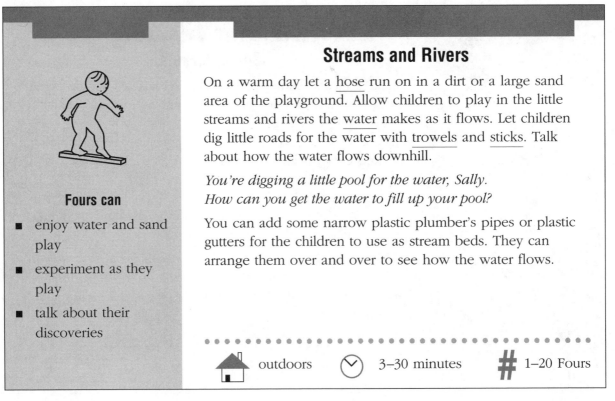

Fours can

- enjoy water and sand play
- experiment as they play
- talk about their discoveries

Streams and Rivers

On a warm day let a hose run on in a dirt or a large sand area of the playground. Allow children to play in the little streams and rivers the water makes as it flows. Let children dig little roads for the water with trowels and sticks. Talk about how the water flows downhill.

You're digging a little pool for the water, Sally.
How can you get the water to fill up your pool?

You can add some narrow plastic plumber's pipes or plastic gutters for the children to use as stream beds. They can arrange them over and over to see how the water flows.

outdoors   3–30 minutes   # 1–20 Fours

372

Fours can

■ do simple matching

Flower Picture Matching Game

Look at How to Make Matching Games for Fours on page 350. Then make a flower matching game with flower pictures that are somewhat different from each other. Show your Fours how to hold a picture card next to each picture on the matching board to find the one that is the same. Put the card on the picture it matches and choose the next flower card. Ask questions that help Fours tell how the flowers are alike or different from each other.

That's a pansy, Katrina. Can you find the other pansy? That's right. It does not match the daffodil. How are they different?

🏠 in or out   🕐 2–15 minutes   # 1–4 Fours

373

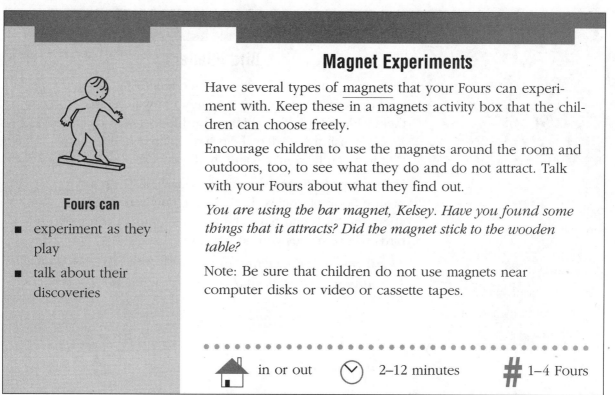

Fours can

■ experiment as they play

■ talk about their discoveries

Magnet Experiments

Have several types of magnets that your Fours can experiment with. Keep these in a magnets activity box that the children can choose freely.

Encourage children to use the magnets around the room and outdoors, too, to see what they do and do not attract. Talk with your Fours about what they find out.

You are using the bar magnet, Kelsey. Have you found some things that it attracts? Did the magnet stick to the wooden table?

Note: Be sure that children do not use magnets near computer disks or video or cassette tapes.

🏠 in or out   🕐 2–12 minutes   # 1–4 Fours

374

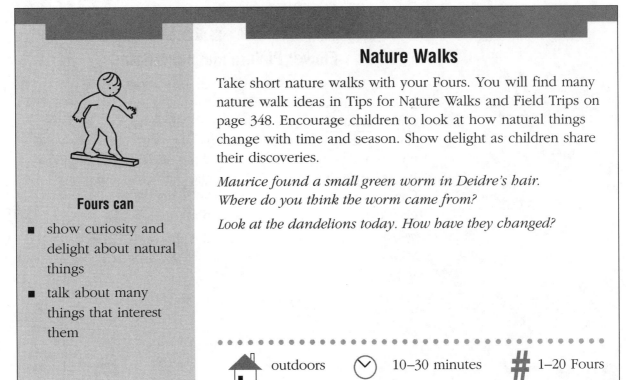

Fours can

■ show curiosity and delight about natural things

■ talk about many things that interest them

Nature Walks

Take short nature walks with your Fours. You will find many nature walk ideas in Tips for Nature Walks and Field Trips on page 348. Encourage children to look at how natural things change with time and season. Show delight as children share their discoveries.

Maurice found a small green worm in Deidre's hair. Where do you think the worm came from?

Look at the dandelions today. How have they changed?

🏠 outdoors   🕐 10–30 minutes   # 1–20 Fours

375

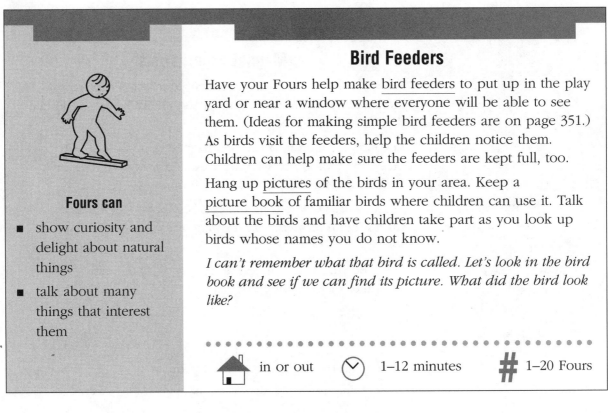

Fours can

■ show curiosity and delight about natural things

■ talk about many things that interest them

Bird Feeders

Have your Fours help make bird feeders to put up in the play yard or near a window where everyone will be able to see them. (Ideas for making simple bird feeders are on page 351.) As birds visit the feeders, help the children notice them. Children can help make sure the feeders are kept full, too.

Hang up pictures of the birds in your area. Keep a picture book of familiar birds where children can use it. Talk about the birds and have children take part as you look up birds whose names you do not know.

I can't remember what that bird is called. Let's look in the bird book and see if we can find its picture. What did the bird look like?

🏠 in or out   🕐 1–12 minutes   # 1–20 Fours

376

Fours can

- show curiosity and delight about natural things

- talk about many things that interest them

Bug Search

Be on the lookout for <u>bugs</u> you and the children can watch. Look for bugs hiding under rocks, walking in the grass, or skittering across the sidewalk. Remind the children that bugs are delicate and should not be hurt. It is usually best to just look and not touch so that the bug can go about its interesting business.

Use <u>posters</u>, <u>pictures</u>, and <u>picture books</u> about insects with your Fours to find out about the insects you and your Fours discover.

Be sure you can tell which insects might bite or sting and protect children from them.

🏠 in or out   🕐 2–15 minutes   # 1–10 Fours

377

Fours can

- recognize familiar sounds

Sounds of Real Things

Use a tape recorder to record sounds of real things the children know. Play the sounds one at a time as your Fours listen. See if the children can figure out what is making each sound. Try some of these sounds on your tape:

children laughing	water running
toilet flushing	dog barking
telephone ringing	carpenter hammering
car horn blasting	cat meowing

You can make a picture game to go with the tape by collecting or drawing <u>pictures</u> that go with the sounds. Put the pictures with the tape for the children to use.

🏠 indoors   🕐 5–15 minutes   # 1–20 Fours

Activities for Learning from the World Around Them   **329**

Fours can

- show curiosity and delight about natural things
- talk about many things that interest them

Caring for Plants

Make safe plants a regular part of your classroom. Teach children how to help care for the plants. They can help you water, fertilize, trim, repot, and be sure the plants get enough light. Keep a small watering can and mister handy for the children to use.

Know the names of the plants in the room and use them as you talk about the plants with the children. Talk about the plant parts, too.

The ivy needs watering, Janice. Feel the dirt. How does it feel? Yes. It is dry. The ivy has dry roots.

Show your Fours pictures of the plants in plant books.

. . . .

🏠 in or out   🕐 2–15 minutes   # 1–5 Fours

379

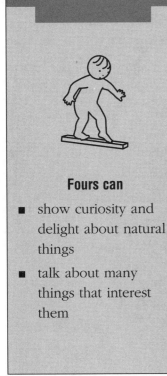

Fours can

- show curiosity and delight about natural things
- talk about many things that interest them

Rock Collections

Show interest in the pebbles and rocks that your Fours find. Make a special place where these can be collected or displayed in the Science and Nature Center. Have picture books and posters about rocks nearby that can be used to find out what types of rocks the children find. Talk about the rocks in many ways with the children—whether they are smooth or rough, and their color, size, and shape.

Maria, your new rock has tiny silver spots in it. I think the silver spots are bits of mica. Where did you find it?

You can add some pretty rocks of different colors to the collection, such as crystal, amber, and turquoise.

. . . .

🏠 in or out   🕐 1–12 minutes   # 1–8 Fours

380

Fours can

- show curiosity and delight about natural things
- talk about many things that interest them

Flower and Seed Hunts

Go on flower and seed hunts with your Fours at different times of the year. You can search for flowers or seeds in the grass during outdoor times or take walks in the neighborhood to hunt for them.

Talk about the colors, sizes, and shapes of the flowers and seeds, as well as how they are parts of a plant's growing cycle.

These impatiens seeds came from a little pod. It popped open, and the seeds shot out. Can you find another pod that has seeds in it? Look carefully.

🏠 outdoors   🕐 3–20 minutes   # 1–20 Fours

381

Fours can

- show curiosity and delight about natural things
- talk about many things that interest them

Magnifying Glasses

Have several safe magnifying glasses in the Science and Nature Center for your Fours to use whenever they are interested in seeing things close up. Plastic or glass magnifiers with thick wooden or plastic frames are best. Encourage children to use them indoors and outdoors.

Those ants are tiny, aren't they, Paul?
You can get a magnifying glass to see them better. Great!
Now can you see the ant's antennae?

Encourage your Fours to talk about the new things they can see when things are enlarged.

🏠 in or out   🕐 1–7 minutes   # 1 Four per glass

Fours can

- show curiosity and delight about natural things

- control sucking and blowing with their mouth

Bubbles of All Sizes

Use liquid dishwashing detergent as the bubble solution for your Fours to use. You can add a little water to thin the detergent, but be sure to try it out before using it with the children. Talk about the rainbow of colors in the bubbles and how the wind carries bubbles away. Let your Fours try these bubble ideas:

- Blow into a cup of bubble solution with a straw to make lots of small bubbles.

- Dip a straw into bubble solution, take it out, and blow softly.

- Use a plastic bubble wand from a jar of bubble liquid.

You can make huge bubbles for your Fours to chase by dipping a stretched-out wire hanger into bubble liquid and then waving it in the air.

in or out   3–20 minutes   # 1–20 Fours

383

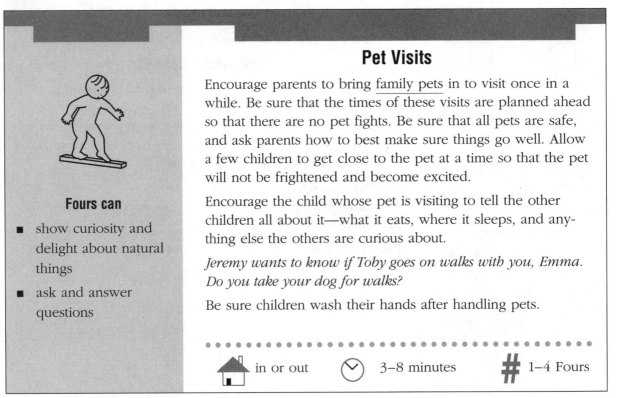

Fours can

- show curiosity and delight about natural things

- ask and answer questions

Pet Visits

Encourage parents to bring family pets in to visit once in a while. Be sure that the times of these visits are planned ahead so that there are no pet fights. Be sure that all pets are safe, and ask parents how to best make sure things go well. Allow a few children to get close to the pet at a time so that the pet will not be frightened and become excited.

Encourage the child whose pet is visiting to tell the other children all about it—what it eats, where it sleeps, and anything else the others are curious about.

Jeremy wants to know if Toby goes on walks with you, Emma. Do you take your dog for walks?

Be sure children wash their hands after handling pets.

in or out   3–8 minutes   # 1–4 Fours

384

Fours can

■ ask and answer questions about things that interest them

Freezing/Melting

On a warm day have some of your Fours pour water into ice cube trays. Then have them help you put them into the freezer. Check on how the water is freezing several times with your Fours. Talk about the changes they see. Let them feel the water as it turns to ice. Later, put the ice cubes into dishpans for outdoor play. Be sure children do not put ice cubes into their mouths. Have crushed ice for eating.

On another day, have children help you freeze juice to make juice bars. Talk about how the juice freezes and melts.

If you have ice outdoors in winter, have the children bring some indoors and put it in a bowl. Then the children can watch and talk about what happens.

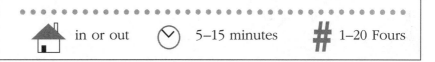

in or out   5–15 minutes   # 1–20 Fours

385

Fours can

■ experiment as they play

■ talk about their discoveries

The Warmth of the Sun

Help your Fours notice how the sun warms things on the earth. Try these ideas:

■ Let them feel warm sunny spots that come through windows in the classroom and the difference between shady and sunny spots outdoors.

■ Have water play outdoors in the sun and in the shade. Talk about how the water temperature differs.

■ Melt ice in the shade and in the sun. See which melts faster.

■ Drink a cup of water that has been in the sun and a cold cup of water. Talk about which is warmer.

in or out   1–12 minutes   # 1–20 Fours

386

Fours can

■ recognize familiar things by touch

Nature Feelie Bag

Make four or five feelie bags by putting plastic margarine tubs into big clean socks. Put one natural thing into each bag, such as a shell, an acorn, a feather, a rock, and a pine cone. Make a picture card showing each natural thing.

Have children look at the picture cards and talk about what the natural things are and how they might feel. Then let a child reach into one of the bags and guess which of the pictured things he is feeling.

How does the thing feel, Carlos? Smooth and soft? What do you think it is? Look at the pictures.

Allow children to play this game on their own or with a friend. Change the natural things and the pictures often.

🏠 in or out   🕐 3–15 minutes   # 1–4 Fours

387

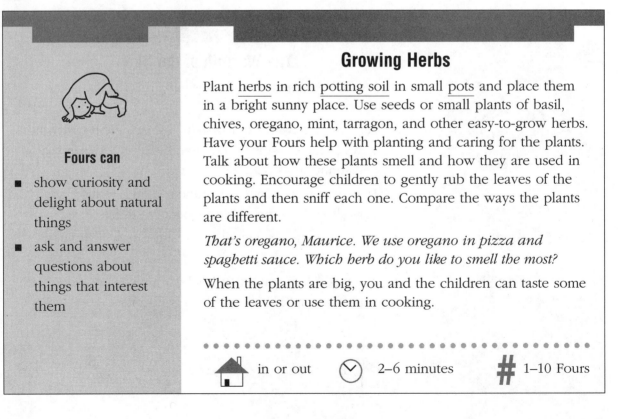

Fours can

■ show curiosity and delight about natural things

■ ask and answer questions about things that interest them

Growing Herbs

Plant herbs in rich potting soil in small pots and place them in a bright sunny place. Use seeds or small plants of basil, chives, oregano, mint, tarragon, and other easy-to-grow herbs. Have your Fours help with planting and caring for the plants. Talk about how these plants smell and how they are used in cooking. Encourage children to gently rub the leaves of the plants and then sniff each one. Compare the ways the plants are different.

That's oregano, Maurice. We use oregano in pizza and spaghetti sauce. Which herb do you like to smell the most?

When the plants are big, you and the children can taste some of the leaves or use them in cooking.

🏠 in or out   🕐 2–6 minutes   # 1–10 Fours

388

Fours can

- show curiosity and delight about natural things

- ask and answer questions about things that interest them

Differences in Trees

Help your Fours notice the things about trees that are the same and different. Inspect the bark, leaves, flowers, seeds, shape, and height through the seasons with the children. Compare when trees get and lose their leaves.

Feel how the bark of this sycamore feels, Mark. That's right, there's some on the ground. It's peeling off.

Have books and posters with pictures of trees where your Fours can look to find out more about trees.

If there are no trees in your area, then help your Fours notice how other plants are the same and different.

🏠 outdoors 🕐 1–12 minutes # 1–10 Fours

389

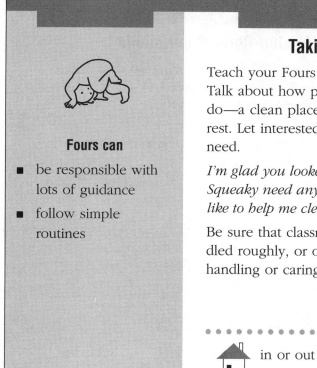

Fours can

- be responsible with lots of guidance

- follow simple routines

Taking Care of Classroom Pets

Teach your Fours how to care for any pets in the classroom. Talk about how pets need many of the same things people do—a clean place to live, healthful food, water, exercise, and rest. Let interested children take part in the care the pets need.

I'm glad you looked at our guinea pig's cage, Deanna. Does Squeaky need anything today? His cage is dirty? Would you like to help me clean it?

Be sure that classroom pets are not disturbed too much, handled roughly, or overfed. Have children wash hands after handling or caring for pets.

🏠 in or out 🕐 3–15 minutes # 1–4 Fours

390

Fours can

- do simple matching
- sort by color, then by other aspects, such as size

Leaf-Matching Game

Collect four or more very different leaves. Find other leaves that closely match the ones you already have in size, shape, and color. Your Fours can help you to collect the leaves. Put all the leaves out for the children to see. See if they can match the leaves that look alike.

This is a maple leaf, Sonya. Can you find another maple leaf that looks the same?

See if children can sort leaves by color, size, shape, or in other ways, too.

How are you sorting the leaves, Dennis? Oh, yes. I see. These are the crunchy ones and these are the soft ones.

🏠 in or out   🕐 3–15 minutes   # 1–4 Fours

391

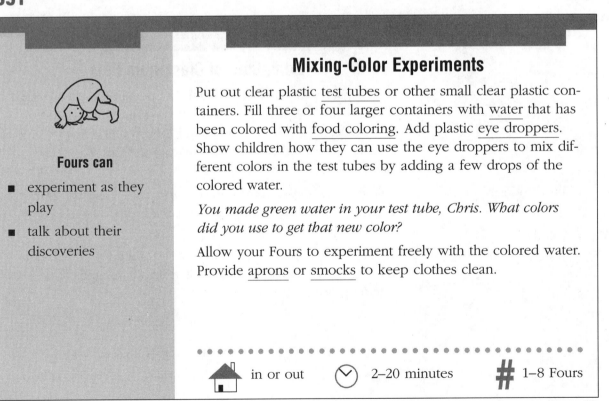

Fours can

- experiment as they play
- talk about their discoveries

Mixing-Color Experiments

Put out clear plastic test tubes or other small clear plastic containers. Fill three or four larger containers with water that has been colored with food coloring. Add plastic eye droppers. Show children how they can use the eye droppers to mix different colors in the test tubes by adding a few drops of the colored water.

You made green water in your test tube, Chris. What colors did you use to get that new color?

Allow your Fours to experiment freely with the colored water. Provide aprons or smocks to keep clothes clean.

🏠 in or out   🕐 2–20 minutes   # 1–8 Fours

392

Fours can

- experiment as they play
- talk about their discoveries

Experimenting with Flashlights

Have several plastic <u>flashlights</u> for your Fours to use freely. Allow them to experiment in many areas of the room: on the ceiling, on the floor, in dark corners, and in bright spaces. Be sure they do not flash them in other people's faces because it is uncomfortable to have light flashed in the eyes. See if the children can talk about how the light changes as the flashlight is used in different places and at different angles and distances.

The light is really dim. How can you make the light really bright, Yolanda?

Explain that flashlights use batteries for energy to make light. Help the children change batteries or bulbs when needed. Remind children to always turn off the flashlight when they are not using it.

🏠 in or out   🕐 2–15 minutes   **#** 1 Four per flashlight

393

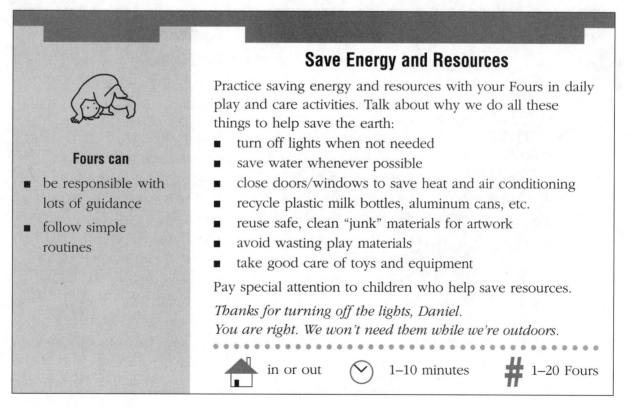

Fours can

- be responsible with lots of guidance
- follow simple routines

Save Energy and Resources

Practice saving energy and resources with your Fours in daily play and care activities. Talk about why we do all these things to help save the earth:

- turn off lights when not needed
- save water whenever possible
- close doors/windows to save heat and air conditioning
- recycle plastic milk bottles, aluminum cans, etc.
- reuse safe, clean "junk" materials for artwork
- avoid wasting play materials
- take good care of toys and equipment

Pay special attention to children who help save resources.

Thanks for turning off the lights, Daniel.
You are right. We won't need them while we're outdoors.

🏠 in or out   🕐 1–10 minutes   **#** 1–20 Fours

394

Fours can

- experiment as they play
- talk about their discoveries
- show some interest in pre-writing

Sink or Float Game

Put a few things that sink and a few that float next to your water table. Let your Fours experiment to find out what each thing does in the water. Talk about sinking and floating with the children.

Some children may be interested in recording what they found out. Encourage any children who are interested to draw pictures of what they discovered—which things sink and which float. Or if children wish, you can help them mark a checklist such as the one on page 352 to show what they discovered.

What do you think the wooden block will do, Jason?
Will it sink or float? Yes, it floats!
Are you going to mark the picture of the block on your checklist?

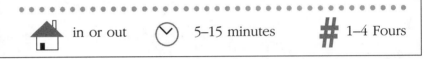

🏠 in or out   🕐 5–15 minutes   # 1–4 Fours

395

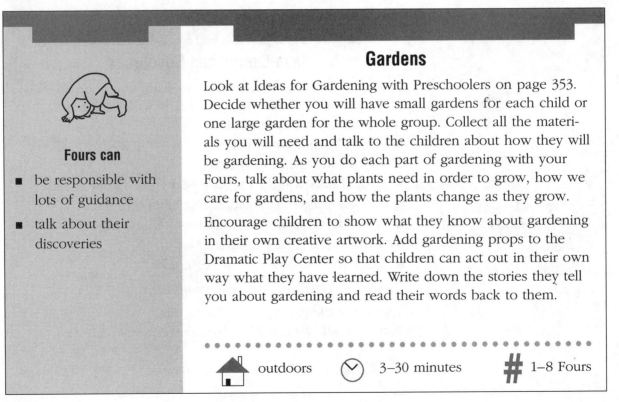

Fours can

- be responsible with lots of guidance
- talk about their discoveries

Gardens

Look at Ideas for Gardening with Preschoolers on page 353. Decide whether you will have small gardens for each child or one large garden for the whole group. Collect all the materials you will need and talk to the children about how they will be gardening. As you do each part of gardening with your Fours, talk about what plants need in order to grow, how we care for gardens, and how the plants change as they grow.

Encourage children to show what they know about gardening in their own creative artwork. Add gardening props to the Dramatic Play Center so that children can act out in their own way what they have learned. Write down the stories they tell you about gardening and read their words back to them.

🏠 outdoors   🕐 3–30 minutes   # 1–8 Fours

Activities for Learning from the World Around Them

396

Fours can

- experiment as they play
- talk about their discoveries

Reflections

Have safe <u>mirrors</u> of many sizes for children to use. Encourage them to experiment with the mirrors in many ways. Talk with the children about how much they can see in smaller or larger mirrors and how they can move mirrors to see different things or people.

Help your Fours notice other reflections in our world, too. Point out reflections in some of these things:

- windows
- puddles of water
- a shiny slide
- a metal spoon
- bright pots and pans

 in or out   1–10 minutes   # 1–10 Fours

397

Fours can

- play simple games, but have trouble with following rules and losing
- do simple matching

Animal Lotto Game

Buy or make an <u>animal-matching or lotto game</u> that has game boards with pictures of animals and matching <u>picture cards</u>. Give one board to each child who wants to play. Then you or another child can hold up one picture at a time for all players to see. Ask who has that same picture on his board. Help your Fours look if necessary. Give the picture card to the child who has the same picture on his board and let him use it to cover that picture. Play until all pictures are used.

Help children understand that the point of the game is to get all pictures covered, not for one person to cover all his pictures first.

Make or buy other matching games with pictures of flowers, fish, trees, birds, or other natural things.

in or out   8–20 minutes   # 2–8 Fours

398

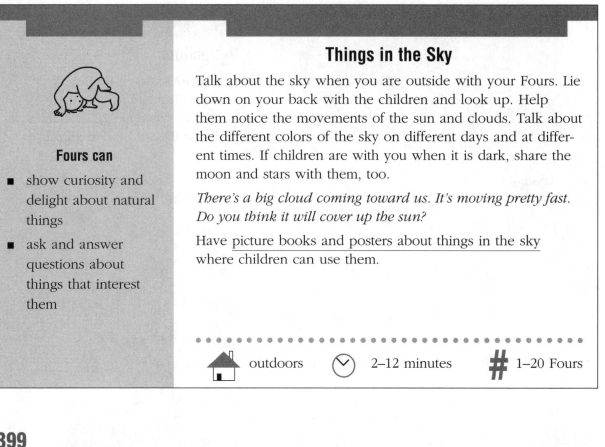

Fours can

- show curiosity and delight about natural things
- ask and answer questions about things that interest them

Things in the Sky

Talk about the sky when you are outside with your Fours. Lie down on your back with the children and look up. Help them notice the movements of the sun and clouds. Talk about the different colors of the sky on different days and at different times. If children are with you when it is dark, share the moon and stars with them, too.

There's a big cloud coming toward us. It's moving pretty fast. Do you think it will cover up the sun?

Have picture books and posters about things in the sky where children can use them.

🏠 outdoors   🕐 2–12 minutes   # 1–20 Fours

399

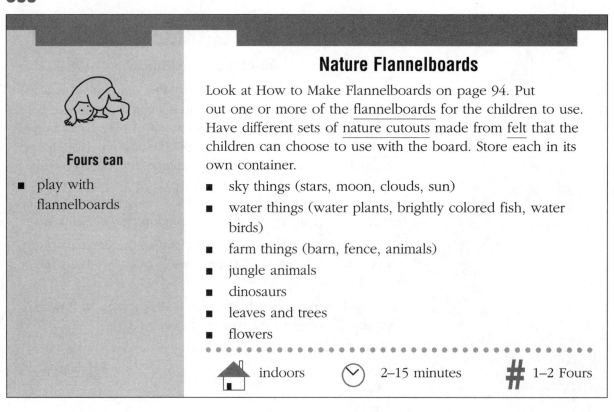

Fours can

- play with flannelboards

Nature Flannelboards

Look at How to Make Flannelboards on page 94. Put out one or more of the flannelboards for the children to use. Have different sets of nature cutouts made from felt that the children can choose to use with the board. Store each in its own container.

- sky things (stars, moon, clouds, sun)
- water things (water plants, brightly colored fish, water birds)
- farm things (barn, fence, animals)
- jungle animals
- dinosaurs
- leaves and trees
- flowers

🏠 indoors   🕐 2–15 minutes   # 1–2 Fours

400

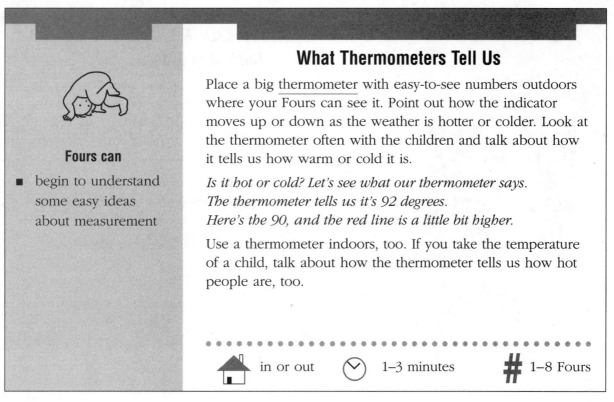

Fours can

- do simple matching
- sort by color, then by other aspects, such as size

Seashells

Have a collection of seashells in the Science and Nature Center for your Fours to inspect. Have several of each kind of shell. See if the children can sort them into piles of shells that look the same. Have books and pictures that show different shells nearby so that you and your Fours can find out more about each kind of shell. Talk about the names of the shells as the children play with them.

You found all the scallop shells, Trina. Do you remember what kind of shell these are? That's right, they are all clam shells.

Add shells to the sand or water table once in a while so that the children can see how they look when found at the beach.

🏠 in or out   🕐 1–20 minutes   # 1–10 Fours

401

Fours can

- begin to understand some easy ideas about measurement

What Thermometers Tell Us

Place a big thermometer with easy-to-see numbers outdoors where your Fours can see it. Point out how the indicator moves up or down as the weather is hotter or colder. Look at the thermometer often with the children and talk about how it tells us how warm or cold it is.

Is it hot or cold? Let's see what our thermometer says.
The thermometer tells us it's 92 degrees.
Here's the 90, and the red line is a little bit higher.

Use a thermometer indoors, too. If you take the temperature of a child, talk about how the thermometer tells us how hot people are, too.

🏠 in or out   🕐 1–3 minutes   # 1–8 Fours

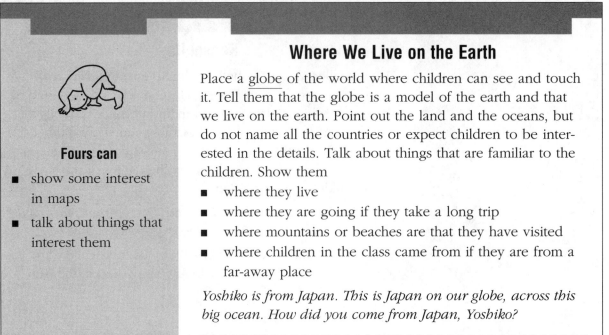

Fours can

- show some interest in maps
- talk about things that interest them

Where We Live on the Earth

Place a globe of the world where children can see and touch it. Tell them that the globe is a model of the earth and that we live on the earth. Point out the land and the oceans, but do not name all the countries or expect children to be interested in the details. Talk about things that are familiar to the children. Show them

- where they live
- where they are going if they take a long trip
- where mountains or beaches are that they have visited
- where children in the class came from if they are from a far-away place

Yoshiko is from Japan. This is Japan on our globe, across this big ocean. How did you come from Japan, Yoshiko?

🏠 indoors　　🕐 2–8 minutes　　# 1–4 Fours

403

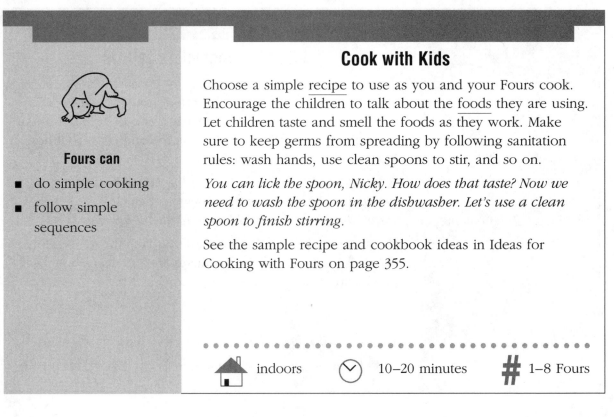

Fours can

- do simple cooking
- follow simple sequences

Cook with Kids

Choose a simple recipe to use as you and your Fours cook. Encourage the children to talk about the foods they are using. Let children taste and smell the foods as they work. Make sure to keep germs from spreading by following sanitation rules: wash hands, use clean spoons to stir, and so on.

You can lick the spoon, Nicky. How does that taste? Now we need to wash the spoon in the dishwasher. Let's use a clean spoon to finish stirring.

See the sample recipe and cookbook ideas in Ideas for Cooking with Fours on page 355.

🏠 indoors　　🕐 10–20 minutes　　# 1–8 Fours

404

Fours can

- learn lots about dinosaurs
- ask and answer questions about things that interest them

All About Dinosaurs

Have a collection of toy dinosaurs for the children to use. You may want to have small and large sets. Be sure to have several of the most popular types to avoid fights over toys.

Place picture books and posters about dinosaurs where children can look and talk about them. Use these with interested children to answer questions and find out more. Help interested children learn the correct name of each dinosaur, what it ate, and how it lived. Explain that dinosaurs lived long ago and are not alive now.

Do you want to know the name of that dinosaur, Charlie? Let's look in a dinosaur book to find out. You found a picture that looks exactly like it! The book says it's called a stegosaurus.

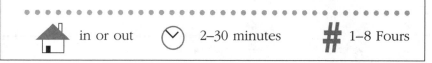

🏠 in or out   🕐 2–30 minutes   # 1–8 Fours

405

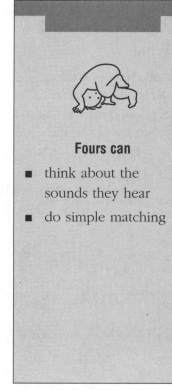

Fours can

- think about the sounds they hear
- do simple matching

Sound-Picture Matching Game

Put one small thing into each of five margarine tubs with lids. Use things that will sound different when shaken in the tub. For example, use a bell, block, crayon, cotton ball, and a scoop of sand. Make a little picture card of each thing in the tub.

Show your Fours how to shake the tubs, listen carefully, look at each picture, and then try to guess which pictured thing is in each tub. Show them how to put each sound tub with its matching picture card. The children can open the tubs to see if they guessed correctly.

Leave the set of tubs and picture cards in a box on a shelf in the Science and Nature Center for children to use on their own once you have shown them how.

🏠 indoors   🕐 4–15 minutes   # 1–3 Fours

406

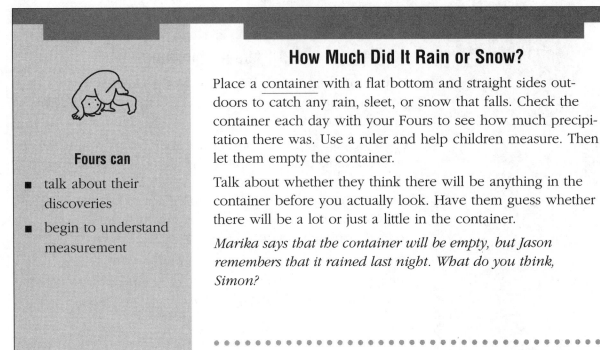

Fours can

- talk about their discoveries
- begin to understand measurement

How Much Did It Rain or Snow?

Place a container with a flat bottom and straight sides outdoors to catch any rain, sleet, or snow that falls. Check the container each day with your Fours to see how much precipitation there was. Use a ruler and help children measure. Then let them empty the container.

Talk about whether they think there will be anything in the container before you actually look. Have them guess whether there will be a lot or just a little in the container.

Marika says that the container will be empty, but Jason remembers that it rained last night. What do you think, Simon?

outdoors   3–10 minutes   1–5 Fours

407

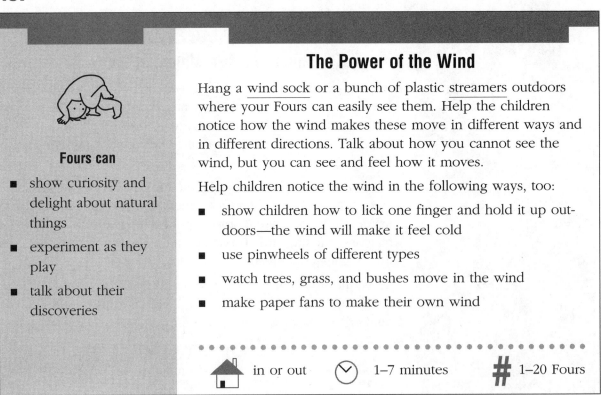

Fours can

- show curiosity and delight about natural things
- experiment as they play
- talk about their discoveries

The Power of the Wind

Hang a wind sock or a bunch of plastic streamers outdoors where your Fours can easily see them. Help the children notice how the wind makes these move in different ways and in different directions. Talk about how you cannot see the wind, but you can see and feel how it moves.

Help children notice the wind in the following ways, too:

- show children how to lick one finger and hold it up outdoors—the wind will make it feel cold
- use pinwheels of different types
- watch trees, grass, and bushes move in the wind
- make paper fans to make their own wind

in or out   1–7 minutes   1–20 Fours

Activities for Learning from the World Around Them

408

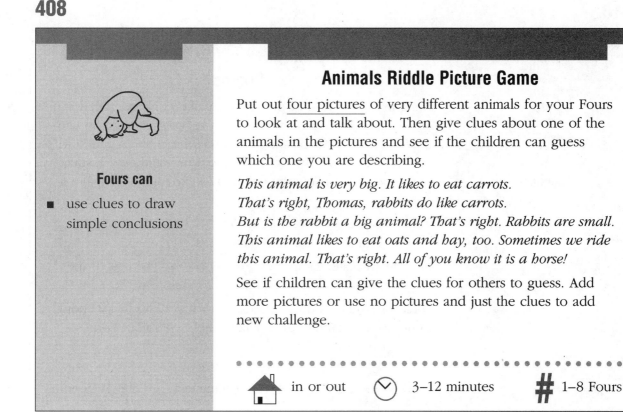

Fours can

- use clues to draw simple conclusions

Animals Riddle Picture Game

Put out <u>four pictures</u> of very different animals for your Fours to look at and talk about. Then give clues about one of the animals in the pictures and see if the children can guess which one you are describing.

This animal is very big. It likes to eat carrots.
That's right, Thomas, rabbits do like carrots.
But is the rabbit a big animal? That's right. Rabbits are small.
This animal likes to eat oats and hay, too. Sometimes we ride this animal. That's right. All of you know it is a horse!

See if children can give the clues for others to guess. Add more pictures or use no pictures and just the clues to add new challenge.

🏠 in or out   🕐 3–12 minutes   # 1–8 Fours

409

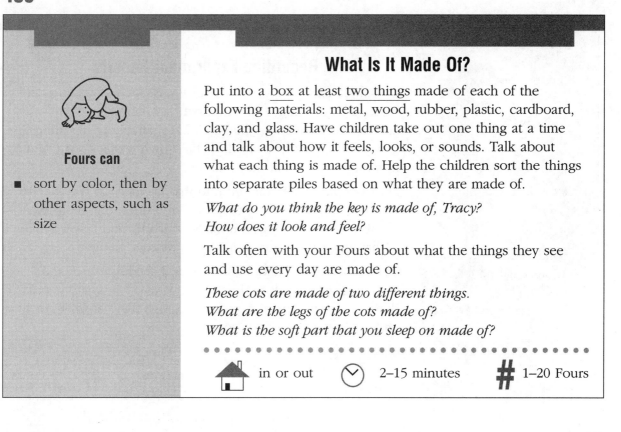

Fours can

- sort by color, then by other aspects, such as size

What Is It Made Of?

Put into a <u>box</u> at least <u>two things</u> made of each of the following materials: metal, wood, rubber, plastic, cardboard, clay, and glass. Have children take out one thing at a time and talk about how it feels, looks, or sounds. Talk about what each thing is made of. Help the children sort the things into separate piles based on what they are made of.

What do you think the key is made of, Tracy?
How does it look and feel?

Talk often with your Fours about what the things they see and use every day are made of.

These cots are made of two different things.
What are the legs of the cots made of?
What is the soft part that you sleep on made of?

🏠 in or out   🕐 2–15 minutes   # 1–20 Fours

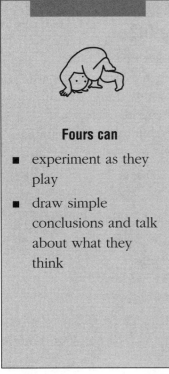

Fours can

- show curiosity and delight about natural things
- experiment as they play

Prisms

Bring in a collection of <u>prisms</u> that make rainbows when sunlight passes through them. Hang crystal prisms in sunny windows and use clear plastic prisms that the children can hold and move to catch the light. Point out the rainbows, inspect the colors, and encourage children to experiment to make a rainbow.

That's right, Chio. I see the rainbow on the wall, too.
Let's see how many colors it has.

Provide art materials in the rainbow colors. Then see if the children begin to include rainbows in their artwork.

Look for rainbows during rainstorms. If you are lucky enough to find one, celebrate the amazing sight with your Fours.

🏠 in or out   🕐 1–7 minutes   # 1–15 Fours

411

Fours can

- experiment as they play
- draw simple conclusions and talk about what they think

Recording Experiment Results

Do simple experiments with your Fours, such as finding out what kinds of things sink and float or what magnets are attracted to. Encourage the children to talk about the things they discover and then to draw their own conclusions (right or wrong) from what they learned.

For example, if the children find that magnets do not stick to wooden pencils, doors, bookcases, and trees, then help them see that all those things are made of wood, and that it is likely that magnets are not attracted to wooden things.

Write down what children say about their discoveries and read their ideas back to them. Do not worry if what they say does not seem correct to you. Encourage them to experiment and think, whatever their conclusions are.

🏠 in or out   🕐 5–20 minutes   # 1–6 Fours

Science and Nature Center

- Have a table where many interesting natural things can be put out for children to inspect.

- Have a sand or water table near the center.

- Make sure there is plenty of light.

- Have a place to put pictures about nature and science. Put up pictures that show natural things children are interested in. Change the pictures often.

- Have a place to put books that give more information about the nature and science things your Fours enjoy.

- Have lots of unbreakable jars, boxes, or containers ready to put natural treasures in. Some will need lids with holes punched in them for air.

- Be sure that nothing in the center is poisonous or dangerous to a child.

- Pay lots of attention to the Science and Nature Center. Show your own curiosity and interest as you share discoveries with the children.

- Change or add to the area often. Help the children notice the changes.

- If a child cares about something he or she has brought in, be sure it is protected and sent home again.

- Add natural things to other areas of the room. Have plants, pets, pictures, or mobiles wherever they can safely fit in.

- If living things are part of the Science and Nature Center, be sure they are well cared for—cages cleaned, food and water provided daily, no rough handling.

- If wild living things are brought in or discovered, encourage your Fours to respect each creature's life, even if the living thing is only a small insect or worm.

- Keep pets such as gerbils or mice out of children's reach. These pets are fun to watch but can bite small fingers, even when children are supervised. And children can easily harm the pets. A sturdy aquarium cage with a lid is the best home for these animals.

- Make sure any animals that children come into contact with are healthy and will not pass on any illness. If any child is scratched or bitten, disinfect the injury and let the parent know what happened.

Tips for Nature Walks and Field Trips

- Most of the trips you take with Fours should be short. Most trips can be walks of no more than 20 to 30 minutes. Very special trips can last a morning, an afternoon, or even a full day, but be sure to keep the children's regular schedule for meals and snacks, toileting, and rest.

- Be sure there are enough adults along and that their full attention is on the children at all times. The longer the trip, the more adults are needed. If a trip is to last a full day, then it is best to have one parent or teacher for every two or three children.

- If a child is difficult to handle, then have one adult care for that child and only one other, more cooperative child.

- Take the same walks over and over again, but look for different things each time.

- If you drive, make sure each child is seat-belted safely with his or her own safety restraint. Seat belts should never be shared.

- Put a name tag on each child.

- Get permission slips from parents. For walks around the block or to a nearby park, one blanket permission for all outings should be enough. But always make sure all parents know where you will be going and when you will be back.

- Let parents know before you take any trip so that they can dress children properly. A note on the parents' message space plus mentioning each trip usually works well.

- Have extra clothing available so that no child ever has to be too cold or too hot.

- Make sure to be back on time. If you will be late, contact someone who can tell the parents.

- If your trip will be longer than usual, take along a snack and anything else you might need for the children.

- If you are going farther than just a few blocks, always bring children's emergency information and a first aid kit.

- Some Fours may want to be independent and wander or run away from adults. If this is a problem, always hold that child's hand and watch carefully. Be serious with the children and explain how important it is for their safety to stay with the adults.

- Whenever possible, encourage children to enjoy plant and animal life in its natural place. For example, instead of picking wild flowers, help children learn to enjoy them but leave them for others, too. Instead of catching bugs, encourage children to watch the bugs do the things they do without being disturbed.

- Some ideas for nature walks and trips with Fours are

walk around the block

visit children's backyards that are nearby

visit a pet store

visit a zoo

explore a big grassy field

tour a children's science museum

visit a farm

visit a forest or woods

visit a park with trees and flowers

tour an aquarium

visit a greenhouse filled with plants

visit a pumpkin patch

visit a Christmas tree farm

visit an orchard (when in flower and when in fruit)

visit a pond, river, or stream (but only with extra supervision)

go to a beach (but only with extra supervision)

go to a duck pond to feed the ducks (but only with extra supervision)

How to Make Matching Games for Fours

- For younger Fours, use eight to ten pictures on a card. Use fewer pictures per card when pictures are difficult to tell apart.

- If the game is too easy for the children, then use pictures that are more alike or use more pictures at a time.

- Pictures of the same thing, but shown differently, may be used for older fours. For example, you may have one picture of a whole apple to match with a picture of an apple cut into slices, or a picture of a bunch of tulips that matches a picture of a single tulip.

1. Collect or draw matching pairs of pictures. You can find matching pictures in two copies of the same catalog, magazine, newspaper ad, or children's activity book.

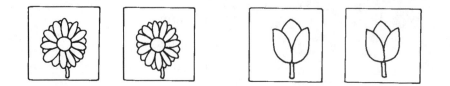

2. Use two sturdy pieces of cardboard that are the same size. Mark each into eight or more same-sized squares or rectangles.

3. Cut one piece of the cardboard along the lines to make eight cards. Leave the other piece whole for the Matching Board.

4. Glue one picture from each pair onto each of the small cards. Glue the other pictures in the squares on the large card.

5. Cover the cards and board with clear contact paper or laminate to protect the pictures.

6. Store cards with boards in individual containers.

Activities for Learning from the World Around Them

Ideas for Making Bird Feeders

1. Mix peanut butter with cornmeal until you can roll the mixture into a doughy, not-too-sticky ball. Your Fours can help knead the mixture with their hands. Add birdseed, if you wish. Make sure there is enough cornmeal in the mixture so that the birds don't choke on the peanut butter.

2. Put a big ball of the mixture into a mesh onion bag. Hang the bag outside.

OR

Cut clean, empty 6-oz cardboard frozen juice containers so that they are 1" in height. Punch a hole through the cardboard at the open end. Tie a loop of string through the hole as a hanger. Have your Fours help you press the mixture into the cans. Hang outside.

Peanut Butter and Birdseed on Toast

1. Toast bread lightly. Stale bread collected from children's parents is fine for the birds. Your Fours may want to taste this before birdseed is added. Use fresh-toasted bread for children to eat.

2. Have your Fours use dull plastic knives to spread peanut butter on toast.

3. Use a dull darning needle to thread a loop of yarn through one corner of the toast.

4. Have children sprinkle birdseed onto the sticky peanut butter.

5. Hang the toast outside for the birds.

Sink or Float Sorting Game Checklist

Mark the things that float.

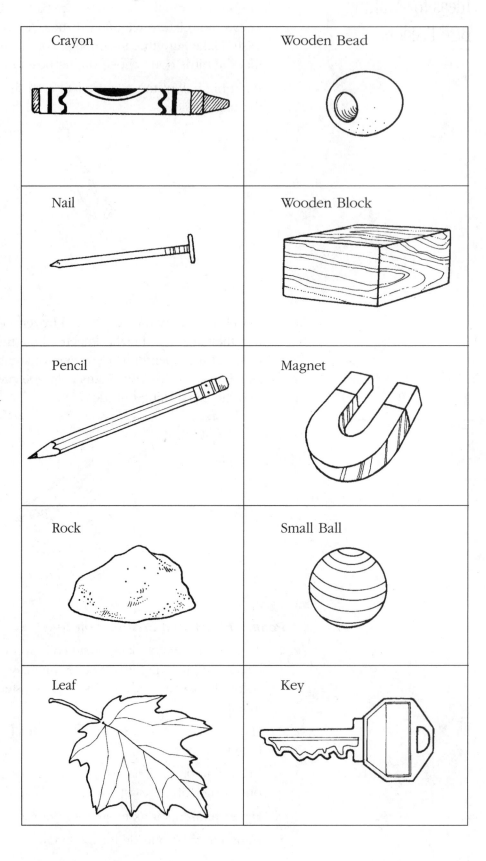

Crayon	Wooden Bead
Nail	Wooden Block
Pencil	Magnet
Rock	Small Ball
Leaf	Key

Activities for Learning from the World Around Them

Ideas for Gardening with Preschoolers

Group Garden

Note: Fours will enjoy growing a garden, but their interest will come and go, depending on what is happening. For example, some children will be interested in planting seeds, others will like watering, and others will want to pick flowers or the foods you grow. Your children will be interested in bits and pieces rather than in the long-term picture that you enjoy so much. This is normal and appropriate for young children.

■ Plant a small garden in a sunny but protected place where children can see it.

■ Plant quick-to-grow vegetables (lettuce, radishes) and flowers (zinneas, marigolds). If your program is open through the summer, plant other things that take longer to grow (tomatoes, green beans, pumpkins, summer squash) but that the children will find interesting to watch.

■ Tend the garden well, keeping it weeded, watered, and harvested. Encourage children to help in every step, but do not expect that they will always be interested.

■ If you do not have a good place for a garden outdoors, plant small vegetables such as radishes, lettuce, or small tomato plants in containers. Dishpans or large flowerpots filled with rich potting soil can be used if kept in a sunny place and watered regularly.

Individual Gardens

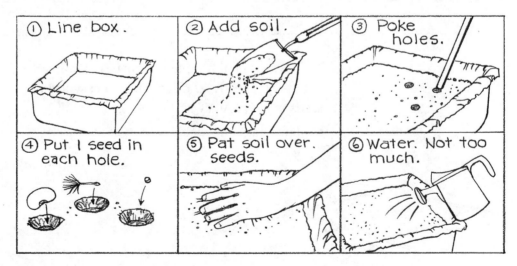

① Line box.

② Add soil.

③ Poke holes.

④ Put 1 seed in each hole.

⑤ Pat soil over seeds.

⑥ Water. Not too much.

Gardening Instructions

■ Copy the garden recipe onto a large chart or onto individual cards.

■ Talk about the pictures with small groups of children before they plant.

- While children make gardens, have them look at the pictures to see what they need to do.

- Help children talk about what they are doing.

- Optional:

  a. If children use plastic dishpans, do not have them line the box (step 1).

  b. Children can use a measuring stick to poke holes. Make a measuring stick by marking a straw, stick, or coffee stirrer 1/4" from one end. Tell children to make holes as deep as the mark.

  c. Place large-holed chicken wire on top of soil. Have the children plant only one seed in each wire space. This avoids overcrowding plants.

  d. Allow children to choose their own seeds. Set up seeds so that children can see how many of each type to take. Provide a picture of what the seed will grow into.

Tip: Give children a piece of masking tape to stick seeds onto until they're ready to plant. They're easy to remove, and small seeds won't blow away or get lost.

- Encourage the children to observe and care for their own gardens.

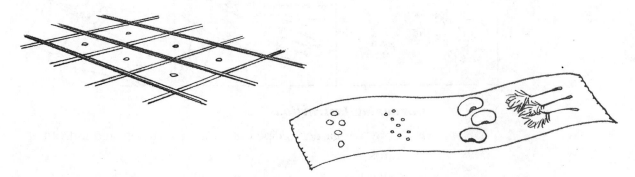

Activities for Learning from the World Around Them

Ideas for Cooking with Fours

1. Copy this recipe on larger pieces of cardboard to make recipe cards.

2. Put each card in a row on a low table or counter from left to right.

3. Put each bowl of fruit in front of its card.

4. Have each child start on the left and take the right amount of fruit to put into his own cup.

FRUIT SALAD

2 apple slices ①

3 banana slices ②

3 pineapple chunks ③

2 orange sections ④

4 raisins ⑤

Stir and eat. ⑥

This recipe is from *Cook and Learn* by Beverly Veitch and Thelma Harms. Menlo Park, CA: Addison-Wesley Publishing Company, 1981. See also *Creative Food Experiences for Children* by Mary Goodwin and Gerry Pollen, Center for Science in the Public Interest, 1755 S. Street N.W., Washington, DC 20009; and *More than Graham Crackers* by Nancy Wannamaker, Kristen Hearn and Sherrill Richarz, NAEYC, 1834 Connecticut Avenue, N.W., Washington, DC 20009.

Materials and Notes

Number, Shape, and Size (Math)

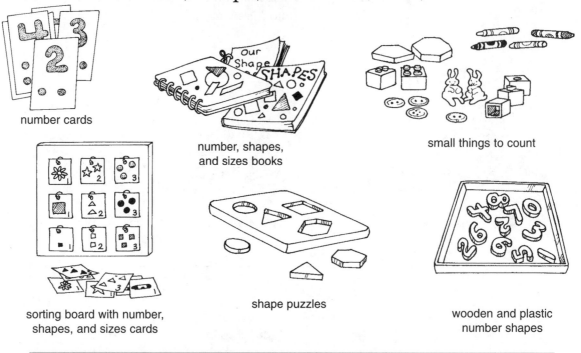

number cards

number, shapes, and sizes books

small things to count

sorting board with number, shapes, and sizes cards

shape puzzles

wooden and plastic number shapes

- Count real things with your Fours often. Talk about numbers of things as you go through the day with the children so that they see how numbers are used and why they are useful.

- Keep number, shape, and size activities fun and interesting for Fours. Do not push children to memorize numbers or turn math into a boring task that children do not enjoy.

- Some children in your group will be able to understand numbers very well, while others will not yet be interested. Challenge each child at his or her own level. Children will learn at their own pace and in their own way.

- A Math Center should be set up in a quiet area of the room where Fours can use a variety of number, shape, and size materials and games.

- Tell parents about some of the number, shape, and size games you play with children. Encourage parents to talk about these things with their children at home.

- Many of the activity ideas for younger and older Fours can be used with either age group. This is because they are open-ended and can be challenging to children with a wide range of abilities.

Activity Checklist

Number, Shape, and Size (Math)

Number, shape and size (math) activities for Fours help children think about and compare how many, how much, and what size or shape as they play games, solve real-life problems, and sing songs. For some older Fours, activities also include reading or writing some of the numbers or drawing shapes, but not all children will be interested in this. Number, shape, and size activities in the preschool focus on real experiences so that mathematical concepts will come more easily later on.

Check for each age group

	48–54 months	54–60 months
1. Children take part in routines in which counting is used, such as setting the table or putting out cots.	❏	❏
2. Adult often counts with interested children and talks about the shapes and sizes of things children see and use.	❏	❏
3. Adult asks questions to help children talk about number, shape, and size but does not quiz children on these things.	❏	❏
4. Number, shape, and size are part of many different activities, not just those in the Math Center. For example, counting is used to keep score for basketball or to see how many blankets are needed for the dolls.	❏	❏
5. Number songs and rhymes are often used with the children.	❏	❏
6. Teaching about number, shape, and size is developmentally appropriate. Hands-on activities are used instead of memorization and worksheets. Interest is encouraged but not forced.	❏	❏
7. A Math Center with number books, age-appropriate games, and lots of small things to count is set up for children to use freely.	❏	❏
8. Adult often plays number games with children and helps when needed.	❏	❏
9. Adult encourages older Fours to estimate numbers of things and then count to check.		❏
10. Interested children can be helped and encouraged to read and write simple numbers, but emphasis is still on hands-on math activities.		❏

412

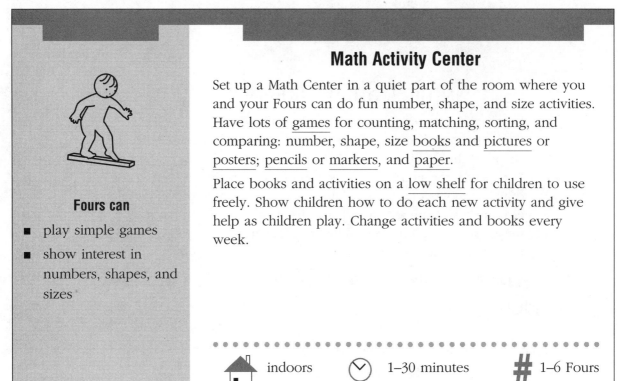

Fours can

- play simple games
- show interest in numbers, shapes, and sizes

Math Activity Center

Set up a Math Center in a quiet part of the room where you and your Fours can do fun number, shape, and size activities. Have lots of <u>games</u> for counting, matching, sorting, and comparing: number, shape, size <u>books</u> and <u>pictures</u> or posters; pencils or <u>markers</u>, and <u>paper</u>.

Place books and activities on a <u>low shelf</u> for children to use freely. Show children how to do each new activity and give help as children play. Change activities and books every week.

🏠 indoors　🕐 1–30 minutes　# 1–6 Fours

413

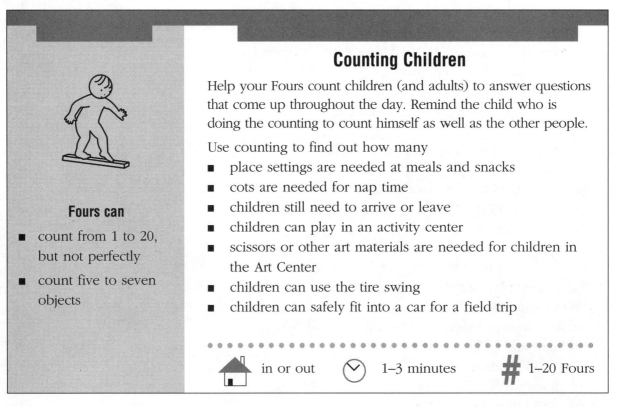

Fours can

- count from 1 to 20, but not perfectly
- count five to seven objects

Counting Children

Help your Fours count children (and adults) to answer questions that come up throughout the day. Remind the child who is doing the counting to count himself as well as the other people.

Use counting to find out how many

- place settings are needed at meals and snacks
- cots are needed for nap time
- children still need to arrive or leave
- children can play in an activity center
- scissors or other art materials are needed for children in the Art Center
- children can use the tire swing
- children can safely fit into a car for a field trip

🏠 in or out　🕐 1–3 minutes　# 1–20 Fours

414

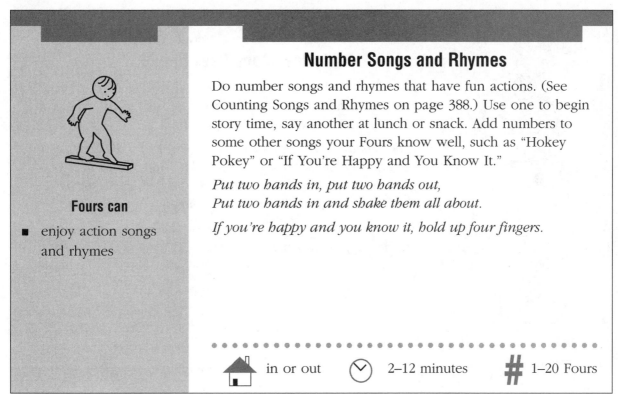

Fours can

■ enjoy action songs
and rhymes

Number Songs and Rhymes

Do number songs and rhymes that have fun actions. (See Counting Songs and Rhymes on page 388.) Use one to begin story time, say another at lunch or snack. Add numbers to some other songs your Fours know well, such as "Hokey Pokey" or "If You're Happy and You Know It."

Put two hands in, put two hands out,
Put two hands in and shake them all about.

If you're happy and you know it, hold up four fingers.

🏠 in or out   🕐 2–12 minutes   # 1–20 Fours

415

Fours can

■ learn a little about
calendars

■ know some time
words, such as *week*
or *next summer*

Birthdays on the Calendar

Hang a colorful calendar where your Fours can easily see and touch it. Explain to interested children that the calendar tells us what day, month, and year it is. Show children what day it is today. Let each child help you mark her birthday and mark your own, as well. Show children when other special days are, too. Talk about the numbers and dates.

Are you trying to find your birthday, Emma?
Here is the September page. Do you see your name?
That's right! It's there on the 9th!

Note: Avoid using the calendar with a big group of Fours. Many children will not be interested, and some will not be able to see. Show and tell about the calendar once in a while, and keep it short—only 1 or 2 minutes.

🏠 indoors   🕐 1–5 minutes   # 1–4 Fours

416

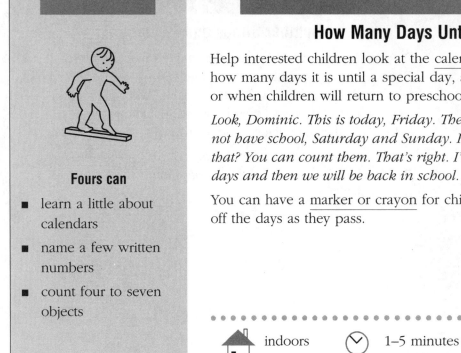

Fours can

- learn a little about calendars
- name a few written numbers
- count four to seven objects

How Many Days Until...

Help interested children look at the calendar and count up how many days it is until a special day, such as the weekend or when children will return to preschool.

Look, Dominic. This is today, Friday. These are the days we do not have school, Saturday and Sunday. How many days is that? You can count them. That's right. I'll miss you for two days and then we will be back in school.

You can have a marker or crayon for children to use to mark off the days as they pass.

🏠 indoors   🕐 1–5 minutes   # 1–4 Fours

417

Fours can

- begin to understand about measurement
- start to measure distances

Measuring with Hands and Feet

Make a line about 4' to 6' long with masking tape indoors or with chalk outdoors. Ask some of the children if they want to measure how long the line is. Show them how many of your feet long the line is by walking toe to heel and counting each step. Then let children find out how many of their feet long the line is. Try measuring the line with hands, carefully putting one hand after the other.

Write the number of hands and feet it took for each child and for you. Then show your children a ruler that is 1' long and measure the line with the ruler.

🏠 in or out   🕐 2–10 minutes   # 1–3 Fours

418

Fours can

- know names of penny, nickel, dime
- see differences in size and color

Money Matching and Sorting Games

Use plastic play money <u>coins</u> or real <u>pennies</u> to make money matching or sorting <u>games</u>. You will find two fun Money Matching and Sorting Games to make on pages 393–394.

Place the games on the shelf for children to choose when they go to the Math Center. Show your Fours how to play. Use the names of the coins, talk about the numbers the children see, and encourage the children to count easy numbers in many ways.

You put the right number of pennies on the card, Sarah. Can you count them?

Show children how to put the games away after playing.

🏠 indoors　　🕐 1–15 minutes　　# 1–2 Fours

419

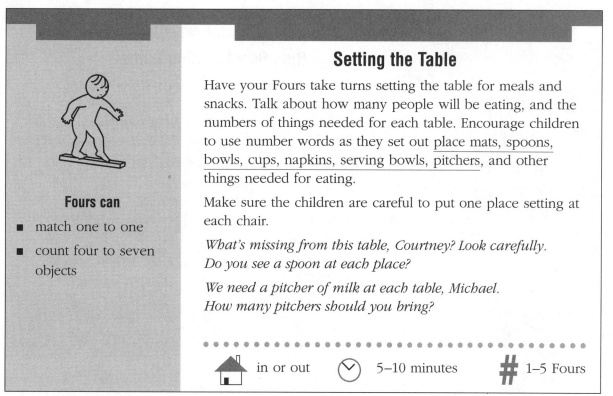

Fours can

- match one to one
- count four to seven objects

Setting the Table

Have your Fours take turns setting the table for meals and snacks. Talk about how many people will be eating, and the numbers of things needed for each table. Encourage children to use number words as they set out <u>place mats</u>, <u>spoons</u>, <u>bowls</u>, cups, napkins, serving bowls, <u>pitchers</u>, and other things needed for eating.

Make sure the children are careful to put one place setting at each chair.

What's missing from this table, Courtney? Look carefully. Do you see a spoon at each place?

We need a pitcher of milk at each table, Michael. How many pitchers should you bring?

🏠 in or out　　🕐 5–10 minutes　　# 1–5 Fours

420

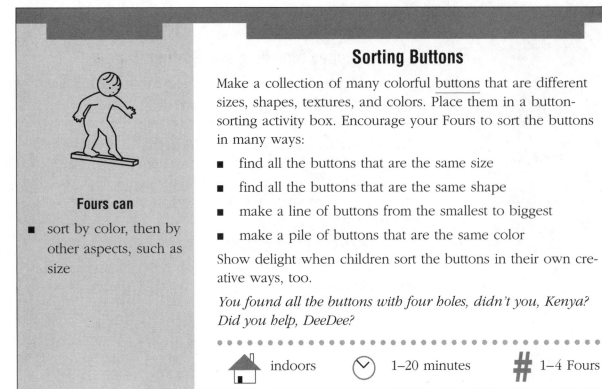

Fours can

- sort by color, then by other aspects, such as size

Sorting Buttons

Make a collection of many colorful buttons that are different sizes, shapes, textures, and colors. Place them in a button-sorting activity box. Encourage your Fours to sort the buttons in many ways:

- find all the buttons that are the same size
- find all the buttons that are the same shape
- make a line of buttons from the smallest to biggest
- make a pile of buttons that are the same color

Show delight when children sort the buttons in their own creative ways, too.

You found all the buttons with four holes, didn't you, Kenya? Did you help, DeeDee?

indoors   1–20 minutes   # 1–4 Fours

421

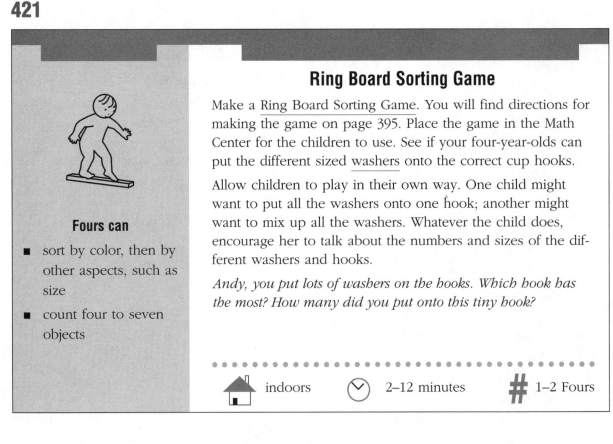

Fours can

- sort by color, then by other aspects, such as size
- count four to seven objects

Ring Board Sorting Game

Make a Ring Board Sorting Game. You will find directions for making the game on page 395. Place the game in the Math Center for the children to use. See if your four-year-olds can put the different sized washers onto the correct cup hooks.

Allow children to play in their own way. One child might want to put all the washers onto one hook; another might want to mix up all the washers. Whatever the child does, encourage her to talk about the numbers and sizes of the different washers and hooks.

Andy, you put lots of washers on the hooks. Which hook has the most? How many did you put onto this tiny hook?

indoors   2–12 minutes   # 1–2 Fours

422

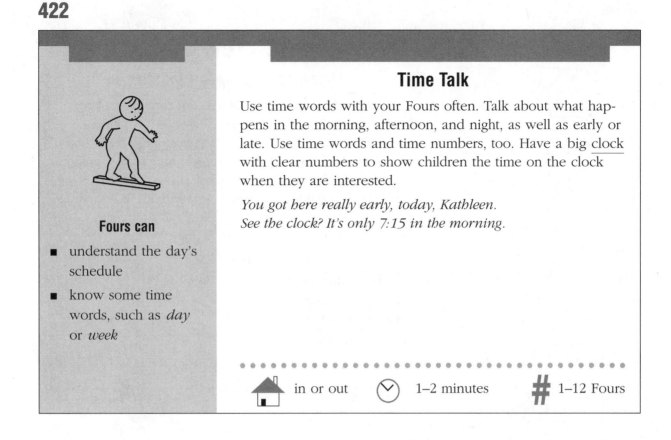

Time Talk

Use time words with your Fours often. Talk about what happens in the morning, afternoon, and night, as well as early or late. Use time words and time numbers, too. Have a big clock with clear numbers to show children the time on the clock when they are interested.

You got here really early, today, Kathleen.
See the clock? It's only 7:15 in the morning.

Fours can

- understand the day's schedule
- know some time words, such as *day* or *week*

in or out   1–2 minutes   # 1–12 Fours

423

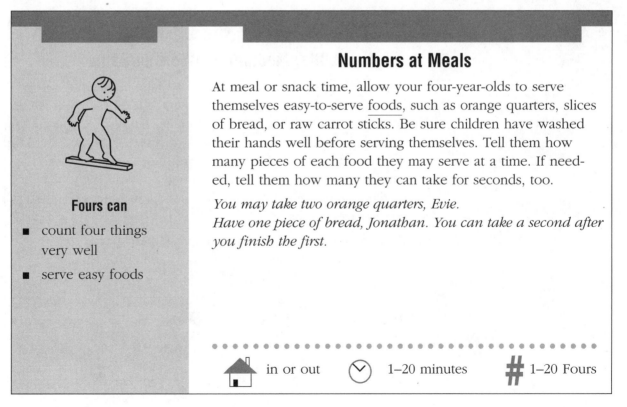

Numbers at Meals

At meal or snack time, allow your four-year-olds to serve themselves easy-to-serve foods, such as orange quarters, slices of bread, or raw carrot sticks. Be sure children have washed their hands well before serving themselves. Tell them how many pieces of each food they may serve at a time. If needed, tell them how many they can take for seconds, too.

You may take two orange quarters, Evie.
Have one piece of bread, Jonathan. You can take a second after you finish the first.

Fours can

- count four things very well
- serve easy foods

in or out   1–20 minutes   # 1–20 Fours

424

Fours can

- do simple puzzles
- name three shapes

Homemade Shapes Puzzles

Cut out two circles, squares, triangles, and rectangles from brightly colored posterboard. Make each shape a different color. Cover all the shapes with clear contact paper. Cut one of each shape in half. Show the whole circle and whole square to an interested child. Put out the pieces for those shapes and see if the child can put the shapes back together. If this is easy, then try more shapes at one time. Talk about the names of the shapes and how the shapes are cut into two pieces.

To add a new challenge try these ideas:

- Cut the shapes into three or four pieces.
- Make all the shapes the same color.
- Have the children put the shapes together without using the whole shapes as a guide.

🏠 in or out   🕐 2–12 minutes   # 1–3 Fours

425

Fours can

- understand *big* and *little*

Little, Medium, Big Sorting Game

Put matching sets of big, medium, and little things into a box. For example, include a big hairbrush, a smaller baby's brush, and a tiny doll's brush; a big cooking spoon, a table spoon, and a baby's spoon; an adult's sock, a child's sock, and a baby's sock; and other different-sized things your Fours would enjoy inspecting. Next to the box, spread out a big, medium, and small cloth. Help children sort things onto the correct-sized cloths.

Talk about the sizes of all the things as the children compare and sort. Leave this activity box in the center for children to choose.

You found the biggest spoon, Paul. Can you find the other two? There they are. Which is the little one?

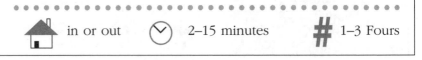

🏠 in or out   🕐 2–15 minutes   # 1–3 Fours

426

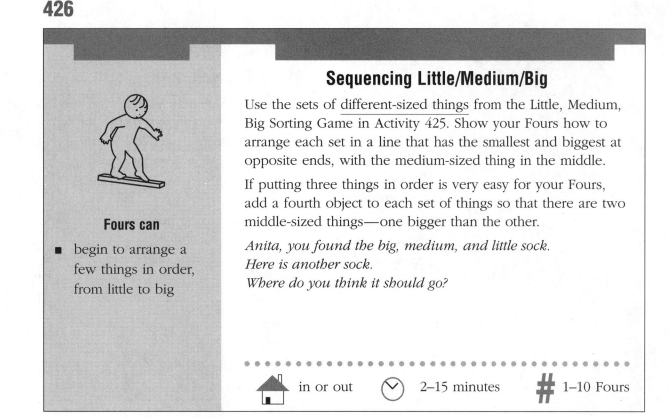

Fours can

- begin to arrange a few things in order, from little to big

Sequencing Little/Medium/Big

Use the sets of different-sized things from the Little, Medium, Big Sorting Game in Activity 425. Show your Fours how to arrange each set in a line that has the smallest and biggest at opposite ends, with the medium-sized thing in the middle.

If putting three things in order is very easy for your Fours, add a fourth object to each set of things so that there are two middle-sized things—one bigger than the other.

Anita, you found the big, medium, and little sock.
Here is another sock.
Where do you think it should go?

🏠 in or out   🕐 2–15 minutes   # 1–10 Fours

427

Fours can

- begin to sort, mostly by color and size

Sorting Feelie Shapes

Cut out five circles, squares, triangles, and rectangles from sturdy cardboard. Use glue to cover one of each shape with sandpaper, fuzzy cloth, satin cloth, bumpy cloth, or vinyl. Trim the edges evenly.

Look at, talk about, and feel the shapes with your Fours. Help them feel corners and curves as you talk about these parts. Put out four shallow boxes with one shape drawn on each. Show the children how to sort the shapes into the boxes.

Children may want to sort the shapes in other ways, too. You can add boxes for sorting textures or colors. Add other shapes, such as hearts, stars, ovals, or octagons to add new interest to this sorting game.

🏠 in or out   🕐 2–20 minutes   # 1–4 Fours

428

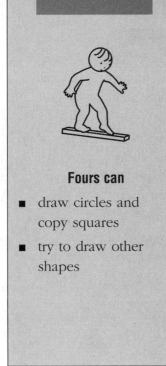

Fours can

- name three shapes
- enjoy creating with art materials

Shape Designs

Have lots of colorful shape stickers for the children to stick onto bigger sheets of plain paper. You can find stickers of different shapes at office or school supply stores. Allow your Fours to make their own creative designs with the shapes. Talk with each child about the shapes, sizes, and ways they can be arranged.

You put a line of circles here, didn't you, Anthony?
Can you tell me about this part of your design?

Children can add to their designs with watercolor markers, pencils, or crayons, too.

🏠 in or out   🕐 2–15 minutes   # 1–6 Fours

429

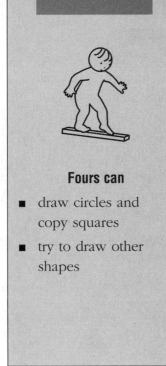

Fours can

- draw circles and copy squares
- try to draw other shapes

Can You Draw This?

Use a crayon or washable marker to draw a square on a piece of paper as the child watches. Talk about the ways the lines go as you draw—how the lines meet, make corners, are straight, go down or across. Next see if the child can copy what you drew. Show delight with how well the child tries. Do not worry if the child's drawings are not perfect.

That's great, Veronica! Look how you got these corners to meet!
Do you want to try the square again or another shape?

Children can also copy the shapes you make in finger paint, in the sand, or with chalk on the sidewalk.

🏠 in or out   🕐 2–6 minutes   # 1–3 Fours

Activities for Learning from the World Around Them

430

Fours can

■ name three shapes

Shapes in Our World

Point out the shapes of things your Fours see every day. For example, point out that the bricks in a building are rectangles, or the "Yield" sign at the end of the road is a triangle. Whenever possible, let children feel the shapes as you talk about them.

Feel the edges of the bricks with your finger, Tiffany.
Feel the pointy corners of the rectangle.
What shape is this window? Feel the edges.

See if the children can tell you what some of the shapes are. Encourage them to point out the shapes they see.

in or out 1–2 minutes # 1–20 Fours

431

Fours can

■ begin to sort, mostly by color and size

Shape-Sorting Boxes

Have one or two shape-sorting boxes on a low shelf in the Math Center for the children to use freely. Show them how to use the boxes. Then let your Fours play with the boxes on their own or with a friend. (Directions for making some shape-sorting boxes are on page 392.)

You are sorting the solid shapes, Brian. Did you already put in the cylinder? Can you figure out where the pyramid fits?

indoors 2–15 minutes # 1–4 Fours

432

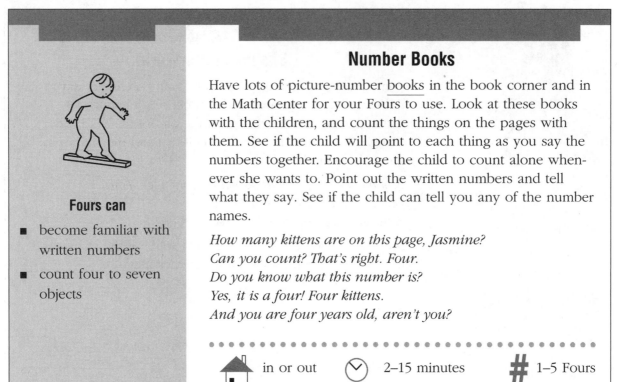

Fours can

- become familiar with written numbers
- count four to seven objects

Number Books

Have lots of picture-number books in the book corner and in the Math Center for your Fours to use. Look at these books with the children, and count the things on the pages with them. See if the child will point to each thing as you say the numbers together. Encourage the child to count alone whenever she wants to. Point out the written numbers and tell what they say. See if the child can tell you any of the number names.

How many kittens are on this page, Jasmine?
Can you count? That's right. Four.
Do you know what this number is?
Yes, it is a four! Four kittens.
And you are four years old, aren't you?

🏠 in or out   🕐 2–15 minutes   # 1–5 Fours

433

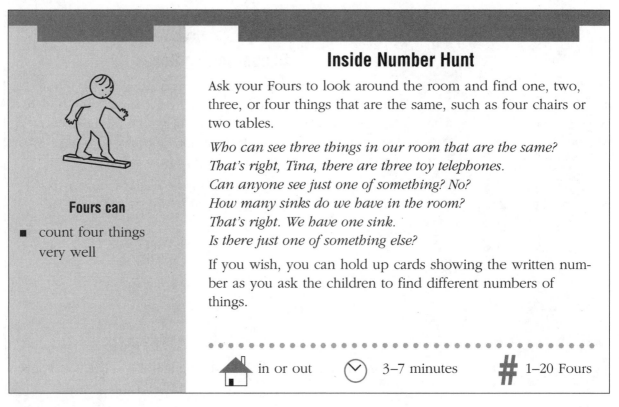

Fours can

- count four things very well

Inside Number Hunt

Ask your Fours to look around the room and find one, two, three, or four things that are the same, such as four chairs or two tables.

Who can see three things in our room that are the same?
That's right, Tina, there are three toy telephones.
Can anyone see just one of something? No?
How many sinks do we have in the room?
That's right. We have one sink.
Is there just one of something else?

If you wish, you can hold up cards showing the written number as you ask the children to find different numbers of things.

🏠 in or out   🕐 3–7 minutes   # 1–20 Fours

Activities for Learning from the World Around Them

434

Fours can

- name three shapes
- tell some things by touch

Shapes Feelie Bag

Make a feelie bag by putting a plastic container into a big, clean sock. Put a flat plastic circle, square, and triangle into the feelie bag. Ask the child to pull out a shape you name. Show a picture of the shape if you need to, and talk about how it feels.

The square has four corners and four straight sides.
Can you feel the square, Jason?

Try these ideas to add new challenges:

- When a child can tell one shape from another, add a rectangle.
- Ask the child to reach into the bag, feel one of the shapes, and then try to guess what it is.

🏠 in or out ⏱ 2–15 minutes # 1–4 Fours

435

Fours can

- begin to sort, mostly by color and size
- name three shapes

Shape-Sorting Board

Put out a sorting board with shape cards to sort. Begin with shape cards that only differ by shape. All shapes should be the same size and color. (Directions for making several sorting boards are on page 396.) Help the child get started by talking about how you sort shapes as you do the first few cards. Then see how much the child can do by herself.

You know this shape, Marta.
That's right, it's a square.
Can you put it in the row with the other square?

🏠 in or out ⏱ 3–15 minutes # 1–2 Fours

436

Fours can

■ count four to seven
objects

Number-Sorting Tubs

Use five clean margarine tubs. Use a permanent marker to write the number 1 in the bottom of the first tub. Make one dot in the bottom of that same tub, too. Continue marking each tub until you have tubs that show 1 through 5.

Put out the tubs with 15 colorful 1/2" beads. Show your Fours how to put one bead into the tub that says 1, two into the tub that says 2, and so on. Then see how the children play the game on their own. Talk about putting one bead into the tub for each dot.

Put a bead on each dot, Javier.
Great! How many beads did you put in this tub?
That's right. Three. That number is three.

 indoors   🕐 3–12 minutes   # 1–2 Fours

437

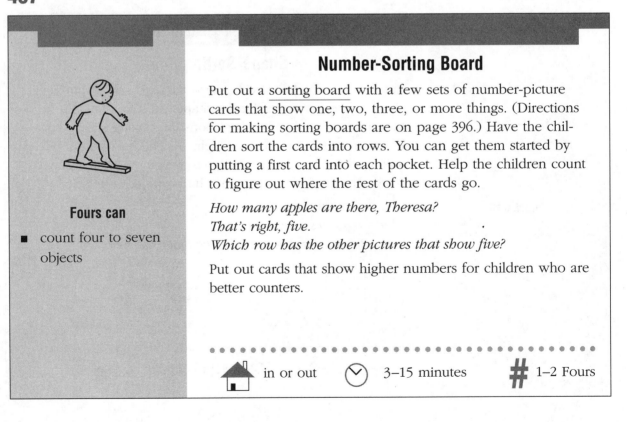

Fours can

■ count four to seven
objects

Number-Sorting Board

Put out a sorting board with a few sets of number-picture cards that show one, two, three, or more things. (Directions for making sorting boards are on page 396.) Have the children sort the cards into rows. You can get them started by putting a first card into each pocket. Help the children count to figure out where the rest of the cards go.

How many apples are there, Theresa?
That's right, five.
Which row has the other pictures that show five?

Put out cards that show higher numbers for children who are better counters.

🏠 in or out   🕐 3–15 minutes   # 1–2 Fours

438

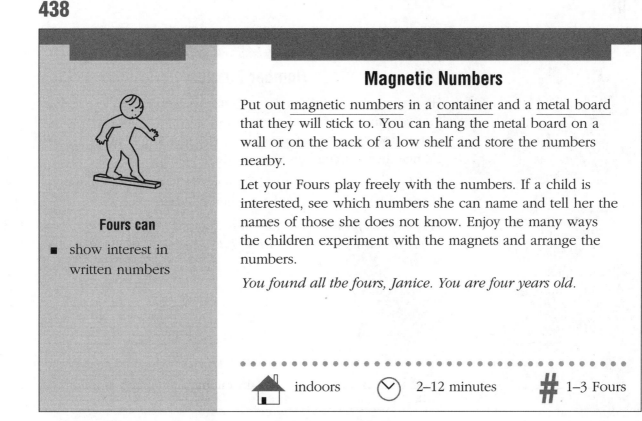

Fours can

- show interest in written numbers

Magnetic Numbers

Put out magnetic numbers in a container and a metal board that they will stick to. You can hang the metal board on a wall or on the back of a low shelf and store the numbers nearby.

Let your Fours play freely with the numbers. If a child is interested, see which numbers she can name and tell her the names of those she does not know. Enjoy the many ways the children experiment with the magnets and arrange the numbers.

You found all the fours, Janice. You are four years old.

🏠 indoors 🕐 2–12 minutes # 1–3 Fours

439

Fours can

- count four to seven objects

Point and Count

Play a counting game with one or two of your Fours. Have them cover their eyes as you put out one to seven small toys to count, such as beads, or small plastic teddy bears. (It's OK if they peek.) Then ask the children to count the toys and tell you how many there are. Help them count by saying a number as they touch each toy.

How many little bears are there, Shane? That's right. Three. Now cover your eyes again. I'm going to add a few more bears.

You can hide your eyes sometimes, too, and then point to and count the toys the children put out.

🏠 in or out 🕐 2–5 minutes # 1–2 Fours

440

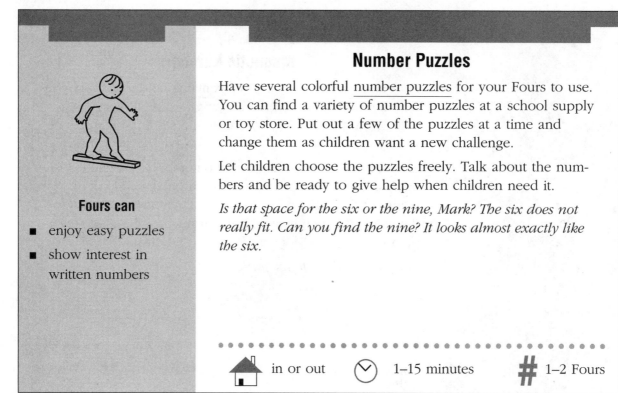

Number Puzzles

Have several colorful number puzzles for your Fours to use. You can find a variety of number puzzles at a school supply or toy store. Put out a few of the puzzles at a time and change them as children want a new challenge.

Let children choose the puzzles freely. Talk about the numbers and be ready to give help when children need it.

Is that space for the six or the nine, Mark? The six does not really fit. Can you find the nine? It looks almost exactly like the six.

Fours can

■ enjoy easy puzzles

■ show interest in written numbers

🏠 in or out　　🕐 1–15 minutes　　# 1–2 Fours

441

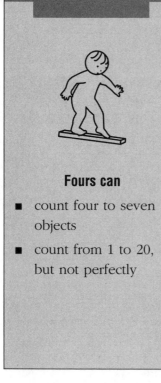

How Old Are We?

Have many informal conversations with your Fours about how old they are. Count how many in the group are each age. Talk about how the numbers will change as people have birthdays.

We have five four-year-olds and three five-year-olds in our group. But Dana's birthday is tomorrow. How old will you be, Dana? You'll be five. Let's count and figure out how many five-year-olds we'll have tomorrow.

If you wish, you can tell the children how old you are, too.

Fours can

■ count four to seven objects

■ count from 1 to 20, but not perfectly

🏠 in or out　　🕐 1–3 minutes　　# 1–10 Fours

442

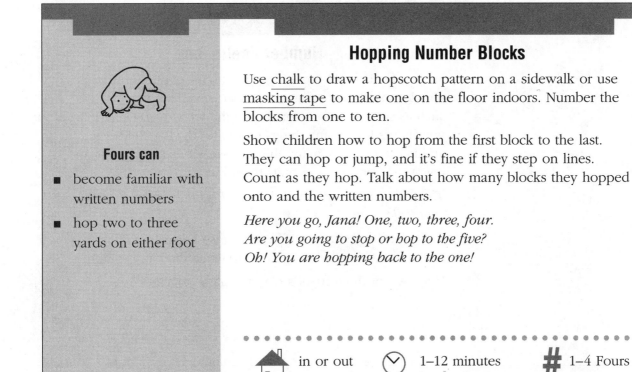

Hopping Number Blocks

Use <u>chalk</u> to draw a hopscotch pattern on a sidewalk or use <u>masking tape</u> to make one on the floor indoors. Number the blocks from one to ten.

Show children how to hop from the first block to the last. They can hop or jump, and it's fine if they step on lines. Count as they hop. Talk about how many blocks they hopped onto and the written numbers.

Here you go, Jana! One, two, three, four.
Are you going to stop or hop to the five?
Oh! You are hopping back to the one!

Fours can

■ become familiar with written numbers

■ hop two to three yards on either foot

in or out   1–12 minutes   # 1–4 Fours

443

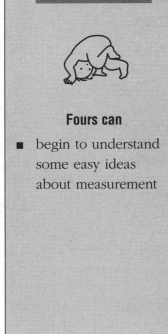

Lots of Measuring

Provide many measuring experiences for children as they play and take part in the daily routines. Have a box of <u>measuring cups</u> and <u>spoons</u> that children can choose as they play with sand or water. Encourage children to measure as they help you prepare art materials, such as paint or play dough. Have cooking activities for the children where they measure foods.

Use measurement words often as the children measure in many ways.

I'm glad you are helping me fill the water table, Patrick.
Let's use these empty gallon milk containers.
How many gallons do you think we will need?
One hundred! That would be a lot of water!

Fours can

■ begin to understand some easy ideas about measurement

in or out   1–20 minutes   # 1–8 Fours

444

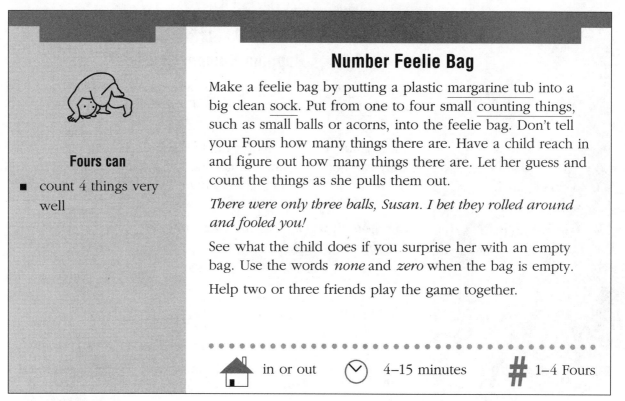

Fours can

- count 4 things very well

Number Feelie Bag

Make a feelie bag by putting a plastic <u>margarine tub</u> into a big clean <u>sock</u>. Put from one to four small <u>counting things</u>, such as small balls or acorns, into the feelie bag. Don't tell your Fours how many things there are. Have a child reach in and figure out how many things there are. Let her guess and count the things as she pulls them out.

There were only three balls, Susan. I bet they rolled around and fooled you!

See what the child does if you surprise her with an empty bag. Use the words *none* and *zero* when the bag is empty.

Help two or three friends play the game together.

🏠 in or out   🕐 4–15 minutes   # 1–4 Fours

445

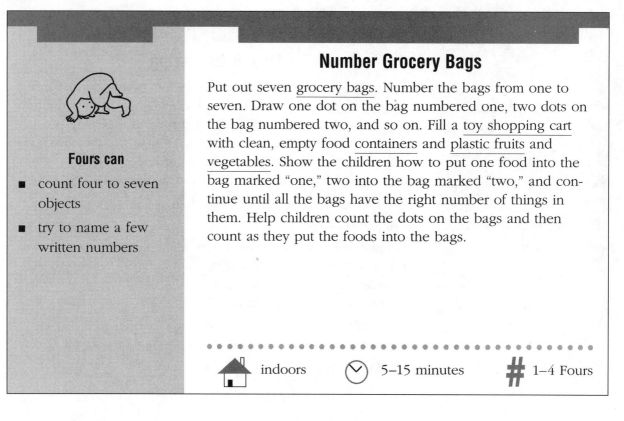

Fours can

- count four to seven objects
- try to name a few written numbers

Number Grocery Bags

Put out seven <u>grocery bags</u>. Number the bags from one to seven. Draw one dot on the bag numbered one, two dots on the bag numbered two, and so on. Fill a <u>toy shopping cart</u> with clean, empty food <u>containers</u> and <u>plastic fruits and vegetables</u>. Show the children how to put one food into the bag marked "one," two into the bag marked "two," and continue until all the bags have the right number of things in them. Help children count the dots on the bags and then count as they put the foods into the bags.

🏠 indoors   🕐 5–15 minutes   # 1–4 Fours

Activities for Learning from the World Around Them

446

Fours can

- begin to understand some easy ideas about measurement

Rulers and Tape Measures

Use rulers and tape measures with your Fours to find out how long or high things are. Have them help as you measure. Encourage them to help count inches, centimeters, or whatever measurement you are using. Point out the written numbers as you measure. Some things you can measure with your Fours are

- the distance between cots for nap
- how tall the children are
- how far children can jump

See if your Fours can think of lots of other things to measure.

Amanda wants to find out how tall Mr. Bunny is.
How can we measure our rabbit?

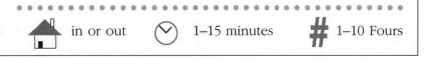

🏠 in or out   🕐 1–15 minutes   # 1–10 Fours

447

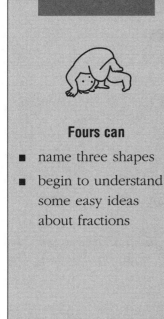

Fours can

- name three shapes
- begin to understand some easy ideas about fractions

Dividing Foods—Sizes, Shapes, and Fractions

Have foods at meals and snacks such as bananas, apples, or sandwiches that can be cut into two, three, or four pieces to serve to children. Let the children watch and help as these are cut up. Count the pieces with your Fours as you take the foods apart and put them back together.

Talk about the sizes and shapes of the pieces. Use fraction words such as *one quarter, one fourth, one third,* and so on to talk about the pieces. See if the children use these words, too.

I cut the sandwich in half, Paul.
Do you want one half or two halves?
OK, here is half a peanut butter sandwich for you.

🏠 indoors   🕐 2–8 minutes   # 1–10 Fours

448

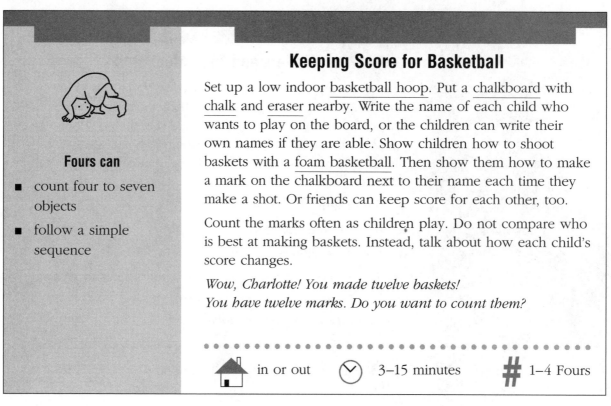

Fours can

- count four to seven objects

- follow a simple sequence

Keeping Score for Basketball

Set up a low indoor basketball hoop. Put a chalkboard with chalk and eraser nearby. Write the name of each child who wants to play on the board, or the children can write their own names if they are able. Show children how to shoot baskets with a foam basketball. Then show them how to make a mark on the chalkboard next to their name each time they make a shot. Or friends can keep score for each other, too.

Count the marks often as children play. Do not compare who is best at making baskets. Instead, talk about how each child's score changes.

Wow, Charlotte! You made twelve baskets!
You have twelve marks. Do you want to count them?

in or out   3–15 minutes   # 1–4 Fours

449

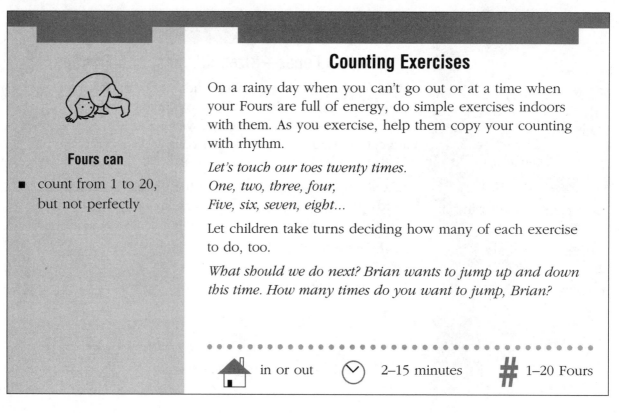

Fours can

- count from 1 to 20, but not perfectly

Counting Exercises

On a rainy day when you can't go out or at a time when your Fours are full of energy, do simple exercises indoors with them. As you exercise, help them copy your counting with rhythm.

Let's touch our toes twenty times.
One, two, three, four,
Five, six, seven, eight...

Let children take turns deciding how many of each exercise to do, too.

What should we do next? Brian wants to jump up and down this time. How many times do you want to jump, Brian?

in or out   2–15 minutes   # 1–20 Fours

450

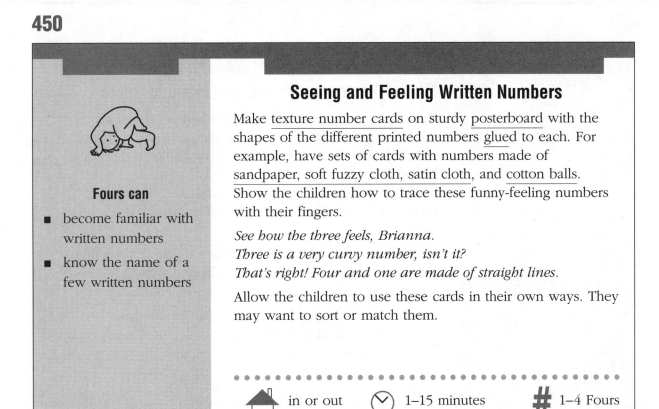

Fours can

- become familiar with written numbers
- know the name of a few written numbers

Seeing and Feeling Written Numbers

Make texture number cards on sturdy posterboard with the shapes of the different printed numbers glued to each. For example, have sets of cards with numbers made of sandpaper, soft fuzzy cloth, satin cloth, and cotton balls. Show the children how to trace these funny-feeling numbers with their fingers.

See how the three feels, Brianna.
Three is a very curvy number, isn't it?
That's right! Four and one are made of straight lines.

Allow the children to use these cards in their own ways. They may want to sort or match them.

in or out   1–15 minutes   # 1–4 Fours

451

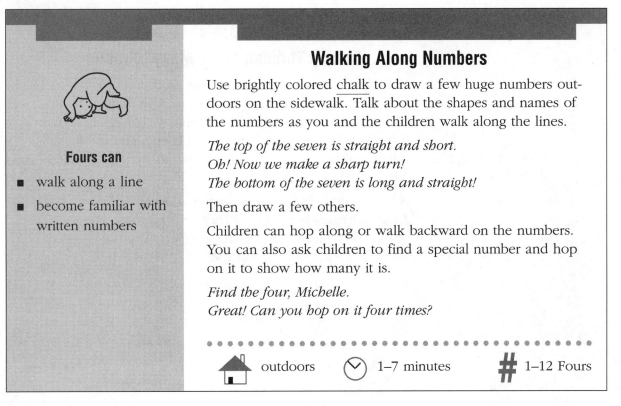

Fours can

- walk along a line
- become familiar with written numbers

Walking Along Numbers

Use brightly colored chalk to draw a few huge numbers outdoors on the sidewalk. Talk about the shapes and names of the numbers as you and the children walk along the lines.

The top of the seven is straight and short.
Oh! Now we make a sharp turn!
The bottom of the seven is long and straight!

Then draw a few others.

Children can hop along or walk backward on the numbers. You can also ask children to find a special number and hop on it to show how many it is.

Find the four, Michelle.
Great! Can you hop on it four times?

outdoors   1–7 minutes   # 1–12 Fours

452

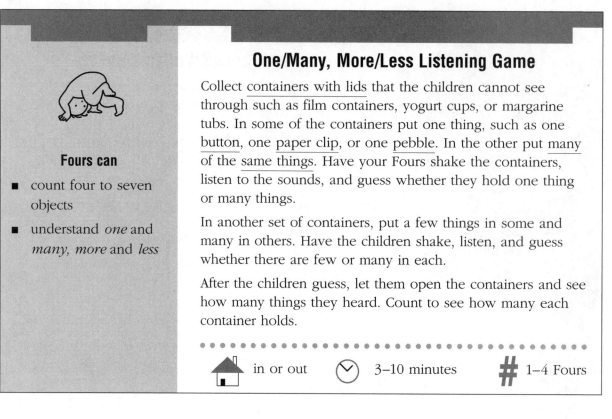

Fours can

- count four to seven objects
- understand *one* and *many, more* and *less*

One/Many, More/Less Listening Game

Collect containers with lids that the children cannot see through such as film containers, yogurt cups, or margarine tubs. In some of the containers put one thing, such as one button, one paper clip, or one pebble. In the other put many of the same things. Have your Fours shake the containers, listen to the sounds, and guess whether they hold one thing or many things.

In another set of containers, put a few things in some and many in others. Have the children shake, listen, and guess whether there are few or many in each.

After the children guess, let them open the containers and see how many things they heard. Count to see how many each container holds.

in or out   3–10 minutes   # 1–4 Fours

453

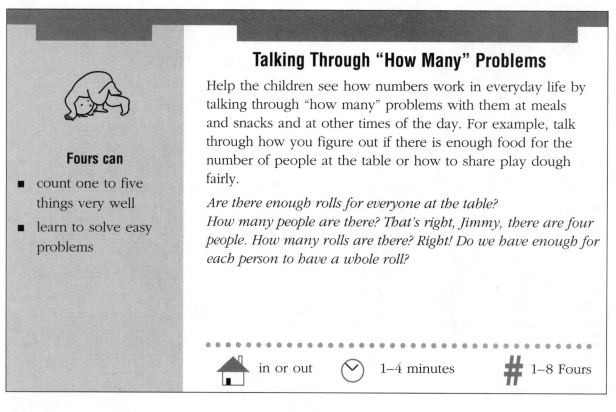

Fours can

- count one to five things very well
- learn to solve easy problems

Talking Through "How Many" Problems

Help the children see how numbers work in everyday life by talking through "how many" problems with them at meals and snacks and at other times of the day. For example, talk through how you figure out if there is enough food for the number of people at the table or how to share play dough fairly.

Are there enough rolls for everyone at the table?
How many people are there? That's right, Jimmy, there are four people. How many rolls are there? Right! Do we have enough for each person to have a whole roll?

in or out   1–4 minutes   # 1–8 Fours

454

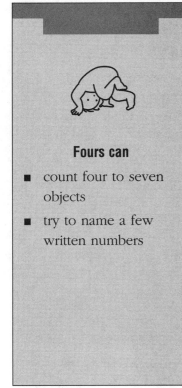

Fours can

■ count four to seven objects

"Which Number Is It?" Riddles

Play easy number riddle games with your Fours. Give clues about the number you want them to guess and see if they can figure out what the number is.

I'm thinking of a very small number.
Good guess, Nicky, but it is not the number one.
We have this many tables in our room.
That's right, it's two!
All of you figured it out.

Allow children to give clues so that you can guess numbers, too. Do not be surprised if the clues are a bit strange and sometimes make no sense. Just enjoy the ways your Fours think, and have fun as children think and talk about numbers.

🏠 in or out   🕐 2–12 minutes   # 1–20 Fours

455

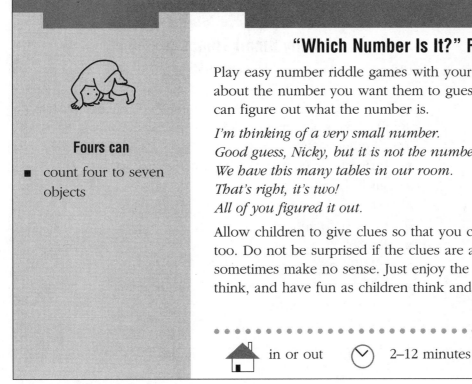

Fours can

■ count four to seven objects

■ try to name a few written numbers

Counting Dinosaurs

Put out a set of sorting tubs that are numbered from one to seven. (To make number-sorting tubs, see activity 436.) Add a collection of small plastic dinosaurs for your Fours to use with the tubs. Show the children how to count the correct number of dinosaurs into each tub.

Shall we see if you put the right number of dinosaurs into each tub, Glenda? You can take the dinosaurs out, one at a time, and help me count.

For lots more counting ideas, see the next activity. Use more tubs for children who count well and fewer tubs for children who who find counting more difficult.

🏠 in or out   🕐 5–15 minutes   # 1–2 Fours

456

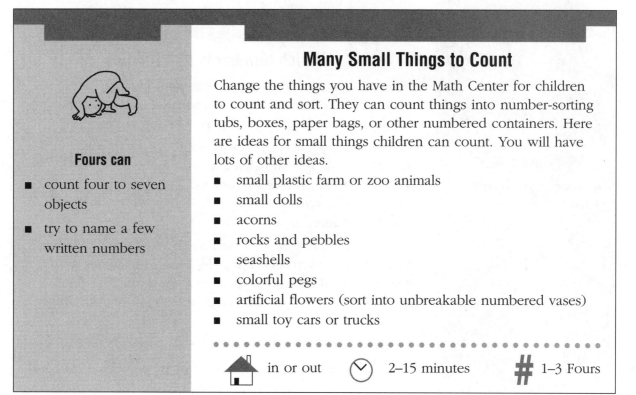

Fours can

- count four to seven objects
- try to name a few written numbers

Many Small Things to Count

Change the things you have in the Math Center for children to count and sort. They can count things into number-sorting tubs, boxes, paper bags, or other numbered containers. Here are ideas for small things children can count. You will have lots of other ideas.

- small plastic farm or zoo animals
- small dolls
- acorns
- rocks and pebbles
- seashells
- colorful pegs
- artificial flowers (sort into unbreakable numbered vases)
- small toy cars or trucks

🏠 in or out   🕐 2–15 minutes   # 1–3 Fours

457

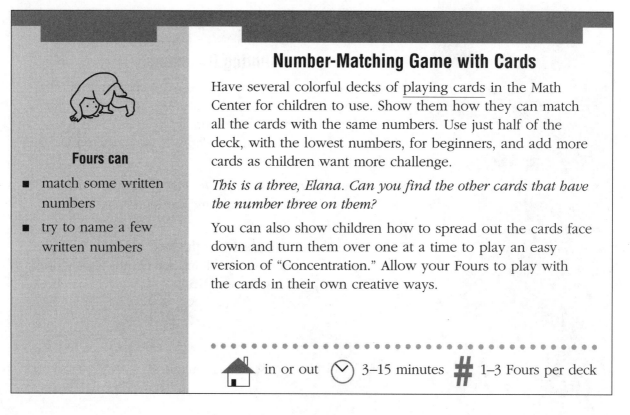

Fours can

- match some written numbers
- try to name a few written numbers

Number-Matching Game with Cards

Have several colorful decks of playing cards in the Math Center for children to use. Show them how they can match all the cards with the same numbers. Use just half of the deck, with the lowest numbers, for beginners, and add more cards as children want more challenge.

This is a three, Elana. Can you find the other cards that have the number three on them?

You can also show children how to spread out the cards face down and turn them over one at a time to play an easy version of "Concentration." Allow your Fours to play with the cards in their own creative ways.

🏠 in or out   🕐 3–15 minutes   # 1–3 Fours per deck

458

Fours can

- sort by color, then by other aspects such as size

Sorting Shoes

Have a group of children who want to play sit with you in a circle. Have everyone take off their <u>shoes</u> and put them into the middle of the circle. Then sort all the shoes into different piles in many ways—by color, type of shoe, the way the shoe fastens, and so on. Encourage the children to decide which pile each shoe should be in.

Kendra says to put all the shoes with laces into this pile. How does this shoe fasten? That's right. It has a buckle. Does it go with the shoes that have shoelaces? Let's make a new pile for shoes with buckles.

Children can find their own shoes to put back on at the end of the game. Try sorting other types of clothing, such as jackets or mittens and gloves.

🏠 indoors 🕐 5–15 minutes # 1–8 Fours

459

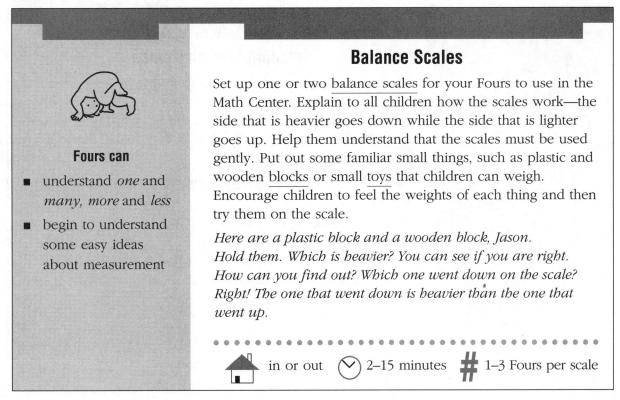

Fours can

- understand *one* and *many, more* and *less*
- begin to understand some easy ideas about measurement

Balance Scales

Set up one or two <u>balance scales</u> for your Fours to use in the Math Center. Explain to all children how the scales work—the side that is heavier goes down while the side that is lighter goes up. Help them understand that the scales must be used gently. Put out some familiar small things, such as plastic and wooden <u>blocks</u> or small <u>toys</u> that children can weigh. Encourage children to feel the weights of each thing and then try them on the scale.

Here are a plastic block and a wooden block, Jason. Hold them. Which is heavier? You can see if you are right. How can you find out? Which one went down on the scale? Right! The one that went down is heavier than the one that went up.

🏠 in or out 🕐 2–15 minutes # 1–3 Fours per scale

460

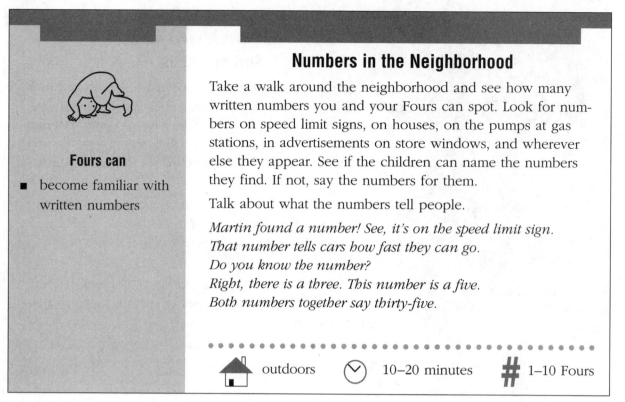

Fours can

■ become familiar with
written numbers

Numbers in the Neighborhood

Take a walk around the neighborhood and see how many written numbers you and your Fours can spot. Look for numbers on speed limit signs, on houses, on the pumps at gas stations, in advertisements on store windows, and wherever else they appear. See if the children can name the numbers they find. If not, say the numbers for them.

Talk about what the numbers tell people.

Martin found a number! See, it's on the speed limit sign.
That number tells cars how fast they can go.
Do you know the number?
Right, there is a three. This number is a five.
Both numbers together say thirty-five.

🏠 outdoors   🕐 10–20 minutes   # 1–10 Fours

461

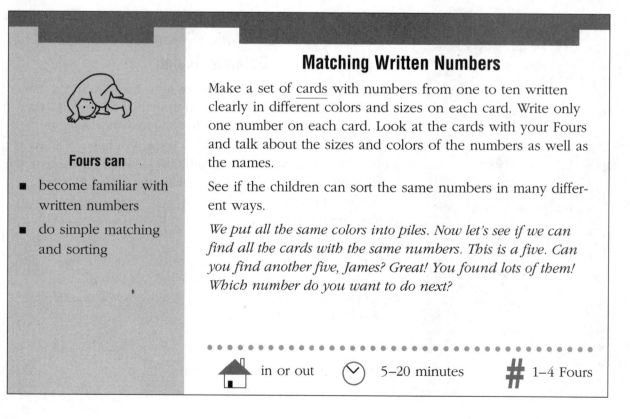

Fours can

■ become familiar with
written numbers

■ do simple matching
and sorting

Matching Written Numbers

Make a set of cards with numbers from one to ten written clearly in different colors and sizes on each card. Write only one number on each card. Look at the cards with your Fours and talk about the sizes and colors of the numbers as well as the names.

See if the children can sort the same numbers in many different ways.

We put all the same colors into piles. Now let's see if we can find all the cards with the same numbers. This is a five. Can you find another five, James? Great! You found lots of them! Which number do you want to do next?

🏠 in or out   🕐 5–20 minutes   # 1–4 Fours

Activities for Learning from the World Around Them

462

Fours can

- begin to understand that adding and subtracting changes numbers of objects

Talking About Real-Life Addition and Subtraction

As you do simple addition and subtraction to figure out real problems, talk about what you are doing and thinking with interested Fours. See if they can help you figure out easy answers when they can see the real things that are being added or subtracted. Use the words *adding* and *subtracting* as you talk.

Let's put the balls into the box so that we can bring them in. I already put two in. Jana is adding one more. How many will we have in the box?

There are four potatoes in the bowl. Zac's going to subtract one and put it on his plate. That means he's going to take one away. How many will be left in the bowl?

🏠 in or out   🕐 2–4 minutes   # 1–10 Fours

463

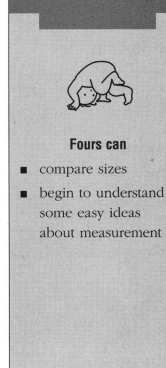

Fours can

- compare sizes
- begin to understand some easy ideas about measurement

Comparing Block Sizes

Put out four wooden unit blocks that are different lengths and a bucket of inch cubes. Line up cubes along the length of a unit block, counting out each one. Count with the children as they put cubes on the other blocks. After they have finished, talk about which blocks held the most cubes and which held the fewest. Compare the sizes of the blocks.

How many cubes did you put on your block, Karen? Which is the longest block? Which block is shortest?

Put out a foot-long ruler so that children can measure their unit blocks in another way.

🏠 inside   🕐 5–10 minutes   # 1–5 Fours

464

Fours can

- match some written numbers

Delivering Mail to Houses

Make ten colorful construction paper houses. Use a marker or crayon to draw windows, doors, and other house parts. Clearly write numbers from 1 to 10 on the house doors. Cover the houses with clear contact paper or laminate to make them sturdy. Number 40 envelopes from 1 to 10, so that you have four sets of envelopes. Mix the envelopes and put them into a tote bag.

Show your Fours how to pretend to be mail carriers. Spread the houses out on the floor or on a table. The children can deliver the mail by matching envelope numbers with house numbers. Use fewer houses to make the game easier. Add people and street names to the addresses to make the game more challenging.

🏠 indoors   🕐 5–20 minutes   # 1–3 Fours

465

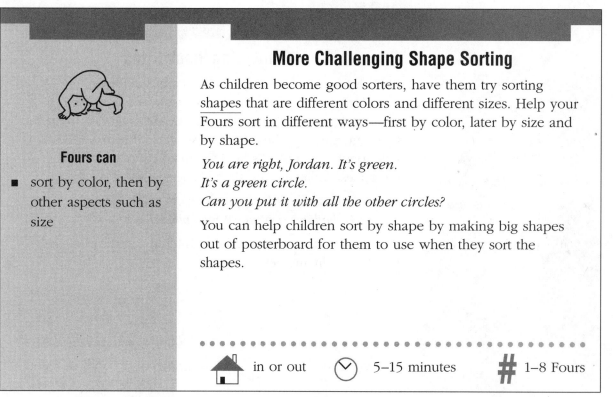

Fours can

- sort by color, then by other aspects such as size

More Challenging Shape Sorting

As children become good sorters, have them try sorting shapes that are different colors and different sizes. Help your Fours sort in different ways—first by color, later by size and by shape.

You are right, Jordan. It's green.
It's a green circle.
Can you put it with all the other circles?

You can help children sort by shape by making big shapes out of posterboard for them to use when they sort the shapes.

🏠 in or out   🕐 5–15 minutes   # 1–8 Fours

466

Fours can

- understand *big/little, tall/short*

- begin to understand some easy ideas about measurement

Graphing Everyone's Height

Make a line graph that shows how tall everyone in your group is. (There is a picture of a line graph in Graph Ideas on page 398.) If there are lots of children, use the wall in a hallway or outdoors. Have each child take a turn standing along the wall and mark the height of each one. Mark the height of the adults in the group, too. Put each person's name near their mark.

Talk about the big graph with your Fours. Measure and write down the heights with interested children. Compare same and different heights. Add marks for other heights, too, such as a classroom pet or children's family members.

Can you find the tallest mark on the graph, Marcia? That's right. It's Tonya's daddy.

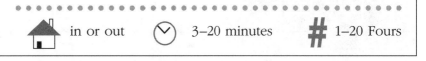

🏠 in or out   🕐 3–20 minutes   # 1–20 Fours

467

Fours can

- understand *one* and *many, more* and *less*

- begin to understand easy ideas about graphing

Using Bar Graphs to Compare

Make bar graphs with your Fours to compare numbers of things that they are interested in. (You will find directions for making bar graphs in Graph Ideas on page 398.) Help children compare the different categories shown on the graphs. Talk about *more, less, equal* (or *the same*) and help your Fours count to find out how many.

You're looking at the new graph we made, Kendra. This bar shows how many boys we have, and this shows how many girls. Can you find your name? Are there more boys or more girls? I think so, too! Let's see how many we have of each. Can you help me count?

🏠 indoors   🕐 3–20 minutes   # 1–20 Fours

468

Fours can

■ sort by color, then by other aspects such as size

Sorting Children

Tell the children that you are going to play a children-sorting game. Ask children who want to play to sit in a big circle. Children can sort themselves in various ways. You can begin by suggesting a way to sort and helping children decide which group to go into. Some aspects to sort by are

color of shirt	type of shoes
color of hair	favorite food
who likes dogs	who has sisters/brothers

Compare the sizes of the different groups. Give children lots of chances to use their own sorting ideas, too.

Wow! Which is bigger—the group of children who like broccoli or the group who does not?

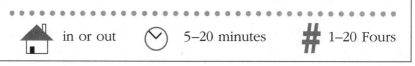

🏠 in or out   🕐 5–20 minutes   # 1–20 Fours

469

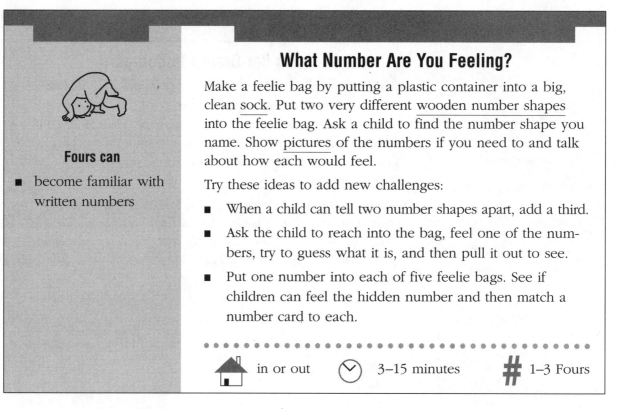

Fours can

■ become familiar with written numbers

What Number Are You Feeling?

Make a feelie bag by putting a plastic container into a big, clean sock. Put two very different wooden number shapes into the feelie bag. Ask a child to find the number shape you name. Show pictures of the numbers if you need to and talk about how each would feel.

Try these ideas to add new challenges:

■ When a child can tell two number shapes apart, add a third.

■ Ask the child to reach into the bag, feel one of the numbers, try to guess what it is, and then pull it out to see.

■ Put one number into each of five feelie bags. See if children can feel the hidden number and then match a number card to each.

🏠 in or out   🕐 3–15 minutes   # 1–3 Fours

470

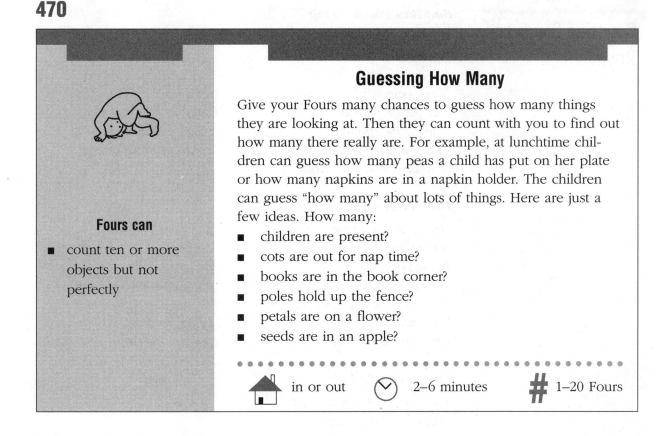

Fours can

- count ten or more objects but not perfectly

Guessing How Many

Give your Fours many chances to guess how many things they are looking at. Then they can count with you to find out how many there really are. For example, at lunchtime children can guess how many peas a child has put on her plate or how many napkins are in a napkin holder. The children can guess "how many" about lots of things. Here are just a few ideas. How many:

- children are present?
- cots are out for nap time?
- books are in the book corner?
- poles hold up the fence?
- petals are on a flower?
- seeds are in an apple?

in or out   2–6 minutes   # 1–20 Fours

471

Fours can

- try to write a few numbers, but not perfectly

Writing Numbers

Give your Fours many chances to practice writing numbers, but only when they are really interested. Have paper, pencils, and markers for them to use. Be sure there are examples of clearly written numbers for them to look at and copy in the Math Center.

Help children write numbers whenever they want to in their play in other areas, too.

You can get a marker and some paper to make some money for your store, Shameeka. You want to help too, Tony?
That must be a four-dollar bill. I see you made a four.

in or out   1–15 minutes   # 1–6 Fours

Counting Songs and Rhymes

Baa Baa Black Sheep

Baa baa black sheep,
Have you any wool?
Yes sir, yes sir,
Three bags full.   (hold up three fingers)
One for the master,   (hold up one finger)
One for the dame,   (hole up two fingers)
And one for the little child   (hold up three fingers)
Who lives down the lane.

The Bee Hive

Here is the bee hive,   (put hands together)
Where are the bees?   (make a fist)
Hiding out
Where nobody sees.   (put hand behind back)
They are coming out now.
They are all alive—   (bring hand out)
One, two, three, four, five.   (put up one finger at a time)

Five in the Bed

There were five in the bed
And the little one said,
"Roll over, roll over!"   (roll one hand over the other)
So they all rolled over
And one fell out.
There were four in the bed
And the little one said, etc.

Five Little Monkeys

Five little monkeys   (hold up five fingers)
Jumping on the bed,   (jump fingers on palm of
                                     other hand)

One fell off   (hold up one finger)
And bumped his head.   (rub head)
They ran for the doctor   (run fingers across other
And the doctor said,   hand)
"No more monkeys jumping
    on the bed!"   (point and shake finger)
(Continue with four, three, two, and one monkey.)

Five Little Pumpkins

Five little pumpkins   (hold up five fingers)
Sitting on a gate.
The first one said,   (hold up one finger)
"Oh my, it's getting late!"
The second one said,   (hold up two fingers)
"There are witches in the air!"
The third one said,   (hold up three fingers)
"But we don't care!"
The fourth one said,   (hold up four fingers)
"Let's have some fun!"
The fifth one said,   (hold up five fingers)
"Let's run, run, run!"
Whooooo went the wind,
And out went the light,
And the five little pumpkins
Rolled out of sight.   (roll one hand over the other)

Johnny Works with One Hammer

Johnny works with one hammer   (pretend to hammer with one
                                        fist)

One hammer, one hammer,
    one hammer
Johnny works with one hammer
Now he works with two.   (pretend to hammer with two
                                        fists)

Continue with:
two hammers   (use both fists)
three hammers   (use two fists, one foot)
four hammers   (use two fists, two feet)
five hammers   (use two fists, two feet,
                                        nod head)

Then he goes to sleep.   (close eyes, put head on
                                        folded hands)

One Little, Two Little, Three Little Children

One little, two little, three little children
Four little, five little, six little children
Seven little, eight little, nine little children
Ten little children right here.
(Sing this, using fingers instead of children.)

One, Two, Buckle My Shoe

One, two, buckle my shoe;
Three, four, open the door;
Five, six, pick up sticks;
Seven, eight, lay them straight;
Nine, ten, a big fat hen!

Six Little Ducks

Six little ducks that I once knew   *(hold up six fingers)*
Fat ones, skinny ones, tall ones too.
But the first little duck with the   *(wiggle one finger)*
    feather on his back,   *(wiggle one finger)*
He led the others with a quack,   *(open and close fingers*
    quack, quack.   *to thumb)*

Down to the river they did go
Wibble wobble, wibble wobble,   *(with palms together, move*
    to and fro.   *hands back and forth)*
But the first little duck with the
    feather on his back,
He led the others with a quack,   *(open and close fingers*
    quack, quack.   *to thumb)*

This Old Man

This old man, he played one, he played nick-nack on my thumb,
With a nick-nack paddy-whack, give a dog a bone,
This old man came rolling home.
Additional verses: (2) shoe; (3) knee; (4) door; (5) hive; (6) sticks;
(7) up in heaven; (8) gate; (9) spine; (10) once again

Three Little Kittens

The three little kittens
They lost their mittens
And they began to cry,
"Oh, mother dear,
We sadly fear
Our mittens we have lost."
"What, lost your mittens?
You naughty kittens!
Then you shall have no pie."
"Meow, Meow, Meow, Meow, we shall have no pie.
Meow, Meow, Meow, Meow, we shall have no pie."

The three little kittens
They found their mittens

And they called out with joy,
"Oh, mother dear,
See here, see here,
Our mittens we have found."
"What, found your mittens?
You good little kittens!
Then you shall have some pie."
"Meow, Meow, Meow, Meow, we shall have some pie.
Meow, Meow, Meow, Meow, we shall have some pie."

Two Little Blackbirds

Two little blackbirds sitting on a hill.
One named Jack and one named Jill.
Fly away Jack, fly away Jill.
Come back Jack, come back Jill.
Two little blackbirds sitting on a hill.
One named Jack and one named Jill.

Two Fat Sausages

Two fat sausages	*(hold thumbs up in front)*
Sizzling in the pan.	*(move thumbs up and down)*
One went POP!	*(put finger in mouth and pop)*
The other went BAM!	*(slap open hands together)*

Homemade Shape-Sorting Boxes

Shoe Box Shape-Sorter

Choose a few different shapes for each box. Make different boxes for different sets of shapes.

1. Choose two to four small table blocks for your shapes.
2. Outline the shapes you want to use on the lid of a sturdy shoe box.
3. Cut out the shapes in the lid with a sharp knife, an X-acto® blade, or a single-edge razor blade.
4. Store one or more of each block in the shoe box. Show the child how to take the blocks out, put the lid on the box, and drop the shapes through the right holes.

Coffee Can Sorting Boxes

1. Collect coffee cans with plastic lids to use as sorting boxes. Use cans with no rough edges. Cover with pretty contact paper if you wish.
2. Choose some shapes. Use small plastic or wooden blocks.
3. Outline one, two, or three shapes on each lid. Cut them out with a sharp knife, X-acto® blade, or single-edge razor blade.
4. Show children how to drop blocks into the correct holes and how to take off and replace the lid to play again.

Giant Shape-Sorting Box

More than one shape may fit into some of the holes on this home-made box. Don't worry if this is so. Talk about the shapes and where they go as the children have fun using them.

1. You can make large shape blocks (circles, squares, triangles, and rectangles) from the plastic foam used to make winter holiday decorations. These blocks will last longer if you cover them with material. Or you can buy foam shapes through school supply companies.
2. Outline your shapes on the sides of a very large, sturdy cardboard box. Use a knife or X-acto® blade to cut the shapes out.
3. Put all the shape blocks into a smaller box next to the big box. Show the children how to match the shape blocks to the holes, drop the blocks in, and get the blocks out to play again.

Money Matching and Sorting Games

Note: Four-year-olds often know that money is a desirable thing to keep. You may notice that they put the money from money games into their pockets or cubbies. Money from these games will also wander to the Dramatic Play Center as children use it in their imaginary play. Avoid making an issue about this. Have extra pennies and play money on hand to replace the pennies that get lost. If money becomes a big problem, have sheets of money pictures the children can cut out for their play. You can also make homemade money by laminating the sheets and then cutting out the money you need for the games.

Real Pennies Matching Game

1. Cut out ten posterboard cards that are about 5" × 7".
2. Glue one penny to the first card, two pennies to the second, three to the next, and so on until you have cards with up to ten pennies glued onto them.
3. Cover the cards with clear contact paper.
4. Place at least 55 pennies into a container. It is best to use a plastic container with a lid.
5. Show your Fours how to put one penny onto each penny on the cards.
6. Talk about the numbers of pennies on each card.

This game is easier when you glue the pennies in rows, but to make the game more challenging, glue the pennies so that they are not in any special pattern.

Coins and Bills Matching Game

1. Use paper play money with 1-, 5-, and 10-dollar bills as well as plastic coins of 1, 5, 10, and 25 cents.
2. Glue one piece of each type of money to its own 5" × 7" card. Cover with clear contact paper.
3. Place several of each coin and bill into a container with the cards.
4. Show children how to spread out the cards and look carefully at the coins and bills. Help the children notice the differences in coin sizes and colors and the different numbers they see.
5. Then show the children how to take one piece of money from the container, look at it carefully, and place it on the card with the matching coin or bill.
6. Make the game easier by
    *   using only coins or bills
    *   using only two coins
    *   having the children sort all the money into two piles (coins and bills)

(Note: Have extra play money on hand to replace what gets lost.)

Activities for Learning from the World Around Them

Ring Board Sorting Game

Note: Look for the materials you need for making this game in a hardware or building supply store.

Note: Look for the materials you need for making this game in a hardware or building supply store.

1. Screw different-sized cup hooks into a plywood board. Make three rows, with hook sizes mixed in each row.

2. Have small, medium, and large washers. Use six or more of each. Place the washers in a container with a lid, such as a margarine tub. Label the container if you wish.

3. Have your Fours fit the correct size washer onto the correct size hook.

How to Make Sorting Boards

Sorting Board 1: Wooden with Cup Hooks

1. Get a rectangular board about 24" wide by 30" long. Make sure it is smooth, with no rough edges.
2. Draw two thick, dark lines down the board to divide it into thirds.
3. Screw in six cup hooks, evenly spaced, in each section. You'll need 18 hooks in all.
4. Small pictures that fit between hooks should be glued to oak-tag or cardboard and covered with clear contact paper. Punch a hole in the top of each picture to hang it up.
5. Hang up one picture from each set on the first hook. Let the child hang the rest.

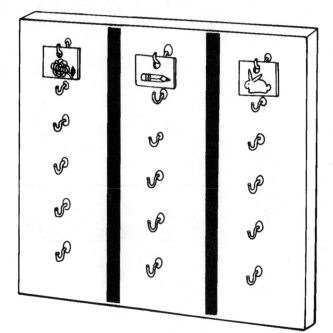

Sorting Board 2: Cloth with Cloth Pockets

1. Cut out 18 cloth 2½" × 5" rectangles. Hem ¼" on all sides of each.
2. Sew the rectangles onto a sturdy piece of 25" × 36" cloth in three rows to make pockets. Be sure to leave the tops (a 5" side) of each pocket open. Sew only the two sides and the bottom.
3. Hang this sorting board on a wall, the back of a bookcase, or a closet door.
4. Make sets of cards to fit into the pockets. Be sure that when the card is in the pocket, most of the picture can still be seen.

A shoe bag also works well as a cloth sorting board for bigger pictures.

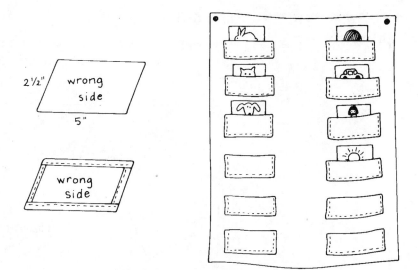

Sorting Board 3: Cardboard with Pockets

(This board is not as sturdy as Boards 1 and 2.)

1. Use 18 sturdy brown envelopes, library card pockets, or envelopes with the flaps turned in and glued down to make them sturdier.
2. Glue the envelopes onto a large posterboard, making six evenly spaced pockets in three lines.
3. Put the sorting board on a low table or floor for children to use. Or try hanging it down low where children can reach it.

Sorting Box

1. Use a grocery box with dividers, such as a box for large soda bottles.
2. Cover the box with colored contact paper, if you want.
3. Use strong tape to make the dividers sturdy.
4. Turn the box on its side so that the dividers become shelves.
5. Put a picture in each space to show children what they will be sorting. Help them get started.

Graph Ideas

Line Graphs

Line graphs are good for comparing children's heights, but bar graphs are better for making other comparisons that Fours will understand.

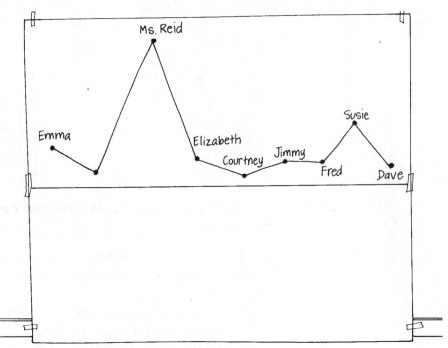

Bar Graphs

Make bar graphs with your Fours so that they can compare numbers of things that interest them.

Children can take part in making these graphs by putting their name cards on the graph to show their choice for certain categories. Then you can help them compare the number of names that were put under each category to see which had more and which had less names.

The easiest graphs for children to help make and understand are graphs that have only two bars. Here are some examples:

- How many children are boys and how many are girls?

- Who likes and who dislikes spinach (or another food)?

- How many children wore a coat today and how many did not?

- How many children wore a dress and how many wore pants?

- How many children do or do not have sisters or brothers?

Harder graphs with more bars can be used when children understand simple bar graphs. Here are some ideas:

- How many children have different kinds of pets?

- How many children enjoy different games?

Activities for Learning from the World Around Them

- How many children like certain foods?

- How many children did different activities over the weekend?

- How many children wore different types of clothes to school?

- How many children have sisters or brothers?

- How many children like which colors the best?

Making Different Types of Bar Graphs:

1. Set up a large graph with bars that can have categories listed at the bottom or side.

Floor Graph

Use a large sheet of plastic that is divided into eight bars. Lines can be made with masking tape or permanent marker. Mark off a large space for the different categories, such as different types of pets, at the bottom of the bars.

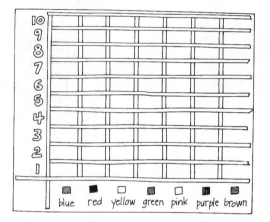

Wall Graph

Use a large sheet of chart paper that is divided into as many bars as there are categories. Make a large space for the category names, such as the names of different types of pets, at the bottom of the bars.

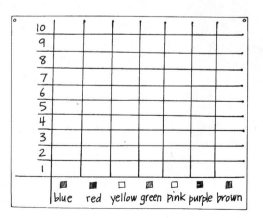

2. Give each child a card made of paper or cardboard with his or her name on it. Be sure each card is of equal size.

3. Help children place their cards on the bars they choose. Look at the categories with the children and help them decide where their names should go. Help children place their cards close together in straight rows. Place the first child's card at the bottom of the bar and add cards so that the bar becomes higher as children add their name cards.

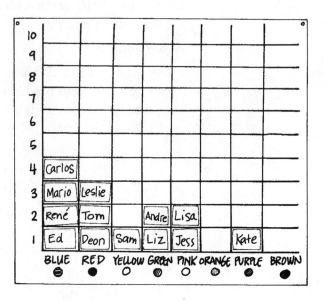

4. Talk about which category has more names, which has fewer, and which categories have the same number.

Activities for Learning from the World Around Them